INNOVATION ACCELERATION

Transforming Organizational Thinking

Donald F. Kuratko, Ph.D.

The Jack M. Gill Distinguished Chair of Entrepreneurship
The Kelley School of Business
Indiana University – Bloomington

Michael G. Goldsby, Ph.D.

The Stoops Distinguished Professor of Entrepreneurship
Miller College of Business
Ball State University

Jeffrey S. Hornsby, Ph.D.

The Jack Vanier Distinguished Chair of Innovation and Entrepreneurship
College of Business
Kansas State University

PEARSON

Boston   Columbus   Indianapolis   New York   San Francisco   Upper Saddle River
Amsterdam   Cape Town   Dubai   London   Madrid   Milan   Munich   Paris   Montreal   Toronto
Delhi   Mexico City   Sao Paulo   Sydney   Hong Kong   Seoul   Singapore   Taipei   Tokyo

Editorial Director: Sally Yagan
Senior Acquisitions Edition: Kim Norbuta
Director of Editorial Services: Ashley Santora
Senior Editorial Project Manager: Claudia Fernandes
Editorial Assistant: Carter Anderson
Director of Marketing: Patrice Lumumba Jones
Senior Marketing Manager: Nikki Ayana Jones
Marketing Assistant: Ian Gold
Senior Managing Editor: Judy Leale
Production Project Manager: Clara Bartunek
Creative Director: Jayne Conte
Cover Designer: Karen Salzbach
Cover Photo: Angelo Cavalli / Digital Vision / Getty Images
Full-Service Project Management: George Jacob / Integra Software Services.
Printer/Binder: STP – RRD / Harrisonburgh
Cover Printer: STP – RRD / Harrisonburgh
Text Font: Times Ten LT Std

Credits and acknowledgments borrowed from other sources and reproduced, with permission, in this textbook appear on appropriate page within text.

Library of Congress Cataloging-in-Publication Data
Kuratko, Donald F.
    Innovation acceleration: transforming organizational thinking / Donald F. Kuratko, Michael G. Goldsby, Jeffrey S. Hornsby. — 1st ed.
        p. cm.
    ISBN-13: 978-0-13-602148-3
    ISBN-10: 0-13-602148-4
    1. Technological innovations—Management. 2. Creative ability in business. 3. Teams in the workplace. 4. Organizational change. I. Goldsby, Michael G. II. Hornsby, Jeffrey S. (Jeffrey Scott), III. Title.
    HD45.K847 2012
    658.4'063—dc22

                                                                                                2011015552

10 9 8 7 6 5 4 3 2 1

ISBN 10:   0-13-602148-4
ISBN 13: 978-0-13-602148-3

Dedication

To my wife, Debbie, and my daughters Christina and Kellie, who have been the light of my life and the inspiration for all my career accomplishments

—Donald F. Kuratko

To my parents, Joe and Sujane Goldsby, and my uncle, Hugh McNeely, who have provided support and encouragement at every stage of my life and career.

—Michael G. Goldsby

With loving thanks to my wife, Peg, and children Dan, Brigid, and Michael. Your love and support are major reasons for my accomplishments.

—Jeffrey S. Hornsby

BRIEF CONTENTS

CONTENTS

PREFACE

INNOVATION IN THE TWENTY-FIRST CENTURY

Whether you want to become a successful innovator within your organization or develop an environment that spawns an innovative perspective, this book can be helpful to you. Accomplished entrepreneurs create successful new ventures and implement them successfully. To do this consistently takes a blend of entrepreneurship, creativity, innovation, and knowing how to make teams work effectively. The concepts behind corporate innovation mirror many of these same principles.

This book will help develop an understanding of an innovative organization, the specific processes involved in corporate innovation, and how to assess your organization's readiness for entrepreneurial activity and innovation. It will help you learn how to get more ideas successfully to market and how to write effective innovation plans for the implementation of innovative ideas. As opposed to simply corporate entrepreneurship or technology entrepreneurship, the principal focus of this book will be new product and service innovation. What distinguishes structures for innovation from the processes for innovation will be explored. The chapter dealing with the corporate innovation process will examine the various stage-gate and other nonlinear models in the new product development literature. Finally, since it is about "acceleration," we explore the outcomes that are being accelerated and specify the kinds of metrics that are involved.

Innovation has long been associated with entrepreneurship and now it is an imperative for organizations to grasp. This book helps you to understand innovation by explaining the four stages of the innovation process, improve your skills in the innovation process, and unleash your personal innovative abilities. In addition, you will find ways to assess the organization's attitudes toward innovation, giving you insights into how to diagnose creative and innovative performance problems in the organization.

For specific areas of interest, we present a quick guide for subtopics within the book.

If your area of interest is to ...	Read Chapter(s)
• get a basic understanding of an innovative organization (I-Organization)	Intro, 1, and 2
• understand the process of corporate innovation and innovative (I-Design)	2, 5, and 6
• learn about individual ideation and innovation (I-Skills)	3 and 4
• develop excellent innovation teams (I-Teams)	8, 9
• increase the innovative performance in an organization	3, 4, 5, 6, and 7
• get more new ideas successfully to market	7, 10, and 12
• learn analytics to measure innovative readiness	
• write effective innovation plans (I-Plans)	11

OBJECTIVES OF THE BOOK

Innovation Acceleration provides an introduction to transforming an organization from the "old" way of thinking to the newer "innovative" ways of thinking and acting. The fundamentals of effectuating an innovative climate within the organization are explored. Beginning with the general understanding of concepts involved with an innovative organization today, this book then explores the fundamental aspects of the individual, the organization, and the implementation. An *I-Organization* is a combination of *I-Skills* developed within individuals, the *I-Design* thinking functions needed to shape innovation, the *I-Teams* that emerge form the HR perspective of structuring the appropriate climate, and the *I-Plans* needed to provide a foundation for implementing any innovative ideas. The book is designed for collegiate or executive education markets. This text is designed for courses in corporate ventures, corporate strategy, or human resources that involve three distinct but related constituencies. First, the textbook is designed to be useful to professors who relate the latest research to each topic as they teach the course. Second, the textbook has been written for students to *read*. The subject matter is presented in an interesting, easy-to-understand style. Finally, the specific needs of active managers charged with the expectation of enhancing the innovative prowess of their organization have been considered. The book's coverage of the key aspects of developing and implementing innovation from the employees' perspective will help them to improve their management effectiveness on the job.

DISTINGUISHING FEATURES

A number of distinguishing features make this book informative, up-to-date, and useful.

COMPREHENSIVE ORGANIZATION

The book has five distinct parts. Each part has a unique subtitle to indicate to the student or practicing manager what is really involved in the chapters ahead.

Part I provides an examination of the "Challenge of Innovation" (*I-Challenge*) that is the aggregate picture of the expectation of innovation in the 21st Century economy. This part discusses the various ways individuals find innovative opportunities in organizations through the basic concepts of entrepreneurial thinking. It explains the opportunities for managers to maximize that ability in people and the characteristics of successful innovative organizations.

In addition the overall process of corporate innovation and entrepreneurship is discussed from the standpoint of new product and service innovations. We have called this part the *I-Organization* in order to characterize the overall nature of the chapters.

Part II presents the ideation and innovation techniques from an individual perspective. Individual creativity and innovative skills are highlighted in these chapters. We have called this part the *I-Skills,* which describes the emphasis placed on the development of skills. How these skills transfer to the process of innovation is a focus of this section.

Part III outlines the elements of design thinking that are needed for innovation. The design-thinking-process stages of define, research, ideate, prototype, choose, implement, and learn are covered. This *I-Design* part focuses on how to shape and model the innovative idea into tangible form for customer development and lean start-up.

Part IV explains the elements needed from an organizational or corporate environment perspective. The climate, structure, and HR challenges are all examined in this part. The basic structures used for new product and new process innovations are also examined. We call this part the *I-Teams* to signify the focus on development of the right personnel in the right form in order to advance innovation.

Part V deals with the implementation of innovative ideas. This part focuses on understanding some key analytics that can be used to measure innovative readiness as well as how ideas move from initial stages to commercialization (or market) . "Accelerating" innovation will be explored from the outcomes perspective with specific metrics presented. Developing effective innovative venture plans is presented in order to have a final tool that can be used for eventual implementation. We call this part the *I-Plans,* which indicates the level of emphasis placed on the planning approach in the implementation of innovation.

The concluding chapter focuses on the challenge of maintaining the momentum in an organization once innovation begins. Attention is directed to unique challenges confronting managers from a human resource perspective as well as a strategic perspective. We call this part the *I-Solution* to represent the final conclusion of this book.

The subject matter of the book moves from consideration of innovative organizations in general to the very specific needs of individual managers charged with this challenge. The underlying theme is effectiveness; that is, the book tells the manager what he or she needs to know in transforming the thinking in an organization to an innovative mind-set in the twenty-first century.

PEDAGOGICAL AIDS

Illustrations

- Numerous tables, charts, and exhibits present data, summarize information, and reinforce important concepts.

Italicized Terms

- Key terms and concepts are highlighted with italics when they are introduced and explained.

Chapter Summaries

- Every chapter concludes with a concise, point-by-point summary of key topics.

Review and Discussion Questions

- Relevant questions address the major chapter concepts at the end of each chapter.

Suggestions for Further Reading

- Numerous endnotes refer readers to primary sources of information—most of them journal articles. These readings can be used to supplement the book material and as sources of information for writing projects.

Subject & Name Index

- A comprehensive index helps students locate information and specific names efficiently.

INTEREST-BASED FEATURES

Innovation-in-Action

- To stimulate the thinking of innovation within organizations, the story of a successful innovative company is featured in each chapter. Many of these boxed inserts have been adapted from key innovative companies featured in *Fortune, Business Week, FSB*; and *Fast Company* magazines or websites.

A Complete Innovation Plan

- A complete innovative venture plan (Suros Surgical) is provided at the end of the book in Appendix A. This is provided as a guide for the manager searching for the exact look and style of a successful plan.

A List of Suggested Innovation Cases

- Also at the end of the book in Appendix B is a list of suggested case studies with information for how to obtain them. The problems posed in these cases are comprehensive and they call for the application of all the material in the chapters as well as the student's experience and prior education.

ACKNOWLEDGMENTS

We are grateful to a number of individuals in the development of this book. Our deepest appreciation goes to Michael H. Morris (Oklahoma State University) and R. Duane Ireland (Texas A&M University), the editors of the Prentice Hall Entrepreneurship Series, for championing this project, providing invaluable feedback on the chapters, and offering insightful guidance. They are truly outstanding scholars and editors!

We are also thankful to our families from whom we took away so much time to pursue this project. Our wives, Debbie, Peg, and Beth, have our love and gratitude for their support and motivation.

A note of recognition and gratitude to the graduate students who worked diligently to research and prepare many of the Innovation-in-Action stories at the end of the chapters, especially Matthew Hallingstad and Jeffrey Mowris, MBAs from the Kelley School of Business at Indiana University; and Kyle Kuntz, MBA, and Maggie A. Ailes, Program Coordinator at the Entrepreneurship Center from the Miller College of Business at Ball State University; as well as the staff at the Center for the Advancement of Entrepreneurship at Kansas State University.

A special thanks to the Prentice Hall team, especially Kim Norbuta and Claudia Fernandes, for their assistance in the production of this book.

Finally, we express our gratitude to our Deans at Indiana University (Daniel C. Smith), Ball State University (Rajib Sanyal), and Kansas State University (Yar M. Ebadi), who have supported our innovative efforts.

Dr. Donald F. Kuratko
Indiana University

Dr. Michael G. Goldsby
Ball State University

Dr. Jeffrey S. Hornsby
Kansas State University

ABOUT THE AUTHORS

Dr. Donald F. Kuratko *(known as Dr. K)* is the Jack M. Gill Distinguished Chair of Entrepreneurship, Professor of Entrepreneurship, and Executive Director at the Johnson Center for Entrepreneurship & Innovation, The Kelley School of Business, Indiana University–Bloomington. Dr. Kuratko is considered a prominent scholar and national leader in the field of entrepreneurship, authoring or coauthoring over 180 articles on aspects of entrepreneurship and corporate innovation in journals such as *Journal of Business Venturing, Entrepreneurship Theory & Practice, Strategic Management Journal, Journal of Business Ethics, Journal of Operations Management, Business Horizons,* and *Journal of Small Business Management.* Professor Kuratko has authored 24 books, including one of the leading entrepreneurship books in the world today, *Entrepreneurship: Theory, Process, Practice,* 8th ed. (2009), as well as *Corporate Entrepreneurship & Innovation* (2011) and *New Venture Management (2009).* In addition, Dr. Kuratko has been consultant on corporate entrepreneurship and innovation to a number of major Fortune 100 corporations and he is the *Executive Director* of the Global Consortium of Entrepreneurship Centers (GCEC), an organization of over 250 top university entrepreneurship centers throughout the world. Professor Kuratko's honors include earning the Entrepreneur of the Year for the state of Indiana; induction into the Institute of American Entrepreneurs Hall of Fame; the George Washington Medal of Honor; the Leavey Foundation Award for Excellence in Private Enterprise; the NFIB Entrepreneurship Excellence Award; the National Model Innovative Pedagogy Award for Entrepreneurship (USASBE); the National Outstanding Entrepreneurship Educator (USASBE); the Riata Distinguished Entrepreneurship Scholar (Oklahoma State University); and a 21st Century Entrepreneurship Research Fellow. Dr. Kuratko was selected as one of the Top Entrepreneurship Professors in the nation by *Fortune magazine* and he was honored by his peers in *Entrepreneur* magazine as the #1 Entrepreneurship Program Director in the nation. In addition, Professor Kuratko has been recognized as one of the Top 50 Entrepreneurship Scholars in the world over the last ten years. The U.S. Association for Small Business & Entrepreneurship honored him with the John E. Hughes Entrepreneurial Advocacy Award for his career achievements in entrepreneurship and the National Academy of Management honored Professor Kuratko with the highest award bestowed in entrepreneurship—the prestigious Entrepreneurship Advocate Award—for his contributions to the development and advancement of the discipline of entrepreneurship. Under Dr. Kuratko's leadership, Indiana University's Entrepreneurship Program has been ranked the *#1* Business School for Entrepreneurship Research by the World Productivity Rankings; the *#1* Graduate Business School for Entrepreneurship, and the #1 Undergraduate Business

School for Entrepreneurship (Public Institutions) by *U.S. News & World Report* and *Fortune* magazines.

Dr. Michael G. Goldsby is the Stoops Distinguished Professor of Entrepreneurship and Executive Director of the Entrepreneurship Center at the Miller College of Business, Ball State University. He teaches creativity, innovation, and design in the university's nationally ranked undergraduate and graduate programs in entrepreneurship. Ball State University's Entrepreneurship Program has continually earned national rankings, including: Top 20 in *Business Week, Success,* and *Entrepreneur* magazines; and Top 10 in U.S. News & World Report's elite ranking. Dr. Goldsby has produced 25 refereed journal articles. His research has been reported in many international media outlets, such as ABC, NBC, CBS, MSNBC, CNN, and the Associated Press. His study on entrepreneurship and fitness was covered by *Runner's World, Prevention Magazine, Muscle and Fitness,* and *Health Magazine,* among others. His article in the *Journal of Applied Management and Entrepreneurship* was selected the winner of the Paul Hershey Award for best paper in the journal. Dr. Goldsby attained his undergraduate degree in business economics and public policy from the Kelley School of Business at Indiana University, his master's degree in economics from Indiana State University, and his doctorate in strategic management and business ethics from the Pamplin College of Business at Virginia Tech. While at Virginia Tech, he was awarded the Jack Hoover Award for Teaching Excellence. He is a member of many management professional organizations, and has served as Vice President and a member of the Board of Directors for the U.S. Association of Small Business and Entrepreneurship (USASBE), of which he has received a distinguished service award. Dr. Goldsby's current research interests focus on opportunity recognition and development, healthy lifestyles for entrepreneurs, design, creativity, and innovation. He specializes in offering guidance during times of creation and change. As such, he is a frequent speaker to companies, communities, and universities, and offers consulting and workshop services. In his spare time, Dr. Goldsby enjoys athletic pursuits, such as running, weightlifting, rock climbing, golfing, skiing, and cycling. He has completed 21 marathons, including 8 Boston Marathons.

Dr. Jeffrey S. Hornsby is the Jack Vanier Distinguished Chair in Innovation and Entrepreneurship, and Professor of Management for the College of Business Administration at Kansas State University. His research has concentrated in the areas of corporate entrepreneurship, entrepreneurial motivation, compensation, team building, and human resource management practices for emerging and entrepreneurial businesses. He has authored or coauthored over 100 refereed journal and proceedings articles appearing in the *Journal of Applied Psychology, Strategic Management Journal, Academy of Management Executive, Journal of Operations Management, Journal of Business Venturing, Entrepreneurship Theory and Practice, Group and Organizational Management, Journal of Small Business Management,* andthe *Journal of Business and Psychology*. He research has earned three conference "best paper awards." Dr. Hornsby has coauthored three books entitled *New Venture Management: The Entrepreneur's Roadmap, The Human Resource Function in Emerging Enterprises,* and *Frontline HR: A Handbook for the Emerging Manager.* Dr. Hornsby is certified by the Society for Human Resource Management (SHRM) as a Senior Professional in Human Resource Management (SPHR) and is Level 3 certified in Simplex Creative Problem Solving. Dr. Hornsby's related experience includes extensive corporate training and consulting in entrepreneurial development, community-based entrepreneurship, team building, corporate entrepreneurship, supervisory management, compensation, market research, and human resource management. He has worked with several firms, including BorgWarner Automotive, Rolls Royce, Bank One, BAA, RCI, Ameritech, Blue Cross and Blue Shield, VEI/IMM (a subsidiary of Community Hospitals), Pathologists Associated, Ontario Systems Corporation, State of Indiana Department of Commerce, Frank Miller Lumber Company, and Muncie Power Products. Dr. Hornsby also coordinates and teaches the SHRM exam-preparation course using the SHRM Learning System. He has been a member of the Executive Board of the U.S. Association of Small Business and Entrepreneurship, serving as Senior Vice President of Programming & Program Chair in 2008, Competitive Papers Chair for the 2007 conference, and Vice President of the Corporate Entrepreneurship Division. Before his appointment at Kansas State, Dr. Hornsby served as the George and Frances Ball Distinguished Professor of Management at Ball State University, where he won several teaching and research awards, including the Dean's Teaching Award for ten consecutive years and the Ball State University 2004 Outstanding Faculty Award.

PART 1

THE INNOVATIVE ORGANIZATION
(I-ORGANIZATION)

CHAPTER 1

UNDERSTANDING THE INNOVATIVE MIND-SET

INTRODUCTION: THE "I-CHALLENGE"

We are all confronting a global innovation challenge. The development, application, and enhancement of new technologies are occurring at a breathtaking pace, and innovation is determining the way business is being conducted. As the number of new ventures, products, technologies, and patents literally explodes worldwide, established companies can either become victims of this innovation challenge or they can answer the call. The world is in the midst of a new wave of economic development, with entrepreneurship and innovation as the catalysts.

The nature of business has been transformed in this fast-paced, highly threatening, and increasingly global environment. Dramatic and ongoing changes are forcing leaders of organizations to reexamine their basic purpose and to become much more innovative with their approach to multiple stakeholders. Organizations today must continually redefine their markets, restructure their operations, and modify their business models. Effective companies in the twenty-first century have made the fundamental discovery that innovation drives success.[1] The ability to continually innovate (to engage in an ongoing process of *entrepreneurial actions*) has become the source of competitive advantage.

While innovative actions are a phenomenon that have captivated the interest of executives in many corporate boardrooms, yet there is a danger that managers can get too caught up in the excitement of a particular innovation or inspiring stories of individual corporate innovators. It is easy to become enamored with the idea of innovation, but the true value of innovation lies in the extent to which it becomes a corporate strategy to create sustainable competitive advantage.[2] The early twenty-first century has been a time when innovative (or entrepreneurial) actions have been recognized widely as the path to competitive advantage and success in organizations of all types and sizes.[3] Moreover, a lack of innovative (or entrepreneurial) actions in today's global economy could be a recipe for failure.

In today's competitive landscape, the opportunities and threats happen swiftly and are relentless in their frequency, affecting virtually all parts of an organization simultaneously. The business environment is filled with ambiguity and discontinuity, and the rules of the game are subject to constant revision. The job of management effectively becomes one of continual experimentation—experimenting with new structures, new reward systems, new technologies, new methods, new products, new markets, and much more. The quest remains the same: sustainable competitive advantage. Innovation and entrepreneurial actions represent the guiding light and the motivating force for organizations as they attempt to find their way down this path.

Achieving innovation (and entrepreneurial actions) is not something that you as a manager can simply decide to do. *Corporate innovation* must be understood by each individual and there must be a realization that it does not produce instant success. It requires considerable training, time, and investment, and there must be continual reinforcement. By their nature, organizations impose constraints on innovative behavior. To be sustainable, innovative thinking must be integrated into the mission, goals, strategies, structure, processes, and values of the organization. The managerial mind-set must become an opportunity-driven mind-set, where actions are never constrained by resources currently controlled.[4] We call this the "innovative mind-set."

Although some earlier researchers concluded that innovation (entrepreneurship) and bureaucracies were mutually exclusive and could not coexist,[5] today we find many researchers examining innovation within the enterprise framework.[6] Leading strategic thinkers are moving beyond the traditional product and service innovations to pioneering innovation in processes, value chains, business models, and all functions of management.[7] Thus, innovative attitudes and behaviors are necessary for firms of all sizes to prosper and flourish in competitive environments.

Developing a corporate innovative philosophy provides a number of advantages. One is that this type of atmosphere often leads to the development of new products and services and helps the organization expand and grow. A second is it creates a workforce that can help the enterprise maintain its competitive posture. A third is it promotes a climate conducive to high achievers and helps the enterprise motivate and keep its best people.

This new millennium has been characterized as an age of instant information, ever-increasing development and application of technology, experimental change, revolutionary processes, and global competition. It is now an age filled with turbulence and paradox. The key descriptive words used about this new "innovation challenge" of the twenty-first century are: *Dreaming*, *Creating*, *Exploring*, *Inventing*, *Pioneering*, and *Imagining*! We believe this is a point in time when the gap between what can be imagined and what can be accomplished has never been smaller. It is a time requiring innovative vision, courage, calculated risk taking, and strong leadership. It is simply answering "*the innovative challenge of the twenty-first century.*" Thus, the "*I-Challenge*" confronts all organizations today.

This book was developed based on the concepts needed for accelerating innovation in your organization. As we mentioned in the Preface, transforming into an innovative organization requires a combination of the needed innovative skills developed within individuals (*I-Skills*: *Part II*), the design-thinking functions needed to shape innovation (*I-Design: Part III),* the development of innovative teams that emerge from the HR perspective of structuring the appropriate climate (*I-Teams*: *Part IV*), and the innovation plans needed to provide a foundation for implementing any innovative ideas (*I-Plans: Part V*). Thus the chapters ahead flow from this organization and provide deeper insights into the ways in which twenty-first-century organizations can transform their thinking toward innovative performance.

INNOVATIVE THINKING

The constantly changing economic environment provides a continuous flow of potential opportunities *if* an individual can recognize a profitable idea amid the chaos and cynicism that also permeates such an environment. Thousands of alternatives exist as every individual creates and develops ideas with a unique frame of reference. Thus, *innovative thinking* has become a critical skill for the twenty-first century. During the last two decades, the entrepreneurial flame has caught on throughout the world with the world's economies searching for the free-enterprise solution through innovative development.

However, *innovative thinking* goes beyond the mere creation of business. The characteristics of seeking opportunities, taking risks beyond security, and having the tenacity to push an idea through to reality combine into a special perspective that permeates innovative individuals. Innovative thinking can be developed in individuals. This mind-set can be exhibited inside or outside an organization, in profit or not-for-profit enterprises, and in business or nonbusiness activities for the purpose of bringing forth creative ideas. As one author stated, "Ideas come from people. Innovation is a capability of the many. That capability is utilized when people give commitment to the mission and life of the enterprise and have the power to do something with their capabilities."[8]

Thus, innovative thinking is an integrated mind-set that permeates individuals and organizations in an effective manner. Let's examine exactly what innovation is and how this mind-set can be nurtured in individuals.

THE CONCEPT OF INNOVATION

INNOVATION, CREATIVITY, AND ENTREPRENEURSHIP

The terms *entrepreneurship, creativity,* and *innovation* are sometimes used interchangeably and while that is understandable, it can be misleading. Creativity and innovation are very similar concepts, but there are some differences. Creativity is typically described as the process of generating new ideas, while innovation takes creativity a step further by being a process that turns those ideas into reality. Innovation is often the basis on which entrepreneurship is built because of the competitive advantage it provides. Innovation is a key function in the entrepreneurial process. Researchers and authors in the field of innovation and entrepreneurship are, for the most part, in agreement with renowned consultant and author Peter F. Drucker about the concept of innovation:

> Innovation is the specific function of entrepreneurship.... It is the means by which the entrepreneur either creates new wealth-producing resources or endows existing resources with enhanced potential for creating wealth.[9]

Thus, innovation is the process by which entrepreneurs convert opportunities (ideas) into marketable solutions. Innovation is a process that transforms ideas into outputs. It is the means by which entrepreneurs become catalysts for change.[10] The emerging perspective of researchers in the field of innovation is to define innovation in the broadest context possible as given in this specific example:

> Innovation is the process of making changes, large and small, radical and incremental, to products, processes, and services that result in the introduction of something new for the organization that adds value to customers and contributes to the knowledge store of the organization.[11]

There are numerous alternative definitions of *innovation*. One popular alternative is to present innovation as an invention that has been exploited commercially.[12] Innovation can also be viewed as the systematic approach to creating an environment based on creative discovery, invention, and commercial exploitation of ideas that meet unmet needs. However, there are millions of innovations that are often much smaller in scale, do not involve an invention, or are not necessarily exploited in the same commercial sense. Therefore, one simplified alternative definition might be:

$$Innovation = Creativity + Exploitation$$

In this sense innovation becomes the composition of creative thoughts and the determination to implement those ideas into a marketable concept. Since there are numerous ways in which individuals apply creative thoughts into exploitation of opportunities there also are numerous ways to categorize innovation.

CATEGORIZING INNOVATION

TYPES

The term *innovation* can be associated with physical products, processes that make products, services that deliver products, and services that provide intangible products. Thus, the basic types of innovation relate to products, processes, and services.

- *Product innovation* is about making beneficial changes to physical products.
- *Process innovation* is about making beneficial changes to the processes that produce products or services.
- *Service innovation* is about making beneficial changes to services that customers use.

METHODS

Whether it is product, process, or service, there are four basic methods that describe the ways that innovation will take place. These extend from new inventions to modifications of existing products or services. In order of originality, these are the four methods:

- *Invention*: creation of a new product, service, or process considered to be "revolutionary."
- *Extension:* expansion of a product, service, or process already in existence (different application).
- *Duplication:* replication of an existing product, service, or process adding the entrepreneur's own creativity to enhance or improve it.
- *Synthesis:* combination of existing concepts and factors into a new formulation (new applications of already-invented items).[13]

TRAJECTORIES

The final way to categorize innovation is through the trajectory that the innovation takes. In this manner there are three major trajectories for innovation: radical, incremental, and disruptive.

1. *Radical innovation* is the launching of inaugural breakthroughs such as personal computers and overnight mail delivery. These innovations take experimentation and determined vision, which are not necessarily managed but *must* be recognized and nurtured. These are considered changes at a significant magnitude. The term *radical* often refers to the level of contribution made to the efficiency or revenue of the organization.[14] Radical innovation can transform the industry itself by changing the existing market and developing the next industry wave.[15] Undertaking radical innovation can not only bring dramatic benefits for an organization in terms of increased sales and profits, but it also carries intensive resource requirements as well as greater risk. Consider pharmaceutical companies that can invest more than $1 billion in drug development with no guarantee that it will ever make it to the marketplace. However, one

major drug breakthrough could be worth billions of dollars every year once it makes it to the marketplace.

2. *Incremental Innovation* refers to the systematic evolution of a product or service into newer or larger markets. Examples include the typical improvements and advances in current products and services. Many times the incremental innovation will take over after a radical innovation introduces a breakthrough. The structure, marketing, financing, and formal systems of a corporation can help implement incremental innovation. Although radical innovations often make headlines, most organizations spread the risk associated with innovation by also looking for incremental innovations to their products, processes, and services. Incremental innovation is less ambitious in its scope and offers less potential for financial gains to the organization, but consequently the associated risks are reduced. Incremental innovations consist of smaller initiatives, making them easier to manage than their radical counterparts. However, organizations may have to undertake numerous incremental innovations to achieve the necessary growth.

3. *Disruptive Innovation* goes beyond radical innovation and transforms business practice to rewrite the rules of an industry. In other words, the business practice of an entire industrial sector could be changed radically. Disruptive innovation often occurs because new sciences and technology are introduced or applied to a new market that offers the potential to exceed the existing limits of technology.[16] (The largest modern disruptive technology to emerge has been the Internet.) Research laboratories and universities are usually a good source of disruptive technologies. Many companies work in cooperation with universities in order to develop the latest disruptive technologies, which can take many years to develop, wait for the outcome of this type of technology, and choose the potential successes that demonstrate market adoption. Organizations must be careful in pursuing the correct disruptive innovations to pursue because the wrong technology can waste scarce resources and place the organization in a position of significant competitive disadvantage. Researchers note that organizations often struggle to achieve a successful balance between developing radical and disruptive innovations while still protecting their traditional business operations.[17]

MISCONCEPTIONS OF INNOVATION

The entire concept of innovation conjures up many thoughts and misconceptions. It seems everyone has an opinion as to what innovation entails. We present some of the common innovation misconceptions, along with reasons why these are misconceptions and not facts:[18]

- *Innovation Is Planned and Predictable.* This statement is based on the old concept that innovation should be left to the research and development (R&D) department under a planned format. In truth, innovation is unpredictable and may be introduced by anyone.

- *Technical Specifications Must Be Thoroughly Prepared.* This statement comes from the engineering arena which drafts complete plans before moving on. Thorough preparation is good but it can sometimes take too long. Quite often it is more important to use a try–test–revise approach.

- *Big Projects Will Develop Better Innovations than Smaller Ones.* This statement has been proven false time and time again. Larger firms are now encouraging their people to work in smaller groups, where it often is easier to generate creative ideas.

- *Technology Is the Driving Force of Innovation Success.* Technology is certainly one source for innovation, but it is not the only one. There are numerous sources for innovative ideas and while technology is certainly a driving factor in many innovations, it is not the only success factor. Moreover, the customer or market is the driving force behind any innovation. Market-driven or customer-based innovations have the highest probability of success.

INNOVATION AND LEARNING

Innovation is a process that needs to be managed within an organization. This includes activities such as encouraging ideas, defining goals, prioritizing projects, improving communications, and motivating teams. For organizations to sustain their mission, they must continuously innovate and replace existing products, processes, and services with more effective ones. Focusing on innovation as a continuous process acknowledges the effect that learning has on knowledge creation within the organization. Learning how to innovate effectively entails managing knowledge within the organization and offers the potential to enhance the way the organization innovates. In addition, entrepreneurs must "learn" from their experiences as well. An organization that can continuously learn and adapt its behavior to external stimuli does so by continuously adding to its collective knowledge store. Researcher Andrew C. Corbett has identified the importance of acquiring and transforming the information and knowledge through the learning process. His research was able to lend credence to the theories about the cognitive ability of individuals to transform information into recognizable opportunities.[19] So, how an organization acquires, processes, and learns from the prior knowledge that it has gained is critical to the complete innovation process.

THE INNOVATIVE MIND-SET IN INDIVIDUALS

In recognizing the importance of the evolution of innovative thinking into the twenty-first century, one integrated definition of entrepreneurship acknowledges the critical factors needed for this phenomenon.

Entrepreneurship is a dynamic process of vision, change, and innovation. It requires an application of energy and passion towards the creation and implementation of new ideas and creative solutions. Essential ingredients include the willingness to take calculated risks—in terms of time, equity, or career; the ability to formulate an effective venture team; the creative skill to marshal needed resources; the fundamental skill of building a solid business plan; and, finally, the vision to recognize opportunity where others see chaos, contradiction, and confusion.[20]

This definition demonstrates that innovative ability is a process that each and every individual could choose to pursue. Today's generation of the twenty-first century may become known as "Generation E" because they are becoming the most entrepreneurial and innovative generation since the Industrial Revolution. Every person has the potential to pursue their ideas and become an innovator. Exactly what motivates individuals to make a choice for innovative thinking has not been identified, at least not as one single event, characteristic, or trait. However, there has been some research associated with specific skills and characteristics.

In the simplest of theoretical forms for studying innovation, innovators cause innovation. That is, $I = f(i)$ states that innovation is a function of the innovator. Thus, an examination of known entrepreneurial or innovative characteristics does help in the evolving understanding of innovative thinking. Below are some of the most commonly cited characteristics.

- *Determination and Perseverance*: More than any other factor, a total dedication to success as an innovator can overcome obstacles and setbacks. Sheer determination and an unwavering commitment to succeed often win out against odds that many people would consider insurmountable. They also can compensate for personal shortcomings.

- *Achievement Drive*: Innovators are self-starters who appear to others to be internally driven by a strong desire to compete, to excel against self-imposed standards, and to pursue and attain challenging goals. This need to achieve has been well documented, beginning with David McClelland's pioneering work on motivation in the 1950s and 1960s.[21] High achievers tend to be moderate risk takers. They examine a situation, determine how to increase the odds of winning, and then push ahead. As a result, high-risk decisions for the average businessperson often are moderate risks for the well-prepared high achiever.

- *Goal Orientation*: One clear pattern among innovators is their focus on opportunity rather than on resources, structure, or strategy. They start with the opportunity and let their understanding of it guide other important issues. They are goal oriented in their pursuit of opportunities. Setting high but attainable goals enables them to focus their energies, to selectively sort out opportunities, and to know when to say "no." Their goal orientation also helps them to define priorities and provides them with measures of how well they are performing.

- *Internal Locus of Control:* Successful innovators do not believe the success or failure of their idea will be governed by fate, luck, or similar forces.

They believe their accomplishments and setbacks are within their own control and influence and they can affect the outcome of their actions. This attribute is consistent with a high-achievement motivational drive, the desire to take personal responsibility, and self-confidence.

- *Tolerance for Ambiguity:* Innovators face uncertainty compounded by constant changes that introduce ambiguity and stress into every aspect of the innovation. Setbacks and surprises are inevitable; lack of organization, structure, and order is a way of life. Yet successful innovators thrive on the fluidity and excitement of such an ambiguous existence.

- *Calculated Risk Taking*: As discussed in the "myths" section, successful innovators are not high-rolling gamblers. When they decide to explore an idea, they do so in a very calculated, carefully thought-out manner. They do everything possible to get the odds in their favor, and they often avoid taking unnecessary risks. These strategies include getting others to share inherent financial and business risks with them.

- *Tolerance for Failure*: Innovators use failure as a learning experience. The iterative, trial-and-error nature of becoming a successful innovator makes serious setbacks and disappointments an integral part of the learning process. The most effective innovators are realistic enough to expect such difficulties. Furthermore, they do not become disappointed, discouraged, or depressed by a setback or failure. Many of them believe they learn more from their early failures than from their early successes.

- *High Energy Level:* The extraordinary workloads and the stressful demands innovators may face place a premium on energy. Many innovators fine-tune their energy levels by carefully monitoring what they eat and drink, establishing exercise routines, and knowing when to get away for relaxation.

- *Creativity:* Creativity was once regarded as an exclusively inherited trait. Judging by the level of creativity and innovation in the United States compared with that of equally sophisticated but less creative and innovative cultures, it appears unlikely this trait is solely genetic. An expanding school of thought believes creativity can be learned. Innovations often have a collective creativity that emerges from the joint efforts of teams of individuals.

- *Vision:* Innovators need to have a vision or concept of what their idea can be. Not all innovators have predetermined visions for their innovations. In many cases this vision develops over time as the individual begins to realize what the firm is and what it can become.

Researchers have continued to examine the psychological and cognitive aspects of entrepreneurs which have helped to expand our understanding of the innovative mind-set.[22] New characteristics are continually being added to this ever-growing list. At this point, however, let us examine some of the most-often-cited entrepreneurial characteristics. Although this list admittedly is incomplete, it does provide important insights into the innovative mind-set.[23]

THE MOTIVATION FOR INNOVATION

Although innovation can be characterized as the interaction of the skills that we listed in the previous section, it is the "motivation" toward innovative behavior that is most important.

The quest for innovative thinking as well as the willingness to *sustain* that thinking is directly related to an individual's **entrepreneurial motivation**. In that vein, one research approach examines the motivational process an entrepreneur experiences.[24] Examining the motivation to sustain entrepreneurial behavior is an effective analogy to the process of innovative behavior. Figure 1.1 illustrates the key elements of this approach.

The decision to behave entrepreneurially (or innovatively) is the result of the interaction of several factors. One set of factors includes the individual's personal characteristics, the individual's personal environment, the relevant business environment, the individual's personal goal set, and the existence of a viable business idea.[25] In addition, the individual compares his or her perception of the probable outcomes with the personal expectations he or she has in mind. Next,

FIGURE 1.1 Model of Enterpreneurial Motivation

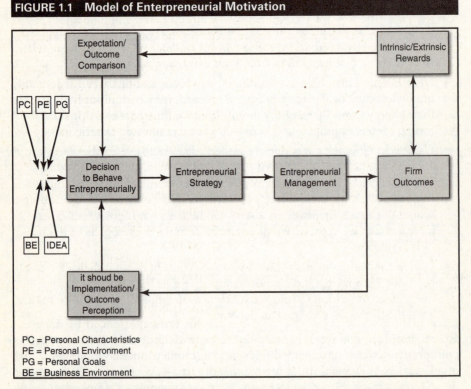

PC = Personal Characteristics
PE = Personal Environment
PG = Personal Goals
BE = Business Environment

Source: Naffziger, D.W., Hornsby, J.S., and Kuratko, D.F. 1994. "A Proposed Research Model of Entrepreneurial Motivation," Entrepreneurship Theory and Practice 18(3):33. Reprinted from *Entrepreneurship Theory and Practice* with the permission of Baylor University. All rights reserved.

an individual looks at the relationship between the entrepreneurial (or innovative) behavior he or she would implement and the expected outcomes.

According to the model, the entrepreneur's expectations are finally compared with the actual or perceived firm outcomes. Future entrepreneurial (innovative) behavior is based on the results of all of these comparisons. When outcomes meet or exceed expectations, the entrepreneurial (innovative) behavior is positively reinforced, and the individual is motivated to continue to behave entrepreneurially (innovatively), either within the current venture or possibly through the initiation of additional ventures, depending on the existing entrepreneurial goal. When outcomes fail to meet expectations, the entrepreneur's motivation will be lower and will have a corresponding impact on the decision to continue to act entrepreneurially (innovatively). These perceptions also affect succeeding strategies, strategy implementation, and management of the firm.[26] Once again we see the importance of the individual in the entrepreneurial (or innovative) process. It is only through individuals that innovation can be initiated and sustained.

AN EXPERIENTIAL VIEW

The prevalent view in the literature is that entrepreneurs and innovators create ventures. While that is a true statement, it misses the complete process of entrepreneurship and innovation due to its narrow framing. This narrow perspective misses much of the reality regarding how ventures and entrepreneurs/innovators come into being. Researchers point out that as with a painting that emerges based on the individual interacting with, feeling, and agonizing over his or her creation, an entrepreneur does not simply produce a venture. Entrepreneurs do not preexist—they emerge as a function of the novel, idiosyncratic, and experiential nature of the venture-creation process. Venture creation is a lived experience that, as it unfolds, forms the entrepreneur. In fact, the creation of a sustainable enterprise involves three parallel, interactive phenomena: emergence of the opportunity, emergence of the venture, and emergence of the entrepreneur. None are predetermined or fixed—they define, and are defined by, one another.[27] Thus, the perspective of the entrepreneurial or innovative experience has gained new momentum in the research of the twenty-first century.

This experiential view of the entrepreneur captures the emergent and temporal nature of entrepreneurship. It moves us past a more static "snapshot" approach and encourages consideration of a dynamic, socially situated process involving numerous actors and events. It allows for the fact that the many activities addressed as a venture unfolds are experienced by different actors in different ways.[28] Moreover, it acknowledges that venture creation transcends rational thought processes to include emotions, impulses, and physiological responses as individuals react to a diverse, multifaceted, and imposing array of activities, events, and developments. This perspective is consistent with the recent research interest in a situated view of entrepreneurial and innovative action.[29]

Drivers (Sources) of Innovation

So, where do innovators seek out sources for the ideas and concepts that result in innovation? Most innovations result from a conscious, purposeful search for new opportunities. This process begins with the analysis of the sources of new opportunities. Renowned business consultant and author Peter Drucker noted that because innovation is both conceptual and perceptual, would-be innovators must go out and look, ask, and listen. Successful innovators use both the right and left sides of their brains. They look at figures. They look at people. They analytically work out what the innovation has to be to satisfy the opportunity. Then they go out and look at potential product users to study their expectations, values, and needs.[30] The following presents some of the most effective sources for the recognition of opportunities.

- *Trends:* Trends signal shifts in the current paradigm (or thinking) of the major population. Observing trends closely will allow an entrepreneur the ability to recognize a potential opportunity. Trends need to be observed in society, technology, economy, and government.

- *Unexpected Occurrences:* These are successes or failures that, because they were unanticipated or unplanned, often end up proving to be a major innovative surprise to everyone.

- *Incongruities:* These occur whenever a gap or difference exists between expectations and reality.

- *Process Needs:* These exist whenever a demand arises for an answer to a particular need. Venture capitalists often refer to this as the "pain" that exists in the marketplace and the entrepreneur must recognize an innovative solution or "painkiller."

- *Industry and Market Changes:* Continual shifts in the marketplace occur, caused by developments such as consumer attitudes, advancements in technology, and industry growth. Industries and markets are always undergoing changes in structure, design, or definition.

- *Demographic Changes*: As mentioned above with the trends, these arise from trend changes in population, age, education, occupations, geographic locations, and similar factors. Demographic shifts are important and often provide new entrepreneurial opportunities.

- *Perceptual Changes*: These changes occur in people's interpretation of facts and concepts. They are intangible yet meaningful. Perception can cause major shifts in ideas to take place.

- *Knowledge-Based Concepts*: These are the basis for the creation or development of something brand new. Inventions are knowledge based; they are the product of new thinking, new methods, and new knowledge. Such innovations often require the longest time period between initiation and market implementation because of the need for testing and modification.

Myths Associated with Innovators

In order to better understand "innovative thinking," we must first examine some of the damaging myths that have prevailed for years due to the lack of understanding surrounding this concept. It should be recognized that some executives and managers reject the "entrepreneurial" concept because of certain long-standing beliefs about entrepreneurship and innovation. These myths have developed through the years and are the result of a slow emergence of research in entrepreneurship and individual innovation. As many researchers in the field have noted, the study of entrepreneurship and innovation is still emerging, and thus "folklore" will tend to prevail until it is dispelled with contemporary research findings. Listed below are five of the most notable myths, with an explanation to dispel each.[31]

"Individuals Are Born to Innovate"   The prevailing idea that innovation cannot be taught or learned, that there are innate traits with which one must be born, has a long history. These traits include aggressiveness, initiative, drive, a willingness to take risks, creative ability, and perseverance. While these traits may certainly have an effect on an individual, they do not dictate nor predict whether one is predisposed to innovative thinking. The recognition of entrepreneurship and innovation as a discipline in universities today has helped to dispel this myth.

"Innovators Must be Inventors"   The idea that innovators are always inventors is a result of misunderstanding and tunnel vision. While many inventors are also entrepreneurs, there are numerous entrepreneurs who encompass all sorts of innovative activity. For example, Steve Jobs did not invent the computer, but his innovative ideas have made Apple one of the leading technology enterprises in the world. A contemporary understanding of innovative thinking covers more than just invention. There must be a complete understanding of innovative behavior in all forms.

"Fitting the Innovator's Profile"   Many books and articles have presented checklists of characteristics of the successful entrepreneurs and innovators. These lists were neither validated nor complete; they were based on case studies and on research findings among achievement-oriented people. Today we realize that a standard entrepreneurial profile is hard to compile. The environment, the idea itself, and the individual have interactive effects, which result in many different types of profiles. Contemporary studies being conducted at universities across the world will, in the future, provide more accurate insights into the various profiles of successful innovators. It is more likely that successful innovators benefit from "entrepreneurial experiences" and innovative education where they can learn rather than conform to a particular profile.

"Innovation Is Being Lucky"   Being at "the right place at the right time" is always an advantage. But "luck happens when preparation meets opportunity" is an equally appropriate adage. Prepared innovators who seize the opportunity when it arises often appear to be "lucky." They are, in fact, simply better prepared to deal

with situations and turn them into successes. What appears to be luck is actually the result of preparation, determination, desire, knowledge, and innovativeness.

"Innovators Are Gamblers"   The concept of risk is a major element in the innovation process. However, the public's perception of the risk assumed by most innovators is distorted. While it may appear that an innovator is "gambling" on a wild chance, the fact is that he or she is usually working on a moderate or "calculated" risk. Most successful innovators work hard through planning and preparation to minimize the risk involved—in order to better control the destiny of their vision.

We present these myths to provide a background for current thinking on innovators. By sidestepping the "folklore," we can build a foundation for critically understanding the processes of innovative thinking.

However, understanding the characteristics, motivations, experiences, and myths associated with innovation is not a shield from the stress that the pursuit of innovation can produce. We must always be aware that the process of innovation may also present a "stressful" experience to individuals.

Innovation and Stress … Beware!   Research studies of entrepreneurs and innovators show that those who achieve goals often pay a high price.[32] For example, in one study a majority of entrepreneurs surveyed had back problems, indigestion, insomnia, or headaches. To achieve their goals, however, these entrepreneurs (innovators) were willing to tolerate these effects of stress.

In general, stress can be viewed as a function of discrepancies between a person's expectations and ability to meet demands, as well as discrepancies between the individual's expectations and personality. If a person is unable to fulfill role demands, then stress occurs. To the extent innovators' work demands and expectations exceed their abilities to perform as idea initiators, they are likely to experience stress. Innovative roles and operating environments can lead to stress.

Many times innovators must bear the cost of their mistakes while playing a multitude of roles, such as salesperson, recruiter, spokesperson, and negotiator. These simultaneous demands can lead to role overload. The innovative mind-set requires a large commitment of time and energy, often at the expense of family and social activities.[33]

SOURCES OF STRESS

Researchers have identified some of the key causes of entrepreneurial stress, which can be applied to the innovation process as well.[34] They include: *insulation*: long hours at work prevent them from seeking the comfort and counsel of friends and family members. Because of this insulation from others they tend not to participate in social activities unless they provide a business benefit; *addiction to the innovation:* One of the ironies of innovation is that successful innovators can become married to their ideas. They work long hours, leaving little time for civic organizations, recreation, or further education; *perfectionist syndrome:* most innovators experience frustration, disappointment, and aggravation with partners, fellow employees, customers, and investors. Successful innovators are to some extent perfectionists and know how they want things done; often they spend a lot of time trying to get other more lackadaisical employees to meet their performance standards. And, frequently, because of irreconcilable conflict, many partnerships are dissolved; *achievement orientation:* the innovator is never satisfied with his or her work no matter how well it was done. They seem to recognize the dangers of unbridled ambition, but they have a difficult time tempering their achievement need. They seem to believe that if they stop or slow down, some competitor is going to come from behind, and everything they have built will fall apart.

MANAGING THE STRESS

It is important to point out that not all stress is bad. Certainly, if stress becomes overbearing and unrelenting in a person's life, it wears down the body's physical abilities. However, if stress can be kept within constructive bounds, then it could increase a person's efficiency and improve performance.

One research study presented stress-reduction techniques.[35] Although classic stress-reduction techniques such as meditation, biofeedback, muscle relaxation, and regular exercise help reduce stress, a few other techniques also help in this purpose. Presented here are six specific ways innovators can cope with stress:

- *Network:* One way to relieve the insulation of the innovator's mind-set is to share experiences by networking with other innovators. The objectivity gained from hearing about the triumphs and errors of others is itself therapeutic.

- *Refresh Yourself:* The best antidote to immersion in an innovation may be a holiday. If vacation days or weeks are limited by valid business constraints, short breaks still may be possible. Such interludes allow a measure of self-renewal.

- *The Personal Touch*: Innovators are in close contact with fellow employees and can readily assess their concerns. The personal touches, such as company-wide outings, flexible hours, and congratulatory celebrations, are many times very useful in helping other employees be not only more productive but also experience much less stress.

- *Gain New Perspectives*: Countering the obsessive need to achieve can be difficult because the innovator's personality is inextricably bound in the fabric of the innovation. Innovators need to get away from their ideas occasionally and become more passionate about life itself. In other words, they need to gain some new perspectives.

- *Delegate:* Implementation of coping mechanisms requires some amount of time. To gain this time, the innovator has to learn to delegate tasks. Innovators can find delegation difficult because they think they have to be involved in every aspect of the innovation. But to gain time for alleviating stress, appropriate delegation must be used.

- *Exercise:* Exercise can often be an excellent method of reducing stress for individuals. As an example, researchers Michael G. Goldsby, Donald F. Kuratko, and James W. Bishop examined the relationship between exercise and the attainment of personal and professional goals for entrepreneurs.[36] The study addressed the issue by examining the exercise regimens of

366 entrepreneurs and the relationship of exercise frequency with the company's sales and the entrepreneur's personal goals. Specifically, the study examined the relationship that two types of exercise—running and weightlifting—had with sales volume, extrinsic rewards, and intrinsic rewards. The results indicated that running is positively related to all three outcome variables, while weightlifting is positively related to extrinsic and intrinsic rewards. This study demonstrates the value of exercise regimens on relieving the stress associated with entrepreneurs and innovators.

MANAGING INNOVATIVE INDIVIDUALS

In order to maintain this "innovative mind-set," managers must assume certain ongoing responsibilities.[37] The first responsibility involves *framing the challenge.* In other words, there needs to be a clear definition of the specified challenges that everyone involved with innovative projects should address. It is important to think in terms of, and regularly reiterate, the challenge. Second, leaders have the responsibility to *absorb the uncertainty* that is perceived by team members. Innovative leaders make uncertainty less daunting. The idea is to create the self-confidence that lets others act on opportunities without seeking managerial permission. Employees must not be overwhelmed by the complexity inherent in many innovative situations. A third responsibility is to *define gravity*—that is, what must be accepted and what cannot be accepted. The term *gravity* is used to capture limiting conditions. For example, there is gravity on Earth, but that does not mean it must limit our lives. If freed from the psychological cage of believing that gravity makes flying impossible, creativity can permit us to invent an airplane or spaceship. This is what the innovative mind-set is all about—seeing opportunities where others see barriers and limits. A fourth managerial responsibility involves *clearing obstacles* that arise as a result of internal competition for resources. This can be a problem especially when the innovation is beginning to undergo significant growth. An expanding and sometimes popular new concept will often find itself pitted squarely against other (often established) aspects of the firm in a fierce internal competition for funds and staff. Creative tactics, political skills, and an ability to regroup, reorganize, and attack from another angle become invaluable. A final responsibility for leaders is to keep their finger on the pulse of the innovative projects. This involves constructive monitoring and control of the developing opportunity.

Sustained efforts with innovation are contingent upon individual members continuing to undertake innovative activities and upon positive perceptions of the activity by the organization's executive management, which will in turn support the further allocation of necessary organizational antecedents.

The dynamic innovative organizations of the twenty-first century will be ones that are capable of merging strategic action with innovative action on an ongoing basis.[38] This type of innovative organization could be conceptualized in the "new thinking" that is needed by today's leaders. As has been shown in much of the recent literature, the strategic mind-set must lean toward the more innovative concepts in leading organizations today. It is our belief that any organization pursuing innovation as their strategy needs to understand the concept of "innovative thinking." It is the techniques and principles of this emerging discipline that will drive the innovative organization in the twenty-first century.

INNOVATION-IN-ACTION

Hiring for Innovative People

According to some experts there are specific strategies that can be utilized to find innovative people to work in your organization. Keeping these points in mind might be helpful when an organization is growing and trying to bring in the right employees.

First, you should always define what kind of innovation or creativity would benefit your organization. You need to distinguish between "breadth creativity," which is the ability to see the big picture and draw connections or spot trends or "depth creativity," which is creativity within a specific knowledge or skill area. The type of desired creativity should be based on the innovative culture of the organization. An organization may not necessarily need too many individuals "seeing the big picture" when specific skills are sought. It may be that the organization should focus on identifying individuals who demonstrate innovative ability in problem solving for a specific job.

The next concept relates to the way in which your organization appears to any potential applicants. Examine how your company's Web pages, career pages, and other materials convey the innovative atmosphere that exists. In order to gain the interest of a more innovative potential employee, the organization needs to showcase itself as an innovative place to be. Examples could include YouTube uploads of interesting company projects, a welcoming Facebook page, or simply tweets or blogs about the passion that employees feel with your organization. The job description should also focus on skills and experiences that demonstrate adaptability versus rigidity. Employees with more challenging life and job experiences are likely to embrace innovation. Finally, utilize your current creative employees for referrals as they are sometimes the best face of the company. Also remember that specific skills for a job can be acquired; it is the innovative part that needs to be sought out.

As a final point to remember, carefully assess the candidate through the interview process.

Pose questions that require candidates to describe previous experiences that involved some innovative skills and abilities that the prospective job requires. Ask questions such as "Describe a recent new problem you have had to deal with on your current job and describe what you did to solve it." If the candidate has too little previous work experiences, you may also use hypothetical questions that provide possible work-related problems and ask them how they would solve them. You could also ask a candidate to create a role-playing scenario, such as dealing with a stubborn team member and turn it into a written exercise. Another example could entail having a candidate being given 30 minutes to outline a strategy for a small innovation within the department. All of these ideas lead to finding and assessing the most innovative employees.

Source: Based on some of the ideas in: http://www.inc.com/magazine/20101001/guidebook-how-to-hire-for-creativity.html accessed March 10, 2011.

Key Terms

Absorb the uncertainty	Gravity
Achievement orientation	I-Challenge
Addiction to the innovation	Imagining
Clearing obstacles	Incongruities
Corporate innovation	Incremental innovation
Creating	Innovative thinking
Disruptive innovation	Insulation
Dreaming	Internal locus of control
Duplication	Inventing
Entrepreneurial action	Perfectionist syndrome
Entrepreneurial motivation	Pioneering
Entrepreneurship, creativity, and	Process innovation
innovation	Radical innovation
Exploring	Sustain
Framing the challenge	Tolerance for ambiguity
Extension	Unexpected occurrences

Discussion Questions

1. What is innovation and how does it differ from entrepreneurship?
2. Identify the three types of innovation.
3. Describe the four methods of innovation—invention, extension, duplication, and synthesis.
4. Explain the different trajectories of innovation.
5. Identify three misconceptions about innovation.
6. Some of the characteristics attributed to innovators include internal locus of control, tolerance for ambiguity, and calculated risk taking. Discuss how these relate to the innovative mind-set.
7. Explain the motivation behind innovation.
8. What are the major drivers of innovative ideas? Explain and give an example of each.
9. What are the key myths associated with innovation? Debunk each.
10. What are four causes of stress among innovators? How can stress be managed?

Endnotes

1. "The World's Most Innovative Companies for 2010," *Fast Company*. Retrieved January 1, 2011, http://www.fastcompany.com/mic/2010 and "The 50 Most Innovative Companies," *Business Week*, 2010. Accessed on January 1, 2011, http://www.businessweek.com/interactive_reports/innovative_companies_2010.html
2. Vanhaverbeke, W. & Peeters, N. 2005. Embracing innovation as strategy: Corporate venturing, competence building, and corporate strategy making, *Creativity and Innovation Management* 14 (3): 246–257.

3. Covin, J. G., Slevin, D. P. & Heeley, M. B. 2000. Pioneers and followers: Competitive tactics, environment, and firm growth, *Journal of Business Venturing* 15: 175–210.
4. Morris, M. H., Kuratko, D. F. & Covin, J. G. 2011. *Corporate Entrepreneurship & Innovation*, 3rd ed. Mason, OH: Cengage/South-Western Publishers.
5. Morse, C. W. 1986. The delusion of intrapreneurship, *Long Range Planning* 19 (2): 92–95; and Duncan, W. J., Ginter, P. M., Rucks, A. C. & Jacobs, T. D. 1988. Intrapreneuring and the reinvention of the corporation, *Business Horizons* 31 (3): 16–21.
6. Kuratko, D. F., Ireland, R. D. & Hornsby, J. S. 2001. The power of entrepreneurial outcomes: Insights from Acordia, inc., *Academy of Management Executive* 15 (4): 60–71; Kuratko, D. F., Ireland, R. D., Covin, J. G. & Hornsby, J. S. 2005. A model of middle level managers' entrepreneurial behavior, *Entrepreneurship Theory and Practice* 29 (6): 699–716; Miles, M. P. & Covin, J. G. 2002. Exploring the practice of corporate venturing: Some common forms and their organizational implications. *Entrepreneurship Theory and Practice* 26 (3): 21–40; Hornsby, J. S., Kuratko, D. F., Shepherd, D. A. & Bott, J. P. 2009. Managers' corporate entrepreneurial actions: Examining perception and position, *Journal of Business Venturing* 24 (3): 236–247.
7. Govindarajan, V. & Trimble, C. 2005. Building breakthrough businesses within established organizations, *Harvard Business Review* 83 (5): 58–68.
8. Brandt, S. C. 1986. *Entrepreneuring in Established Companies.* Homewood, IL: Dow-Jones-Irwin, 54.
9. Drucker, P. F. 1985. *Innovation and Entrepreneurship.* New York: Harper & Row, 20.
10. Schroeder, D. M. 1990. A dynamic perspective on the impact of process innovation upon competitive strategies. *Strategic Management Journal* 11: 25–41.
11. O'Sullivan, D. & Dooley, L. 2009. *Applying Innovation.* Thousand Oaks, CA: Sage Publications.
12. M. J. C. Martin. 2004. *Managing Innovation and Entrepreneurship in Technology Based Firms.* New York: Wiley.
13. Based on: Kuratko, D. F. 2009. *Entrepreneurship: Theory, Process, & Practice,* 8th ed. Mason, OH: Cengage/South-Western Publishing.
14. MacLaughlin, I. 1999. *Creative Technological Change: The Shaping of Technology and Organizations.* London: Routledge.
15. Christensen, C. M. 1997. *The Innovator's Dilemma.* Boston, MA: Harvard Business School Press; Utterback, J. M. 1996. *Mastering the Dynamics of Innovation.* Boston, MA: Harvard Business School Press.
16. Christensen, *The Innovator's Dilemma.*
17. O'Reilly III, C. A. & Tushman, M. L. 2004. The ambidextrous organization, *Harvard Business Review* 82 (4): 74–81.
18. Adapted from: Drucker, P. F. 1985. The discipline of innovation, *Harvard Business Review* 63 (May/June): 67–72.
19. Corbett, A. C. 2005. Experiential learning within the process of opportunity identification and exploitation, *Entrepreneurship Theory and Practice* 29 (4): 473–491; and Corbett, A. C. 2007. Learning asymmetries and the discovery of entrepreneurial opportunities, *Journal of Business Venturing* 22 (1): 97–118.
20. Kuratko, D. F. 2009. *Entrepreneurship: Theory, Process, & Practice,* 8th ed. Mason, OH: Cengage/South-Western Publishing.

21. McClelland, D. C. 1961. *The Achieving Society.* New York: Van Nostrand; and McClelland, D. C. 1962. Business drive and national achievement, *Harvard Business Review* 40 (4) (July/August): 99–112.

22. Mitchell, R. K., Busenitz, L., Lant, T., McDougall, P. P., Morse, E. A. & Smith, J. B. 2004. The distinctive and inclusive domain of entrepreneurial cognition research. *Entrepreneurship Theory and Practice* 28 (6): 505–518; and Baron, R. A. and Ward, T. B. 2004. Expanding entrepreneurial cognition's toolbox: Potential contributions from the field of cognitive science. *Entrepreneurship Theory and Practice* 28 (6): 553–574.

23. For some articles on entrepreneurial characteristics, see Kickul, J. & Gundry, L. K. 2002. Prospecting for strategic advantage: The proactive entrepreneurial personality and small firm innovation, *Journal of Small Business Management,* 40 (2): 85–97; and Brigham, K. H., DeCastro, J. O., and Shepherd, D. A. 2007. A person-organization fit model of owners-managers' cognitive style and organization demands. *Entrepreneurship Theory and Practice* 31 (1): 29–51.

24. Reprinted from *Entrepreneurship Theory and Practice* with the permission of Baylor University. All rights reserved.

25. Reuber, A. R. & Fischer, E. 1999. Understanding the consequences of founders' experience. *Journal of Small Business Management* (February) 37 (2): 30–45.

26. Kuratko, D. F., Hornsby, J. S. & Naffziger, D. W. January 1997. An examination of owner's goals in sustaining entrepreneurship. *Journal of Small Business Management* 35 (1): 24–33.

27. See: Morris, M. H., Allen, J. A., Kuratko, D. F. & Brannon, D. 2010. Experiencing family business creation: Differences between founders, non-family managers, and founders of non-family firms, *Entrepreneurship Theory & Practice* 34 (6): 1057–1084; and Morris, M. H., Kuratko, D. F. & Schindehutte, M. 2012. Framing the entrepreneurial experience, *Entrepreneurship Theory & Practice,* January, In–press.

28. Politis, D. 2005. The process of entrepreneurial learning: A conceptual framework, *Entrepreneurship Theory and Practice* 29 (4): 399–424.

29. Davidsson, P. 2004. A general theory of entrepreneurship: The individual-opportunity nexus, *International Small Business Journal* 22 (2): 206–219; Berglund, H. 2007. Entrepreneurship and phenomenology: Researching entrepreneurship as lived experience. In J. Ulhoi & H. Neergaard (eds.), *Handbook of Qualitative Research Methods in Entrepreneurship* (pp. 75–96). London: Edward Elgar.

30. Adapted from Taylor, W. 1990. The business of innovation, *Harvard Business Review* (March/April): 97–106; and George, G. & Bock, A. J. 2009. *Inventing Entrepreneurs: Technology Innovators and Their Entrepreneurial Journey.* Upper Saddle River, NJ: Pearson/Prentice Hall.

31. Kuratko, D. F. 2009. *Entrepreneurship: Theory, Process, & Practice,* 8th ed. Mason, OH: Cengage/South-Western Publishing.

32. Akande, A. 1992. Coping with entrepreneurial stress, *Leadership & Organization Development Journal* 13 (2): 27–32; and Buttner, E. H. 1992. Entrepreneurial stress: Is it hazardous to your health? *Journal of Managerial Issues* 4 (2) (summer): 223–240.

33. Buttner, Entrepreneurial stress; see also Rabin, M. A. 1996. Stress, strain, and their moderators: An empirical comparison of entrepreneurs and managers, *Journal of Small Business Management* 27 (4) (January): 46–58.

34. Boyd, D. P. & Gumpert, D. E. 1983. Coping with entrepreneurial stress, *Harvard Business Review* 61 (2) (March/April): 46–56.

35. Boyd & Gumpert, Coping with Entrepreneurial Stress.

36. Goldsby, M. G., Kuratko, D. F. & Bishop, J. W. 2005. Entrepreneurship and fitness: An examination of rigorous exercise and goal attainment among small business owners, *Journal of Small Business Management* 43 (1) (January): 78–92; see also: Levesque, M. & Minniti, M. 2006. The effect of aging on entrepreneurial behavior, *Journal of Business Venturing* 21 (2): 177–194.

37. McGrath, R. G. & MacMillan, I. 2000, *The Entrepreneurial Mindset*. Boston, MA: Harvard Business Press.

38. Ireland, R. D., Hitt, M. A., Camp, S.M. & Sexton, D. L. 2001. Integrating entrepreneurship actions and strategic management actions to create firm wealth, *Academy of Management Executive* 15 (1): 95–106.

CHAPTER 2

THE PROCESS OF CORPORATE INNOVATION

INTRODUCTION

As we discussed in the Preface, companies cannot be static—they must continually adjust, adapt, or redefine themselves. The twenty-first century is witnessing corporate strategies focused heavily on innovation. The contemporary thrust of innovative thinking has become the major force *inside* enterprises.[1] Successful corporate innovation has been used in many different companies and today a wealth of popular business literature describes a new "corporate revolution" taking place thanks to the infusion of innovative thinking into large bureaucratic structures.[2] This infusion is referred to as *corporate entrepreneurship, corporate innovation,* or *intrapreneurship*, and represents innovative activity inside of the organization where individuals (innovators) will "champion" new ideas from development to complete reality. Corporations enhance the innovative abilities of their employees, and increase corporate success through the creation of new products, markets, or methods. Successfully applying the innovative process within larger, established organizations requires that the manager appreciate the unique nature of corporate entrepreneurship or corporate innovation.[3]

However, corporate innovative activity can be difficult since it involves radically changing traditional forms of internal corporate behavior and structural patterns. Yet, the desire to pursue corporate innovation (entrepreneurship) has arisen from a variety of pressing problems including (1) increased global competition; (2) continual downsizing of organizations seeking greater efficiency; (3) dramatic changes, innovations, and improvements in the marketplace;

(4) perceived weaknesses in the traditional methods of organizational management; and (5) the exodus of innovative-minded employees who are disenchanted with bureaucratic organizations.

However, the pursuit of corporate innovation as a strategy to counter these problems creates a newer and potentially more complex set of challenges on both a practical and theoretical level. On a practical level, organizations need some guidelines to direct or redirect resources toward establishing effective innovation strategies. They also need to continually reassess the components or dimensions which predict, explain, and shape the environment in which corporate innovation flourishes. There have been only a limited number of studies focusing on various factors contributing to, or enhancing, the establishment of corporate innovation. This chapter presents an overview of the concept of corporate innovation from an organizational perspective by outlining recommended steps for a strategy in corporate innovation and entrepreneurship based upon the critical factors that enhance the development of innovative-minded employees.

OBSTACLES TO CORPORATE INNOVATION

A number of researchers have attempted to examine particular factors which are associated with success in corporate innovation. For example, issues such as financial factors, incentive and control systems, market and entry approaches, and market-driven versus technology-driven demand have all been examined as possible causal factors in the success or failure of corporate innovative activity.[4]

However, a number of researchers have explained the process of innovation from the perspective of obstacles. They have identified a large set of obstacles that reflect aspects of organizational culture that prevent innovation from occurring. Today, many corporations are viewed to have obsolete ideas about cooperative cultures, management techniques, and values of management and employees. Organizations have to stimulate, support, and protect innovative individuals.

The entrepreneurial/innovative process does not conform to standard operating procedures as innovation represents the antithesis of standard operating procedures. Innovation requires individuals willing to challenge "business as usual." Michael H. Morris, Donald F. Kuratko, and Jeffrey G. Covin[5] presented critical obstacles in the corporate innovation process, including lack of time, lack of rewards, lack of resources, *turfism*, and lack of a sponsor. Let's examine each of these.

NO TIME

Because of increased global competition and the birth of the information age, business professionals are extremely busy keeping up with a wealth of available information and changes in technology. There just isn't a lot of time during the workday to engage in innovation. A few companies encourage their employees to spend a portion of their time on ideas outside their normal course of duties. However, this lack of time should not prevent an innovative individual who has a passion for an idea from putting together a team, writing a business plan, harnessing the necessary internal resources, and making the innovation a reality.

POOR REWARDS

Traditionally, corporations do not necessarily reward (financially or otherwise) employees for being innovative. Many companies have recently implemented reward systems for cost-saving suggestions or ideas presented through structured suggestion programs. But, with few exceptions, rewards for innovative thinking and behavior are not built into organizational performance systems.

UNDERFUNDED

Without financing, a corporate innovator's idea will remain only a vision. For this reason, the successful innovator must either develop knowledge about financial projections and calculations, or recruit a member of their team who has this knowledge and is willing and able to develop this aspect of the venture plan. Executives are not going to invest money in a new venture unless the entrepreneur can demonstrate the potential for a return on the investment that the company needs to achieve. As with any organization, funds are limited, and support of new products and services is determined by extensive market research, detailed financial projections, and contingency plans in case the sales projections are overestimated.

JOB DOMAIN

Trying to be innovative in an established company, an individual may find that departments are more concerned with protecting their "domain" than they are with developing new ideas that will benefit the organization. Frequently, the corporate innovator will run into "power plays" and battles for control over decision making occurring between vice presidents and/or their respective areas. The successful innovator needs to avoid these power plays, if at all possible, and be willing to work beyond the traditional boundaries of a particular job.

NO ALLIES

To help them in their assessment of these political wars, the corporate innovator needs an ally higher in the organization who oversees the progress of the corporate venture. These allies also act as buffers guarding innovators against unnecessary organizational bureaucratic interference. This allows the corporate entrepreneur to concentrate on his/her venture. Sponsors can also act as coaches for corporate innovators. They are most effective if they have personally championed an idea earlier in their career. In the latter case, they also serve as role models who can offer empathy and optimism through a critical but trusting attitude.

FELLOW EMPLOYEES

The greatest of all the obstacles may actually be with fellow employees. Management may be able to fix the structure and remove bureaucratic rules and procedures, but the challenges involved in getting employees to embrace innovative thinking, change the way they do things, collaborate on projects involving new ideas, and give up resources to support innovative initiatives can be especially challenging. Innovative ideas not only can represent tremendous opportunity to the firm, but they can also threaten individuals inside the firm. For many employees, innovative ideas could mean that current products will be eliminated, budgets will be reallocated, or processes will be modified. As a result, many new ideas are blocked by:

- making premature and uninformed judgments;
- *neophobia*—the dread of anything new or novel, fear of the unknown; sense of embarrassment or humiliation that accompanies the admission that existing products or procedures are inferior to new proposals;
- caution—it's safer to have "the me-too-later" attitude;
- politics—new ideas frequently pose a threat to the corporate stature and vested interests of managers who are anxious to maintain the existing hierarchical structure.

These obstacles share a common element—namely, they represent situations in which to meet the needs of a new project, the corporate innovator must attempt to convince someone or some unit to change current behavior patterns from what the person or unit might otherwise prefer to do. Therefore, two methods for handling some of the obstacles are building social capital and acquiring resources.

BUILDING SOCIAL CAPITAL

Corporate entrepreneurs must rely on their ingenuity and persistence to build influence. They need to build "*social capital*," which is defined as an inventory of trust, gratitude, or obligations that can be "cashed in" when the new project is in demand (Blau, 1964). Building this capital can be accomplished a number of ways, including:

- Sharing information
- Creating opportunities for people to demonstrate their skills and competence
- Building and using influence networks[6]

RESOURCE ACQUISITION

The major method of securing the necessary resources is through co-optation or leveraging of the resources currently underutilized by the firm. Stark and MacMillan identified four distinct strategies for co-optation:

- *Borrowing*: Borrowing strategies are employed to temporarily or periodically secure the use of assets or other resources, on the premise that they will eventually be returned.

- *Begging*: Begging strategies are employed to secure resources by appealing to the owner's goodwill. In this way, venture managers gain the use of the resources without needing to return them, despite the fact that the owner recognizes the value of the assets. In her research, Kanter (1983) identifies many cases of "tincupping," in which venture managers begged or scrounged resources from the rest of the firm.

- *Scavenging*: Scavenging strategies extract usage from goods that others do not intend to use or that they might actually welcome an appropriate opportunity to divest themselves of. This approach involves learning about unused or underused resources (e.g., obsolete inventory, idle equipment, or underutilized personnel).

- *Amplifying*: Amplification is the capacity to leverage far more value out of an asset than is perceived by the original owner of the asset.[7]

These ideas may help the innovator to secure resources that would otherwise have to be secured by economic exchange at a much greater cost. There are three critical benefits of relying on these methods of resource acquisition: by appropriating underutilized resources venture managers reduce the cost of start-up, they reduce the risk of start-up by dramatically bringing down the initial investment, and they increase the return on assets of the venture.

CORPORATE INNOVATION AS A STRATEGY

Operational definitions of corporate innovation and corporate entrepreneurship have evolved over the last 30 years. For example, one researcher[8] noted that corporate innovation is a very broad concept that includes the generation, development, and implementation of new ideas or behaviors. An innovation can be a new product or service, an administrative system, or a new plan or program pertaining to organizational members. Another researcher[9] observed that corporate innovation may be formal or informal activities aimed at creating new businesses in established companies through product and process innovations and market developments. These activities may take place at the corporate, division (business), functional, or project levels. Sharma and Chrisman[10] established one of the most cited definitions of corporate entrepreneurship when they described it as a process whereby an individual or a group of individuals, in association with an existing organization, creates a new organization or instigates renewal or innovation within the organization. Under this definition, strategic renewal, innovation, and corporate venturing are all important and legitimate parts of the corporate innovation process.

Morris, Kuratko, and Covin[11] cited two phenomena as constituting the domain of corporate entrepreneurship—namely, corporate venturing and strategic entrepreneurship. *Corporate venturing* approaches have as their commonality the adding of new businesses (or portions of new businesses via equity investments) to the corporation. This can be accomplished through three implementation modes—internal corporate venturing, cooperative corporate venturing, and external corporate venturing. By contrast, *strategic entrepreneurship* approaches have as their commonality the exhibition of large-scale or otherwise highly consequential innovations that are adopted in the firm's pursuit of competitive advantage. These innovations may or may not result in new businesses for the corporation. With strategic entrepreneurship approaches, innovation can be in any of five areas—the firm's strategy, product offerings, served markets, internal organization (i.e., structure, processes, and capabilities), or business model.[12]

As the field has further evolved, the concept of a corporate innovation as a strategy began to develop. Ireland, Covin, and Kuratko define a corporate entrepreneurial (innovative) strategy as "a vision-directed, organization-wide reliance on entrepreneurial behavior that purposefully and continuously rejuvenates the organization and shapes the scope of its operations through the recognition and exploitation of entrepreneurial opportunity."[13] Today we see a number of companies that have adopted this innovative perspective. Apple, Google, Intel, Samsung, and Amazon are companies that continually appear on the lists of the "most innovative companies." This type of achievement can only come through an organization-wide commitment to a *corporate innovation strategy*.

For corporate entrepreneurship/innovation to operate as a strategy, it must "run deep" within organizations. Eisenhardt, Brown, and Neck[14] perhaps best captured where firms' strategies lie along the "innovation" continuum in their observations that firms with entrepreneurial strategies remain close to the "edge of time," judiciously balancing the exploitation of current entrepreneurial opportunities with the search for future entrepreneurial opportunities. Top managers are increasingly recognizing the need to respond to the entrepreneurial imperatives created by their competitive landscapes. Minimal responses to these entrepreneurial imperatives, reflecting superficial commitments to corporate innovation strategy, are bound to fail. Moreover, while top management can instigate the strategy, it cannot dictate it. Those at the middle and lower ranks of an organization have a tremendous effect on and significant roles within entrepreneurial and strategic processes.[15] Without sustained and strong commitment from all levels of the organization, innovative behavior will never be a defining characteristic of the organization.

An innovation strategy is hard to create and, perhaps, even harder to perpetuate in organizations. The presence of certain external environmental conditions may be sufficient to prompt an organization's leaders into exploring the possibility of adopting such a strategy. However, the commitment of individuals throughout the organization to making an innovation strategy work and the realization of personal and organizational innovative outcomes that reinforce this commitment will be necessary to insure that innovation strategy become a defining aspect of the organization. Alignments must be created in evaluation and reward systems such that congruence is achieved in the innovative behaviors induced at the individual and organizational levels. Thus, while external conditions may be increasingly conducive to the adoption of a corporate

innovation strategy, managers should harbor no illusions that the effective implementation of these strategies will be easily accomplished.

THE CRITICAL ELEMENTS

Many companies that have made systematic efforts to learn how to conduct
effective corporate innovation programs have found them to be viable and effective. They have proved that an effective innovative process can be developed.
However, what elements are involved in such programs? Since a corporate innovation strategy is sometimes difficult to grasp, let alone develop, five critical elements
have been suggested in the implementation of any innovation strategy: vision,
innovation, environment, managers, and teams.[16] In this section, we examine these
five elements in order to identify what it takes to establish a successful program.
These elements become the critical steps for any executive seeking to establish the
foundation for an innovation strategy within the organization.

CREATE THE VISION

The first step in planning a corporate innovation strategy for the enterprise
is sharing the vision of innovation that the corporate leaders wish to achieve.[17]
The vision must be clearly articulated by the organization's leaders; however,
the specific objectives are then developed by the managers and employees of
the organization. Because it is suggested that corporate innovation results from
the creative talents of people within the organization, employees need to know
about and understand this vision. Shared vision is a critical element for a strategy
that seeks innovative pursuits of the managers and employees. This shared vision
requires identification of specific objectives for corporate innovation strategies
and of the programs needed to achieve those objectives.

ENCOURAGE INNOVATIVE THINKING

The second step is encouraging innovation as the specific tool of the
corporate entrepreneur. Corporations must understand and develop innovation as the key element in their strategy. Numerous researchers have examined
the importance of innovation within the corporate environment.[18] Described as
chaotic and unplanned by some authors[19], other researchers insist it is a systematic discipline.[20] Both of these positions can be true depending on the nature of
the innovation. As we explained in Chapter 1, one way to understand the concept
of innovation is to focus on three different trajectories of innovation: radical,
incremental, and disruptive.

- *Radical innovation* is the launching of inaugural breakthroughs that take
  experimentation and determined vision (such as personal computers,
  Post-it Notes, disposable diapers, and overnight mail delivery), where as
  incremental innovation refers to the systematic evolution of a product or
  service into newer or larger markets (such as microwave popcorn or popcorn
  used for packaging to replace Styrofoam). The structure, marketing, financing, and formal systems of a corporation can all contribute to incremental
  innovation. *Disruptive Innovation* goes beyond radical innovation and

transforms business practice to rewrite the rules of an industry. In other words, the business practice of an entire industrial sector could be changed radically. Radical, incremental, and disruptive innovations require vision and support. This support takes different steps for effective development. For example, it has been widely recognized that innovative activity needs a champion—the person with a vision and the ability to share it. In addition, both types of innovation require an effort by top management to develop and educate employees concerning innovation and entrepreneurship.

- *Encouraging innovation* requires a willingness to not only tolerate failure, but also to learn from it. For example, one of the early founders of 3M, Francis G. Oakie, had an idea to replace razor blades with sandpaper. He believed that men could rub sandpaper on their face rather than use a sharp razor. He was wrong and the idea failed. But, his ideas continued until he developed waterproof sandpaper for the auto industry—a blockbuster success! In the process, 3M's philosophy was born.

Innovation is often a numbers game; the more ideas a company has, the better the chances for a successful innovation. This philosophy has paid off for 3M. Antistatic videotape, translucent dental braces, synthetic ligaments for knee surgery, heavy-duty reflective sheeting for construction signs, and, of course, Post-it Notes are just some of the great innovations developed at 3M. Overall, the company has a catalogue of 60,000 products that contributed to over $10.6 billion in sales. Today, 3M follows a set of innovative rules that encourage employees to foster ideas.[21] Two key rules are:

- *Don't Kill a Project* If an idea can't find a home in one of 3M's divisions, a staffer can devote 15 percent of his or her time to prove it is workable. For those who need seed money, as many as 90 Genesis grants of $50,000 are awarded each year.
- *Tolerate Failure* By encouraging plenty of experimentation and risk taking, there are more chances for a new product hit. The goal: divisions must derive 25 percent of sales from products introduced in the past five years. The target may be boosted to 30 percent.

ESTABLISH AN INNOVATIVE ENVIRONMENT
The third step and possibly the most critical element is establishing an innovative environment. In establishing the drive to innovate in today's corporations, there must be a commitment to invest heavily in *innovative* activities that allow new ideas to flourish in an innovative environment. This concept, when coupled with the other specific elements of a strategy for innovation, enhances the potential for employees to become innovation developers. In fact, in developing employees as a source of innovations for corporations, researchers have found that companies need to provide more nurturing and information-sharing activities. In addition to establishing innovative ways and nurturing innovators, there is a need to develop a climate that will help innovative-minded people reach their full potential. The perception of an innovative climate is critical for stressing the

importance of management's commitment to not only the organizations' people but also to the innovative projects. The importance of establishing the proper organizational climate is made clear by Morse when he questioned the ability of organizational bureaucracies to foster innovation due to the problem of reward structures which do not compensate in line with the expectations of innovative personnel. In addition, personal autonomy is usually not granted sufficiently for innovators to work on special projects as the corporate climate tends to promote stability and efficiency as opposed to the adaptability needed for innovation.[22]

Specific organizational antecedents of an organization's innovative actions have been identified in the literature—top management support, work discretion, rewards/reinforcement, time availability, and organizational boundaries.[23] Employee perception of these factors for an innovative environment is critical for stressing the importance of management's commitment (Ireland, Kuratko & Morris, 2006).[24] Thus it is not enough to simply believe these factors are in place; they must be perceived by the employees as strong.

DEVELOP INNOVATIVE MANAGERS

The fourth step is to develop individual managers for corporate innovation leadership. As a way for organizations to develop key managers for innovative leadership, a corporate innovation training program (Corporate Innovation Training) often induces the change needed in the work atmosphere. It is not my intent to elaborate completely on the content of a training program here, but a brief summary of an actual program is presented to provide a general understanding of how such a program is designed to introduce an innovative environment in a company. This award-winning training program was intended to create an awareness of innovative opportunities in organizations. The Corporate Innovation Program consists of seven modules, each designed to train participants to support corporate innovation in their own work area. The modules and a brief summary of their contents follow:

1. *The Innovative Experience.* An enthusiastic overview of The Innovative Experience in which participants are challenged to think innovatively with an emphasis on the need for innovation strategies in today's organizations.

2. *Innovative Thinking.* The process of thinking innovatively is foreign to most traditional managers. The misconceptions about thinking innovatively are reviewed, and a discussion of the most common inhibitors is presented. After completing an innovation inventory, managers engage in several exercises designed to facilitate their own innovative thinking.

3. *Idea Acceleration Process.* Managers generate a set of specific ideas on which they would like to work. The process includes examining a number of aspects of the corporation, including structural barriers and facilitators. Additionally, managers determine resources needed to accomplish their projects.

4. *Barriers and Facilitators to Innovative Thinking.* The most common barriers to innovative behavior are reviewed and discussed. Managers complete several exercises that will help them deal with barriers in the workplace. In addition,

video case histories are shown that depict actual corporate innovators that have been successful in dealing with corporate barriers.

5. *Sustaining Innovative Teams.* Managers work together to form teams based on the ideas that have been circulating among the entire group. Team dynamics is reviewed for each group to understand.

6. *The Innovation Plan.* After managers examine several aspects of facilitators and barriers to behaving innovatively in their organization, groups are asked to begin the process of completing a plan. The plan includes setting goals, establishing a work team, assessing current conditions, and developing a step-by-step timetable for project completion and evaluation.

7. *Assessing the Innovative Culture.* A survey instrument is provided and described which assesses the level of innovative culture within the organization. Participants complete the survey as a posttraining phase and results will be fed back to all participants. Areas for improvement are then addressed.

Corporate innovation training that is viewed as a one-time activity cannot succeed. The more widespread the understanding of corporate innovation, the more likely it is that real culture changes will occur in the organization. The organizations who have utilized the training understand this idea. They all have attempted to repeat the program for as broad an audience as possible.

To validate the training program's effectiveness, an instrument entitled the *"Corporate Entrepreneurship Assessment Instrument" (CEAI)* was developed to provide for a psychometrically sound instrument that measured key innovative climate factors. The responses to the CEAI were statistically analyzed and resulted in five identified factors. The CEAI was originally developed as an "intapreneurial" instrument to measure the perceptions of managers on the critical factors necessary for an innovative environment to exist (Kuratko, Montagno & Hornsby, 1990; Hornsby, Kuratko & Montagno, 1999).[25] The CEAI has been further refined by Holt, Rutherford, and Clohessy (2007)[26] and Rutherford and Holt (2007).[27] In essence, Ireland, Kuratko, and Morris (2006)[28] have argued that the CEAI provides a sound basis for managers to effectively manage, facilitate, and improve corporate innovation activities.

Thus, several studies have tried to isolate the organizational factors that promote corporate innovation. Specifically, Hornsby et al. (2002) Kuratko et al. (2005) and Ireland et al. (2006a; 2006b)[29] have taken steps toward answering this question by attempting to empirically and theoretically identify a parsimonious set of factors that influence corporate innovation. The results suggested that there are five stable organizational antecedents of middle-level managers' innovative behavior. These antecedents are:

1. *Management support* (the willingness of top-level managers to facilitate and promote innovative behavior, including the championing of innovative ideas and providing the resources people require to take innovative actions);

2. *Work discretion/autonomy* (top-level managers' commitment to tolerate failure, provide decision-making latitude and freedom from excessive

oversight, and delegate authority and responsibility to middle-level managers);

3. *Rewards/reinforcement* (developing and using systems that reward based on performance, highlighting significant achievements, and encouraging pursuit of challenging work);

4. *Time availability* (evaluating work loads to ensure that individuals and groups have the time needed to pursue innovations and that their jobs are structured in ways that support efforts to achieve short- and long-term organizational goals); and

5. *Organizational boundaries* (precise explanations of outcomes expected from organizational work and development of mechanisms for evaluating, selecting, and using innovations).

In interpreting their results, Hornsby et al. (2002)[30] highlighted the importance of middle-level managers receiving information from top-level managers regarding their position relative to the five antecedents and then effectively communicating that information to operating-level managers. In Chapter 7, we cover the instrument and its applications in greater depth.

COMMIT TO INNOVATION TEAMS

The fifth step is to encourage the creation and use of *innovation teams* as they hold the potential for producing innovative results and productivity breakthroughs. Companies that have committed to an innovation team approach often label the change they have undergone a "transformation." This new breed of work team is a powerful strategy for many firms. They have been referred to as self-directing, self-managing, high-performing, and empowering; although in reality an innovation team includes all of those characteristics (Francis & Sandberg, 2002).[31] In Chapter 9, we develop the concept of teams in further detail.

In examining many of the successful innovative developments within established corporations, innovative activity is not the sole province of the company's founder or top managers. Rather, it is diffused throughout the firm where experimentation and development go on all the time, as the company searches for new ways to build on knowledge accumulated by its workers. It has been referred to as "collective entrepreneurship," where individual skills are integrated into a group and their collective capacity to innovate becomes greater than the sum of its parts. Over time, as group members work through various problems and approaches, they learn about each other's abilities. Specifically, they learn how they can help each other to perform better, what each can contribute to a particular project, and how they can best take advantage of one another's experience. Each participant is constantly on the lookout for small adjustments that will speed and smooth the evolution of the whole.

The net result of many such small-scale adaptations, affected throughout the organization, is to propel the enterprise forward. There are, in fact, specific key roles that must be filled on the venture team. In putting together the venture team, management must ensure that certain key roles are filled. The following roles are the most significant:

- *Innovator*: The person who has made the major technical innovation.
- *Venture Manager*: The internal entrepreneur responsible for the overall progress of the project.
- *Champion*: Any individual who makes a decisive contribution to the project by promoting its progress through the critical early stages, particularly up to the point of implementation.
- *Innovative CEO*: The individual who is in charge of the venture and controls the allocation of resources (e.g., a sub-CEO, a division manager, or a venture division manager).
- *Sponsor*: The high-level person in the parent company who acts as buffer protector and modifier of rules and policies and who helps the venture obtain the needed resources.

SUSTAINING CORPORATE INNOVATION

So, the question is, "how does an organization sustain the corporate innovation process?" The answer lies in the actions of senior managers. In order to maintain this innovative mind-set in an organization, managers must assume certain ongoing responsibilities.[32] The first responsibility is to establish a clear definition of the specified challenges that everyone involved with innovative projects should address. Second, managers have the responsibility to make the uncertainty of pursuing innovative projects less daunting and create the self-confidence within all employees that they can act on innovative opportunities without seeking managerial permission. Employees must not be overwhelmed by the complexity inherent in many innovative situations. Finally, managers need to clear out any obstacles that arise as a result of the innovative project progress. This can be a problem especially when the innovation begins to undergo significant growth. The ability to regroup and reorganize becomes invaluable. Organizational leaders must monitor and take control of the developing innovation.

From another perspective, it becomes apparent that change is inevitable in the organizational structure if innovative activity is going to exist and prosper. The change process consists of a series of emerging constructions of the people, the organizational goals, and the existing needs. In short, the organization will encourage innovation by relinquishing controls and changing the traditional bureaucratic structure.

One process model adapted from a number of researchers illustrates the critical elements needed for sustained corporate innovation activity.[33] Specifically, the model integrates and extends previous models that have examined the organizational or individual components of innovative activity. The model provided additional theoretical foundation emphasizing the importance of perceived implementation–output relationships at both the individual and organizational

FIGURE 2.1 A Model of the Corporate Innovation Process

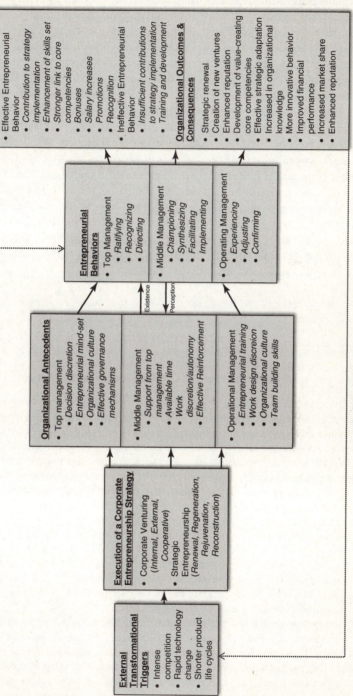

levels. The perceived satisfaction of these relationships provides the basis for whether or not a corporate innovation activity will be sustained.

The model shows that change or transformational triggers cause organizations to pursue strategies for innovative activities and to institute certain internal organizational factors to ensure their implementation. As demonstrated in this model, it is the degree of ongoing innovative behavior of individuals and the perceptions of an organization's executive management toward innovative activities that need to be focused upon. This model provides insights for understanding the entire corporate innovation process from both the individual and organizational levels.

Researchers Michael H. Morris, Donald F. Kuratko, and Jeffrey G. Covin warn that corporate innovation does not produce instant success. It requires considerable time and investment, and there must be continual reinforcement. By their nature, organizations impose constraints on innovative behavior: "To be sustainable, entrepreneurial thinking must be integrated into the mission, goals, strategies, structure, processes, and values of the organization. Flexibility, speed, innovation, and entrepreneurial leadership are the cornerstones. The managerial mindset must become an opportunity-driven mindset, where actions are never constrained by resources currently controlled."[34]

INNOVATION-IN-ACTION

"Innovation for the Sake of Dominance"

When the landscape of technology is surveyed, there is little doubt that the two most powerful companies in the world are Microsoft and Google. Microsoft long ago claimed dominance over the desktop, and Google has been working diligently to stake its claim on online applications. So, it would seem that the two companies might be resigned to live happily alongside one another, each overseeing its own domain with little attention paid to the other. The problem lies in the fact that their two worlds are colliding and slowly merging into a single realm where consumers glide from desktop to online without distinguishing between the two. As a result, the two companies have begun an epic battle to prove their dominance through innovation.

Beyond Microsoft's dominant position in operating systems, with the ubiquitous Windows series, it has also controlled the market in office suites with Microsoft Office and Internet browsers with Internet Explorer. Google, on the other hand, has largely been restricted to its namesake search engine, which has approximately 70 percent of the search-advertising market. Thus, the stage is set for the two companies to discover ways in which each can intrude on the other's turf.

Google's approach has become evident with the introduction of its own Internet browser, Google Chrome. The company's plan is to integrate the browser with its existing Google Apps and Google search in order to offer a full-scale operating system as a service, which will be known as Google Chrome. Google is banking on consumers' movement toward smaller laptops, known as netbooks, which have less capacity and, thus, benefit from online applications which do not take up storage space or processing power.

Microsoft's approach is to wrangle the search-advertising market away from Google with its own search engine by taking its existing Live Search and rebranding it as Bing. Despite Microsoft's reputation as an archaic company which is too lethargic to compete with more innovative companies such as Google, the company has surprised industry experts by gaining market share since its launch, slowly edging in on Yahoo's second-place position. Given that Microsoft's search-advertising market share had been declining for more than two years, the shift in trajectory is notable. According to analysts, every percentage point of market share is equivalent to $100 million of revenue, so even small gains can mean big dollars.

The question is no longer what approach the companies will take in their efforts to steal market share from the other, but rather how successful they will be in their attempts. Despite Google's impressive track record, many analysts are skeptical of its ability to profit from Chrome. After all, out of all of the tools Google has developed, it has only managed to monetize the use of its search engine, resulting in the company being labeled as a "one-trick pony." And, though Microsoft's gain in search-advertising market share has been impressive, analysts point to its $150 million PR effort as the only reason for the gain, leading them to speculate whether Microsoft's gain is merely a short-term by-product of its marketing push.

Moreover, the two companies did not ascend to supremacy blithely. Each took care to ensure that once they gained control of their respective markets that they would be able to retain it. Google's distribution deal with the popular Firefox browser has guaranteed that it will not be easily toppled from its market position, and Microsoft's first-mover advantage with its operating system, Internet browser, and office suite will force Google to take on every business's biggest competitor: the status quo. Users have grown accustomed to using Microsoft's software, and consumer behavior can be difficult, if not impossible, to change.

In the end, the possibility exists that neither company will be able to claim absolute victory, but competition breeds innovation, and innovation breeds new technology and, in turn, more choices for consumers. So, for the sake of the consumer, let the fighting commence.

Sources: Adapted from Goldman, D. (July 2009). "Bing Gaining on Google and Yahoo." Retrieved July 25, 2009, *CNNMoney.com*, http://money.cnn.com/2009/07/15/technology/bing_google_yahoo_search/index.htm; Goldman, D. (July 2009). "Google Chrome: Microsoft killer?" Retrieved July 25, 2009, *CNNMoney.com*, http://money.cnn.com/2009/07/08/technology/google_chrome_microsoft/index.htm; and Vogelstein, F. (July 2009). "Why Is Obama's Top Antitrust Cop Gunning for Google?" Retrieved July 27, 2009, *Wired Magazine*, http://www.wired.com/print/techbiz/it/magazine/17-08/mf_googlopoly

Key Terms

Amplifying
CEAI
Champion
Corporate entrepreneurship
Corporate innovation
Corporate innovation strategy

Corporate innovation, or intrapreneurship
Corporate venturing
Disruptive innovation
Incremental innovation
Innovation teams

Innovative
Inside
Neophobia
Social capital

Sponsor
Strategic entrepreneurship
Turfism

Discussion Questions

1. What are two reasons that such a strong desire to develop corporate innovators has arisen in recent years?
2. What are some of the corporate obstacles that must be overcome to establish a corporate innovation environment?
3. What are the two major domains that comprise corporate entrepreneurship?
4. Define a "corporate innovation strategy."
5. Identify the five key elements on which managers should concentrate to develop a corporate innovation strategy.
6. Explain the differences between radical and incremental innovation.
7. Identify the five specific innovative climate factors that organizations need to address in structuring their environment.
8. Why are innovation teams emerging as part of a new strategy for many corporations?
9. Identify the key roles that members of an innovation team could fulfill.
10. Describe the elements that are involved in sustaining corporate innovation.

Endnotes

1. Morris, M. H., Kuratko, D. F. & Covin, J. G. 2011. *Corporate Entrepreneurship & Innovation.* Mason, OH: Cengage/SouthWestern Publishers.
2. Hamel, G. 2000. *Leading the Revolution.* Boston, MA: Harvard Business School Press.
3. Kuratko, D. F., Ireland, R. D. & Hornsby, J. S. 2001. Improving firm performance through entrepreneurial actions: Acordia's corporate entrepreneurship strategy, *Academy of Management Executive* 15 (4): 60–71.
4. Sykes, H. B. & Block, Z. 1989. Corporate venturing obstacles: Sources and solutions, *Journal of Business Venturing* 4 (winter): 159–167.
5. Morris, Kuratko & Covin. *Corporate Entrepreneurship & Innovation.*
6. Blau, P. 1964, *Exchange and Power in Social Life.* New York: John Wiley & Sons.
7. Starr, J. A. & MacMillan, I. C. 1990. Resource co-optation via social contracting: resource acquisition strategies for new ventures, *Strategic Management Journal* 11 (Summer): 79–92.
8. Damanpour, F. 1991. Organizational innovation: A meta-analysis of effects of determinant and moderators, *Academy of Management Journal* 34: 355–390.
9. Zahra, S. A. 1991. Predictors and financial outcomes of corporate entrepreneurship: An exploratory study, *Journal of Business Venturing* 6: 259–286.
10. Sharma, P. & Chrisman, J. J. 1999. Toward a reconciliation of the definitional issues in the field of corporate entrepreneurship, *Entrepreneurship Theory & Practice* 23 (3): 11–28.
11. Morris, Kuratko & Covin. *Corporate Entrepreneurship & Innovation.*

12. Ireland, R. D. & Webb, J. W. 2007. Strategic entrepreneurship: Creating competitive advantage through streams of innovation. *Business Horizons* 50 (1): 49–59.
13. Ireland, R. D., Covin, J. G. & Kuratko, D. F. 2009. Conceptualizing corporate entrepreneurship strategy, *Entrepreneurship Theory and Practice* 33 (1): 19–46.
14. Eisenhardt, K. M., Brown, S. L. & Neck, H. M. 2000. Competing on the entrepreneurial edge. In G. D. Meyer & K. A. Heppard (eds.), *Entrepreneurship as strategy* (pp. 49–62). Thousand Oaks, CA: Sage Publications.
15. Hornsby, J. S., Kuratko, D. F., Shepherd, D. A. & Bott, J. P. 2009. Managers' corporate entrepreneurial actions: Examining perception and position, *Journal of Business Venturing* 24 (3): 236–247.
16. Kuratko, D. F. 2009. *Entrepreneurship: Theory, Process, & Practice*, 8th ed. Mason, OH: Cengage/South-Western Publishing.
17. Collins, J. C. & Porras, J. I. 1996. Building your company's vision, *Harvard Business Review* (September–October): 65–77.
18. Schroeder, D. M. 1990. A Dynamic perspective on the impact of process innovation upon competitive strategies, *Strategic Management Journal* 2: 25–41; and Fiol, C. M. 1995. Thought worlds colliding: The role of contradiction in corporate innovation processes, *Entrepreneurship Theory and Practice* 20 (3): 71–90.
19. Peters, T. 1990. Get innovative or get dead, *California Management Review* 33: 18–26.
20. Drucker, P. F. 1985. The discipline of innovation, *Harvard Business Review* 63 (May/June): 67–72.
21. Von Hipple, E., Thomke, S. & Sonnack, M. 1999. Creating breakthroughs at 3M, *Harvard Business Review* 77 (September–October): 47–57.
22. Morse, C. W. 1986. The delusion of intrapreneurship, *Long Range Planning* 19 (2): 92–95.
23. Kuratko, D. F., Montagno, R. V. & Hornsby, J. S. 1990. Developing an entrepreneurial assessment instrument for an effective corporate entrepreneurial environment, *Strategic Management Journal* 11 (Special Issue): 49–58; Hornsby, J. S., Kuratko, D. F., & Montagno, R. V. 1999. Perception of internal factors for corporate entrepreneurship: A comparison of Canadian and U. S. managers. *Entrepreneurship Theory and Practice*, 24(2): 9–24.
24. Ireland, R. D., Kuratko, D. F. & Morris, M. H. 2006. A health audit for corporate entrepreneurship: Innovation at all levels—Part I, *Journal of Business Strategy* 27 (1): 10–17.
25. Kuratko, D. F., Montagno, R. V. & Hornsby, J. S. 1990. Developing an entrepreneurial assessment instrument for an effective corporate entrepreneurial environment, *Strategic Management Journal* 11 (Special Issue): 49–58; Hornsby, J. S., Kuratko, D. F., & Montagno, R. V. 1999. Perception of internal factors for corporate entrepreneurship: A comparison of Canadian and U. S. managers. *Entrepreneurship Theory and Practice*, 24(2): 9–24.
26. Holt, D. T., Rutherford, M. W. & Clohessy, G. R. 2007. Corporate entrepreneurship: An empirical look at individual characteristics, context, and process, *Journal of Leadership & Organizational Studies* 13 (4): 40–54.
27. Rutherford, M. W. & Holt, D. T. 2007. Corporate entrepreneurship: An empirical look at the innovativeness dimension and its antecedents, *Journal of Organizational Change Management* 20 (3): 429
28. Ireland, R. D., Kuratko, D. F. & Morris, M. H. 2006a. A health audit for corporate entrepreneurship: Innovation at all levels— Part I, *Journal of Business Strategy*, 27 (1): 10–17.

29. Ireland, R. D., Kuratko, D. F. & Morris, M. H. 2006a. A health audit for corporate entrepreneurship: Innovation at all levels—Part I, *Journal of Business Strategy* 27 (1): 10–17; Ireland, R. D., Kuratko, D. F. & Morris, M. H. 2006a. A health audit for corporate entrepreneurship: Innovation at all levels—Part II. *Journal of Business Strategy* 27 (2): 21–30.
30. Hornsby, J. S., Kuratko, D. F. & Zahra, S. A. 2002. Middle managers' perception of the internal environment for corporate entrepreneurship: Assessing a measurement scale, *Journal of Business Venturing* 17: 49–63.
31. Francis, D. H. & Sandberg, W. R. 2002. Friendship within entrepreneurial teams and its association with team and venture performance, *Entrepreneurship Theory and Practice* 25 (2): 5–25.
32. McGrath, R. G. & MacMillan, I. 2000. *The Entrepreneurial Mindset.* Boston, MA: Harvard Business Press.
33. Adapted from: Ireland, R. D., Covin, J. G. & Kuratko, D. F. 2009. Conceptualizing corporate entrepreneurship strategy, *Entrepreneurship Theory and Practice* 33 (1): 19–46; Kuratko, D. F., Ireland, R. D., Covin, J. G. & Hornsby, J. S. 2005. A model of middle-level managers' entrepreneurial behavior, *Entrepreneurship Theory & Practice* 29 (6): 699–716; and Kuratko, D. F., Hornsby, J. S. & Goldsby, M. G. 2004. Sustaining corporate entrepreneurship: A proposed model of perceived implementation/outcome comparisons at the organizational and individual levels. *International Journal of Entrepreneurship and Innovation* 5 (2): 77–89.
34. Morris, Kuratko & Covin. 2011. *Corporate Entrepreneurship & Innovation*, pp. 420–421.

PART 2

INDIVIDUAL INNOVATION SKILLS
(I-SKILLS)

CHAPTER 3

UNLEASHING INDIVIDUAL CREATIVITY

INTRODUCTION

"Ideas are like fish. If you want to catch fish, you can stay in the shallow water. But if you want to catch the big fish, you've got to go deeper. Down deep, the fish are more powerful and more pure. They're huge and abstract. And they're beautiful."[1]

Finding *ideas* for new products and services may be one of the hardest challenges a manager faces today; however, it is critically important that *creativity* and innovation become the backbone of a company's operations. Lower wages, easily accessible communication networks, and enhanced supply chain management allow competitors around the world to compete against more well-known companies. The deciding factor in today's hypercompetitive markets is creatively offering better products and services that serve customers in new ways.[2] Unfortunately, many managers have been educated and trained to increase the efficiency of doing what has been successful in the past. Additionally, education is often based on getting "the" right answer, instead of learning to work with the ambiguity and uncertainty found in innovative activities.

Clayton Christensen of the Harvard Business School states that this mind-set can lead to the demise of company, as the organization continues to deliver what the customer expects, without looking to new opportunities in the marketplace. When better products come out by entrepreneurial start-ups and more innovative competitors, the established company has difficulties meeting the new challenges.[3] A big reason for this is the inertia found in established companies. Hit with deadlines and performance goals, managers often focus on meeting production and shipping deadlines and generating revenues, at the expense of developing new markets. Thinking about new products and services becomes a sideline activity, but it is innovative products and services that likely got the company where it is today.[4] Thus, managers must regain the entrepreneurial edge by being more creative.

The entrepreneurial process inside an organization is guided by a manager or employee who has identified a unique, new opportunity or idea, as well as the self-discipline and perseverance to commercialize the new opportunity or idea. The origin of the new opportunity or idea is the beginning of the entrepreneurship process, and creative thinking on the part of the individual is the foundation of the birth of the idea.

The crucial component is an individual who has a vision of a new way of doing things or a unique insight. The entrepreneurial process begins with discovering a new problem to be solved or a new opportunity to be capitalized on resulting from the personal creativity of individual workers and managers. Later, entrepreneurial thinking creates a solution to the problem or opportunity in the form of a new service or product. However, it is creativity that begins the entrepreneurial process.

In this chapter, we explain what creativity is and is not, the elements that support creative activity, the four phases of the creative process, and areas where people can focus their creativity. In the process, you will learn how your brain comes up with new ideas, and what steps you can take to develop your own and your employees' creativity. We begin by examining the concept of creativity.

THE NATURE OF CREATIVITY

Creativity is one of the most misunderstood topics in our society. It is prized and coveted while being feared and mistrusted at the same time. Most people see it as magical and incorrectly believe that only a genius can be creative. Most people also assume that some people are born creative and others are not, or only the highly intelligent person is capable of generating creative ideas and insights. The authors of this book do not accept these views; neither does Nancy C. Andreasen of the University of Iowa, who has done extensive studies of science, business, and art, and found that everyone's creative potential can be enhanced. As Andreasen states, "We know that even prehistoric people possessed the gift of creativity—the capacity to see something new that others could not. Someone picked up a stone and saw a tool. Someone realized that it could be made sharp and pointed by chipping away at it. Someone recognized that a group of people could join together and hunt large food-rich animals, using their collective intellect and strength. Someone suspected that seeds could be planted and crops grown, thereby creating a more secure food supply. Someone figured out how to concentrate light or to chip flints together to create a fire and cook. Someone worked out that circular wheels could facilitate moving heavy objects. ... We have so many amazing examples of human creativity from human prehistory and history—an ongoing progression of varied and enduring human creative achievements.[5]"

Thus, to be human is to be creative, but as is the case with many *domains* like athletics and arts, some people have developed and improved their abilities more than others. This chapter explains how creativity is a skill set for how to look at the world in new and different ways. Since creativity is a set of thinking skills, it can be developed. Anyone can become more creative. Creative skills are built through developing the habit of looking for new problems, trends, and opportunities for making things better for the people of the world.

Creative workers and managers have a different mind-set than their peers. They use alternative ways of looking at the world and overcome the limitations of conventional thinking. They amaze others around them in their company, because they are capable of thinking in new ways that are different from the rational, linear, analytical, and logical ways we are taught in school and in many business environments. Steve Jobs and Steve Woczniak, for example, amazed an entire generation when they saw the potential in everyone owning a computer. When they made these bold statements, they were met with laughs and shrugs. In the 1970s, only large institutions like Fortune 500 firms and research universities used computers, but that changed with the personal computer revolutions spearheaded by Apple. Similarly, tomorrow's great successes will be those managers in entrepreneurial companies that exploit opportunities where others only see crises or impossibilities. Creativity makes this possible. But the first question that needs to be answered in order to make this happen is, what is creativity?

POPULAR MISCONCEPTIONS SURROUNDING CREATIVITY

Sir Ken Robinson proclaims that creative capacities are the greatest resource available to an organization, but in order to maximize that potential people must first understand the real nature of creativity[6]. Creativity is a tricky concept to understand. Many people are interested, but few understand its true nature. One way we can gain a better understanding of what the concept is is by understanding what it is "not." Creativity is enshrouded with misconceptions. If we pursue our goals by following these misconceptions, we will miss our mark. As we discussed in Chapter 1 with the myths associated with innovation, misconceptions mislead our thinking and keep us from developing skills. By following commonly accepted wisdom instead of empirically verified guidelines, we return to making the same mistakes over and over. Once the misunderstanding is rectified, we can approach creative pursuits with the right practices. Leading creativity scholar Keith Sawyer states that the following misconceptions are the leading culprits of preventing people from developing their creative potential.

CREATIVITY COMES TOTALLY FROM THE UNCONSCIOUS

While the unconscious plays a role in various stages of creative activity, conscious awareness and focused effort are also important. Without a certain degree of structure, breakthroughs are not made. Sawyer has observed that "creativity rarely comes in a sudden burst of insight. Instead, scientists have discovered that creativity is mostly conscious, hard work."[7] This is because creative individuals have invested a lot of time and energy learning a domain. With the knowledge gained, they can then search for problems, knowledge gaps, and opportunities in the area of study. A newcomer rarely, if ever, makes a major breakthrough in a field. Stories of such success are usually myths themselves. In *Outliers*, Malcolm Gladwell tells the real stories behind such successes as Bill Gates. Long before Bill Gates was a billionaire he was learning computer programming in his middle school in 1968. His mother, along with other parents in the school, bought a mainframe computer for the students in the school to use. Gates took advantage of this opportunity and began logging thousands of hours on the school's system. By the time Gates was 16 years old, he was one of the top 50 programmers in the world. It is no wonder he achieved a fortune based on software at a young age.[8] Warren Buffett has a similar story. His position as one of the world' richest people has its foundation in his studies as a young man. Buffett had a keen interest in business and finance as a boy, operating a pinball machine business in his hometown. When he went to Columbia University to learn finance, he studied under the legendary investor Benjamin Graham. Professor Graham gave his only A+ to Buffett. Buffett applied Graham's teachings to building his own investment company, and, after a slow start, Bershire Hathaway eventually became one of the most successful entrepreneurial ventures over the last 40 years.[9] The true story of creativity and success has a long road of hard work and learning on it.

CHILDREN ARE MORE CREATIVE THAN ADULTS

This is one of the most repeated statements in our society. Children are portrayed as having a pure reservoir of ideas that spontaneously spring forth, with schools and society squashing their creativity over time. Sawyer points out that this is a myth which science has disproved. Children actually aren't very creative, and, in fact, school and society provide stimuli and knowledge that children apply as adults later in their creative pursuits. Experience and knowledge matter. In order to generate new ideas, a person needs a collection of concepts in his or her brain to reassemble into new combinations. While it's true that biases and paradigms can sometimes limit creativity, a bank of knowledge is what new ideas are drawn from. In fact, Anders Ericsson, the leading authority on expertise, has proven Nobel Prize winner Herbert Simon's belief that great contributions in a field require a person to first partake in 10,000 hours, or roughly 10 years, of hard, deliberate practice on a topic.[10] When skills and knowledge are gained, then a person can recognize what their field needs and values. So, while children clearly can be spontaneous and fun loving, they do not have the requisite training or knowledge to be truly creative.

CREATIVITY IS SPONTANEOUS INSPIRATION

Much of this myth is the result of nineteenth-century idealistic images of the creative artist that exists to this day. We have an image of the great artist shunning social conventions and traditions and working in isolation, rebuffing social critics, and rejecting the approaches of art schools. Sawyer says that that vision of the art world could not be further from the truth. While the public still believes that artists reject convention, an increasing number of people are entering art school to be trained in the mechanics and methodologies of painting and sculpting.

In fact, many of the world's greatest artists hold a Masters in Fine Arts. Formal schooling does not squash an artist's creative contribution, but rather provides the training needed to develop advanced techniques through their career. In whatever endeavor, formal training and conscious deliberation are important components of a creative individual. As Louis Pasteur stated, "Chance favors the prepared mind."

CREATIVE WORKS GO UNRECOGNIZED AND ARE DISCOVERED LATER

According to Sawyer, "One of our most stubborn creativity myths is that unrecognized genius is quite common."[11] In actuality, creative output of high quality normally does get recognized in a society. In order to generate work of quality, a person is likely well networked in his or her field. Additionally, if the output is needed or interesting to a market, it will most likely receive a positive reception. One often-cited example of overlooked genius is Gregor Mendel and his experiments on crossbreeding peas. Credited for being the pioneer of modern genetics, legend has it that it took 35 years for his work to be known. In fact, his work was well received during his lifetime. The main problem with the legend is that others from his era were also doing work that had an equal or larger impact on genetic research. Mendel's main contribution was developing a method for using ratios that later scientists used to discover genes and inheritance, but he was one of many during his era who impacted the field's development. Another classic example of overlooked genius is the artists of the impressionist movement in France. While it is true that their works were not displayed in the French academy, their art was still displayed in many galleries in Europe and the United States, resulting in fortunes for some of the artists. As these examples demonstrate, creativity is dependent to a certain degree on quality as well as originality. Therefore, original, high-quality work, if properly promoted, will usually find an appreciative audience.

EVERYONE IS CREATIVE

We sometimes assume that everyone is generating original work, but unfortunately this is not the case. Since what is deemed creative is largely dependent on societal acceptance, selection factors in a culture often do not recognize a lot of artistic, scholarly, scientific, and economic outputs. *Evaluation* criteria by members of a domain select what original work is accepted and what is forgotten. While it is true that everyone has *potential* to create original work, the hard work and training needed to shape an idea into acceptance is not followed by all. Making an original contribution requires putting in many hours of structured work to learn what gaps in a field need to be addressed. Then, the person must work equally long hours to bring the concept to fruition. Most entrepreneurial successes have a rich, complex story that is often overly simplified in popular accounts and legends. This leads many to think that they are not capable of original contributions due to lacking special gifts or intelligences, when the truth is that with proper training and work habits creative outcomes are possible. Breakthroughs are not the work of superhuman geniuses, but rather hardworking, real people with a desire and persistence to find solutions and answers.

DEFINING CREATIVITY

Now that we know what creativity isn't, we are better prepared to learn what it is. The science of creativity is relatively new. It was not until J. P. Guilford's presidential address to the American Psychological Association in 1950 that the scientific community began to consider it as worthy of study. Since then creativity has slowly begun to be studied more, but through its development there has been debate as to what its true nature is. The aforementioned myths illustrate that there are many different interpretations in society as to what creativity is. As E. Paul Torrance observed in 1988, "Creativity defies precise definition. This conclusion does not bother me at all. In fact, I am quite happy with it. Creativity is almost infinite. It involves every sense—sight, smell, hearing, feeling, taste, and even perhaps the extrasensory. Much of it is unseen, nonverbal, and unconscious. Therefore, even if we had a precise conception of creativity, I am certain we would have difficulty putting it into words. However, if we are to study it scientifically, we must have some approximate definition."[12]

Since Torrance's statement, leading researchers have taken on the challenge of defining the elusive concept. The major advancement in the study of creativity was when the social nature of creativity was identified as a key factor. Creativity was no longer seen as the process of a lone individual, but rather a socially constructed phenomenon. Robert Sternberg and colleagues, for example, defined creativity as the "ability to produce work that is novel (i.e., original, unexpected), high in quality, and appropriate (i.e., useful, meets task constraint)."[13] Thus, in order to generate ideas that have impact, a person must ensure certain attributes are contained in it to gain acceptance. This acceptance is derivative of a person's understanding of a domain. According to Howard Gardner:

> "A person isn't creative in general—you can't just say a person is
> 'creative.' You have to say a person is creative in X, whether it's writing,
> being a teacher, or running an organization. People are creative in
> something….People who are creative are always thinking about the
> domains in which they work. They're always tinkering. They're always
> saying, "What makes sense here, awhat doesn't make sense?' And if it
> doesn't make sense, 'Can I do something about it?' "[14]

Recognizing the role of external standards and influences led the psychologist Mihaly Csikszentmihalyi to provide the most-often-cited view of creativity: "Creativity occurs when a person, using the systems of a given domain such as music, engineering, business, or mathematics, has a new idea or sees a new pattern, and when this novelty is selected by the appropriate field for inclusion into the relevant domain."[15] That is, it is not enough to develop ideas, but rather the ideas must also be of interest and use to others. This view serves entrepreneurial managers well since new products, regardless of how original and unique, must also be accepted by their company and the market in order to be successful. Therefore, in an organizational setting, we can say that creativity occurs when a manager has a new idea or sees an opportunity that is feasible and profitable for the company.

Now that we have debunked the misconceptions of creativity and gained a better understanding of the concept's true nature, we can now examine what elements can bring about more of it. By understanding what factors increase creative behavior, we can begin to inculcate creativity into our own lives.

THE THREE ELEMENTS OF CREATIVITY

If we want to increase our creative output, we must include three elements in our pursuit: domain skills, creative-thinking skills, and *intrinsic motivation*. Teresa Amabile of the Harvard Business School compares the mixing of these elements to making a stew : "The essential ingredient, something like vegetables or the meat in a stew, is expertise in a specific area: domain skills. These skills represent your basic mastery of a field…Creative thinking skills are like spices and herbs you use to bring out the flavor of the basic ingredients in a stew. They make the flavors unique, help the basic ingredients to blend and bring out something different…Finally, the element that really cooks the creative stew is *passion*. Creativity begins to cook when people are motivated by the pure enjoyment of what they are doing."[16] In the following sections, we examine these ingredients in more depth.

DOMAIN SKILLS

Neuroscience has proven that creativity is not supernatural. Ideas do not come out of thin air or from the whisper of a mysterious muse, but instead are a result of new combinations of old and new concepts stored in brains. Domain skills, also known as expertise, encompass the ability to perceive and handle the challenges and intricacies found in a field, and provide a solid foundation for generating new ideas. As Steven Johnson explains in his study of scientific pioneers, "Ideas are built out of self-exciting networks of neurons, clusters of clusters, with each group associated with some shade of a thought or memory or emotion. When we think of a certain concept, or experience some new form of stimulus, a complex network of neuronal groups switches on in synchrony."[17] The more clusters of information we have, the more potential for more new combinations to draw from. Figure 3.1 depicts this view and shows how our brains are complex networks of circuits of skills and knowledge that interconnect and share information.

The best way to develop expertise is to immerse ourselves in a domain, and is done in two ways. One form of immersion is external. To more fully understand a domain, we must interact with experts in that field and place ourselves in the middle of thought leadership in an area when possible. Economists point out that this is the main reason urban areas are expensive to live in. There is a market premium on living near others who are experts in their fields. This is why businesses usually locate in larger cities because they know the rewards from interaction with others in their domain will be worth it.[18] As mentioned previously, the archetype of a lone genius making breakthrough ideas is myth. Michelangelo, for

FIGURE 3.1 **The Shape of an Idea Forming in the Brain**

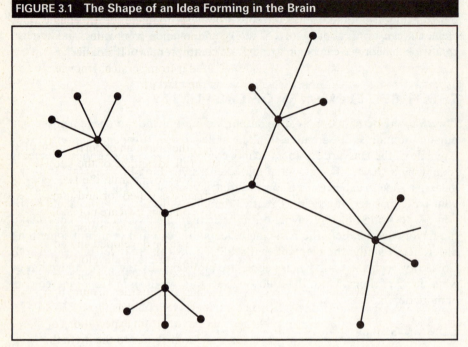

Source: Based on Steven Johnson, The Invention of Air. New York: Riverhead Books.

example, produced his masterpieces in Florence, Italy, where other greats like Donatello and Giotto were located, not in a small village like Caldine. It pays to be near the action in your field. We need to interact with others to help us develop our ideas.

The second form of immersion in a domain is internal. As previously mentioned in the section dealing with myths, Anders Ericcson found that 10,000 hours, or roughly 10 years, of studying and working in a domain is required to be an expert, and experts are more likely to make significant contributions to society. Again, Bill Gates' rise to entrepreneurial stardom exemplifies this well. In 1968, when Gates was in eighth grade, the mothers of his school's students invested in a computer terminal and started a computer club at a time when most colleges didn't even own computers. Young Gates practically lived in the computer room from that moment on. In his senior year, he even spent the spring writing computer code for the Bonneville Power Station in southern Washington State. By the time Gates dropped out of Harvard as a sophomore and started his own company, he had put in well past 10,000 hours of computer programming. While Gates may have been young when he made his fortune, he was not a newcomer to computers born to write code. The truth is closer to say he was a seasoned programmer who happened to be young. Thus, if someone wants to make breakthroughs like Gates did, they must first gain knowledge in a domain. This is best done by locating near where others in the domain are and interacting with that group whenever possible. If a company doesn't have knowledge of a domain, then it must hire experts from it if they are to make breakthroughs. This is why larger companies often buy smaller, innovative companies, and concurrently why this is often an exit strategy for entrepreneurs. It's easier and faster sometimes to acquire that knowledge than build it from scratch. Knowledge and asymmetric information bring a high price in the market.

CREATIVE-THINKING SKILLS

Once a person has sufficient domain knowledge, they have an opportunity to generate more ideas on a topic. However, to take full advantage of the knowledge, they must be able to diverge, converge, and be able to separate the two types of thinking—that is, there are times where *divergence* is called for and times when *convergence* is needed. Knowledge and expertise on their own are not enough. We have to be able to apply them in a creative fashion to come up with more new ideas. Since divergence and convergence are skills, they can be developed and honed.

Divergence, also known as ideation, is perhaps the least-developed thinking skill in business, but one that is critical to creativity. Divergent thinking is the process of generating many possible options and possibilities around a topic of focus. This skill can be just as difficult for experts in a field as those new to it. If one has a lot of experience in a field, they may have certain expectations or biases that limit their exploratory nature.[19] This fault contributes to the myth that children are more creative than adults, because kids are often very divergent; but, the more experience a person has the more opportunity for creative output if he or she can generate a larger quantity of ideas to choose from. Domain knowledge mixed with divergent thinking creates a world of possibilities.

Perhaps no group is better known for generating new ideas and technologies in this way than the Imagineers of the Walt Disney Company. Imagineers are the creative arm of Disney parks and resorts worldwide, and have created everything from the audio-animatronics of the moving characters in landmark theme rides, such as the Pirates of the Caribbean and the Haunted Mansion, to the man-made mountains, like Space Mountain, which are found in all the Disney Parks. Imagineers make these breakthroughs by following a "Blue Sky" philosophy and supporting ideation throughout their ranks. "Blue Sky" means that the sky's the limit. Anything is possible. Imagineers are given a general goal, such as designing a ship for the Disney Cruise Line, and then go to work taking reams of blank paper and capturing ideas. Constraints and considerations are not to be taken into account during this stage of the creative process. In the words of the Imagineers, "Limitations only weigh on the wings of an idea as it soars wild and free on the updrafts of possibility. Creative freedom allows us to do anything imaginable, anything at all."[20] This mind-set is utilized whether a team is working on a new store design, new ride, or an entirely new park layout. Every company would benefit from utilizing the "Blue Sky" philosophy.

The approach that Disney follows as a part of its daily routines can be developed in any business. Min Basadur and colleagues found that ideation is a skill that can be developed with training. In an experiment, Basadur had 65 engineers participate in a three-day (24-hour) training program on ideation. The first step included training participants on the concept of ideation with exercises that captured the concept. The second step included more application of the concept. Participants were given a problem from a case, asked to offer solutions for the case, and then shared their answers with others. The participants discovered that there are different ways of looking at a problem and finding solutions. This recognition led to the engineers applying the knowledge on divergence to their own work settings and improving performance.[21]

It is important that if you want to develop your creative output you gain this perspective as well. Basadur provides seven guidelines in developing these critical-thinking skills.[22] First, withhold evaluating ideas while diverging. The more ideas you have the better. In order to do this, it is important we avoid using the inadvertent killer phrases that are often used in human communication, such as "Naah," "Can't," "That's the dumbest thing I've ever heard," "Yeah, but if you did that …," and "It's not in the budget." People may not intentionally stop a creative idea, but these simple, negative phrases preclude people from thinking any further.[23] Second, don't worry about being right. There is a time for evaluating ideas laterbut during this stage you want to open up your mind and the minds of others to possibilities. From these ideas, something better may come later. Third, generating a lot of ideas is the goal of this stage. From quantity, quality comes. Fourth, don't interrupt a stream of thought. Write everything down and capture it on paper, as in a frantic creative work session, ideas can be easily lost. Fifth, reach for radical, impossible ideas. Some of history's greatest ideas appeared to be a little insane when first proposed, but later were shaped into acceptable form. Often in outlandish thoughts, there is a deep kernel of truth. Just look at the power of great comedians and their observations. Sixth, think in pictures. Draw your ideas on paper, and search for possible connections. Seventh, build on others ideas. One idea can be a launching point for many other ideas. This is why it is important to never critique or analyze ideas during this stage. Utilizing these seven principles repetitively will generate divergent thinking skills and be a major step toward being a more creative person.

While it is important to generate a lot of ideas, there also comes a time to select the best options given your goals and tasks. This thinking skill is known as *convergence* in that we converge down to the best options. While many people have trouble generating ideas, "big idea" people often struggle with picking something and moving forward. They stay in dream mode, and love every idea that crosses their mind. This is why some people procrastinate. They seek perfection and big hits, instead of focusing on progress. In almost any creative pursuit, however, we will make mistakes and miscalculations. These missteps though provide feedback for us and allow us to learn and correct our mistakes. As W. H. Murray, the Scottish adventurer and rock climber, once said:

> Until one is committed, there is hesitancy, the chance to draw back,
> always ineffectiveness. Concerning all acts of initiative (and creation),
> there is one elementary truth the ignorance of which kills countless

ideas and splendid plans: that the moment one definitely commits oneself, the providence moves too. A whole stream of events issues from the decision, raising in one's favor all manner of unforeseen incidents, meetings and material assistance, which no man could have dreamt would have come his way. I learned a deep respect for one of Goethe's couplets: 'Whatever you can do or dream you can, begin it. Boldness has genius, power and magic in it!'[24]

Thus, there comes a point where we must move forward, and start getting results. Again, with regard to making creative breakthroughs, Walt Disney understood this. In 1953, he picked a site in Anaheim, California, to build Disneyland. He gave himself two years to build the theme park. There had never been anything built like Disneyland before, and many people thought it was destined for failure. Critics called it "Disney's Folly," but in two short years he completed the major construction. The park opened on July 17, 1955, on time. The opening day was not smooth by any means, and was referred to by Walt and his executives as "Black Sunday." More people showed up to the park than expected on an unusually hot day, visitors passed out from heat exhaustion, food and beverage stands went empty, and many other mini-catastrophes occurred, but Disney believed in the power that action can bring to making projects a reality. He and his colleagues corrected the problems found on opening day, and within a few weeks the park was operating smoothly.

Disney often said, "Dream and do," and "The way to get started is to quit talking and begin doing."[25] Had it not been for him making decisions, setting deadlines, and getting the team and resources together to move forward, Disneyland would never have occurred. While Disney loved big ideas and encouraged his employees to stretch themselves, he also appreciated convergent behavior. As he once said, "Get a good idea, and stay with it. Dog it, and work at it until it's done, and done right."[26] The "Blue Sky" thinking got the projects started, but the pragmatic follow-through ensured the movies, parks, and hotels were produced. To be a good leader, you must be open to possibilities and not thwart ideas, but you also must be willing to make the tough calls and expect results.

So, how can we decide what ideas to move forward on? First, we have to decide what is important to us. One place to start is our value system. What do we value? What do we stand for? What are we selling? What is our mission as an organization? For Disney, it was providing happiness to those that watched his movies and visited his park. If a park employee was grumpy to customers, he or she was told to cheer up or leave. In designing the parks, Disney tried to instill the same sense of aesthetics and values that the movies had. If a project strayed from those guidelines, it was modified or terminated.

The second thing to consider in choosing an idea is referring back to the original problem or issue you were trying to address and solve. Ask yourself, what are the critical success factors in addressing this issue? Then choose the one that appears to be the best. For example, when Disney was entertaining different ways to build a mountain in Disneyland, he originally thought he would build a place in the park where guests could take sled rides on real snow … in the middle of July in Anaheim, California! He gave this challenge to his Imagineers and waited for their designs and plans. Finally, he accepted the Imagineers' advice that creating Snow Mountain would be too costly and its melting would cause problems with runoff. While he understood the Sisyphean nature of his idea, he did not let the concept of a mountain in Disneyland die. While on a movie shoot in Switzerland in 1958, Walt could often be found for hours looking at a mountain in the distance called the Matterhorn. A few days later he sent a post-card of the mountain to his Imagineers in California with two words scribbled on it: "Build this!" Those marching orders led to the 1959 opening of the Matter-horn Sled Ride in Disneyland.[27] While the mountain was made of concrete and steel, rather than dirt and snow, Disney got his mountain. Because of his use of the skills of divergence and convergence, Disney was quite literally able to move mountains—he moved the Matterhorn from Switzerland to Anaheim.

Like Disney and the Imagineers, we too can move mountains if we become good at using both divergence and convergence. Thus, a third critical-thinking skill is *deferral of judgment*, or being aware of the difference of when to diverge and converge. In developing thinking skills, before they become second nature, we must consciously separate the steps and follow the previously mentioned guidelines to get to creative ideas that others accept. We must withhold judgment and generate many possibilities when diverging, and then make good decisions and move forward to get results. If we do not perform these skills regularly, we limit our creative output. This approach has led to Disney creating stories for the silver screen that we still watch today and new experiences in its theme parks that people flock to from all over the world. These same skill sets can revolutionize any company's culture and its creative output, whether it is in the entertainment business or the mining industry.

INTRINSIC MOTIVATION

The final element of the creative stew is intrinsic motivation, commonly referred to as passion. While it is important to have the requisite knowledge on a topic in order to make significant contribution and the thinking skills to work with ideas, it is perhaps most important to be passionate about what you are working on. Creative breakthroughs require a lot of work to bring them into reality, and with-out the firm belief and commitment to an idea, it is much harder to see them through to completion. Fortunately, passion and exuberance are qualities that can be found in all achievements throughout history and available to everyone if properly channeled. As Louis Pasteur observed, "The Greeks understood the mysterious power of the hidden side of things. They bequeathed to us one of the most beautiful words in our language—the word 'enthusiasm'—*en theos*—a god within. The grandeur of human actions is measured by the inspiration from which they spring. Happy is he who bears a god within, and who obeys it."[28]

So it would make sense that we are better off pursuing ideas that inspire us, but can we really know where passion comes from? And is it possible to develop it in a person? The answer to both questions is "yes." Some places are very adept at creating superstars in certain fields, and give us living labs for learning how to ignite passion in people. In his study of nine talent hotbeds around the world, Daniel Coyle found that future superstars became deeply interested in a subject when one or more of the following events occur. The first, and perhaps most important, factor is that a tiny idea about a topic is introduced to the person and it resonates deeply within them. A *spark* has been lit that builds into a roaring fire of curiosity and passion. They feel compelled to work on their endeavor and make a personal commitment to devote time and energy to become good at it. This factor plays a more important role than IQ and physical factors in reaching stardom. Albert Einstein, for example, became interested in physics when he was five and his father gave him a small, magnetic compass. Einstein spent hours studying how the needle always pointed to the north. Later in his life, he pointed to this moment as the spark to examining the underlying order behind the physical world. Howard Gardner says this deep connection to an idea like the one experienced by Einstein "essentially moves you to take steps to learn more about the thing that interests you, and to discover its complexities, its difficulties, its strengths and obscurities. From that initial love of doing something comes persistence."[29] From persistence comes the development of knowledge and skills to make breakthroughs.

The second factor Coyle pinpoints for igniting passion in a person is *the role of a good mentor or teacher.* A good teacher can guide the person on what to examine and how to learn the intricacies of complex domains. Left on our own, we may wander aimlessly searching for knowledge, but a good teacher can break a domain down into its critical elements and steer us to better performance. More efficient learning can save us years of frustration and put us on a path to better performance at a younger age. Better performances then motivate us and help us create a positive self-image of ourselves. Belief in ourselves is the fuel needed to develop our abilities. Without it, we are less likely to be accepting of our shortcomings during the early days of skill acquisition. Karen Connolly Armitage, a senior concept designer at Walt Disney Imagineering, shares a moment like this that occurred early in her life and set her on a path to her future career:

> "My mom told a story in later years about an airy drawing of mine with
> a bold dash of blue under a magnificent swirl of pink. She would recall
> that I presented it proudly. 'What is it, dear heart?' she asked. I stuck
> my four-year-old chin out and with all the indignation of a misunder-
> stood genius, and retorted, "It's an elephant getting out of the bathtub!"
> Soon it was framed, matted, under glass, and hung with pride in the hall.
> My self-belief was started."[30]

While your employees may not be drawing elephants getting out of bathtubs, they may occasionally come up with the ideas that make you scratch your head. At that point, encourage the effort, offer support on where the idea can go, and start building the belief that the person has in him- or herself. Doing otherwise could shut the person down, and prevent them from presenting you in the future with an idea that might actually be a big hit.

The third factor stimulating intrinsic motivation is finding *a role model* you can relate to. If we can relate to a creative person on a human level and find similarities between them and us, it shows us that we too can achieve similar accomplishments if we work hard enough. The role model creates perhaps the most motivating thought our heads can hold: "I want to be like them. If she can do it, why can't I?" Once this thought has been embedded in a person's head, the next one is just as powerful and gets the job done: "Better get busy."

Coyle gives the example of Roger Bannister and the four-minute mile as a great example of this phenomenon. Physiologists and athletes alike used to believe that it was physically impossible to run a mile in under four minutes. Bannister didn't agree with the commonly accepted wisdom and trained specifically to go sub-four by running many, many quarter mile repeats in 60 seconds. It worked. When Bannister ran a sub-four mile in 1954, it was deemed the greatest athletic accomplishment of the twentieth century by *Sports Illustrated*. Once Bannister did it, others thought, "If a medical student in Britain can do it, I can too." Then, within three years' time, seventeen other runners accomplished the once-impossible feat. Bannister had provided a role model to the other runners that it could be done, and then they got busy and trained with that goal in mind. It is for this reason that you should read biographies of your personal heroes, because it is likely the real story of how they attained success varies from popular cultural accounts. You'll see that you too can go on to big accomplishments, if you apply yourself and give yourself time to become an expert. You'll engrain in your mind the important knowledge that great leaders and innovators achieve breakthroughs by devoting years learning a field and working hard to learn its intricacies. Once we see that creative legends are not superhuman, we learn that we too can make similar leaps if we apply their lessons.

Coyle found that taking people with an interest in a topic and placing them with great teachers and role models produces unusual numbers of exceptional performers in their fields. What is most encouraging about his findings is that we do not have to be blessed with the best and latest technologies and facilities for this to occur. Brazilian youths learn soccer on dirt fields and in crowded streets, and yet produce nine hundred players who are picked up every year by professional European clubs. The Spartak Tennis Club in Moscow produced five of the top ten women's professional players and the men's Davis Cup champions on one single indoor court led by a 77-year-old master teacher named Larisa Preobrazhenskaya. Coyle believes the key way these places ignite passion is by continually sending primal cues—people, images, and ideas—that tell a person that they too can achieve great things. Thus, state-of-the-art workplaces are not necessary if you want to train your employees and yourself to be more creative. What is required is that when you see a spark in someone's eyes when they are working on a project that you support the idea and let them run with it. It doesn't mean that you have to fully accept it, but be open to where the person goes with the idea, because that spark may lead to a creative outburst that you have never recognized in the person before. Once it appears the person is serious about the idea, surround them with mentors who have championed ideas in the past. Practices that have been proven to work in your company can be applied to the new idea, and with proper coaching and support the employee will see that their vision can become a reality.

It is important to celebrate the person's effort, regardless of whether their project is eventually green-lighted or not. For example, it's impossible for every student of the Spartak Tennis Academy to win Wimbledon, but the players are appreciative of the opportunity to train there and that they are given a shot at the big time. Employees of creative companies feel the same way, for they know they are part of a unique organization that provides them with the opportunity to reach for their best. Not every project in your company can be implemented, but with enough people embracing a creative mind-set, odds are favorable that it will produce more new hits rather than turning out the same products and services. Companies with this type of culture will win out in today's marketplace.

In summary, domain knowledge, creative-thinking skills, and intrinsic motivation are the three key elements of creativity. If we have this combination, we greatly increase our odds of generating more creative output. However, we still need guidance on how to actually work with ideas and bring them into reality. In the following section, we examine the actual process people go through when they create new things.

THE CREATIVE PROCESS

Creativity is a process that can be developed and improved.[31] This process comes easier for some because they have been raised and educated in an environment that encouraged them to develop their creativity. For others, the process is more difficult because they have not been positively reinforced; if they are to be creative, they must learn how to implement the creative process.[32] The creative process has four commonly agreed-on phases or steps. Most experts agree on the general nature and relationships among these phases, although they refer to them by a variety of names.[33] Experts also agree that these phases do not always occur in the same order for every creative activity. For creativity to occur, chaos is necessary—but a structured and focused chaos. We shall examine this four-step process using the most typical framework.

PHASE 1: BACKGROUND OR KNOWLEDGE ACCUMULATION

Successful ideas are generally preceded by investigation and information gathering. This usually involves extensive reading, conversations with others working in the field, feedback from stakeholders like customers and suppliers, attendance at professional meetings and workshops, and a general absorption of information relative to the problem or issue under study. Additional investigation in both related and unrelated fields is sometimes involved. This exploration provides the individual with a variety of perspectives on the problem, and it is particularly important to the manager, who needs a basic understanding of all aspects of the development of a new product or service.

Managers must use their existing knowledge base to identify an actual opportunity; that knowledge serves as the basis for interacting with the new experience. This knowledge base could take the form of general industry knowledge, prior market knowledge, prior customer understanding, specific-interest knowledge, or any previous knowledge that helps the manager to better identify opportunities. Every manager in a creative organization needs to use his or her previous knowledge base to interpret the unusual sources of innovative ideas into a potential opportunity. Thus, each individual's experiences are uniquely valuable to generating new ideas for products, services, and processes.[34]

People practice the creative search for background knowledge in a number of ways. Some of the most helpful are:

1. read in a variety of fields,
2. join professional groups and associations,
3. attend professional meetings and seminars,
4. travel to new places,
5. talk to anyone and everyone about your topic,
6. scan magazines, newspapers, and journals for articles related to the subject,
7. develop a subject library for future reference,
8. carry a small notebook and record useful information,
9. devote time to pursue natural curiosities, and
10. survey stakeholders.[35]

PHASE 2: THE INCUBATION PROCESS

After we acquire knowledge on our subject, it is often good to get away from it for a while. Creative individuals allow their subconscious to mull over the tremendous amounts of information they gather during the preparation phase. Neuroscience supports this approach with the computational theory of mind, which posits that the brain is essentially a pattern-recognition machine. In order to assemble these patterns, it needs time to store and process the large amounts of data it holds. During the *incubation* process, the brain clumps information together in similar mental clusters, places new data with similar preexisting clusters, and reorganizes the clusters as we experience new events. Figure 3.2 illustrates this mental mechanism.[36] As noted cognitive scientist Stephen Pinker states, "The mind owes it power to its synaptic, compositional, combinatorial abilities. Our complicated ideas are built out of simpler ones, and the meaning of the whole is determined by the meanings of the parts and the meanings of the relations that connect them."[37] Essentially, the brain is trying to make sense of its world by organizing and reorganizing knowledge and new data, and then predicting future possibilities related to your goals, desires, needs, and survival. Your brain then matches up input from the external world with mental models

FIGURE 3.2 New Information Linking with Knowledge for Insight

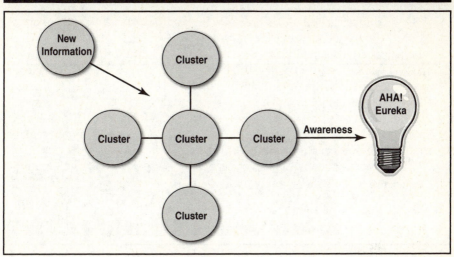

you have constructed, in order to determine what the best possible outcome will be among various options. When there is a disconnect between input and stored patterns, your brain makes adjustments for a wider range of possible scenarios in the future and selects the one that makes the most sense to you. Thus, we are capable of developing new business ideas by consciously gathering new information on a market or societal trend and letting our subconscious relate it to past experience and knowledge.[38]

Incubation spurs new idea formulation by giving our brains time to recombine the information into new combinations, which is essentially what creativity is. We drop our evaluative frame of mind and relax our mental filters, and then the subconscious goes to work. From this perspective, we can imagine the mind resembling an iceberg, with a majority of cognition taking place below the surface of consciousness.[39] Figure 3.3 illustrates how this subconscious mechanism is comprised of hidden networks of neurons that share information with each other. As medical researcher Robert Burton explains, "The hidden layer is a powerful metaphor for the brain's processing of information. It is in the hidden layer that all elements of biology (from genetic predispositions to neurotransmitter variations and fluctuations) and all past experience, whether remembered or long forgotten, affect the processing of incoming information. It is the interface between incoming sensory data and a final perception, the anatomic crossroad where nature and nurture intersect. It is why your red is not my red, your idea of beauty isn't mine, why eyewitnesses offer differing accounts of an accident, or why we don't all put our money on the same roulette number."[40] It is also why one person may come up with a new business idea that is different from others looking at the same situation. The incubation phase brings forth new ideas by stirring the creative stew.

FIGURE 3.3   Iceberg Model of the Brain

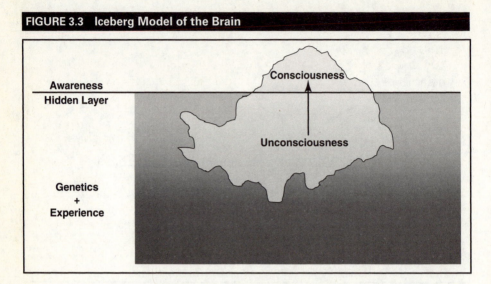

The incubation process often occurs while people are engaged in activities totally unrelated to the subject or problem. It happens even when they are sleeping. This accounts for the advice frequently given to a person who is frustrated by what seems to be an impossible challenge: "Why don't you sleep on it?" Getting away from a problem and letting the subconscious mind work on it allows creativity to spring forth. Some of the most helpful steps to induce incubation are to:

1. engage in routine, "mindless" activities (cutting the grass, painting the house, etc.),
2. exercise regularly,
3. play (sports, board games, puzzles),
4. think about the project or problem before falling asleep,
5. meditate, and
6. sit back and relax on a regular basis.[41]

PHASE 3: THE IDEA EXPERIENCE

This phase of the creative process is often the most exciting, because it is when the idea or solution the individual is seeking is discovered. When the brain makes a connection that makes logical sense for that person, it is thrown into conscious awareness to be considered for action. The subconscious has made a connection that appears to solve a puzzle or challenge you've been grappling with, and your body has sent you a signal that tells you that this is indeed something to be excited about. It's this powerful feeling that often brings us back to pursuing creative endeavors over and over again. It can almost be addictive.

Sometimes referred to as the "eureka moment," this phase is also the one the average person incorrectly perceives as the only component of creativity. While it is the phase most chronicled in popular accounts of breakthroughs, we must always remember the preparation, hard work, and time that go into attaining a powerful idea.

As with the incubation process, new ideas often emerge while the person is busy doing something unrelated to the investigation (e.g., taking a shower, driving on an interstate highway, or leafing through a newspaper). Sometimes, the idea appears as a bolt out of the blue. In most cases, however, the answer comes to the individual incrementally. Slowly but surely, the person begins to formulate the solution. Because it is often difficult to determine when the incubation process ends and the idea-experience phase begins, many people are unaware of moving from Phase 2 to Phase 3.

Following are ways to speed up the idea experience: 1) daydream and fantasize about your project, 2) practice your hobbies, 3) work in a leisurely environment (e.g., at home instead of at the office), 4) put the problem on the back burner, 5) keep a notebook at bedside to record late-night or early-morning ideas, and 6) take breaks while working.[42]

The awareness of how the brain gets ideas will assist you in becoming more creative. You will have a better understanding of how to gather information and let your subconscious work for you. You will also develop more patience and persistence, traits that are of supreme importance in creative pursuits. If you haven't found an idea that you think has potential, you will realize that is not due to a lack of ability on your part but rather on a lack of relevant information. Don't worry. Frustration and confusion are normal feelings during the creative process. When you come across pertinent information that would be helpful in creating new business ideas, your brain will let you know!

PHASE 4: EVALUATION AND IMPLEMENTATION

This is the most difficult step of a creative endeavor and requires a great deal of courage, self-discipline, and perseverance. Successful managers can identify ideas that are workable and that they have the skills to *implement*. More importantly, they do not give up when they run into temporary obstacles. Often they will fail several times before they successfully develop their best ideas. In some cases, managers will take the idea in an entirely different direction or will discover a new and more workable idea, while struggling to implement the original one.

Another part of this phase is the reworking of ideas to put them into final form. Frequently an idea emerges from Phase 3 in rough form, so it needs to be modified or tested to achieve its final shape. Some of the most useful suggestions for carrying out this phase are to: 1) increase your energy level with proper exercise, diet, and rest, 2) educate yourself in the innovation process and what steps are needed to make the idea a reality, 3) test your ideas with knowledgeable people, 4) take notice of your intuitive hunches and feelings, 5) educate yourself in how to persuade others on your idea, 6) examine organizational policies and practices on bringing ideas to market, 7) seek advice from others (friends, experts, etc.), and 8) view the problems you encounter while implementing your ideas as challenges.[43]

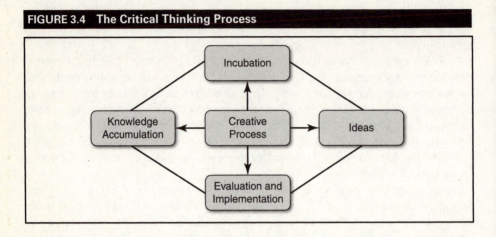

FIGURE 3.4 The Critical Thinking Process

Figure 3.4 illustrates the four phases of the creative-thinking process. If a person encounters a major problem while moving through the process, it is sometimes helpful to go back to a previous phase and try again. For example, if an individual is unable to formulate an idea or solution (Phase 3), a return to Phase 1 often helps. By immersing him- or herself in the data, the individual allows the unconscious mind to begin anew processing the data, establishing cause–effect relationships, and formulating potential solutions.

AREAS IN WHICH PEOPLE ARE CREATIVE

Remember, everyone has the potential to be creative. Some are creative all the time while others stifle it, and most of us fall somewhere in between the two. The reality is that people often do not recognize when or how they are being creative. Furthermore, they fail to recognize the many opportunities for creativity that arise within their jobs on a daily basis. Creativity researcher William Miller argues that people often do not recognize when they are being creative, and they frequently overlook opportunities to be creative. He suggests that the path to creativity begins by first recognizing all the ways in which we are, or can be, creative. People in organizations can channel their creativity into seven different areas:[44]

1. *Idea creativity:* thinking up a new idea or concept, such as an idea for a new product or service or way to solve a problem.
2. *Material creativity:* inventing or finding new uses for materials for products, services, or processes, such as using carbon fiber for reinforcing skateboard decks.
3. *Organization creativity:* organizing people or projects and coming up with a new organizational form or approach to structuring things. Examples include organizing a project, starting a new business division, putting together or reorganizing a work group, and changing the policies and rules of a group.

4. *Relationship creativity:* a creative approach to achieving collaboration, cooperation, and win–win relationships with others. The person who handles a difficult situation well or deals with a particular person in an especially effective manner is being creative in a relationship or one-on-one context.

5. *Event creativity:* producing an event such as an awards ceremony, team outing, or annual meeting. The creativity here also encompasses décor, ways in which people are involved, sequence of happenings, setbacks, and so forth.

6. *Inner creativity:* changing one's inner self; being open to new approaches to how one does things and thinking about oneself in different ways; achieving a change of heart or finding a new perspective or way to look at things that is a significant departure from how one has traditionally looked at them.

7. *Spontaneous creativity:* acting in a spontaneous or spur-of-the-moment manner, such as coming up with a witty response in a meeting, an off-the-cuff speech, a quick and simple way to settle a dispute, or a creative appeal when trying to close a sale.

When working in one of these areas, remember to apply the principles of creativity covered in this chapter. Immerse yourself into the issues around the topic, use divergent thinking to generate possible solutions, apply convergent thinking to make a decision to move forward on, and believe in your abilities to reach your goals. If you consistently practice these principles in more personal and work settings, you will become more creative.

Summary

This chapter examined the importance of creativity in generating new business ideas and remaining competitive in today's business climate. The nature of creativity was examined by first examining the common myths surrounding it, and then defining it. The three elements needed to increase creativity were then covered. The four phases of the creative process were also presented. The chapter concluded with the areas where people can generate new ideas.

INNOVATION-IN-ACTION

Scientific Research on the "AHA!" Moment

Recent research in neuroscience is shedding light on how the brain works. Scientists used to believe the only way to understand mental mechanisms was by indirectly studying behavior and attitudes; however, medical technology in the form of magnetic resonance imaging (MRI) has provided a new set of tools to peer into the once-mysterious realms of the brain. Using a technique called functional magnetic resonance imaging (fMRI), neuroscientists can study what areas of the brain become activated by different thoughts and stimuli. Researchers Read Montague and Gregory Berns took special

(continued)

interest in utilizing the technology to answer the question, "What do people find reward-ing?" Or put another way, what do people really want? The way to finding the answer to this age-old question is by measuring the amount of dopamine released in the brain. Dopamine is the "feel good" chemical in the brain, and is your body's way of reinforcing behaviors. In a sense, it's natural "dope." Those things that bring a dopamine release are repeated because they feel good. If a thought, action, or stimuli is enjoyable to the person, it's due to dopamine being released in greater quantities. It's your body's way of telling you what to pursue and what to avoid. While it's difficult to actually measure dopamine itself, scientists do know that the striatum—a small area in the brain with the densest dopamine concentration—lights up during an fMRI when dopamine is released. Scientists from all realms, as well as economists, are searching to see what things stimu-late the striatum.

So, after all these studies, what have scientists found that stimulates the striatum the most? Novelty. When you go into new territory, whether physically or mentally, new information comes into your brain and your striatum goes into overdrive. The challenge and the risk of new situations stimulate an increased release of dopamine that focuses your attention on the new stimuli. As you contemplate and address the new situation or topic, your brain changes at the molecular level, and lays down new tracks and connections. The new neuronal networks we build are the foundation of learning, which brings satisfaction with ourselves and our world. As a result, we are driven to seek new challenges and accept the risk involved if we subconsciously calcu-late that the rewards of the search outweigh the costs. Some people get these feelings through risky, physical activities like skydiving and rock climbing, while others find it through more cerebral pursuits that stretch their minds.

Even the expectation of something good can release dopamine. This is the source of curiosity, and once piqued we feel compelled to follow through. Thus, when we seek an answer to a problem that we think could bring future rewards, we search until we find a solution. When we finally find a solution to a problem, we are rewarded with a larger release of dopamine. This dopamine release is the essence of the "Aha!" moment. In a sense, we can become addicted to this experience—but in a good way. When we've experienced this pleasurable, satisfying moment, we seek out further challenges. This incredible mechanism leads us to conquer new lands, markets, and fields. It may also be why some people are serial entrepreneurs, because they return again and again to the exciting challenges and thrills found during the early days of a start-up company.

Source: Based on Gregory B. 2005. *Satisfaction: Sensation Thinking, Novelty, and the Science of Finding True Fulfillment.* New York: Henry Holt and Company.

Key Terms

A role model	En theos
Convergence	Evaluation
Creativity	Ideas
Deferral of judgment	Implementation
Divergence	Incubation
Domains	Intrinsic motivation

knowledge accumulation
Outliers
Passion

Potential
Spark

Discussion Questions

1. Describe creativity. Explain how it is important for managers in a company.
2. What are the eight myths of creativity?
3. What are the three elements of creativity? How could a manager incorporate these elements into their company? How could a manager use these elements to become more creative themselves?
4. What is the difference between divergent and convergent thinking? Why are these important skills?
5. Why is Disney such a creative company?
6. What role does a mentor or teacher play in shaping creativity?
7. Explain each phase of the creative process.
8. How does your brain come up with new ideas?
9. Describe the seven areas in which people can be creative.
10. What steps can you take today to become more creative in your own work?

Endnotes

1. Lynch, D. 2006. *Catching the Big Fish: Meditation, Consciousness, and Creativity* New York: Penguin.
2. Kao, J. 2007. *Innovation Nation: How America Is Losing Its Innovation Edge, Why It Matters, and What We Can Do to Get It Back.* New York: Free Press.
3. Christensen, C. M. 2003. *The Innovator's Dilemma: The Revolutionary Book that Will Change the Way You Do Business.* New York: Harper Business Essentials.
4. Schwartz, E. I. 2004. *Juice: The Creative Fuel that Drives World-Class Inventors.* Boston, MA: Harvard Business School Press.
5. Andreasen, N. C. 2005. *The Creating Brain: The Neuroscience of Genius.* New York: Dana Press.
6. Robinson, K. *Out of Our Minds: Learning to Be Creative.* West Sussex: Capstone.
7. Ibid., p. 18.
8. Gladwell, M. 2008. *Outliers: The Story of Success.* New York: Little, Brown, and Company.
9. Colvin, G. 2008. *Talent Is Overrated: What Really Separates World-Class Performers from Everybody Else.* New York: Portfolio.
10. Ericsson, K. A. 1996. The acquisition of expert performance: An introduction to some of the issues. In K. Anders Ericsson (ed.), *The Road to Excellence: The Acquisition of Expert Performance in the Arts and Sciences, Sports and Games* (pp. 1–50). Mahwah, NJ: Lawrence Erlbaum Associates.
11. Sawyer, *Explaining Creativity: The Science of Human Innovation*, p. 22.
12. Torrance, E. P. 1988. The nature of creativity as manifest in its testing. In Robert J. Sternberg (ed.), *The Nature of Creativity: Contemporary Psychological Perspectives.* (pp. 43–75). New York: Cambridge University Press.
13. Sterberg, R. J, Kaufman, J. C. & Perez, J. E. 2002. *The Creativity Conundrum.* New York: Psychology Press.

14. Goleman, D, Kaufman, P. & Ray, M. 1993. *The Creative Spirit.* New York: Plume, p. 26.
15. Csikszentmihalyi, M. 1996. *Creativity: Flow and the Psychology of Discover and Invention.* New York: HarperCollins.
16. Goleman, D, Kaufman, P. & Ray, M. 1993. *The Creative Spirit.* New York: Plume.
17. Johnson, S. 2008. *The Invention of Air: A Story of Science, Faith, Revolution, and the Birth of America.* New York: Riverhead.
18. Harford, T. 2008. *The Logic of Life: The Rational Economics of an Irrational World.* New York: Random House.
19. Johnson-Laird, P. N. 1988. Freedom and constraint in creativity. In R. J. Sternberg (ed.), *The Nature of Creativity: Contemporary Psychological Perspectives* (pp.55–75). Cambridge, England: Cambridge University Press.
20. The Imagineers, 1996. *Walt Disney Imagineering: A Behind the Dreams Look at Making the Magic Real.* New York: Disney.
21. Basadur, M, Graen, G. B. & Scandura, T. A. 1986. Training effects on attitudes toward divergent thinking among manufacturing engineers, *Journal of Applied Psychology* 71 (4): 612–617.
22. Basadur, M. 1999. *Simplex: A Flight to Creativity.* Hadley, MA: The Creative Education Foundation Press.
23. Biondi, A. M. 1986. *The Creative Process.* Hadley, MA: The Creative Education Foundation.
24. Murray, W. H. 1951. *The Scottish Himalayan Expedition.* London: Dent.
25. Smith, D. 2001. *The Quotable Walt Disney.* New York: Disney.
26. Ibid.
27. Surrell, J. 2007. *The Disney Mountains: Imagineering at Its Peak.* New York: Disney.
28. Dubos, R. J. 1950. *Louis Pasteur.* Boston, MA: Little, Brown.
29. Goleman, D, Kaufman, P. & Ray, M. 1993. *The Creative Spirit.* New York: Plume.
30. The Imagineers, 2003. *The Imagineering Way: Ideas to Ignite Your Creativity.* New York: Disney.
31. de Bono, E. 1992. *Serious Creativity: Using the Power of Creativity to Create New Ideas.* New York: HarperBusiness.
32. Mellow, E. 1996. The two conditions view of creativity, *Journal of Creative Behavior* 30 (2): 126–143.
33. de Bono, E. 1985. *Six Thinking Hats.* Boston, MA: Little, Brown; and de Bono, E. 1995. Serious creativity, *The Journal for Quality and Participation* 18 (5): 12.
34. Ardichvili, A, Cardozo, R. & S. Ray, 2003. A theory of entrepreneurial opportunity identification and development, *Journal of Business Venturing* 18 (1): 105–123; and Davidsson. P & Honig, B. 2003. The role of social and human capital among Nascent entrepreneurs, *Journal of Business Venturing* 18 (3): 301–31.
35. Raudsepp, E. 1981. *How Creative Are You?* New York: Pedigree; Van Gundy, A. B. 1983. *108 Ways to Get a Bright Idea and Increase Your Creative Potential.* Englewood Cliffs, NJ: Prentice Hall; and Roger L. Firestein, R. L. 1989. *Why Didn't I Think of That?* Buffalo, NY: United Education Services.
36. Johnson, S. 2008. *The Invention of Air: A Story of Science, Faith, Revolution, and the Birth of America.* New York: Riverhead.
37. Pinker, S. 1997. *How the Mind Works.* New York: Norton.
38. Hawkins J. & Blakeslee, S. 2004. *On Intelligence.* New York: Times Books.
39. Stevenson, L. 2004. *Ten Theories of Human Nature.* New York: Oxford.

40. Burton, R. A. 2008. *On Being Certain: Believing You Are Right Even When You're Not.* New York: St. Martin's.
41. Harman W. W. & Rheingold, H. 1984. *Higher Creativity: Liberating the Unconscious for Breakthrough Insights.* Los Angeles: Tarcher; and Goleman, D, Kaufman, P. & Ray, M. 1993. *The Creative Spirit.* New York: Plume.
42. Osborn, A. F. 1963. *Applied Imagination,* 3rd ed. New York: Scribner's; Gordon, W. J. 1961. *Synetics.* New York: Harper & Row; and Pollock, T. April 1995. A personal file of stimulating ideas, little-known facts and daily problem-solvers, *Supervision* 4: 24.
43. Keil, J. M. 1985. *The Creative Mystique: How to Manage It, Nurture It, and Make It Pay.* New York: Wiley; and Brandowski, J. F. 1990. *Corporate Imagination Plus: Five Steps to Translating Innovative Strategies into Action.* New York: The Free Press.
44. Miller, W. C. 1999. *Flash of Brilliance.* Reading, PA: Perseus Books.

MANAGERIAL SKILLS FOR THE INNOVATION PROCESS

INTRODUCTION

As we discussed in Chapter 1, creativity and *innovation* can be very similar concepts, but there are some differences. Creativity is typically described as the process of generating new ideas, while innovation is a process that turns those ideas into reality. It is for this reason that some refer to innovation as applied creativity.[1] To further complicate the concept, innovation is conceptualized as not only a process, but also as an outcome based on change. As Donald Marquis clarifies, "When an enterprise produces a good or service or uses a method or input that is new to it, it makes a technical change. The first enterprise to make a given technical change is an innovator….Another enterprise making the same technical change is presumably an imitator….Thus, an innovation can be thought of as the unit of technical change."[2]

Change is the key word in innovation. The more we do something that fundamentally changes our market and forces our competitors to react to us, the more innovative we are. While efficiency and cost control are important for effectively running a business, we eventually reach a plateau where increased efforts on improving current *products, services*, and processes bring minimal improvements on return. Innovation, therefore, is required to take us to new heights. Legendary track-and-field athlete Sergei Bubka understands the value of using innovation to go to new heights. After pole-vaulting to a world-record height of 6 meters (19 feet 8 ¼ inches), he was asked if he would ever reach 7 meters (22 feet 11 ¾ inches). He replied, "No, there will have to be another technical revolution before that height can be reached. There's only so high you can jump using a bending fiberglass pole."[3] There's also only so high a company can go in its market if it continues to offer the same products and services. In order to raise the bar, a company must embrace innovation, but this isn't always easy.

The first step in changing attitudes and behaviors is to use a diagnostic tool to identify your personal innovation style. Table 4-1 provides an adapted version of the Kirton Adaption-Innovation instrument for gauging whether you embrace routine or change.[4]

TABLE 4-1 Adapted Kirton Adaption-Innovation Inventory

The following questions are about your style of work behavior (e.g., decision making) in your organization. Please respond to the question based on your assessment of yourself. Please read all the questions first, and then respond.

1 = Not at all (NA)

2 = To a slight extent (SE)

3 = To a moderate extent (ME)

4 = To a great extent (GE)

5 = To a very great extent (VGE)

You are a person who:	NA	SE	ME	GE	VGE
1. Conforms.	1	2	3	4	5
2. Will always think of something when stuck.	1	2	3	4	5
3. Enjoys detailed work.	1	2	3	4	5
4. Would sooner create than improve.	1	2	3	4	5
5. Is prudent when dealing with authority.	1	2	3	4	5
6. Never acts without proper authority.	1	2	3	4	5
7. Never seeks to bend or break the rules.	1	2	3	4	5
8. Likes bosses and work partners who are consistent.	1	2	3	4	5
9. Holds back ideas until obviously needed.	1	2	3	4	5
10. Has a fresh perspective on old problems.	1	2	3	4	5
11. Likes to vary set routines at a moment's notice.	1	2	3	4	5
12. Prefers change to occur gradually.	1	2	3	4	5
13. Is thorough.	1	2	3	4	5
14. Is a steady plodder.	1	2	3	4	5
15. Copes with several new ideas at the same time.	1	2	3	4	5
16. Is consistent.	1	2	3	4	5
17. Can stand out in disagreement against group.	1	2	3	4	5
18. Is stimulating.	1	2	3	4	5
19. Readily agrees with the team at work.	1	2	3	4	5
20. Has original ideas.	1	2	3	4	5
21. Masters all details painstakingly.	1	2	3	4	5
22. Proliferates ideas.	1	2	3	4	5
23. Prefers to work on one problem at a time.	1	2	3	4	5
24. Is methodical and systematic.	1	2	3	4	5

25. Often risks doing things differently.	1	2	3	4	5
26. Works without deviation in a prescribed way.	1	2	3	4	5
27. Imposes strict order on matters within his control.	1	2	3	4	5
28. Likes protection of precise instruction.	1	2	3	4	5
29. Fits readily into the system.	1	2	3	4	5
30. Needs the stimulation of frequent change.	1	2	3	4	5
31. Prefers colleagues who never "rock the boat."	1	2	3	4	5
32. Is predictable.	1	2	3	4	5

Source: Monavvarrian, A. 2004. Administrative reform and style of work behavior: Adaptors-innovators, *Public Organization Review: A Global Journal* 2: 141–164.

After taking the inventory, add up your scores. Kirton has concluded that the mean score across the general population is 96. If you scored less than 96, you are an *adaptor* who tends to focus on reducing conflict, minimizing risks, and solving *problems* in a disciplined manner. Adaptive skills are very helpful in structuring work and getting results. If you scored above 96, you are a more natural *innovator* who is comfortable with increased risk, uncertainty, and imprecision. Innovators are more flexible in where they search for opportunities and are constantly toying with ideas. The further less you are of 96, the more adaptive you are. The further more of 96, the more naturally innovative you are. It is important to note that adaptors are very capable of making innovative breakthroughs. As Kirton notes, "Everyone is a *potential* agent of change."[5] However, adaptors may find innovative activities a bit messy and take them out of their comfort zone. By mixing some ingredients for innovation into your work life, described in the following section, adaptors can become more innovative and open to change. Innovators will benefit from these conditions, too.

INGREDIENTS FOR ENHANCING INNOVATION AT WORK

As we learned in the last chapter, good ideas do not come out of thin air, but are the result of combining knowledge, new information, and thinking skills with hard work. Innovation requires even more effort, but an individual *transformation* is possible by incorporating the tried and true practices of the world's most innovative companies. In this section, some of those practices are spelled out.

INNOVATION MENTORSHIP

For innovative behavior to take place in a company, it must be supported by upper management. One way of demonstrating this support is by providing mentorship. Employees benefit from a coach or teacher who can guide them in developing the skills required to be more innovative. This process will not always be easy, and may require pushing the employees out of their comfort zone. Consider the example of Jack Welch and General Electric (GE). In 1988, GE faced a crisis when millions of compressors in their refrigerators were recalled. Welch and human resources chief Bill Conaty put Jeff Immelt in charge of this situation, even though he had no *experience* with recalls. Immelt handled the crisis well with Welch's guidance, and later he went on to replace Welch as CEO. Immelt credits that experience with helping him to become CEO.[6] Companies should provide similar leadership in developing innovative employees. If the company's executives do not have the ability to mentor employees in this way, they should hire talent to do so and/or contract with innovative and applied creativity consultants to provide such guidance. As a manager, you should always be searching for the most innovative people in your network who can serve as sounding boards and guides on your ideas.

INCENTIVES FOR THE INNOVATIVE EMPLOYEE

A company's culture has a significant impact on innovative activity. Smaller companies can provide great opportunities for learning about how to spot opportunities and bring them to market. Without the more formalized organizational structures and policies, employees have more flexibility to work on all aspects of a project. However, that does not rule out opportunities in a large firm. A major advantage large organizations have over smaller competitors is that they have a wealth of human capital within business units. People often think of smaller companies as being naturally more entrepreneurial, but commanding vast human resources might actually give large corporations the edge in innovation. K. Anders Ericsson has extensively studied high achievers and found that people need to spend 10 years in a domain before they attain expert status.[7] Clearly, corporations have a large wealth of experienced talent from which to draw. In a large company, you will have a larger selection of people to develop relationships with, and you may also have access to more resources.

The key for any department, division, or company is to examine how they support and reward the development of innovative and entrepreneurial pursuits. Do the senior managers of the organization select, develop, and reinforce innovative behaviors among their charges? Do the organizational structure and practices foster and facilitate innovation within their organizations? Do senior managers adequately reward such behavior? Due to agency theory, lower-level managers tend to be more risk averse and need to be encouraged by tying risk taking to pay outcomes. Innovation should be rewarded, since it is a signal as to what the senior managers value and support.[8] In your organization, make sure rhetoric about innovation is matched by its outcomes, such as the number of new products and services the company has supported and experiences the company has gained over the years.

INNOVATIVE BEHAVIOR

A key way you can incorporate innovation into your work life is by instituting *deliberate practice* into your daily routines. *Deliberate practice* is the use of regular, structured, and intense repetition of activities deemed important in becoming highly skilled at something. High performers not only work harder, but work on the right things to make themselves better.[9] By studying what separates great innovators from their peers, entrepreneurship researchers can now provide practices that others can replicate. Innovation best practices include enthusiastic immersion in a domain, collaborating with others in the sharing and development of ideas, and clear direction on what organizational priorities to address.[10]

The previous chapter emphasized the importance of domain expertise in generating new ideas. Besides deep knowledge, a person also gains new perspectives on a problem by collaborating with others.[11] Big breakthroughs happen within a network of motivated people excited about some core issues. The European Renaissance, for example, would not have happened had it not been for the Medici family funding and coordinating many of the era's top artists and scientists.[12] The Medici family created an environment that brought many of history's greatest minds together. In more modern times, many of civilization's leading innovations occurred through similar large-scale communities. The Manhattan Project is one example of collaboration that had a massive impact on the world: The atomic bomb would never have been built during World War II without bringing together the country's greatest scientists in the deserts of New Mexico. Its project director Robert Oppenheimer understood the power of collaboration, motivating and organizing perhaps the most brilliant, and eccentric, group of individuals ever brought together. Scientists were later brought together again in large government and corporate collaborations to put people into space. Bell Labs was the corporate version of NASA. During its heyday, Bell Labs held seminars and invited guests to exchange knowledge with its research scientists and technicians; however, many of their breakthroughs occurred from informal interactions in the hallways. At one time, Bell Labs housed many of the world's top scientists. As a result, Bell Labs was able to develop cellular telephone technology, laser, and transistors. As these examples illustrate, the lone genius making a breakthrough in an isolated lab in the mountains is largely myth. Even moments of insight that appear to have been made in seclusion are the result of collaboration, as the information affecting the thought most likely came from another person.[13]

Today, Google is able to attract some of the brightest technology experts by creating an environment that encourages its employees to pursue innovative ideas. At Google headquarters, aka the Googleplex, you might find employees sharing work cubes and huddle rooms, employees bicycling down the hall to get to meetings, outdoor seating for idea-discussion sessions, and health-food cafes. Google also supports its employees spending 30 percent of their work time on innovative projects that interest them.[14] Even during the recession of 2009, Google's new offerings have enabled it to increase its stock price from $279 per share to $446 per share. You should search for or create areas in your company where people get together to discuss ideas. If there aren't too many options currently available for you, organize salon-style get-togethers where colleagues can socialize and share their thoughts, whether that's at a home, bar, or ball game.

Another practice that is critical for innovation is *opportunity* recognition, or the ability to find or create untapped sources of potential profit.[15] Research reveals that entrepreneurs have been found to be more alert to opportunities than managers in traditional organizations. Clearly, managers would benefit from thinking like an entrepreneur and developing skills to recognize opportunity.

Fortunately, entrepreneurial alertness is a skill that can be improved with experience in recognizing and developing opportunities. Professors DeTienne and Chandler were able to help their students improve this skill by having them keep an opportunity-alertness notebook. Each day students were required to capture 5–10 business opportunities in the world around them and write them into their notebook. They found that students did indeed improve their ideas-development skills by following this practice.[16]

Consider the examples of Leonardo da Vinci and Thomas Edison, two of history's greatest innovators. While da Vinci was famous for his artistic and scientific breakthroughs, historians often have more interest in his notebooks. His great paintings were the result of his active scholarship on light, matter, form, and function. Da Vinci was an avid note taker, as was Edison. Edison believed every idea should be captured for possible future development. He was so committed to this principle that he had notebooks positioned throughout his workshops, so that his team and he got into the practice of writing down all possible ideas regarding problems in the world of their day. Thus, da Vinci and Edison indeed worked on large-scale, organized projects, but they also kept their minds open to serendipity. Side observations led to the invention of the phonograph, one of Edison's greatest inventions.

If the aforementioned ingredients of personal innovation are adhered to, you will become more innovative. As you pursue innovation, however, there are two different approaches you can take. The following section explores *closed innovation* and *open innovation*.

APPROACHES TO INNOVATION

Innovation occurs when two questions are successfully answered: "What is possible?"—which concerns research, discovery, and invention—and "What is needed?"—which concerns business and social *needs*. Answering these questions is complicated because developing new products, services, and experiences may take a while and what is wanted in the future may vary from what customers buy now. As Mark Stefik and Barbara Stefik observe, "You can't easily ask a future customer what they will want."[17] There are two approaches you can take in getting to these answers. Closed innovation is a more traditional approach that utilizes in-house resources and maintains secrecy about the project until it is brought to market. Open innovation is an approach where collaborations with external parties are used to help bring forward ideas. There are pros and cons with each approach. The traditional approach protects intellectual property well, but often proceeds in a calculated, slow way. The open approach embraces the advantages of the social and digital networks, but makes company activities more transparent. In a quickly changing world, companies are increasingly turning to open innovation and accepting the trade-off of collaboration for loss of ownership. Both approaches have been found successful by different companies, so it is a manager's call as to which they want to use.

CLOSED INNOVATION

The questions "What is possible?" and "What is needed?" may be answered by different people at different times in the innovation process. In traditional research and development (R&D) models, there is a linear process to innovation: basic research to applied research to development to production. Basic research begins the process by asking "What is possible?" Led by their curiosity, scientists search for answers to this question without any thought of practicality. While this may seem antithetical to business success, many of today's most innovative and popular products and services, such as microwaves and cell phone service, are the result of such scientific searches. As Donald Stokes found in his survey of breakthrough innovations, basic research is the "powerful dynamo of technological progress as applied research and development convert the discoveries of basic science into technological innovations to meet the full range of society's economic, defense, health, and other needs."[18] When interesting discoveries are made, applied scientists, researchers, and engineers seek ways to make them practical for everyday life. There may be a considerable time lag between scientific discovery and practical application, but once found technological revolutions occur and the economy becomes invigorated. It is for this reason that the government and other large institutions commit large resources to basic science projects. Once possible applications are found, the discoveries, inventions, or insights can be developed into commercial products, services, or experiences. The company then puts the organizational support in place to produce and deliver the commercial offering. Basic and applied sciences are beyond the reach of this book, but the principles of research and development can be applied to any company.

The closed approach to innovation is an attempt to generate new business breakthroughs through the utilization of the people, knowledge, and technology within the company's boundaries. Figure 4-1 demonstrates the traditional approach to R&D.

FIGURE 4-1   The Closed Paradigm for Managing Industrial R&D

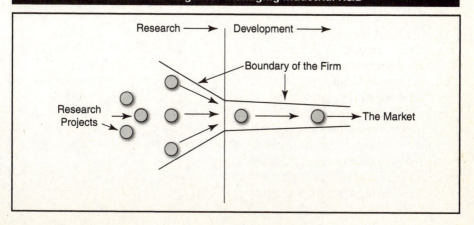

This system has an internal focus and is based on the following principles:[19]

1. Hire the best and brightest people, so that they work for you and not your competitors.
2. Make discoveries and development yourself, so that your company brings new products and services to market.
3. Discover something first so that you're the first to market it.
4. Invest great amounts in R&D, in order to insure that your company generates the best ideas and stays ahead of the competition.
5. Control intellectual property, in order to ensure that your company profits from it and not your competitors.

OPEN INNOVATION

While closed innovation is still the dominant paradigm in industry, some companies are starting to rely on an approach variously known as open-source innovation, open-market innovation, or, more simply, open innovation. Open innovation implies that the firm is not solely reliant upon its own resources for new technology, product, or business development. Rather, the firm acquires critical inputs to innovation from outside sources. Additionally, the firm may choose to commercialize its innovative ideas through external pathways that operate beyond the bounds of the firm's current business(es).

Through open innovation, firms move from a traditional, closed-system model of innovation, where they generate, develop, and commercialize their own innovative ideas, to one in which the organizational boundaries of innovation are porous and innovative ideas flow into and out of the organization with ease. Figure 4-2 demonstrates this dynamic.

FIGURE 4-2 The Open Innovation Paradigm for Managing Industrial R&D

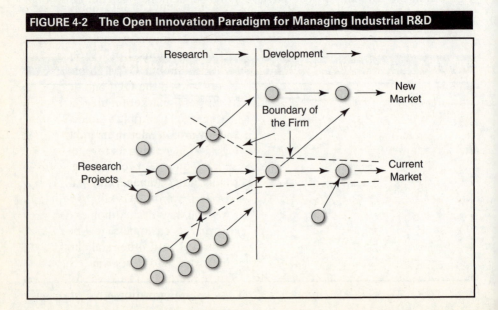

The open-innovation model encourages firms to exploit creative ideas through different innovation modes. Open innovation can entail, for example, licensing arrangements in which the firm sells its technology and/or acquires technology from others, joint ventures, corporate spin-offs of new businesses that are enabled by the firm's resources but not central to the firm's strategy, venture capital investments, and participation in external R&D consortia/alliances. In short, open innovation enables others' innovative ideas to enter the firm's innovation process and the firm's innovative ideas to be exploited outside the firm's organizational boundaries by the firm itself or by others, to the firm's benefit. As Keith Sawyer observes,

> Innovation today isn't a sudden break with the past, a brilliant insight that one lone outsider pushes through to save the company. Just the opposite: Innovation today is a continuous process of small and constant change, and it's built into the culture of successful companies. When I ask creators where their ideas come from, they always tell stories about collaboration and connection, about innovations that emerge from a creative space that spreads out across the entire company—and sometimes beyond its boundaries (p. 155).[20]

Collaboration has always been the key to great breakthroughs, and companies are realizing that communications technology and enhanced supply chains provide more possibilities for innovation. A firm's innovation processes, activities, and capabilities depend on the information resources provided by its social networks. Being "plugged in" to information networks allows a firm to be alert to new opportunities in its environment. This is a "give and take" approach that is not entirely accidental. Managers can and do influence their information networks strategically. The more a manager is connected to others, both inside and outside the firm, the better their chance to obtain superior information about opportunities in their environment. These sources can come from many different areas, and the firm needs to be open to possibilities. Famous examples in innovation have happened because of these types of interactions. In 1979, Steve Jobs toured the Xerox PARC laboratories and learned about GUI (graphical user interface). For three days, he and his engineers studied the GUI and developed the idea for the Apple Lisa. Although the Lisa was a market failure, the knowledge and technology gained from its development led to Apple's later computer successes. Proctor and Gamble is another innovation leader in its industry. An $80-plus billion company, it sets an annual goal of increasing its revenues 5 percent each year. This is not an easy task, as it is equivalent to creating a brand leading product, like Tide, each year. To do this, it has managers immerse themselves in their customer's life experiences. In its *Living It, Working It* program, employees actually live with consumers for several days in their homes and take part in their daily lives. P&G *wants* to learn what its customers' real needs and wants are.[21] Companies can generate relationships with other stakeholders as well. Distributors may have more insight into what end users want. Suppliers may have new materials that could revolutionize products. The key is to be open to opportunity wherever it presents itself. As open-innovation advocate Henry

Chesbrough observes, "Today it is not necessary or even feasible to lock up vital knowledge and ideas in silos, where they will only be used when and if a company's internal business needs dictate. A world of opportunity awaits the company that can harness ideas from its surrounding environment to advance its own business and that can leverage its own ideas outside its current business (p. 195)."[22]

Successful innovation has occurred with both approaches, because closed and open innovation share a similar goal: finding and seizing market opportunities. Unfortunately, many managers do not know how to pursue and develop opportunities. There are many books that provide direction on how to work with existing intellectual property or how to commercialize new technology, but little guidance is given with regard to opportunity recognition. This chapter provides guidance on how you can find opportunities starting from scratch. The first step in finding opportunity is knowing where to look for it.

SOURCES OF OPPORTUNITY

All innovative activity begins with an opportunity where a favorable set of circumstances creates a need or an opening for a new business concept or approach. Sometimes the opportunity is clear and other times it is revealed through a rigorous search. The reality is that many new business ideas fail because there was no opportunity in the first place. In these situations, the management team likely didn't have a true understanding of who their customer truly was. While one product may have been successful for the company, there is no guarantee the next one will be. The following questions are examples that can help guide you in gaining insights about your customer's background, attitudes, and behavior:

What common physical features do the customers have, if any?
What common activities do they do?
What do they typically wear?
What are typical jobs they hold?
Where do they typically live?
What is the most interesting thing about these customers?
What one word or phrase best describes these customers?

Interviews, observation, and consultation can be used in answering these questions. Apply the principles of creativity from the previous chapter. Use divergent thinking to list as many answers to the questions as you can, and then converge on the most intriguing facts, gaps, and revelations. Answers can come from fellow employees, outside experts, suppliers, customers, and yourself. If you already have intellectual property that you wish to develop into a commercial opportunity, first diverge and converge on potential markets and customers for the technology. Once you have selected a target market, answer the questions.

Once we have a profile of our potential customer, our next step in identifying opportunity is to understand why our target market buys particular goods and services in the first place. The simplest and most accurate answer is that everyone buys things in order to make their life better. Some transactions are simply to meet the physiological and safety needs of survival, such as food, water, sex, a constant body temperature, safety from dangerous elements, and medical attention.[23] People need to eat, need to clothe themselves, and need to have shelter. A market for satisfying these needs will always exist. Since everyone has different tastes, *life goals*, and means, how they satisfy these needs will vary though. When survival and safety needs are met, most people turn their attention to buying things to meet their desires and wants. These transactions often account for a large share of people's consumption, as they buy products they want but don't necessarily need. As social critic Arthur Asa Berger summarizes, "It boils down to this: Needs are finite but desires are infinite. We don't need all the stuff we buy; but we feel that having things will make our lives better, make us feel more alive."[24] So in a capitalist society where desires are never fully met, companies will always have the opportunity for product and service innovation. Goals for living a better life and being accepted or admired in society are two of the most common sources of these desires. Unsolved problems are another popular source of innovation potential. Most customers' buying patterns can be captured by one or more of these three categories. By considering these categories, you will have a better understanding of how to satisfy the customer.

SOCIAL GOALS

One way customers pursue their vision of the "good life" is by buying products and services that signal to others their values, rank, and preferred self-image. Everyone covets their uniqueness and wants to feel special. This goal is often achieved in our society through the purchase of the things we wear, the objects we use, and the things we do. Evolutionary psychologist Geoffrey Miller asserts that the underlying drive of this consumer behavior is to demonstrate to others your worth. The clothes you wear, the car you drive, and the house you live in are visible indicators of your professional and financial status. From an evolutionary perspective, these are signs or proxies of good genes, good health, and good social intelligence, which others are drawn and attracted to. As Miller notes, "Almost every animal species has its own fitness indicators to attract mates, intimidate rivals, deter predators, and solicit help from parents and kin. Male guppies grow flag-like tails, male lions sport luxuriant manes, male nightingales learn songs, male bowerbirds build bowers, humans of both sexes acquire luxury goods (13)."[25] In a consumer society, this will likely be an ongoing shopper arms race that will offer unlimited innovative opportunities for companies, with marketing providing the vehicle for persuading customers that the new products and services meet these underlying desires. Corporations even evidence this behavior through branding and symbols of prestige. Banks are often housed in large, marble buildings to show stability and wealth, and Fortune 500 companies host professional golf events that bring celebrities and athletes together under a corporate presence.

While Miller addresses the competitive nature of people in pursuing mates, status, and possessions, he also notes the social side of human nature. As social creatures, we seek products and services that allow us to communicate and socialize more frequently and easily. Music preferences, Web pages, and clothing help us to advertise our interests, so that we can interact with people like ourselves. Coffee shops and other social settings allow us to have places to meet and socialize. Cell phones and PDAs make it easier for people to stay in touch on a more regular basis. LinkedIn is a social networking website that brings professionals together to share ideas and contacts. There will always be business opportunities for creating new ways to help people come together and share their dreams, concerns, and problems. The following questions can offer insights into your customer's *social goals*.

> How does this customer usually communicate with others?
> What are this customer's favorite places to go?
> Why do they like these locations so much?
> What about the locations they frequent stand out to you?
> Is there anything unusual about these locations?
> Is there anything about these locations that could be applied in different settings?
> Is there anything interesting about the people that could be applied to a different group of people?
> Is there anything from a different setting or a group of people that could apply to this setting?
> How do the people interact with each other in this setting?

Apply the principles of creativity from the previous chapter. Use divergent thinking to list as many answers to the questions as you can, and then converge on the most intriguing facts, gaps, and revelations. Answers can come from fellow employees, outside experts, suppliers, customers, and yourself. You might be surprised by what trends begin to appear. Uncovering an unmet, and perhaps consciously unknown, want is a big step in making a breakthrough innovation.

LIFE GOALS

Beyond the social nature of consumption, shopping plays an immensely personal role in people's lives. As author Jim Pooler asserts, "Shopping is important, and it is underestimated. It's one of the most common things we do, and it dominates our lives....Never before has so much emphasis been placed on shopping, and never before has it assumed the central place in our lives that it now does. Shopping for emotional and psychological reasons has become the new mantra of modern society."[26] In short, shopping has become a pathway toward the good life and feeling fulfilled...at least in the short term. People shop to attain health and alleviate illness, to achieve gusto and thrills and reduce sluggishness and misery, to feel secure and avoid physical threats, to feel loved and admired and not hated and shunned, to be considered an insider and not an outsider looking in, to feel confident and not insecure, to feel serene and relaxed and not tense and anxious, to feel beautiful and not ugly, to feel rich and not poor, to feel clean and not dirty, to feel knowledgeable and not ignorant, to feel in control of life and not at the mercy of events, to feel entertained and not bored, among other reasons.[27]

Shopping also serves a self-reward for enduring the trials and challenges of life. In a busy world where people take on the responsibilities of work and family, they often do not receive the recognition from others they may feel they deserve. Shopping provides an opportunity to indulge in buying something extra like an unneeded tool, gadget, or piece of clothing. Savvy marketers advertise this theme in many commercials broadcast in the middle of people's busy days. Although at opposite ends of the entertainment spectrums, Las Vegas and the Disney theme parks pamper their customer base in meeting this underlying motivation with *escapism* and self-renewal. Ironically, some people even reward themselves for doing a good job of shopping. Finding bargains gives psychological comfort for buying more goods and services. While some managers struggle for new business ideas, the aforementioned discussion on shopping motivations evidences that there should never be a shortage of opportunities if human nature is understood and utilized. The following questions can serve to find out more about your customers' life goals.

What do they seem to enjoy doing?
What are their hobbies?
What activities do they pay to do?
What are they passionate about?
How could the customer improve themselves physically, intellectually, or
    spiritually?
What seems to be missing in their lives?
What changes, issues, problems, and opportunities for improvement do you
    visualize?

Again, apply the principles of creativity from the previous chapter. Use divergent thinking to list as many answers to the questions as you can, and then converge on the most intriguing facts, gaps, and revelations. Answers can come from fellow employees, outside experts, suppliers, customers, and yourself. This is an important *fact-finding* stage of your innovation journey.

PROBLEMS

Problems are great sources for innovation. A problem is a situation where there is a gap between where a person is now and where they want to be, but they don't know how to find a way to cross that gap.[28] The bigger that gap is and/or the more difficult it is to figure out how to cross it, the bigger the problem. If it's a big enough problem, then finding a solution to it will be very important to a person. They will be willing to pay a lot to have it solved. If enough people feel the same way, there is a great market opportunity for the company that can solve it. The problem with a lot of innovation attempts is that the chosen solution doesn't adequately cross the gap, the gap is not a big enough concern to the customer to warrant interest, or there are not enough people who have the problem to make it profitable for the company. Thus, innovation requires finding the right problems to solve and offering solutions that are worthwhile to enough people. The astute manager can ask the following questions to have a better idea as to what problems to pursue for innovation opportunities :

Is there anything that appears to be frustrating this customer?
What activities or responsibilities are placing unwanted financial strain on the customer?
Where are the bottlenecks in the customer experience?
What red tape does the customer face in their daily life?

The following questions apply more to business-to-business situations:

What performance goals are being missed regularly in the industry?
What issues and problems could be alleviated through partnerships with other organizations?
What will be the biggest challenges companies in the industry will face over the next three years?
What technology issues are hindering progress in the industry?

Again, apply the principles of creativity from the previous chapter. Use divergent thinking to list as many answers to the questions as you can, and then converge on the most intriguing facts, gaps, and revelations. Answers can come from fellow employees, outside experts, suppliers, customers, and yourself.

FACT-FINDING

Once we have identified a need, want, or problem that we think is worth exploring, we need to learn more details about it. Professor Min Basadur emphasizes the importance of fact-finding on an opportunity before moving forward on offering a solution to the customer. Fact-finding gives us a better idea of what we are dealing with and also often uncovers issues we might have overlooked in our previous analyses. Diverge on the following questions to gather more facts about the need, want, or problem you selected:[29]

What do you know, or think you know, about this opportunity?
What do you not know about this opportunity (but you'd like to know)?
Why is this a problem or an opportunity?
How does the customer currently deal with this issue?
What have you and your competitors already thought of or tried?
If this opportunity were met, what would the customer have that they don't have now?
What might you be assuming about the need, want, or problem that you don't have to assume?

After answering these questions, you should have a better idea of the underlying structure of the opportunity. You may want to fact-find and research more than one opportunity, and then select the one that has the most market potential. This fact-finding exercise will help you in better addressing the need, want, or problem. Once you feel confident this is an opportunity worth pursuing, it is time to seize it and move forward in developing your innovation.

SEIZING OPPORTUNITY

Once an opportunity has been recognized, a company must seize it. The best way to develop an innovation is to collaborate with others and have a particular challenge to focus on. Business teams perform better when they have specific issues to address rather than working on ambiguous goals.[30] Taking the previously selected need, want, or problem, it is now time to convert it into a commercial product. For example, let's assume we found out from our research that runners find it difficult to get motivated to run after a long day at work. They want to get their run in, but they feel drained when they get up away from their desk at the end of the day. We could address this problem by asking, "How might we help runners find the motivation they need to get their runs in when they get off work?"

Now we can pursue a solution to the problem. There are five ways a company can fulfill a customer need or want. It can sell a commodity that provides the materials or ingredients the customer can use for fulfilling their need or want; it can sell a finished good that is already assembled and can be put to immediate use by the customer; it can provide a service that accomplishes a specific task for the client; or it can stage an experience that more fully engages the customer. At the highest level of offerings is transformation where the business has a deeply personal impact on a customer, but this is rare. For example, let's assume we found that the running customer would like a drink they could consume that would pep them up and give them a good workout. We decide that coffee could meet this need, and we start thinking about what type of coffee product would interest these runners. Let's also assume we found a coffee bean that not only wakes the person up but has a performance benefit for endurance athletes. We could sell these coffee beans, which are a commodity, directly to the runners, and have them grind them up themselves and brew the coffee at home before their workout. Of course, that takes a little time, so the customers may be willing to pay a little more for an instant version of coffee at the grocery store that they can put right into their Mr. Coffee machines. This more finished product will bring a higher price tag at the store than the scoop of coffee beans, however. Busier people may bypass the brewing process altogether and pay a little more for someone else to make it. The runners may drive through at a fast-food restaurant that serves it, and take the coffee with them on the way to the gym or park where they'll do their run. However, they may want to socialize with other runners before they work out, so they pay a little more for the experience of drinking the coffee at the Endorphin Café. Providing a transformative experience with coffee would be difficult, but maybe we offer coaching and motivational talks at the café that inspire the runner to do better workouts and run personal records. Because of this transformative approach, the runners feel more confident and proud, which carries over into the rest of their lives. They receive promotions at work and set new records on the course, all of which they credit to the Endorphin Café. The Endorphin Café becomes hugely successful in the running community, and we realize we can charge country club memberships to customers who drink coffee there. After considering who our customers are, we decide that the best approach to meeting the customer's needs is to offer a coffee product that boosts endurance performance. We package it so that it can be drank cold or easily warmed up in a microwave, and sell it in supplement stores, on running websites, and at marathon expos. We are intrigued by the Endorphin Café idea but decide that there are very few areas in the country with a dense concentration of runners to support it. This line of thinking can be applied to any customer need, want, or problem we are addressing. It ensures that we don't overlook a more profitable business idea, and that we truly offer something the customer will be interested in.

The form of commercial offering we deliver is a critical business decision. It is important that you understand the nature and benefits of each approach. B. Joseph Pine II and James H. Gilmore point out that "each successive offering greatly increases in value because the buyer finds each more *relevant* to what he truly wants."[31] Major breakthroughs can occur when a company successfully moves from its traditional industry category into another. For example, McDonald's commoditized the restaurant business by standardizing products and services, and became very popular by creating the "fast food" category. Starbucks, on the other hand, created an experience for the coffee drinker by placing emphasis on product variety, quality, and customer service in a relaxing, hip atmosphere. As a result, McDonald's prices products at a low price, while Starbucks charges a premium. The following discussion examines offerings in more detail.

COMMODITIES AND MATERIALS

Commodities are resources that are obtained from the natural world, such as animals, minerals, and vegetables, and are the first source of opportunity in an economic system. All products are made from something, and great fortunes have been made in acquiring and selling commodities. The market for commodities is immense. Most of the world we live in today is a human-created environment—a built environment. We design, build, and plan things to satisfy our needs and wants. Look outside your window, and chances are that even the grass and trees you see were engineered, grown, and planted by someone.[32] Table 4-2 presents a breakdown of common materials used in manufacturing and building.

Commodities trade based on supply and demand, and since most commodities are bought in a raw state and easily acquired, their economic value is usually at the bottom of the value chain. Innovation can occur, however, when we find new compounds and materials for medicine, architecture, and manufacturing; however, most of the land on earth has been explored, leaving fewer chances of discovery of new materials and compounds. A few remote rain forests, the deep ocean, and other planets may hold the opportunity for new discoveries, but increasingly scientists and researchers are exploring ways to create new materials

TABLE 4-2   Family of Materials

Group	Subgroup	Examples
Metallics (metals and alloys)	Ferrous	Iron
		Steel
		Cast iron
	Nonferrous	Aluminum
		Tin
		Zinc
		Magnesium
		Copper
		Gold
	Powdered metal	Sintered steel
		Sintered brass
Polymerics	Human-made	Plastics
		Elastomers
		Adhesives
		Paper
	Natural	Wood
		Rubber
	Animal	Bone
		Skin
Ceramics	Crystalline compounds	Porcelain
		Structural clay
		Abrasives
	Glass	Glassware
		Annealed glass
Composites	Polymer based	Plywood
		Laminated timber
		Impregnated wood
		Fiberglass
		Graphite epoxy
		Plastic laminates
	Metallic based	Boron aluminum
		Primex
	Ceramic based	Reinforced concrete
		CFCC
	Cermets	Tungsten carbide
		Chromium alumina

Group	Subgroup	Examples
Others	Other	Reinforced glass
	Electronic materials	Semiconductors
		Superconductors
	Lubricants	Graphite
	Fuels	Coal
		Oil
	Protective coatings	Anodized aluminum
	Biomaterials	Carbon implants
	Smart materials	Shape memory alloys
		Shape memory polymers

Source: Adapted from Jacobs, J. A. & Kilduff, T. F. 2000. *Engineering Materials Technology: Structures, Processing, Properties, and Selection.* Columbus, OH: Prentice Hall, 57.

in laboratories. Materials science creates new resources for manufacturing and building, bioengineering designs new foods, and nanotechnology changes the molecular structure of compounds. Once these new materials and composites are created, they are patented and can generate tremendous financial returns. Some companies sell the new materials to others, while others use them in their own products as a source of competitive advantage.

Another source of innovation is finding new ways to use existing commodities and materials. Many entrepreneurs today are building companies that specialize in sustainable business practices and construction. As the green movement takes hold, there will be increasing needs for retooling existing structures and building new houses and facilities that are sustainable. The innovative companies will gain an edge in those markets, but it is likely that once a dominant design has taken hold, green building technologies will standardize, and more companies will enter the market. These building materials will then become more of a commodity and lose some of their economic value. Additionally, commodities require the purchaser to shape and mold the materials themselves. To receive more compensation from customers, we must offer them something they can put to immediate use—a product.

PRODUCTS

A common way to seize opportunity is to create a unique product—one that is not being offered today but would be in great demand if it were. The next-best way is to adapt something that is currently on the market or extend the offering into an area in which it is not presently available. The first approach is often referred to as *new-new* the second as *new-old*.

The new-new approach is a more innovative way to enter a market. Typical examples include smartphones, MP3 players, high-definition televisions, and global positioning systems (GPS). All of these products and more have been introduced as a result of research and development efforts by major corporations. What we must realize, however, is that unique ideas are not produced only by large corporations. Small companies are often able to more easily fill product niches overlooked by bigger firms. Moreover, the rate at which new products enter the market has caused the public to expect many of their goods to improve continually. There will always be a place for small and large companies in our economic system.

How does one discover or invent new products? One of the easiest ways is to make a list of annoying experiences or hazards encountered with various products during a given period of time. Common examples include objects that fall out of one's hands, household chores that are difficult to do, and items that are hard to store. Can certain innovations alleviate these problems? Indeed, people often get ideas for new products this way. For example, an engineer once observed the mechanism for recording the revolutions of a ship's propeller. As he watched the device tally the propeller's revolutions, he realized that the idea could be adapted to the recording of sales transactions—a problem he had been trying to solve for some time. The result led, eventually, to the development of the traditional cash register.

Most business ideas tend to come from people's experiences. In general, the main sources of ideas are prior and current jobs, hobbies or interests, and personally identified problems. This new-new approach indicates the importance of people's awareness of their daily lives (work and free time) for developing new business ideas.

Most new products, however, do not start with a totally unique idea. Instead, a company "piggybacks" on someone else's ideas by improving a product—hence the term "new-old" approach. There are several ways this can be done. First, competitors may not be offering products that fully meet the needs of the customer, and thus offer avenues for a company to deliver more value with better products. Second, there may be locations that are being overlooked by other companies where there is a substantial enough potential customer base to warrant selling the product there. Walmart is a classic example of this type of scenario. When Sam Walton focused on towns of less than 50,000 people to build his business, critics thought he was destined to fail. The small-town platform, however, helped him to gain a foothold in communities across the country that led to its current position as a retail leader. Third, in markets where the product is radically innovative, early pioneers rarely end up in the number one spot in the long run. With radical innovation, customers usually aren't demanding the new product because they have no experience with it, and thus don't realize the impact it would have on their lives. As a result, the potential market can be quite small for a while until the product starts to catch on. In the mean time, established firms usually focus on generating enough revenues to support current operations and planned growth. It becomes quite a paradox. If a company pursues a lot of different avenues, it may become unfocused and lose efficiencies. If it doesn't maintain its exploratory activities, it may miss out on profitable markets in the long term.[33] The solution many companies take is to stay abreast of technological developments and bring entrepreneurial small companies into their networks. The small company benefits from the support, and the larger company develops new markets with its resources and experience. It is for this reason that many start-ups have acquisition as their exit strategies.

Sometimes it pays to be a fast-second in the market rather than the original developer. Thus, while the new-new approach is the one we often associate with innovation, we must be very aware of the benefits of the new-old approach as well. Established companies would be wise to follow a portfolio approach when pursuing an innovation strategy.

SERVICES

Sometimes customers want more from companies than merely products. They want companies to perform tasks for them they would rather not do themselves, or they seek out expert counsel on matters they don't understand. In the latter half of the twentieth century, the economy increasingly moved from being industrial-based to being service-based. In a service-based business, companies provide specific tasks customers want done but don't want to do themselves. It is a step beyond products, because there is usually more interaction between the company and the customer. Companies that provide services that better meet the individual needs of their clients will receive more compensation. Services tend to be much more personal than selling products. Therefore, listening to the customer and finding out what their needs and problems are is essential. It is then up to the company to offer a service that leaves the customer satisfied in meeting those demands, if they are to attain return business.

Just as products can be new-new and new-old, services can be as well. One hot area of service innovation is Internet social utilities, such as Facebook and MySpace. Facebook was founded by Mark Zuckerberg, a Harvard University student who was frustrated by the lack of networking facilities on campus. The company was founded in February 2004 and is now the largest source for photos and one of the most trafficked sites on the Internet. In two short years, the company attracted offers of $750 million from Viacom[34] and $900 million from Yahoo.[35] Common new-old examples of service offerings are offering new varieties of restaurants, clothing stores, or similar outlets in homogenous shopping districts. Of course, these kinds of operations can be risky because competitors can move in easily. Potential companies considering this kind of market should try to offer services that are difficult to copy. For example, a computerized billing and accounting service can be successful if the business serves a sufficient number of doctors to cover the cost of computer operators and administrative expenses in order to turn an adequate profit. Better yet, if a company wants a sustainable advantage in its market it will transform its services into a hard-to-match experience.

EXPERIENCES AND TRANSFORMATIONS

Services increasingly resemble commodities as companies search for new ways to handle tasks for customers in cheaper and more efficient ways. Airline travel was once a high-end service, but now resembles bus rides. Airline companies having already cut meal services, now charge for refreshments that were once complimentary. Many people no longer have a personal relationship with an insurance agent, but rather search for the best deals on the Internet. Fast-food restaurants continue to pop up all over America offering quick and cheap ways to get daily calories. Taco Bell, for example, offers triple layer nachos for 79 cents and cheesy double bean burritos for 99 cents, and proclaims, "Why pay more?" Some companies are meeting that challenge by offering experiences rather than merely services.

As Pine and Gilmore state, an experience "occurs whenever a company intentionally uses services as the stage and goods as props to engage an individual. While commodities are fungible, goods tangible, and services intangible, experiences are memorable. Buyers of experiences—we'll follow Disney's lead and call them guests—value being engaged by what the company reveals over a duration of time."[36] This observation is quite evident during the 2008–2009 recession. Few would consider theme parks one of life's necessities, and during a time of cash crunch we would expect people to curtail their spending on such activities. This has happened but to different degrees. Six Flags which offers thrill rides to its customers has filed Chapter 11 bankruptcy, but the Disney theme parks have maintained their attendance during the same period.[37] How can this be? The main reason is that Disney stages an experience that goes beyond rides to consider how to interact with every customer in a positive way throughout the entire park. Disney delivers inviting sensations from the majestic photo ops in front of castles and mountains to the sweet smells being pumped into the air down Main Street. While some parks like Kings Island have a few cartoon characters strolling the grounds, the Disney parks bring their animated features into three dimensions, letting customers interact with the characters and settings. This makes the visit more memorable and personal.

Pine and Gilmore provide Disney as the exemplar of these interactions because they deliver on all four experience realms: esthetics, escapist, educational, and entertainment. *Esthetics* make an environment more inviting, and encourage a guest to enjoy the setting. Guests sit down, relax, and hang out. Walt Disney World creates awe among its guests by employing 5,000 maintenance and engineering workers, including 750 horticulturists and 600 painters, to keep the grounds clean and majestic.[38] The *escapist* aspect draws a guest in and encourages them to participate in the setting. Whether it's interacting with "tour guides" on the Jungle Cruise ride or getting a picture taken with Goofy, guests have many opportunities to feel connected to the park. The *educational* component occurs when guests learn something from taking part in the activities of the experience. Shows, such as *It's a Bug's Life,* present facts about nature in an amusing fashion. The *entertainment* aspect makes the experience more fun and enjoyable.

The best indicators of Disney's success in this area are the smiles, ooh's, and ah's guests emit during their visit. Pine and Gilmore point out that it's not required to deliver on all four of these realms to be successful, but the more you do the more memorable the customer's experience is.

You don't have to operate a theme park to deliver a world-class experience. Companies from very different industries create memorable moments with customers that bring them back again for future purchases. Southwest Airlines is well known for turning discount air travel into an experience. Funny and caring flight attendants can actually make hours in the air fun and relaxing. On the other end of the price spectrum, British Airways and Singapore Air pamper travelers with luxuries and access to services not found on traditional flights. Their customers are willing to pay significantly more money to make travel time more pleasant and satisfying. In the food industry, the Hard Rock Café provides a dining experience where customers can interact with hip food servers and bartenders while checking out museum-quality artifacts from the music industry. Many people make it a point to dine at these theme restaurants when on vacation and purchase memorabilia to commemorate the visit.

In an increasingly competitive world, developing innovative experiences can help differentiate a company from its competitors. Pine and Gilmore believe the highest stage of experience is transformative in nature in that the customer changes in some fundamental way from the interaction. In a transformation, the customer is the product. The company looks for ways to help customers realize their aspirations along the physical, emotional, intellectual, or spiritual dimensions. The first place to start in a transformation is with a diagnostic tool that allows the customer to know where they stand on an issue. Then it's the company's responsibility to lead and guide the customer to the desired change. This approach is quite common in good university programs and churches, and may account for the strong attachments and loyalties people have with those institutions. Companies that can develop innovative transformative experiences would have very appreciative customers who would pay a premium for these results. One can imagine an innovative healthcare company focusing on changing its clients into healthy and productive individuals instead of focusing on efficient, cost-based treatment. A transformative hospital might be more expensive, but patients might travel great distances to be treated in an inspirational, caring way.

This section examined sources of possible opportunities for new innovations. We first examined who the customer is, then uncovered their wants, needs, and problems. We then explored ways to meet these opportunities. A company can find, develop, or use new materials; create new products; offer unique services; deliver experiences that fully engage their customers; and/or transform their behaviors and attitudes. As evidenced in this section, needs, wants, and problems are prime opportunities for innovation. After developing a list of the best opportunities, it is time to offer a deliverable to the customer. The following section provides a methodology for shaping the idea into a commercial product, service, or experience.

CONVERTING OPPORTUNITY INTO INNOVATION

Assuming that you have found an opportunity for commercialization, it is time to convert it into an actual product, service, or experience. We now examine new product development. Keep in mind what a commercial offering actually becomes in the market is rarely identical to the original idea it was based on. Attributes and features might be added or subtracted and modifications will occur as a natural result of R&D efforts and commercialization.

NEW PRODUCT DEVELOPMENT

CONCEPT DEVELOPMENT

The first step in converting an opportunity into an innovation is to develop a clear concept of what you want to achieve. The opportunity must be developed into a clear concept that can be defined and evaluated. For example, using the coffee example from earlier in this chapter, we could frame a challenge such as "What type of coffee product could we offer runners that would give them pep and boost endurance?" We can now explore different ways to meet this challenge by utilizing the creative skills of divergence and convergence.

Leading design and development company Ideo employs this approach as a regular way of doing business. At Ideo, creative teams address challenges by undergoing a "deep dive" and immersing themselves in the problem space. With a specific challenge in mind, they study and interact with the customer and their surroundings in any way possible. General manager Tom Kelley says they act like anthropologists, "getting out of the office, cornering the experts, and observing the natives in their habitat."[39] In a classic Nightline episode, Ted Koppel presents Ideo with a distinct challenge: "Take something old and familiar, like say the shopping cart, and completely redesign it in just five days."[40] After visiting grocery stores, talking to managers, watching parents and children use shopping carts, talking to professional buyers who purchase shopping carts, and interviewing a cart repairman, three goals emerged from the research: make the cart more child-friendly, redesign the shopping experience so that is more efficient, and increase safety. The team then broke into different groups and diverged on possible ways to meet these goals in a new shopping cart design. After each group had developed their solutions, they shared them with the larger group. Each individual then selected the solutions they thought best met the stated goals of the project. After everyone converged on their favorite solutions, the team as a whole discussed why they chose what they did. After much discussion, the group came to agreement on what the best concept would be for the new shopping cart design.

Once a concept is defined, it can now be tested with relevant audiences, including customers, to gauge potential interest in the new product. Focus groups, interviews, and surveys are often used to do this. Industry analysis can also be helpful in preparing the product for new market entry. Areas such as competition, customer definition, technological assessment, regulatory concerns, and economic measures are all considerations for such research.[41] Once potential benefits are identified, marketing and sales are then considered before moving forward with product development. How much will shipping and handling cost to sell the product? Where will the product be stored? How can you get the product into proper distribution channels? How tough is the competition in this sector, and what are they doing to deliver products, services, and experiences?[42] If these factors are addressed and the idea still holds up, business cases can be prepared for the most promising surviving concepts. A preliminary outline of the business case can include the concept and the related goals it meets; the needs, wants, or problems it addresses; the milestones you'll need to achieve in bringing the concept to market; and the potential obstacles you'll have to overcome to be successful.[43]

PROTOTYPING

Once the concept is well defined and evaluated, it is time to start to transform it into a physical product, service delivery model, or customer experience. Managers must assemble a team who can establish the exact technical requirements for designing and producing the product, ensuring these requirements can be met on a reasonable time and cost schedule. Design professionals may conceive different versions of the product (or service delivery system) based on the many trade-offs that must be made among product attributes. Next comes technical product or service testing, which subjects the innovation to a rigorous examination of tolerances and performance capabilities under differing circumstances. Products, services, and experiences can then be placed in customer locations (or beta test sites) and their use is monitored.

FINAL EVALUATION

After a *prototype* is modeled, profitability analysis is performed to determine breakeven points in terms of initial investment as well as rates of return that will be realized through selling the product based on projected cash flows. To confirm initial sales projections and finalize decisions regarding price, packaging, promotion, and distribution, test marketing is then performed using a representative subset of the intended market. Market launch efforts have become fairly complex, and sophisticated undertakings often require a year or more of planning and staging before a product or service hits the market. In these situations, the firm is attempting to successfully penetrate the innovators and early adaptors, while laying the groundwork for penetration of the more general market.

A UNIQUE SWOT ANALYSIS APPROACH

In this section we offer another approach to uncovering opportunities by utilizing a **SWOT** (Strengths, Weaknesses, Opportunities, and Threats) analysis in an unconventional manner. A SWOT analysis is predominantly used in strategy sessions, but it can also be helpful as a tool for generating new product or service ideas. Following the steps below will help uncover additional opportunities.

DIVERGE ON THE STRENGTHS, WEAKNESSES, OPPORTUNITIES, AND THREATS OF YOUR ORGANIZATION

You have probably performed these steps before. It will look familiar, but we provide a few twists to SWOT analysis. First, gather a diverse group of organizational members and diverge on strengths, weaknesses, opportunities, and threats—that is, capture all the strengths the group can come up with on large sheets of easel paper, and then do the same with weaknesses, opportunities, and threats. Be sure to write each fact in a complete sentence. For example, "Communication between the sales force and the marketing team is bad" is a better-stated fact than "bad communications." Full sentences discipline us to think in more clear and precise terms, and ensure we understand what each other is saying. As you fill a page, have another participant tape the page to a wall in the room. Continue until the group comes to a standstill. Remember there are no wrong answers. The key is to capture as many ideas as possible.

CONVERGE ON THE MAIN STRENGTHS, WEAKNESSES, OPPORTUNITIES, AND THREATS

After you have developed a full list of each factor, count how many facts were obtained in each segment. Multiply each segment's total by 10 percent and write that number at the top of each segment. For example, if a group had 22 strengths, 35 weaknesses, 10 threats, and 18 opportunities, write 2 on strengths, 4 (rounding up) on weaknesses, 1 on threats, and 2 (rounding up) on opportunities. Now ask each participant to put a sticky dot on the 2 strengths, 4 weaknesses, 1 threat, and 2 opportunities that they think will have the biggest impact on the company's future well-being.

CLARIFY AND SELECT THE KEY STRENGTHS, WEAKNESSES, OPPORTUNITIES, AND THREATS

Now look at the statements in each column that received the most "sticky dots" and ask the people who selected them why they did so. When there is consensus among the group as to the most important strengths, weaknesses, opportunities, and threats, circle the selections, and ask if there are any facts that were overlooked by the group that should be given further consideration. Once consensus is reached, draw a line under the strengths column and write underneath "core competencies."

ADD CORE COMPETENCIES TO THE STRENGTHS COLUMN

Explain to the group that core competencies are another type of strength that can be useful for capitalizing on opportunities. Core competencies are specific factors your company does well that are central to the way it delivers benefits to its customers. Core competencies distinguish your company from its competition, and are applied over a range of products and services. If the company has an official list of what its core competencies are, write them in the strengths column. If not, have the group diverge and converge on what the core competencies of the company should be.

EXPLORE HOW STRENGTHS AND CORE COMPETENCIES CAN BE LEVERAGED

Ask the group to diverge on how the company can leverage its strengths and core competencies to take advantage of the opportunities that were converged on. Once a list is generated, have the group converge on the ideas with the most market potential.

EXPLORE WAYS TO IMPROVE WEAKNESSES

Ask the group to consider how it could improve weaknesses in the company. For example, there may be process or service improvements that could be pursued for innovative solutions.

DISCUSS THREATS

Ask the group to consider how it could prevent threats from hurting the company. You can also ask what alternatives the company has for minimizing the threats it faces.

This SWOT Analysis approach provides participants, after they leave the meeting, with a list of general challenges that they can start designing solutions for. When the group meets again, each person will present their ideas. Write the ideas on easel paper, then ask each participant to converge on the two ideas that have the most potential for the company. Ask the group why they made their selections as they did. The group should now discuss which ideas they want to move forward.

COMMERCIALIZATION

The moment that management has decided the product, service, or experience is ready to launch is called the *point of commercialization*. Final designs are confirmed, manufacturing and operations requirements are put in place, and distribution channels are authorized. It is now critical that the marketing component of the innovation be firmed up. Chapter 10 will explore this component in more detail.

Summary

An innovative company is composed of innovative employees. Innovation is a way of life for people in these organizations. While scientists discover and inventors create, innovators find ways to adapt new products and services so that they are accepted in the market. This chapter examined how a manager can become more innovative. The ingredients for innovation were first covered. The approaches of closed innovation and open innovation were then examined. Sources of opportunity were covered in depth. The chapter next explained how to recognize and seize an opportunity. It concluded with guidelines on how to develop an opportunity into an innovation.

INNOVATION-IN-ACTION

Nike's History Of Innovation

Since his graduation from Stanford University, Phil Knight, the founder of Nike, has changed the way everyone thinks about athletic shoes. With $500 and a handshake, Knight and his college track coach, Bill Bowerman, created Nike in 1964 and the innovations began immediately. The two made their first shoe order and began ripping the shoes apart, trying to find ways to improve the running shoe. Before long, Nike was revolutionizing running shoe technology and changing the way runners and the general public looked at the gym shoe.

Nike's innovative spirit has always played a key role in developing the athletes who utilize the technology. Athletes, including Michael Jordan, Steve Prefontaine, Tiger Woods, Michael Johnson, and Lance Armstrong, have sought Nike for their design techniques, looking to better their already-incredible talents. In the 1970s, Steve Prefontaine, one of the greatest track runners of all time, was one of the first to sport Nike's first innovative technology. Bowerman drew inspiration from a common kitchen appliance when he created a shoe with an outsole that had waffle-type nubs for traction but were lighter than traditional training shoes. Prefontaine served as Nike's first international spokesman.

Perhaps Nike's most influential ambassador, Michael Jordan, began his relationship with Nike in the 1980s and created his first signature basketball shoe. The Jordan brand was launched in 1986 after Jordan was drafted into the National Basketball League. The sky proved to be the limit and Nike and the Jordan brand are still creating custom shoes. His footwear remains the standard for not just basketball shoes, but for popular culture as well.

Olympic gold medalist Michael Johnson asked Nike to design a shoe that was light enough to shave a tenth of a second off of his personal best sprint times. Nike created a 112-gram track spike, the lightest track shoe ever made. The lightweight shoe proved to be the perfect catalyst, and at the 1996 Olympics, Johnson set the world record in the 200-meter sprint and also won gold in the 400-meter sprint.

Lance Armstrong began his relationship with Nike shortly before he was diagnosed with cancer. Standing by his side, Nike remained one of the few sponsors of the young cyclist and in 1999, on the wings of Nike equipment, Armstrong won the first of his seven Tour de France titles. Throughout his career, Nike developed equipment and apparel that would give Armstrong an edge, and today, every rider in the field utilizes the technologies that Nike pioneered.

The list of athletes who wear Nike shoes and clothes, swing Nike golf clubs, and sport the Nike Swoosh on their chest goes on and on. Nike continues to design and create the world's most important sports technology and to push the limits of what the athlete can achieve.

Source: Based on: NikeBiz, Company Overview: History, http://www.nikebiz.com/company_overview/history, Accessed on January 13, 2011.

Key Terms

Adaptor	Living It, Working It
Change	Needs
Closed innovation	New-new
Commodities	New-old
Concept development	Open innovation
Deliberate practice	Opportunity
Educational	Point of commercialization
Entertainment	Potential
Escapism	Problems
Escapist	Products
Esthetics	Prototyping
Experience	Relevant
Fact-finding	Services
Final Evaluation	Social goals
Innovation	SWOT Analysis
Innovator	Transformation
Life goals	Wants

Discussion Questions

1. What is the difference between creativity and innovation?
2. What is the difference between an adaptor and an innovator?
3. Why is mentorship important?
4. What are the deliberate practices of innovation?
5. What is the difference between closed innovation and open innovation?
6. When would a company use closed innovation? Open innovation?
7. Why is collaboration important for innovation?
8. Where can managers find opportunities for new business?
9. Why do customer wants provide opportunities for new business?
10. What is the difference between a need and a want?
11. What avenues do managers have for seizing an opportunity?
12. Provide your own example of a customer experience. What makes it unique?
13. Explain the four realms of customer experience. Provide your own example of a company that delivers value in these four realms.
14. Provide your own example of a transformative experience. Why are transformative experiences like this rare?
15. What is the process for converting an opportunity into an innovation?

Endnotes

1. Basadur, M. 1999. *Simplex: A Flight to Creativity.* Hadley, MA: The Creative Education Foundation Press.
2. Marquis, D. 1972. Innovation. In E. Mansfield (ed.), *Research and Innovation in the Modern Corporation.* New York: Norton.

3. Foster, R. 1986. *Innovation: The Attacker's Advantage.* New York: Summit Books.
4. Monavvarian, A. 2002. Administrative reform and style of work behavior: Adaptors-innovators, *Public Organization Review: A Global Journal,* 2: 141–164.
5. Kirton, M. J. 1987.Adaptors and innovators: Cognitive style and personality. In Scott G. Isaksen (ed.), *Frontiers of Creativity Research.* Buffalo: Bearly Limited.
6. Colvin, G. 2008. *Talent Is Overrated: What Really Separates World-Class Performers from Everybody Else.* New York: Portfolio.
7. Ericsson, K. A. 2006. The influence of experience and deliberate practice on the development of superior expert performance. In K. A. Ericsson, N. Charness, P. J. Feltovich & R. R. Hoffman (eds.), *The Cambridge Handbook of Expertise and Expert Performance.* New York: Cambridge University Press.
8. Hayton, J. C. & Kelley, D. J. 2006. A competency-based framework for promoting corporate entrepreneurship, *Human Resource Management* 45 (3): 407–427.
9. Ericsson, K. A., Prietula, M. J. & Cokely, E. T. The making of an expert, *Harvard Business Review* 85 (7/8): 114–121.
10. Colvin, G. 2008. *Talent is Overrated: What Really Separates World-Class Performers from Everybody Else.* New York: Portfolio.
11. Gladwell, M. 2008. *Outliers: The Story of Success.* New York: Little, Brown, and Company.
12. Johansson, F. 2006. *The Medici Effect: What Elephants and Epidemics Can Teach Us About Innovation.* Boston, MA: Harvard Business School Press.
13. Sawyer, K. 2007. *Group Genius: The Creative Power of Collaboration.* New York: Basic Books.
14. Corporate Information: The Google Culture, http://www.google.com/corporate/culture.html. Accessed July 30, 2009.
15. Hills, G. E. & Shrader, R. C. 1998. Successful entrepreneurs' insights into opportunity recognition. In P. D. Reynolds et al. (eds.), *Frontiers of Entrepreneurship Research* (pp. 30–43). Babson Park, MA: Babson College Press.
16. DeTienne, D. R. & Chandler, G. N. 2004.Opportunity identification and its role in the entrepreneurial classroom: A pedagogical approach and empirical test, *Academy of Management Learning & Education* 3 (3): 242–257.
17. Stefik, M. & Stefik, B. 2004. *Breakthrough: Stories and Strategies of Radical Innovation.* Cambridge, MA: MIT Press.
18. Stokes, D. 1997. *Pasteur's Quadrant: Basic Science and Technological Innovation,* Washington, D.C.: Brookings Institution Press.
19. Chesbrough, H. 2003. *Open Innovation: The New Imperative for Creating and Profiting from Technology.* Boston, MA: Harvard Business School Press.
20. Sawyer, K. 2007. *Group Genius: The Creative Power of Collaboration.* New York: Basic Books.
21. Laffley, A.G. & Charan, R. 2008. *The Game-Changer: How You Can Drive Revenue and Profit Growth with Innovation.* New York: Crown Business.
22. Chesbrough, H. 2003. *Open Innovation: The New Imperative for Creating and Profiting from Technology.* Boston, MA: Harvard Business School Press.
23. Maslow, A. 1943. A theory of human motivation, *Psychological Review* 50: 370–396.
24. Berger, A. A. 2005. *Shop 'til You Drop: Consumer Behavior and American Culture.* Lanham, MD: Rowman & Littlefield.
25. Miller, G. 2009. *Spent: Sex, Evolution, and Consumer Behavior.* New York: Viking.
26. Pooler, J.. 2003. *Why We Shop: Emotional Rewards and Retail Strategies.* Westport, CT: Praeger.

27. O'Shaughnessy, J. 1987. *Why People Buy.* New York: Oxford University Press.
28. Hayes, J. 1980. *The Complete Problem Solver.* Philadelphia, PA: The Franklin Institute Press.
29. Basadur, M. 1999. *Simplex: A Flight to Creativity.* Buffalo, NY: The Creative Education Foundation Press.
30. Sawyer, K. 2007. *Group Genius: The Creative Power of Collaboration.* New York: Basic Books.
31. Joseph Pine II, B. & Gilmore, J. H. 1999. *The Experience Economy: Work Is Theatre & Every Business a Stage.* Boston, MA: Harvard Business School Press.
32. McClure, W. R. & Bartuska, T. J. 2007. *The Built Environment: A Collaborative Inquire into Design and Planning.* Hoboken, NJ: John Wiley & Sons.
33. Christensen, C.. 2003. *The Innovator's Dilemma: The Revolutionary Book that Will Change the Way You Do Business.* New York: Harper.
34. Rosenbush, S. 2006. "Facebook's on the Block," *BusinessWeek Online,* Retrieved March 28, 2006, http://www.businessweek.com/technology/content/mar2006/tc2006o327_215876.hum. Accessed on October 3, 2006.
35. Hansell, S. 2006. "Yahoo Woos a Social Networking Site," *New York Times Online,* Retrieved September 22, 2006, http://www.nytimes.com/2006/09/22/technology/22facebook.html?ex=1316577600eten=09f3d5e70aa0r977etei=5008eparte nr=rssnyetemic=rss. Accessed on October 3, 2006.
36. Joseph Pine II, B. & Gilmore, J. H. 1999. *The Experience Economy: Work Is Theatre & Every Business a Stage.* Boston, MA: Harvard Business School Press.
37. Barnes, B. 2009. "Struggles at the Box Office Weigh on Disney's Profit," *New York Times Online,* Retrieved May 5, 2009, http://www.nytimes.com/2009/05/06/business/media/06disney.html?_r=1&ref=media. Accessed on July 21, 2009.
38. Disney by the Numbers. http://www.disneybythenumbers.com/wdw/wdw.html. Accessed on July 21, 2009.
39. Kelley, T. & Littman, J. 2001. *The Art of Innovation: Lessons in Creativity from IDEO, America's Leading Design Firm.* New York: Currency Books.
40. Nightline: Deep Dive. http://www.youtube.com/watch?v=z6z-3ejvvGE. Accessed on January 22, 2011.
41. Gruenwald, G. 1997. *How to Create Profitable New Products—from Mission to Market.* Chicago, IL: NTC Business Books.
42. Gorman, T. 2007. *Innovation.* Avon, MA: Adams Business.
43. Nochur, K. 2009. *Executing Innovation.* Boston, MA: Harvard Business Publishing.

PART

3

THE DESIGN FUNCTION IN INNOVATION
(I-DESIGN)

THE DESIGN-THINKING PROCESS

INTRODUCTION

Herbert A. Simon, professor and 1978 Nobel Laureate in Economics, once said, *"Engineers are not the only professional designers. Everyone designs who devises courses of action aimed at changing existing situations into preferred ones."*[1]

The Great Pyramids of Egypt and the Hoover Dam, while separated by thousands of years, are both great achievements in design. We marvel at their appearance and imagine the labor that went into building them. But the immense structures would not be there at all, if someone had not first devised a plan to build them. The plans were not perfect, and no doubt many mistakes were made in the construction of both. Slaves were likely crushed by the huge blocks of limestone that canvassed across the sloped faces of the pyramids and, in building the Hoover Dam, the U.S. Department of the Interior cites 96 "industrial fatalities," such as from drowning, blasting, fall rocks, slides, falls from the canyon walls, truck accidents, and equipment issues.[2] But through perseverance and adjustment, each great vision was achieved. Although most things around us are not on par with these man-made marvels, everything around us is an outcome of a design of some sort.

A good business idea is important in getting the innovation process going, but it is design that brings it into reality. Design is the process that converts ideas into form, whether that is a plan of action or a physical thing. Some companies are much better at design than others, and practice it at a higher level. The differences are evident in comparing products and services of companies from the same industry. In the computer industry, for example, Apple is widely recognized as the most innovative company among its peers, but it is also lauded for its design as well. Apple products are sleek, powerful, and fun to use, and, as a result, the company has became one of the hottest buys in the stock market, going from $159 per share in 2009 to $279 per share in 2010. There may be other reasons for these differences in performance, but design is no doubt a major driver of Apple's success. After all, computers at their essence are data and information machines. Most teenagers in the 1970s did not put the Altair 8080 at the top of their Christmas lists, but much has changed over the last 30 years. iPhones, iMacs, iPods, and iPads are now icons of hipness. Apple, through its design process, has made plastic boxes of silicon cool.

If companies like Apple have garnered media attention and consumer dollars for their design prowess, why aren't more companies following suit? After all, design is one of the most popular topics covered in the business press. The average business traveler can't enter a kiosk at the airport without seeing "design" plastered on magazines and books. One key reason managers may not be incorporating design more into their practices is that they do not understand the *concept*.

DESIGN

In the previous chapters, we examined the concepts of creativity and innovation. We have also discussed entrepreneurial activity within an organization. In this chapter, we turn to the role design can *play* in making us more innovative. Creativity, design, innovation, and entrepreneurship are related terms and influence each other. Creativity is a set of thinking skills that help bring novel, acceptable ideas into the world. Using divergent and convergent thinking we can be more creative in everything we do. Design is the process of shaping an idea into an *artifact*, which is something we can observe and manipulate. Keep in mind that this artifact could be a product, a service, a process, or a business model. When we design, we bring an idea into the world for others to comprehend. We don't have to ask the designer what the idea means. The artifact speaks for itself. A well-designed artifact is embraced by the target audience, whereas bad design leaves the user confused and/or uninterested in the artifact. Innovation is the extended process of providing the artifact to a larger audience. The more impact a product or service has on a society, the more innovative it is deemed to be. However, sustaining and growing the delivery of the innovation requires an entrepreneur to champion the product or service. Without entrepreneurial behavior, the idea will die on the vine.

Figure 5.1 demonstrates how the concepts are related. Understanding the differences and interrelationships of these concepts will make you a more successful manager in today's world where companies must be diligent in pursing and capitalizing on the opportunities available to them. A designer—which can be anyone who comes up with a new artifact—has an idea and then tweaks and transforms it into a desirable or needed form. He or she becomes an innovator when they convert the design into a marketable product for production. That same person becomes an entrepreneur when they overcome the obstacles, garner the resources to manufacture the product, and champion the final implementation of the innovation to the

FIGURE 5-1 Relationship Between Design, Innovation & Entrepreneurship

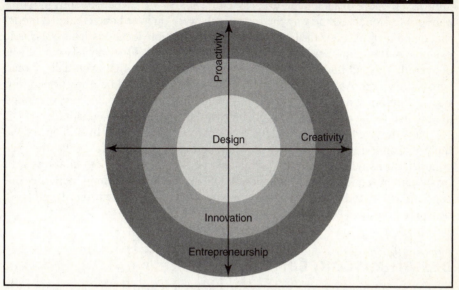

target audience. Designing a product or service that is worthwhile will drive innovation, and the more innovation a company generates, the more entrepreneurial it can be. Supporting all this activity is creativity and proactiveness. The project is shepherded by a *proactive* champion who maintains the discipline to shape the idea into a viable commercial product or service. If a manager applies creativity and remains proactive, then all three elements will be amplified. Thus, being more creative and proactive leads to better design, better design leads to more innovation, and more innovation leads to increased entrepreneurial activity.

Understanding the interrelationship of these concepts explains why Peter Drucker used McDonald's as a prime example for getting across his points in his classic book *Innovation and Entrepreneurship*. As Drucker observed:

> McDonald's first designed the end product; then it redesigned the entire process of making it; then it redesigned or in many cases invented the tools so that every piece of meat, every slice of onion, every bun, every piece of fried potato would be identical, turned out in a precisely timed and fully automated process. Finally, McDonald's studied what 'value' meant to the customer, defined it as quality and predictability of product, speed of service, absolute cleanliness, and friendliness, then set standards for all of these, trained for them, and geared compensation to them (p. 17).

The above observation captures how McDonald's became so successful utilizing design, innovation, and entrepreneurship. The hamburger was designed to be affordable and tasty to a wide market. McDonald's were innovative in how they made the hamburgers, transforming the cooking operations from a grease cook approach to more of a manufacturing assembly line in the kitchen. Finally, the company professionalized the way the restaurants were operated and created a model that could be replicated easily and profitably in multiple locations. This is a classic example of designing a system around the hamburger and the way in which it was delivered. This led the way to designing a scalable system that eventually spread across the world. As Drucker notes, if hamburger stands can be transformed into business empires, nearly anything can if enough creativity and business discipline are applied to the practices of design, innovation, and entrepreneurship.

Now that we have examined the concept of design, we now turn to one of the main reasons why design is often not pursued in the managerial ranks: the misconceptions associated with it. Much like we have seen in previous chapters with myths and misconceptions in innovation and creativity, examining these misconceptions associated with design will help you overcome major hurdles in applying design in your own company.

DESIGN MISCONCEPTIONS

There are also many misconceptions surrounding design that keep people from pursuing design in their jobs. Some of the most notable design misconceptions and an explanation to dispel each one follows.

ONLY ARTISTS, ENGINEERS, AND ARCHITECTS USE DESIGN

Artists, engineers, and architects are most commonly associated with design because they build things that we can see. Artists work with different mediums to bring what is inside their minds onto the canvass. Some artists provide the same process through graphic design to encapsulate the branding of a business through product packaging and advertisements. Engineers work with a variety of product and operational problems to design solutions to bring a company's offerings to the marketplace. Architects design buildings to satisfy client requests and make philosophical and aesthetic statements to the greater society. While these professions do incorporate design, they need not be the only ones to do so. Managers can also bring a design mind-set to their work by utilizing the same principles the aforementioned professionals do to their realms. Doing so, however, requires a different approach to work and business opportunities than most managers are acquainted with. Design requires a flexible approach to work, in which product specifications may evolve over time. The manager must become a facilitator during the design process, rather than just a boss.

RESEARCH AND DEVELOPMENT DEPARTMENTS ARE WHERE COMPANIES SHOULD DO DESIGN

It is true that a lot of design takes place in the *research and development* (R&D) departments of companies, but it is time for more managers to engage in the design process. Markets are changing rapidly, and keeping design solely in the R&D departments will limit the opportunities. While R&D departments will always play an important role in large corporations, other employees must be allowed to participate in the innovation process with scientists and engineers. Everyone in a company has unique insights that could lead to new products and services if they are allowed to develop an idea. The twenty-first-century business leaders can unleash a wealth of new product ideas by teaching other employees the processes that go on in their laboratories. Design, like entrepreneurship and creativity, is the practice of a universal set of principles that can be applied in any domain. As has happened with corporate entrepreneurship and creativity, design is quickly becoming the next practice that will become democratized by forward-thinking companies.

DESIGN IS TOO COMPLEX TO BE USED BY THE AVERAGE MANAGER IN THE COMPANY

This misconception is related to the first one. Since technical professionals use design in their daily jobs, design is seen as the province of craftsmen and artisans. Indeed, if a manager were to attempt to design a building or engineering a product, they would find it an arduous task. But there are equally challenging aspects of their jobs that engineers and architects would find perplexing as well. Once managers understand design they can work more easily with the technical professionals in their company. The technical professionals will benefit by having more original material to work with as well. When business professionals incorporate design principles into their work, they will gain more technical literacy. On the flip side, when technical professionals are working more closely with managers, they will gain more financial and marketing literacy. Design can bring the two often opposing worlds of technology and business together, so that a company can perform at a higher level.

DESIGN WOULD CUT INTO A MANAGER'S DAILY SCHEDULE AND ONLY LEAD TO FRUSTRATION

Managers often spend their days thinking about hitting financial numbers and achieving organizational goals. Coupled with the demands that come with leading employees in their business units, managers may feel they don't have time to implement design into their jobs. While this is an understandable concern, these managers would be wrong. Utilizing design principles would actually help a manager to design their department's work processes and policies to be more effective and efficient. Too many managers give their employees orders without taking the time to consider the true impact of their decisions. Design principles can help a manager build a better functioning team. Additionally, managers that get involved in designing new products and services are more likely to find enjoyment in their work. In *Drive*, Daniel Pink explains how financial incentives work well with manual labor jobs, but in more cognitively focused jobs, people work harder when they feel they are doing more meaningful and purposeful work. Thinking of ways to create products and services that benefit customers would actually lead to a manager becoming more engaged in their work. Top-performing organizations like Google encourage all their employees to design products to satisfy their customers' needs and wants.[3]

DESIGN WILL SLOW DOWN THE INNOVATION PROCESS

In today's competitive world, time may be our most valuable resource. Executives are expected to quickly get results, or else risk losing their jobs. Under these conditions, managers may not feel that they have the luxury to be involved in design. They may say to themselves, "Better to leave it to the experts in the R&D department. We've got work to do." This sentiment is understandable, but it may actually lead to setbacks in the innovation process. Good design speeds up the innovation process. Customers, experts, technicians, and other managers should be brought into product discussions. By incorporating a diverse group of relevant stakeholders early in the innovation process, setbacks can be averted or minimized. Design requires that managers face the reality of what really matters to their customers and what their company can realistically produce. Thus, design is the mixing of what currently exists with a possible future to be built.

DESIGN IS TOO FUZZY AND WILL TAKE THE MANAGER AWAY FROM THE REALITIES OF BUSINESS

Many managers may think that design is a practice for eccentric artists or engineers, but design properly understood is grounded in the realities of business. While early stages of design can be fuzzy, as a manager seeks out needed information, takes *feedback*, and fixes concerns with the idea, a product or service that is in tune with the company's market will occur. The best managers will develop the ability to manage and lead their organizations to hit current goals while looking for new opportunities. This mind-set will not happen overnight, but the more managers integrate design into their work the better they will be able to do this. Managers must develop an awareness of this need, be patient to hone it, and have the discipline to transform their daily practices and workplace.

DESIGN IS JUST ANOTHER BUSINESS FAD

Many business practices seem to be the "flavor of the month" in management theory. In the 1980s, total quality management and continuous improvement were the rage. The 1990s brought the re-engineering movement and e-commerce. In the twenty-first century, design may be the most popular new trend in business. While critics may cynically call these movements "fads," experienced managers know that these trends are now established in many successful companies. It is almost second nature for managers to consider quality and cost efficiency delivering products and services. The re-engineering movement is still evident today because most Fortune 500 companies seek ways to become more lean and productive.

With companies operating with better efficiencies, executives now realize they must become entrepreneurial to increase their revenues. As a result, they are turning to innovation to create new products and services. Understanding design can make a company more innovative. It is likely that in 10 years, the world's leading companies will have entrepreneurial designers spread throughout their ranks.

DESIGN IS THE SAME THING AS INNOVATION

Design and *innovation* are used together in conversations quite often. While the terms are related, there are some differences. *Innovation* covers the entire process of bringing an idea to market, whereas *design* encompasses the iterative component of shaping the idea into a finished product or service. The critical reason for covering design is that too many companies rush an idea into the marketplace before it has had the opportunity to evolve into a better product or service. In meeting the call of innovation, some companies actually hurt their business by bringing worse products to the market than they already have. Good design slows a company down in the short run but speeds up the innovation process in the long run. Business history is riddled with the New Cokes and Ford Edsels that while different were not embraced by the market because of poor design. Understanding these subtle differences will help the manager to become more effective in the innovation process.

DESIGN IS TOO QUIRKY FOR A BUSINESS ENVIRONMENT

Design often gets a bad rap in business. This may be because professions traditionally related to design are often comprised of flamboyant characters. At the Walt Disney Company, for example, there is a big difference in the cultures found among the Imagineers and the business executives. The Imagineers may wear wild clothes and jewelry while the executives would be able to fit in well at other Fortune 500 companies, but when it comes to developing a new ride or hotel for one of their parks the executives appreciate the big ideas of the Imagineers. While there is some creative tension, the co-development that takes place on projects bridging the aesthetic with the financial targets gives Disney a huge advantage over its competition. As a result, a Disney theme park rarely misses its mark, and their customers come back repeatedly to see what the company dreams up next. While Disney is in an industry focused on delivering high-quality experiences, every company has the opportunity to include design in the way they do business.

These misconceptions have been presented to provide a background for today's current thinking on design. By sidestepping the folklore, we can build a foundation for better understanding what *design thinking* is and how the design process works.

DESIGN THINKING

Now that we have examined what design is and what it isn't, we can look at how to think like a designer. Just as executives have incorporated entrepreneurial principles into the practices and strategies of firms, design is now a hot topic in the business world. The demand is becoming so great that universities are now building programs that take a general approach to design rather than concentrating it in just technical schools like architecture and engineering. Mirroring the general design approach of companies like IDEO that tackle problems in industries ranging from medicine to consumer products, Stanford University has founded the Institute of Design (also known as the D-School) and the Rotman School of Management at the University of Toronto has built a curriculum based on "harnessing the power of design thinking."[4] The goal of such programs is to train future business leaders to incorporate design thinking into their general practices. Companies, such as Proctor and Gamble and Microsoft, are also embracing this approach, but any company can utilize design principle through their ranks if they employ the following elements of design thinking offered by design firm IDEO CEO Tim Brown[5].

ELEMENTS OF DESIGN THINKING

ACCEPT THAT CONSTRAINTS ARE PART OF DESIGN

Good designers are always faced with choices in how they develop a new product or service. They would like to be able to make a product fast, good, and cheap, but they are almost forced between picking two of these qualities. If a product is made fast and good, it may require a lot of resources to pull off the achievement in such a short time. If a product is made good and cheap, it may take a while to refine the production process because organizational resources haven't been supplied in great amounts. And if it is made fast and cheap, the quality may suffer. This is the reality of design, but the best designers see it as an invigorating challenge to handle rather than shrink from. The best designers take a can-do attitude about "wicked" problems and use *constraints* as a source of *inspiration*.[6] As Brown explains, "The mark of a designer is a willing embrace of constraints. Without constraints design cannot happen, and the best design—a precision medical device or emergency shelter for disaster victims—is often carried out within quite severe constraints. The willing and even enthusiastic acceptance of competing constraints is the foundation of design thinking."

SEEK THE PEACEFUL COEXISTENCE OF DESIRABILITY, FEASIBILITY, AND VIABILITY

A designer must always consider another collection of restraints to be resolved in great design. The best-designed products are desired by their customers, can be reasonably built, and make business sense for the company. This is attained by designing the product with the user in mind. The designer observes, researches, and interacts with the customer to attain a good idea of what the customer likes and responds positively to. Aesthetics are taken into consideration that the customer will find pleasing and interesting for that particular group. Thus, aesthetics may vary greatly from one region or segment of the market to another. The products should be reliable and easy to use for the intended customer. The products must also be feasible for the company to manufacture. If the product is too complicated or intricate to be produced in great numbers, the company will have to strongly consider whether it should be produced. Thus, a major aspect of commercializing a product is deciding what materials, components, and fabrication techniques make the most sense for manufacturing. And finally the *business viability* of the product must be considered. The product might be interesting and well received but if it doesn't make business sense to produce it, it may need to be modified or dropped. Brown points out that "a competent designer will resolve each of these three constraints, but a *design thinker* will bring them into a harmonious balance."

From our own experience, we offer the following elements of design thinking in addition to the aforementioned points. We have found them useful in working with clients and students on new product ideas.

INSPIRATION

In Chapter 4, we learned how to find ideas to work on, which is the first critical step of design. All designers are inspired by a problem they want to solve or an opportunity that they feel motivated to seize. Without working on meaningful projects, people will not be willing to put in the long hours of work required to shape an idea into an innovative product.

PROACTIVITY

Inspiration is an important starting point for working on a project, but a more important element of design thinking is a proactive disposition. Most people get excited by the possibility of where an idea may go, but don't have the grit to persevere through the difficult paths that are likely to arise. One source of this reticence is that people struggle with the thought of facing the unknown. Thus, being proactive means embracing risk. The person might put a lot of time into something that doesn't pan out, and the person will be proven wrong. Some people may not know where to start or who to turn to. There will be a lot to learn and do to make it happen. They doubt their abilities to make it happen and others think that innovators who achieve great *breakthroughs* are made of something different. Action brings understanding. These are all misconceptions that can be overcome by being proactive. Anyone who has made a big discovery has had to make the decision, and move forward. If you are inspired by an idea and think realization of it will bring significant rewards to your company, and yourself, then it's time to take a leap of faith and pursue it. Designers don't live in the past; they create the future.

HUMILITY

A humble approach to designing products or services is one of the most important thinking characteristics you can have. This may seem contradictory to some high achievers, but *humility* properly understood leads to better results. As Charles Koch, CEO of Koch Industries, told one of the authors recently, "Humility doesn't mean looking down at your shoes and saying, 'Aw Shucks.' It means knowing what you don't know and being willing to admit that to yourself and others. From that state of mind, you can get the answers you need to get things done." When you approach others for knowledge that would be useful to you and ask for their thoughts on your project, you accelerate the design process. Instead of wandering through a scattered collection of resources haphazardly, approach content experts with specific questions. Experts are busy people, and they will appreciate your consideration of their time. Showing up with a clear agenda will assist with the process. If you are well prepared for the meeting, you will all find it an enjoyable experience. Since this type of interaction is rare in most meetings, you may sense the expert quickly developing a positive opinion of you.

At the end of any meeting, ask the person if they know of any good resources, such as books, videos, and websites. And never forget the most important phrase you can utter at the end of a session with an expert: "Thank you for your time. Is there anyone else you know that may be helpful to me in this process?"

Author Stephen Covey states that this type of behavior is one of the seven habits of highly effective people and defines what makes someone an interdependent person. As Covey explains, "If I am intellectually interdependent, I realize that I need the best thinking of other people to join with my own. As an interdependent person, I have the opportunity to share myself deeply and meaningfully, with others, and I have access to the vast resources and potential of other human beings."[7]

FLEXIBILITY

One of the biggest pitfalls of people working on an idea is that they hold too tightly to their original insight. A good designer maintains an open mind about the possibilities of what an idea can become by seeking and using the input of others. The idea that inspires you is just your beginning point to get the design process started. Too many people think the idea is everything, but few products or services turn out the way they were originally imagined. And those that do are usually failures in the market place. As a caveat, if you attain a successful product launch, remember to maintain a *flexible mind*. Sometimes success can cause a person to think they have all the answers. Being arrogant and shutting out ideas from others is a recipe for failure. If you continue to hone the way of thinking that brought the success, you can have an even greater impact in the future.

FOCUS

This element is one of the hardest to master. You need to keep the focus on the idea and not yourself. Always remember, you and the idea are separate. Criticism about the idea is not criticism about you. As you receive feedback on your idea you want them to know you will not be offended by comments they have about your idea. Good designers want honest feedback about their ideas. If you approach design with this mind-set, you will amass information and opinions that will help you build a better product or service, and you can benefit in the long run. Thus you endure a few bruises. This approach can be difficult because we often perceive feedback as criticism of us: after all we came up with the original idea, so isn't an indictment of the concept a backhanded insult to us? No! That is a very limiting perspective to have; one person does not have all the answers and successful people know that. Appreciate that they care enough to give feedback which is one of the most beneficial favors someone can do for you. Increasingly research supports this position. More wisdom occurs when projects are collaborative. In the book, *Smart Swarm,* it explains how groups are correct more often than individuals. It uses the game show *Who Wants to be a Millionaire* as evidence of this phenomenon. Contestants have three "lifelines" they can use on questions they are unsure of. They can poll the audience, phone a friend, and choose 50/50 (the option of taking two of the answers away). When contestants called a smart friend as their lifeline, they were right 63 percent of the time, but when they polled the studio audience for help they were right 91 percent of the time. Peter Miller points out that there may not be any particular person in the audience as intelligent as the friend on the other end of the phone, but as a group the audience knows more than the smart friend.[8] Keep the same perspective in your projects. If you do, you will find yourself far more successful in your final results. It is still your decision how you choose to use the information. Your experts might not be right, but if you start to see a pattern of consistent answers and insights, you would be wise to seriously consider those positions and work them into your project.

DESIGN GUIDELINES

Once we know how successful designers think, we can now look at how they act. Tilman Lindberg, Christine Noweski, and Christoph Meinel of the Hasso Plattner Institute of the University Potsdam, provide design-thinking education specifically to nondesigners. The curriculum adheres to the following guidelines. Each guideline includes insights from our own experience training others in design thinking.[9]

PARAPHRASE A DESIGN CHALLENGE INTO A FORM WORTH WORKING ON

As discussed in the previous section, the original idea is a starting point. Once you've received feedback from others, you may find that major revisions are required. When your idea receives general support from others, you may proceed in taking more serious design steps. In a study of more than 700 product-development teams, Gary S. Lynn and Richard R. Reilly found that the most successful product launches came from a clear vision of what the team wanted to accomplish. This vision was clarified through the use of "project pillars" that focused the design efforts. For example, the project pillars for the Palm Pilot were: (1) fits in pocket, (2) synchronizes seamlessly with PC, (3) fast and easy to use, and (4) costs no more than $299. Within those constraints, the Palm Computing Company was able to build the world's first successful personal digital assistant. Meeting those constraints required a lot of trial and error, but it provided targets to focus the team's creative energies.[10] Once you have nailed the general design concept, this approach leads to more innovative outcomes than wandering aimlessly from one idea to another. This is a tricky guideline to master because you have to balance direction with an open mind. Lindberg, Noweski, and Meinel point out that it may require a lot of formulating and reformulating of the vision and criteria before you move forward on the project. But it's important to know what your design goals are.[11]

UTILIZE RESTRICTION-FREE THINKING TO AVOID PREMATURE JUDGMENTS

All actions begin with the thoughts we entertain. One of the key guidelines for behaving like a designer is to think like one, too. Our awareness of the need to think this way will better our odds of designing truly innovative products and services. In Chapter 3, we discussed divergent thinking. This thinking skill is critically important during design. We have to be open to where an idea can go. Biz Stone, the cofounder of Twitter, says that "Everyone should study design because you learn that every problem has many good possible solutions."[12]

GATHER INFORMATION FROM A VARIETY OF SOURCES AND ARRANGE THE KNOWLEDGE INTO AN ASSOCIATIVE NETWORK

As you research and seek feedback on your idea, document everything you learn. The designer's best friend is their notebook. Capture everything you come across that pertains to your topic. As you pursue your idea, you may at times be overwhelmed by the mass of information you gather. Keeping information and thoughts in notebooks and folders can alleviate that problem. After all, your memory is fallible. If you don't maintain notebooks, you are likely to recall the information incorrectly or forget it altogether. Also, you can periodically reexamine your notebooks to pull together ideas and insights. Notebooks are a wonderful way to remind us of important points on our projects that can be forgotten as we move forward. It lessens the stress that comes with gathering information on big projects. We don't have to worry about forgetting anything because it's in our notebooks. This practice can move projects along much faster because we don't risk retreading familiar ground because of forgetfulness or sloppiness.

GENERATE AND REFINE IDEAS UNTIL THEY ADAPT TO THE SECTION OF THE WORLD FOR WHICH THEY ARE INTENDED

We may have what we think are great ideas, but our target audience may disagree. Design is sometimes different than straight problem solving because we are bringing into the world something that may not have existed before. Therefore, before we make a massive commitment of resources to a project, it is beneficial to get signals from our target audience that we are moving in the right direction. However, if we include the customer in the design process, we receive immediate feedback that can be used for quick design fixes. An innovation will always be a bit of a gamble, but we lessen the risk when we include a wide variety of perspectives in the design of the product. This doesn't mean though that you have to deliver what the customer expects or asks for. Use their feedback as on source of information along with experts' ideas, too. In the *Innovator's Dilemma,* Clayton Christensen explains that simply meeting expectations can lead to stale product development. To design a radical innovation, it is better to consider customers' deepest values and interests rather than past purchasing behavior. The key to good design is interaction with a range of stakeholders at each stage of development.[13]

IDEAS SHOULD BE TRANSLATED INTO DIFFERENT PROTOTYPES (E.G., VISUALIZATION, MOCK-UPS, MODELS)

This is perhaps the heart of the design process because it is so effective in advancing an idea into a better form. When we have an insight, it's only in our head, so we try to communicate that idea verbally; others will understand the insight. Verbal communication, however, is often misunderstood. A better way to communicate your idea is to capture in a visual format. This can be done through such ways as sketches, mechanical drawings, or 3-D computer programs. After all, as the old saying goes, a picture is worth a thousand words. However, if a picture is worth a thousand words, an actual physical representation is worth a million words. If you want to get great feedback on your idea, build a *prototype*. Nothing gets your idea across better than something people can view from different angles and provide questions and feedback. One of the reasons managers struggle with this guideline is that they fear a lot of craftsmanship and expertise is required to build a prototype, but this is not necessarily true. Prototypes can be inexpensive and basic. The key point is to build something you can receive feedback on and return to rebuild as soon as possible. Moreover, with available technologies today, it's getting easier to make prototypes. Chapter 6 will provide more information on how this can be accomplished.

DESIGNERS SHOULD CONSCIOUSLY SELECT SOLUTION PATHS

Once you move a project along, you are likely to face design issues. This is the point where success or failure is often determined. Some people may give up because the problems seem too overwhelming to solve. Shutting down the project may be the right thing to do. Throwing good money after sunk costs is not rational but often done because of personal commitment to the project. If you do terminate the project, keep all your notes. A change in conditions or your knowledge may warrant revisiting the idea again in the future. Keep a project file for future reference. On the other hand, too many projects are ended prematurely because the designer wasn't persistent enough to work through the problems. The key for working through these tough patches is to recognize each problem as a *design challenge* of its own. Utilizing the same principles on a smaller scale as you applied to the larger design challenge can help you overcome the hurdles. Additionally, if you can overcome these challenges, it will give you a competitive advantage over other companies, because you will have gained particular knowledge and a distinct product for the market.

SEARCH FOR FEEDBACK AND INVOLVEMENT FROM PEOPLE WITH DIVERSE BACKGROUNDS AND TALENTS

The main design challenge is finding a compelling idea for building a product or service to offer customers. If an idea is original and interesting, it will attract the attention of others. Search for feedback from a diverse group of potential customers, suppliers, fellow managers, employees, and content experts. You may get a lot of suggestions, but only a few might be really useful (that's okay; design is a journey). You never know when someone will give you an unexpected insight that would have been overlooked had you not searched out a lot of the opinions of others. When an idea starts to consistently generate excitement that you have discussed with others, you'll know you're on the right path.

ITERATIONS: THE SECRET SAUCE

The previous section examined the design and *commercialization* processes. It was mentioned that developing a concept doesn't have to be a costly endeavor, and, as such, a company would benefit from having its ranks of employees explore and design new business ideas. But this is a new practice for most people who are used to implementing orders and maintaining the way a company operates. So how does a manager work with an idea to bring it into reality? And more importantly, how do they learn to design? The key practice that brings forth a great design is the practice of *iteration*. The iterative process is composed of three steps that occur over and over until a design is considered worthy for implementation into a company's operations. In the first step, we work with an idea and tinker with it until we think we have come upon something that is worth showing to others. We call this step *"play"* because it requires the designer to be playful and work with many possible combinations until something feels right. When the designers like what they have, they show it to others for their feedback. We call this step *"display."* After the designer displays their idea, he or she asks for feedback from the group for suggestions on how it could be made better. We call this step *"watch the replay,"* because the activity is reminiscent of sports announcers who break down a replay when there is a break in the game and offer their thoughts on how the player could have performed. If you are videotaping the feedback sessions, you can literally watch the replay. Take the feedback and go back to the drawing board to address it. After playing with the new information, redesign your idea and display the idea to the group again. You may also want to display your reformulated idea to another group that might have a different perspective. Continue this process until it appears that you are receiving consistent interest and approval from others. When support is given, display the idea to the appropriate executives so that you can receive sponsorship that will shepherd the idea further through the system. When you display the idea to an executive team, it should be polished enough to generate a "wow" effect. The iterative process will polish the idea to shape it into that form.

Once approved, you will need to continue to play, display, and watch the replay continuously until the idea reaches the market or is implemented into company practice. The iterative process is present in all aspects of design. In the following sections we examine the three stages of iteration in more detail.

STEP 1: PLAY

Play is a vital aspect of the design process. It can even be found throughout nature. A famous example of play is the dolphin that rides the waves in front of large sea vessels. The activity is actually quite dangerous for the dolphin, and offers little in regard to survival needs, but appears to be done for the sheer sake of thrill and enjoyment. Successful entrepreneurs often describe a similar rush of enthusiasm when considering market opportunities, and continue to pursue new ventures long after they have made their fortune. Legendary inventor and entrepreneur Thomas Edison, for example, was famous for pursuing numerous projects simultaneously, and reworking ideas until he found a solution that was both technologically and economically feasible. Although some entrepreneurs may have been lucky enough to have had success with an instant insight into the market, it is more likely that most learned from trial and error and playful contemplation in developing an idea. However, while play is a natural behavior, it is unfortunately often conditioned out of people over time, especially inside large organizations. Thus, it is imperative that managers regain a playfulness to working with business ideas. If not, companies will find it difficult to renew themselves and remain competitive in the marketplace. To gain a perspective of playfulness, you must understand that a business idea needs to go through an evolutionary development. Avoid being locked into protecting an idea. Instead, see it as something to be played with. You must set aside your ego and work with different variations of the idea in different contexts until you are sure you have a possible winning combination.

Like entrepreneurs who dream big, you should also set high aspirations for your ideas. Keith Sawyer (2008) has found that more creative outputs occur when people set expectations that their ideas must be truly unique and valuable. If your idea does not pass that test, then you should continue playing with it until you are excited about it. In business, unique means something new to a market or something that is better than rival products or services. Valuable means that value is attained when the customer feels the derived benefits from the product or service exceed the costs of purchasing it. If the value of your idea is low, then you will need to search for ways to provide more benefits. More features, ease of adoption, lower switching costs, better customer service, ease of use, and lower costs to the consumer are common methods for increasing value.[14]

Once the product is determined to be unique and valuable, the designer should consider whether your company is capable of bringing the product to market, or whether partnering with another company or acquiring a business that has the ability to make it should be considered. It is possible the technical requirements of bringing the idea to market exceed your company's capability.

Another key question you must consider is whether you have enough legitimacy in the market among the necessary stakeholders—such as customers, suppliers, investors, and the media—to make the product successful. You may need to look for other markets where the product will be accepted, or you may need to adjust the idea to better fit your technical capabilities. Scaling back the idea may be required. With time, though, you may be able to scale up the idea as you gain market traction and develop new skills.

Many companies make the mistake of going to market with an underdeveloped idea. Thus, the play stage is when more systematic approaches can be used for better defining the market problem to be solved. The name of this stage may contain a bit of irony. Good old-fashioned hard work and a total commitment of the manager's time and energy to the business idea is what this stage of the process requires. However, it is at this stage where you really begin to take the idea to the next level by playing with various combinations of inputs to find a true entrepreneurial insight into the market. It takes a tremendous amount of genuine passion and love of the business idea—passion and love that will sustain you through the most difficult times in developing truly innovative products and services. To find that right combination of business inputs requires a "stick to it" or "never give up" attitude, and the good health needed for the designer to work a demanding schedule. Things you can do to strengthen this resolve are, to be sure, that you have chosen a business idea that you know you'll absolutely love. Avoid choosing a business idea solely because you think you'll acquire a promotion or a raise because of its success. In the *Art of the Start*, Guy Kawasaki says he has never seen a business be successful when it was built with money in mind rather than the creation of something meaningful to the world. Research from behavioral economics supports Kawasaki's position.[15] Meaningfulness trumps financial rewards as a motivator of cerebral activity.

Once you have an idea, it is time to more fully develop it. After all, it probably is not ready yet for implementation and may require further development and *refinement*. This is where the hard work starts. There may be unforeseen contingencies with the idea, or it may just simply appear to be missing something to make it more feasible. Confusion and frustration may result, and you may be tempted to call a halt to the process. But always keep in mind: those that persist and solve the problems of the idea will receive the reward of insight. Experienced designers understand, seek, and relish the insight moment, also known as the "Eureka" or "aha!" moment. When you attain a sudden deep understanding of a situation, you are flooded with feelings of joy and relief that you finally found a solution that had been eluding you. Mayer (1995: 3) describes this moment as a time when "a problem solver goes suddenly from a state of not knowing how to solve a problem to a state of knowing how to solve it."[16] Or, as Dominowski and Dallob (1995) state, "to gain insight is to understand (something) more fully, to move from a state of relative confusion to one of comprehension."[17] Good designers find the challenge of solving design problems as stimulating and enjoyable. As you discover how to solve problems more efficiently you will become more confident and proficient in your design and you will also seek out more opportunities to design new products and services.

STEP 2: DISPLAY

Once the concept has been fully developed, it is now ready to be displayed. It is time to see if what was in your head matches up with the hard realities of the world. A short pitch is given to anyone who might be able to provide insight on your idea. Thus, a physical representation of the business idea, whether it be a visual representation, prototype, feasibility study, business plan, or I Plan, provides something for you to receive the feedback about the validity of your idea. You must be very open to feedback at this stage. This is where your conception of what will be accepted in the outside world is tested against realistic assumptions of that reality. You may be tempted to simply seek confirmation of your concepts in this stage, but that would be a mistake. You should instead be open to complaints and criticisms others may have with the product or service. When you address these issues, you will return later with a strong idea. If necessary, you may need to consider starting again with an empty slate if initial displays prove too negative. Humbling yourself to receive this feedback is difficult but it pays dividends later.

Ultimately, design is a gamble. The market may respond favorably to your product or it may not comprehend it. Thus, you will want to take the time to develop a clear concise description of what you are producing. This requires calculated risk taking. A creative contribution requires venturing into new territory but you must also be careful not to make any overly risky moves. In the end it is your call. Ideally, though, if you have taken an intellectually honest approach in getting feedback from others, you will have increased your odds of making the right design decisions. If you still have a good gut feeling about your idea after displaying it, it is time to reflect on how you will refine the concept and continue moving forward.

STEP 3: WATCH THE REPLAY

The third step of the iterative process is called "Watch the Replay" because it is time to reflect on others' feedback—much like a broadcast analyst or a coach breaks down a player's performance on tape. As every sports fan knows, the best athletes watch a lot of game film to improve their performance.

You have a lot of effort put in developing your idea but now it is time to search for more knowledge you will need to fix any problem areas. You may need to seek out new experts, who can point you in the right direction. Design is not only a creative process, it is more importantly a learning process. Having specific design issues provides a frame of reference for experts to apply their knowledge and teach you what you need to learn.

After receiving expert advice, you might (1) go back and rework major areas of the concept where the expert feels you fall short, (2) search for another market for the idea and adapt it by doing research on the new domain, (3) scrap the idea and pursue new ideas to explore, (4) scrap the idea and put your focus on projects that you have previously set aside, or (5) fix any minor issues that the experts think needs refinement and move forward into the next stage of development.

Always remember that if one of the first four options is taken, the hard work was not done in vain. New skills were gained and, additionally, major losses of investment may have been prevented. As you innovate, you will cycle through these steps—playing with an idea, displaying it to others for feedback, reflecting on the advice, and refining the concept for showing again—over and over again through the design process.

AN IMPORTANT CAVEAT TO THE BEGINNING DESIGNER

We have found successful designers become immersed in their projects, playful in working with their ideas, excited to show what they have to others, appreciative of the feedback they receive, carefully consider what the feedback means for their idea's success, and willing to go back and play with possible ways to work the feedback into a better product to show again later. On the other hand, we have found novice designers are often either overly confident about their original idea, or, on the other end of the spectrum, lack confidence and work with the first idea they get because they fear they may not get another. Another problem those new to the design process may have is not recognizing which ideas are feasible for the company to pursue. Clearly, companies should encourage creative thinking among its employees. However, for a design to be taken further in the organization it must fit with the company's strategy. Given limited time, money, and other resources, you must insure that the design meets the vision, mission, and goals of the company. From a strategic perspective, the design may be interesting, but not good for the present competitive situation. If this situation occurs, you may find yourself frustrated with the company and consider leaving to build your own start-up where you can implement the idea. The decision to leave should be seen as beneficial for both parties. You need to feel fulfilled, and the company doesn't need a disgruntled employee in its ranks. A company may decide to take a huge risk and change its business model and organizational mission to adopt a breakthrough design. This strategy is risky and rare but it does occasionally happen in business.

SUMMARY

Design is the process that converts ideas into form. A designer is anyone who comes up with a new artifact by tweaking and transforming an idea into a desirable or needed form. Designing a product that is worthwhile drives innovation, and the more innovation a company generates the more entrepreneurial it can be. The most common misconceptions of design were covered in this chapter. This chapter explained how designers think. Guidelines were also given to assist people with becoming designers in their own work environments. Steps were also given for converting ideas into innovations using the design process. The chapter concluded with an overview of the power of using an iterative approach to designing products and services and solving problems.

INNOVATION-IN-ACTION

From Designers To Design Thinkers

IDEO is one of the most famous names in the design world today. They are a design and consulting firm responsible for thousands of products, services, retail environments, and digital experiences you probably take for granted. IDEO has influenced products like the computer mouse, the modern toothbrush, and the first laptop. Companies like Anheuser-Busch, Gap, HBO, Kodak, Marriott, Pepsi, and PNC have sought the "design thinking" expertise of IDEO to redesign products that they can call their own.

The shift from being traditional designers to "design thinkers" proved to be the catalyst for IDEO's amazing success since its inception in 1991. "We moved from thinking of ourselves as designers to thinking of ourselves as design thinkers," explains cofounder David Kelley. Whether it's the redesign of a shopping cart, creating a new customer experience for a popular retailer, or creating the laptop from scratch, IDEO uses a long-proven method. According to Kelley, design thinking requires the utilization of a process very similar to the scientific method: a precise, refined system of steps that guide the designer. This method often contradicts common misconceptions about creativity and innovation. Rarely does a flash of insight spark the light bulb above the designer's head. Instead, design thinkers often start by asking a seemingly simple question—what is the problem? Only when that question is answered, can design thinkers begin to reshape a product, process, or customer experience, and realizing the nature of that problem is generally half the battle won.

The idea of rethinking the status quo isn't unique to IDEO's clients. IDEO itself is often forced to reshape its own processes. As often as fashion trends change, so also do consumers' wants and needs. Even today, after over 20 years of experience, IDEO has to analyze markets of consumers and shift its own approaches in order to truly benefit its clients. This self-evaluation and recalculation is often the most important lesson IDEO can teach its clients. While IDEO may be redesigning a child's toothbrush, they are teaching their customers to become design thinkers, and in the end, that is the true advantage.

Source: Based on: "A Designer" by L. Tischler, *Fast Company*, 10859241, February 2009. (132): 78–101.

Key Terms

Art of the Start	Concept
Artifact	Constraints
Breakthroughs	Design
Business viability	Design challenge
Commercialization	Design thinker

Design thinking   Inspiration
Display   Iteration
Drive   Play
Feedback   Proactive
Flexible mind   Prototype
Humility   Refinement
Innovation   Research and development
Innovation and Entrepreneurship   Watch the replay

Discussion Questions

1. What is the difference between design and creativity?
2. What is the difference between design and innovation?
3. What factors can enhance design, innovation, and entrepreneurship?
4. What is design?
5. How does a designer think?
6. How does a designer handle challenges and opportunities?
7. What was Peter Drucker's favorite entrepreneurial example? Why?
8. What are the various myths of design? Why are they myths?
9. What role do constraints play in design?
10. What is humility? Why is it good for design?
11. What guidelines do good designers follow?
12. How do designers convert opportunities into innovations?
13. Why is iteration such an important part of design?
14. Describe the three steps of iteration.
15. What caveat must the designer consider when working on an idea?

Endnotes

1. Simon, H. A. 1996. *The Sciences of the Artificial,* 3rd ed. Cambridge, MA: M.I.T. Press.
2. U.S. Department of the Interior, http://www.usbr.gov/lc/hooverdam/History/essays/fatal.html
3. Pink, D. H. 2005. *A Whole New Mind: Moving from the Information Age to the Conceptual Age.* New York: Riverhead Books.
4. http://www.rotman.utoronto.ca/index.html
5. Kelley, T. & Littman, J. 2005. *The Ten Faces of Innovation: IDEO's Strategies for Beating the Devil's Advocate & Driving Creativity Throughout Your Organization.* New York: Random House, Inc.
6. Ibid.
7. Covey, S. R. 1999. *The 7 Habits of Highly Effective People: Powerful Lessons in Personal Change.* New York: Simon & Schuster, Inc.
8. Miller, P. 2010. *The Smart Swarm: How Understanding Flocks, Schools, and Colonies Can Make Us Better At Communicating, Decision Making, and Getting Things Done.* New York: Penguin Publishing.

9. Lindberg, T., Noweski, C. & Meinel, C. 2010. Evolving discourses on design thinking: How design cognition inspires meta-disciplinary creative collaboration. *Technoetic Arts: A Journal of Speculative Research* 8 (1): 31–37.
10. Lynn, G. S. & Reilly, R. R. 2002. *Blockbusters: The Five Keys to Developing Great New Products.* New York: Harper Collins Publishers.
11. Ibid.
12. Biz Stone, www.twitter.com/biz
13. Christensen, C. M. 2003. *The Innovator's Dilemma: The Revolutionary Book That Will Change the Way You Do Business.* New York: Harper Collins Publishers, Inc.
14. Sawyer, R. K. 2007. *Group Genius: The Creative Power of Collaboration.* New York: BasicBooks.
15. Kawasak, G. 2004. *The Art of the Start: The Time-tested, Battle-hardened Guide for Anyone Starting Anything.* New York: Penguin Publishing.
16. Mayer, R. E. 1995. The search for insight: Grappling with Gestalt psychology's unanswered questions. In R.J. Sternbert & J. E. Davidson (eds.), *The Nature of Insight* (pp. 3–32). Cambridge, MA: A Bradford Book, The MIT Press.
17. Dominowski, R. L. & Dallob, P. 1995. The search for insight: Grappling with Gestalt psychology's unanswered questions. In R. J. Sternbert & J. E. Davidson (eds.), *The Nature of Insight* (pp. 33–62). Cambridge, MA: A Bradford Book, The MIT Press.

DESIGN-DRIVEN INNOVATION

INTRODUCTION

In the previous chapter, we discussed how to utilize design principles to shape an idea into a commercial concept. The next challenge is how to get the product actually manufactured. If you're like many other managers, you may not have an extensive technical background. That's okay. You don't have to attain technical expertise to get a product manufactured. All you have to do is gain some basic technology literacy so that you can communicate with the people in your company who have that expertise. In this chapter, we provide an overview of *engineering* and *prototyping* so that you can gain a bit of fluency in the language of technology. You will learn the basic principles engineers employ in their daily practices. You will also be given guidelines on how you can prototype your ideas. Although it would take a long time to become an expert in these areas, our goal is to help you become technology literate so that you can interact better with engineers and other technical experts. This knowledge will help you to get your ideas through the corporate system better.

Your main role as a corporate innovator is to be a facilitator. Your success will be determined by how well you shepherd good ideas—your own or the employees'—through your organization. This may seem like a daunting task if you've been trained to read financial statements and develop marketing campaigns; however, being able to take part in discussions with technology-savvy colleagues holds advantages for a corporate innovator. The manager who can speak geek, as well as talk money, will be able to acquire needed feedback and gain the support of technical colleagues. Engineers and production managers can become valuable partners in your innovation journey. They will help you shape your ideas into more feasible and exciting products and services.

If you've traveled to another country, you know that having a rudimentary knowledge of the local language helps get you around easier. When you enter the laboratory or machine shop, you may feel like you just landed in a foreign land, but you'll be able to navigate through the labs and the shop floors better by speaking the language of the locals. A more thorough understanding of what the technical people in your organization do will help you gain their support, involvement, and feedback as you design your product. We first examine engineers—the chieftains of the technology landscape—in order to gain an appreciation for how they contribute to innovation and design.

ENGINEERING

Woody Norris is an inventor who has made millions creating products like a non-lethal acoustic weapon that has been used to ward off pirates, a bone-induction headset, radar that can scan the human body, and a tapeless tape recorder—and yet he says, "Virtually nothing has been invented yet. We're just now starting to understand the laws of nature."[1] Popular science writer Matt Ridley, after interviewing the world's leading technologists and economists, also concluded that innovation is limitless. He encapsulates this view with the following observation:

> There is not even a theoretical possibility of exhausting the supply of ideas, discoveries, and inventions. This is the biggest cause of all for my optimism....If you were to combine any of the 100 chemical elements into different alloys and compounds in different proportions ranging from one to ten, you would have 330 billion possible chemical compounds and alloys to test, or enough to keep a team of researchers busy testing a thousand a day for a million years. Yet if innovation is limitless, why is everybody so pessimistic about the future?[2]

Better yet, why do so few people offer solutions? We believe a major reason most people are pessimistic and apathetic is that they don't possess entrepreneurial and innovative skills. Most people feel more comfortable with the status quo. They fear change, instead of embracing it. That is unfortunate, because a structural shift is taking place in the economy. Just as a manufacturing economy replaced agrarianism in the nineteenth century and was later replaced itself by an information society, the economy of the latter twentieth century is being supplanted by one based on creativity and openness. Richard Florida captures this economic transformation in his seminal book, *The Rise of the Creative Class*. He envisions a world where people with artistic and technical knowledge thrive as members of the Creative Class:

> If you are a scientist or engineer, an architect or designer, a writer, artist, or musician, or if you use your creativity as a key factor in your work in business, education, health care, law or some other profession, you are a member....Because creativity is the driving force of economic growth, in terms of influence the Creative Class has become the dominant class in society.[3]

If managers are going to succeed in this new economic reality, they must be able to work in technical and artistic domains that they may have ignored in the past. Understanding design can help in bringing about this *transformation*. As Roger Martin, dean of the Rotman School of Management, said, "Business people don't need to understand designers better. They need to be designers."[4] One way business people can become better designers is by becoming more proficient in technology. If managers embrace technology, they will find the economic shift providing more opportunities than ever before. At a round table discussion, investor Warren Buffett, Microsoft CEO Steve Ballmer, and General Electric CEO Jeff Immelt predicted a bright future based on more technological advancement and invention than during the Internet era. Ballmer stated, "I am very enthusiastic about what the future holds for our industry and what our industry will mean for growth in other industries." Buoyed by new technologies that tie together computers, phones, televisions, and data centers, new products will be spun out at an amazing rate. Immelt added that more manufacturing may take place in the country as well due to better production technologies and service centers. And Buffet resolutely stated, "This country works. The best is yet to come."[5] Unfortunately, many managers do not have the same view. New opportunities bring new challenges. Managers will have to stretch themselves to learn design and technology. They will have to gain a more artistic sensibility to go along with their comfort of numbers and analyses. This terrain may be disconcerting to a lot of managers, but if they embrace the future they may find it better than anything they've experienced before.

So what is a good first step for better understanding technology? We suggest the manager acquire a rudimentary knowledge of engineering because it is the profession that designs, builds, and maintains the objects in our world. Engineering has been around in some form for thousands of years, but in recent history the impact of the engineer has been huge. Alfred P. Sloan, Jr., the longtime president of General Motors, stated, "Without his genius and the vast contributions he has made in design, engineering, and production on the material side of our existence, our contemporary life could never have reached its present standard."[6] But, as C. C. Furnas and Joe McCarthy observed in 1966:

> Despite the essential part the engineer plays in the progress and well-being of humanity, to many he is a blurred figure, his exact role imperfectly understood. One reason for the hazy impression left by the modern engineer is his close association with the scientist. Both men look alike, talk alike, worry over similar mathematical equations; the guard at the gate who checks their identification badges often cannot tell which is which. In fact, in such industries as plastics and communications, it is difficult to determine where the scientist's work ends and the engineer's begins.[7]

Aside from the gender insensitivity of the quote, much of Furnas and McCarthy's sentiments hold today, but that need not be the case if one understands the different goals that a scientist and an engineer pursue. Jay B. Brockman, an engineering professor at Notre Dame University, clarifies the difference:

> The main business of engineering is to apply technology in concert
> with natural phenomena to develop these things that we need or want.
> Whereas the natural sciences traditionally seek to discover how things
> are, engineering focuses on the question, what form should we give to
> this thing so that it will effectively serve its purpose?[8]

As the above quote points, scientists focus on discovery in the natural world, whereas engineers are trained to utilize a problem-solving process to address issues in the constructed world. Therefore, you can sum up engineering in one phrase: problem solving. So, understanding more about engineering also teaches you more about problem solving. And since most design issues are actually problems to be solved, you can quickly see why you would benefit from having a basic comprehension of engineering. Yet, everyone is taught science in school but not engineering, even though we are affected every minute of the day by the handiwork of engineers. It is not in the scope of this book to provide a complete education on engineering, so we will simply summarize some of the basic approaches engineers apply in their jobs.

ENGINEERS ARE VERY GOAL ORIENTED

If you approach an engineer with an idea, give them a good idea of what you intend to accomplish and what is important in the project. Engineers want to know that they are working toward clearly defined goals, and they also want to know what constraints must be adhered to. Engineers want to know the parameters of the tasks and goals they are pursuing. Ranges of values with which to work within are helpful. It is also important that the criteria are in alignment with the project mission. If you do not come to engineers with this information, you may find them becoming frustrated with you, and they will not be interested in working on your project. The eternal conflict between marketing and engineering can be curtailed with a little understanding and empathy on your part. Keep in mind that marketing professionals often believe engineers are not creative, and engineers often believe that marketers' ideas are too fuzzy and unrealistic. However, coming prepared to a meeting with an engineer with a well-formed idea, design goals, evaluation criteria, and project constraints will ensure better interactions.

ENGINEERS APPROACH PROBLEMS LIKE AN ECONOMIST

Engineers understand the old economic adage that "there is no such thing as a free lunch." Time is money. As such, an experienced engineer will first search for solutions that may already exist for the problem. If the solution adequately fits the situation, they may advise that route be followed, since time can be saved and used on other problems requiring more thinking. A very important point for managers new to technology to understand is: Most inventions and new products are simply a new combination of what already exists. That is why very few products are made of truly original components. When possible, the engineer will use off-the-shelf components to build a product. As you more closely examine how products are designed, you'll quickly discover that most are simply made with already-existing parts with a new innovation or two added in.

The aesthetic qualities may appear original, but the inside components are usually from preexisting products. Why do engineers use already-existing technology instead of innovating totally original products? Because it saves a lot of money. Why put a lot of dollars into R&D when a parts distributor can sell you something that already works?

ENGINEERS SEEK THE MOST EFFICIENT SOLUTION TO A PROBLEM

Complexity expert W. Brian Arthur points out that understanding this important fact makes technology a much less daunting subject.: "If you open up a jet engine (or aircraft gas turbine power plant, to give it its professional name), you will find components inside—compressors, turbines, combustion engines. If you open up other technologies that existed before it, you find some of the same components....Technologies inherit parts from the technologies that preceded them, so putting such parts together—combining them—must have a great deal to do with how technologies come into being. This makes the abrupt appearance of radically novel technologies suddenly seem much less abrupt. Technologies somehow must come into being as fresh combinations of what already exists." Solutions that have been useful in the past may be useful to working on new design projects. However, while efficiency and economics are common design constraints, an innovative engineer is always on the lookout for a better way to do something. Balancing the new with the tried and true is the ultimate design challenge.

With knowledge of how engineers approach their jobs, you can ask questions in a way to get more help on the technical aspects of your product. You will also approach opportunities with the eye of an engineer as well as a designer. As technology experts often say: You'll know just enough to be dangerous. With that in mind, we now provide information about the different engineering disciplines so that you'll have a general idea of who to go to for help.

THE ENGINEERING DISCIPLINES

If you are turning to an engineer for help in developing your product, you'll want to approach one who is from the discipline that pertains most to your design question. In *Engineering Your Future,* William Oakes, Les Leone, and Craig Gunn provide new university students with an overview of the most common areas of engineering. Their descriptions are also useful to managers new to engineering.[9]

CHEMICAL ENGINEERING

Chemical engineers apply chemistry to industrial processes. They change the composition or properties of substances for the manufacturing of drugs, cements, paints, lubricants, pesticides, fertilizers, cosmetics, and foods. Chemical engineers also work with oil refining, combustion, and extraction of metals from ores, and assist with the production of ceramics, brick, and glass. They can be very helpful in explaining what materials would work best in your product. They may also help create new materials needed for producing the product you are designing. Some industries are transformed by the use of more efficient or affordable materials, such as aerospace, automotive, biomedical, electronic, environmental, space, and military applications. Material innovation is one of the greatest sources of new technology in our society.

CIVIL ENGINEERING

Civil engineers design the infrastructure that supports our communities. They deal with the design, construction, and maintenance of structures in built environments, such as buildings, bridges, roads, canals, and dams. They are very engaged in projects involving rapid transit systems, highway systems, skyscrapers, industrial plants, and recreational facilities. Because of their involvement in construction, they also often work in materials science and deal with concrete, aluminum, steel, polymers, and carbon fibers. Civil engineers also help lay out roads, tracks, and pipelines as surveyors. If a new facility needs to be built, a civil engineer is a likely first expert to consult.

ELECTRICAL ENGINEERING

Electrical engineering is the largest discipline of engineering. Over 300,000 engineers design and develop electronic systems and products in the United States.[10] They may work on electronics, solid-state circuitry, communications systems, computers, instrumentation, power generation and transmission, and industrial applications. If a product needs power to operate, it is likely an electrical engineer had a hand in the development. We can expect electrical engineering to continue to grow, especially as people use PDAs and smart phones more. In addition, with advances in medical technology, electrical engineers will be called upon to power up new devices that will be used in prosthetics and implants.

COMPUTER ENGINEERING

Computer engineering combines electrical engineering with computer science to develop new computer systems. Robotics, artificial intelligence, industrial automation, and computer hardware and software are just a few of the many areas that computer engineers work in today's digital world. As new digital technologies become utilized in more areas of work and leisure, the role of the computer engineer will continue to grow.

INDUSTRIAL ENGINEERING

If you've designed a product, chances are an industrial engineer will assist in the manufacturing. Industrial engineering applies engineering principles and techniques to efficiently produce goods. As such, industrial engineers are very concerned with the optimal allocation of people, materials, and equipment to increase productivity in their areas. Industrial engineering is also known as management science, systems engineering, or manufacturing engineering. The information industrial engineers provide on the manufacturing needs of your product will be very helpful when you put together an I Plan later.

MECHANICAL ENGINEERING

Mechanical engineering is a vital area of new product development. It deals with the design, development, production, control, operation, and service of machines and mechanical devices. Mechanical engineers provide detailed layout and assembly of the components of products and machines. They ensure the parts of a product fit together and operate as intended. Because of their expertise on components and parts, they can be found in many related areas, such as bioengineering, robotics, aerospace engineering, nuclear engineering, ocean engineering, applied mechanics, and manufacturing.

INDUSTRIAL DESIGNERS

Although not technically an area of engineering, *industrial design* is an area that applies many engineering concepts to designing products. Ergonomics, usability, design-for-manufacturing, and design for end-of-life management are some of the areas involved in industrial design. Industrial designers work to improve the function, value, and appearance of products. Since they focus on the form of the product, they can come from different backgrounds, such as architecture, art, and engineering. Industrial designers, such as Jonathon Ive of Apple, have garnered worldwide recognition for their products. Their products are admired for their artistic relevance as well as their commercial success. Other aesthetic professionals, such as graphic designers, set designers, and fashion designers, are influencing new product development as well. As prototyping technologies become more accessible in price and availability and design principles propagate through the greater public, we will see more companies and innovators implementing the principles of industrial design into their products.

Understanding the basic roles of the aforementioned engineers will be very useful when you try to develop a product in the future. As you design the function, shape, and components of your product idea, you may need to turn to one of these experts to help you work through design issues. You should be aware we did not provide you with an exhaustive list of engineering categories. Many fields and industries have their own engineering specialists as well, such as nuclear engineering and petroleum engineering. If you are interested in learning more about engineering and technology, you can obtain free online lectures by visiting the following websites: TED (www.ted.com), M.I.T.'s OpenCourseWare (ocw.mit.edu), and the Stanford Technology Ventures Program (stvp.stanford.edu). For up-to-date information on the latest technologies and science trends, visit www.wired.com, news.cnet.com, www.popsci.com, www.technologyreview.com, and www.popularmechanics.com. The Bureau of Labor Statistics also provides more information on the engineering disciplines at www.bls.gov/oco/ocos027.htm.

In the following section, we will examine another important aspect of new product design: prototyping. To the average person, prototyping seems like a task best left to technical professionals; however, as we will see, prototyping technologies have been democratized where anyone can build basic prototypes. This skill set will come in very handy as you work with your product idea.

PROTOTYPING

Burt Rutan, the American aerospace engineer who won the Ansari X Prize, believes that experimentation and exploration are important aspects of the human condition. He said, "I think we need to explore. I think if we stop exploring that we will run into mediocrity and we all will get bored." Yet, how many companies are mediocre because managers and employees through the ranks accept the status quo and hold back their ideas? One key reason why managers may hold back their ideas is they're not quite sure what to do with the ones they have. Their reticence to explore the practical side of technology was not always the case in the developed world. Peter Wright, former assistant director of MI 5—the British Intelligence service— once observed that World War II was won by having a large group of inquisitive people who sought practical solutions to complex problems. He states:

> Science in wartime is often a case of improving with the materials at hand, solving a problem as best you can at the time, rather than planning ten or fifteen years ahead. The war shaped my later approach to technical intelligence. It taught me the value of improvisation and showed me, too, just how effective operations can be when men of action listen to young men with a belief in practical, inventive science. Sadly, by the end of the war this attitude had all but disappeared, the dead hand of committees began to squeeze the life out of England.[11]

These sentiments pertain to many businesses today as well. How many managers behave like the committees Wright describes? Overanalyzing and micromanaging employee activities can squeeze out any innovation taking place in a company. Managers should instead be role models for innovative behavior and support their employees in exploring the development of ideas.

In previous chapters, we discussed the general principles that managers and employees can follow to design new products and services. Unfortunately, most books that cover innovation stop there, and the reader is not given any direction on how to actually shepherd the idea into production. We rectify this gap by providing practices you can employ to shape an idea into an actual product. As Chapter 4 covered, the innovation process begins with an insight of an opportunity to explore. Chapter 5 discussed how to apply the design process to develop the insight into a practical and refined concept. This chapter extends the design process into prototyping and manufacturing.

A prototype is a physical representation of your idea, and is useful for attaining more in-depth feedback. A model of your idea makes it more realistic. It's no longer just on paper, so others can look at it from every angle. Therefore, a prototype is rich with details of what you are hoping to build. After all, visual communication is usually more informative than verbal communication. If a picture is worth a thousand words, a prototype is worth a million words. The next time you have a meeting with your boss to discuss an idea, bring a prototype. If you start off describing the idea with a polished pitch, they'll probably nod and say something like, "Okay, sounds interesting." But if you then put a well-designed prototype in their hand, they might respond, "Oh, wow! Now I get it! Let me see more. Tell me how this works." If you've piqued their interest with the prototype, the floodgates might open with feedback and support to make the next version better. And you'll probably start to separate yourself from the rest of the employees in your company who go through their days pushing paper.

PROTOTYPING IN FIVE STEPS

Many people avoid learning about prototyping because they think it is too complicated or expensive. This need not be the case. Prototypes do vary in their sophistication and costs, but in the early stages of design, anyone can create inexpensive models made of simple materials like paper and tape to capture the most basic elements of an idea. As we display the prototype for feedback, we can modify the concept with another inexpensive model. As you can see, the iterative process of "play, display, and watch the replay" holds true for prototyping as well. Once enthusiastic support has been received for the simple prototype, we can build a more advanced *conceptual prototype*. The conceptual prototype is not necessarily polished or expensive, but it is more sophisticated than the earlier rough prototypes. Conceptual prototypes are also known as surface prototypes, because on the surface they start to take on the appearance of what the final product may look like. You may have to create a few conceptual prototypes until you have a winning concept. When you are pleased with the conceptual prototype, you can begin building a *working prototype*. Although it doesn't necessarily have to be the case, it's likely that more costs will be incurred on this model, because a working prototyping has to actually *work*. It goes beyond merely looking like the final product it needs to demonstrate how it functions. After a working prototype is found acceptable, some designers build a *presentation prototype* to demonstrate a polished version of how the actual product will look and work. It doesn't have to be an exact replica of the real product, but it should appear to be. Sometimes companies substitute less costly materials that wouldn't be used in the actual product, but paint and final detailing is applied to give it a polished look. If the working prototype gets across enough information and garners support for follow-through, some executives may give the go-ahead to bypass the presentation model and go straight to production with the technical *drawings*, concepts, and working prototype as guides for setting up the manufacturing processes.

Now that you have a basic understanding of what prototyping is and the various types of prototypes, you're now ready to learn how to actually build one. The following five steps provide guidance on how to take your idea through the various stages of prototyping and ready your concept for production.

STEP 1: DRAWING

SKETCHES

When you get an idea, the first thing you should do is draw a quick sketch and jot down notes. The sketch doesn't have to be particularly artistic or technical. It just needs to get a basic point across to someone else. This exercise doesn't require much in terms of materials or costs. A good pen and something to write on will get you going. Many great companies were founded by someone having an idea for a new business and writing it on the back of a napkin. For example, market leader Southwest Airlines was started this way. When Rollin King and Herb Kelleher met for dinner in 1967 at a San Antonio, Texas, restaurant, they had an idea for a new airline. Grabbing a napkin, King drew a triangle representing flight routes between Dallas, Houston, and San Antonio. They would offer airline services that catered to frequent fliers who did business between the three cities. Southwest would later be innovative in its company culture and operations as well, but it all got started when King and Kelleher drew out the idea.

Sketching is also a good way to document your ideas. Whenever you have an idea, draw it out and capture it. Notebooks are also important for writing as well as drawing. It is important to write notes on the parameters, criteria of success, and possible issues and ideas in your notebook. This is why engineers, designers, and inventors keep notebooks handy. They know that an idea is safe and won't be lost if it is written down. Another benefit of keeping an active notebook is that it supports the design principles of "play, display, and watch the replay." You can track the changes in your idea. Furthermore, if someone suggests you do something you've already tried, you can pull out your notebook and show them what you did and explain why it didn't work.

TECHNICAL DRAWING

As you progress with an idea, you may want the assistance of an engineer or draftsman to draw more technical *sketches* of the product. Drawings that capture the width, height, and depth along with measurements, parts, and components will communicate how an object should be made. Rudimentary skills in *technical drawing* can be developed by taking art classes and mechanical drawing courses; however, open-source software, such as Google SketchUp, can be used to craft digital 3D drawings of your idea as well.

The best way to gain proficiency in drawing is to do it whenever you have an idea. Rest assured that even if you don't see yourself as artistic, the more you do it the better you will get. You don't even have to always draw products to develop your artistic skills though. Simply carry a notebook around and draw what you see around you. Examine objects on your desk, such as a computer mouse, pens, and coffee cups, and examine with a designer's eye the shape, colors, and small details of the object. Try drawing them. Observe how the object reflects light. Take a guess at what it is made of. Try to figure out how it was put together. Think about the characteristics of objects as you draw them, and as you do so you will develop a designer's eye. Ask yourself how the product could have been made better. What are its weaknesses? What are the good characteristics of the object? Why? What is interesting about the object? What do you think the designer was trying to achieve when the concept was developed? How would you modify the object for a different market? Drawing the world around you with a critical eye will help you develop skills that will be helpful when you design your own products.

STEP 2: MODEL BUILDING

MAKING IT REAL

A complement to drawing is *model building.* Designer and University of Rhode Island Teaching Fellow Karl Aspelund describes a model as "any kind of sample, mock-up, or attempt at physical representation of an idea, ranging from a standard architectural model to a sample garment on a mannequin. The creation of models and samples at this stage of any design is an attempt to bring the idea into the real world and help us understand how the design will function there."[12] Again, like drawing, model building can be an informal and relaxed method for capturing your idea, except now instead of being on paper it will be captured in 3D physical form. As Apelund points out, "The model is real, but it's not the real thing."[13]

If there were one phrase to sum up this stage of prototyping, it would be "Build it." You may have had a good conversation with someone on a business idea and even drawn it on the back of a napkin, but if you want to really get across your idea, get some paper, cardboard, tape, and a pair of scissors and start building a mock-up. The same principles you utilized in drawing apply here. Use whatever is available that you can piece together to capture your idea. As Tom Kelley, general manager of IDEO, states, good designers "delight in how fast they take a concept from words to sketch, to model, and yes, to a successful new offering."[14] In *The Ten Faces of Innovation,* he recalls how IDEO used modeling to develop a concept for a breakthrough medical instrument for nasal surgery. IDEO met with the medical advisory board of surgical tool company Gyrus ENT to discuss what surgeons wanted in the new device. Ideas were flying around the meeting about what the instrument should look like, but the group was having a hard time grasping the general design of the product. Kelley recalls,

> Then one of our young engineers bolted from the room. Outside the conference room, seizing on the 'found art' of materials lying around the office, he picked up a whiteboard marker, a black plastic Kodak film canister, and a clothes-line clip. He taped the canister to the white board marker and attached the clip to the lid of the film canister. The result was an extremely crude model of the new surgical tool. He asked, 'Are you thinking of something like *this?*' To which a surgeon replied, 'Yes, something like THIS!' That initial crude prototype got the project rolling.[15]

MATERIALS FOR MODEL BUILDING

As the IDEO example demonstrates, you can make mock-ups with whatever is handy around you. However, if you want to be more adept at building models, you may want to invest a little money into a few basic tools and materials that can be found at any good art store or craft shop. Paper, illustration board, heavy cardboard, poster board, bristol paper, chipboard, museum board, foamcore, canson paper, balsa wood, and basswood are good materials to have on hand. A utility knife, a craft knife, a retractable blade knife, a handheld board cutter and beveler, dividers, a metal ruler, a T square, a 30-degree-by-60-degree triangle, a 45-degree triangle, and an ample supply of pencils, pens, markers, and charcoal are handy tools to design and shape the parts and frames of your prototype. Adhesives are important to hold your creation together. White glue, rubber cement, spray adhesive, balsa wood cement, and sticky tape can work wonders in building fairly sturdy prototypes.

TIPS FOR BUILDING MODELS

Building models is comprised of gathering materials, drawing out what you want to cut, cutting out the pieces, and gluing or fastening them together. Be sure to carefully measure your drawings on the materials so that you ensure the parts fit together well. When you extract the parts out of the materials, slice against a metal straight edge such as a T square to ensure an even cut, and put a protective object underneath the material you are cutting so that you avoid damaging your table surface and dulling the knife blades. It is also important to wear safety goggles. Just snipping a metal can shoot a metal shard into the eye. Attentiveness during any cutting maneuver is essential. If you use glue to attach the parts, only apply as much as is minimally necessary, in order to avoid making messy models. And replace blades whenever they become dull.[16]

The materials at this stage are inexpensive, so don't be afraid to make mistakes. That is the only way you can learn to develop prototyping skills. You will get better with time. If you are particularly adventurous and want to build a small model shop, you might consider purchasing some fairly inexpensive power tools and machines. A scroll saw and a chop saw are easy to use and very effective in working with wood and foamboard to build slightly more realistic prototypes. Portable hand drills, a rotary shaft tool, a floor model drill press, and a hack saw are worth considering as well. A shop vacuum cleaner and a draftsman table will complete your workshop. Clay and plaster are other materials you might also want to add to your supply shelf. You may find it worthwhile to build a small shop in your home to experiment with your ideas as well.

As you begin to build inexpensive prototypes, you will start looking differently at the world around you. You'll become curious as to how something was made, why it was made that way, and how it could have been made better. You might even find yourself picking up a copy of *Make* magazine or *Popular Mechanics* instead of your traditional business periodicals. Technology will no longer be a foreign concept to you. Also, as you iterate and build more models, you'll learn prototyping shortcuts and new ways to display the details of your ideas. And, as your prototyping skills improve, people will get a better idea of what is going on inside your head. You'll no longer have to struggle with trying to find the right words to get across your ideas. Your models will do the talking for you.

BUSINESS VIABILITY

In the previous chapter, we noted how IDEO defines good design as a product or service that meets the constraints of consumer desirability, technical feasibility, and *business viability*. The consumer desirability component of design has been covered in Chapter 4. Chapter 5 extended coverage of this component when it provided guidance on how to design products with customer feedback. The early part of this chapter has addressed technical feasibility. The rough prototype stage is an excellent time to cover business viability. Figure 6.1 provides a simple method for getting a general idea about the business viability of your product. Experienced innovators, executives, investors, and designers can run these calculations in their head, but you'll likely need to work these calculations out on paper. These are rough calculations. When you address financial aspects in your I Plan, you'll apply more sophisticated techniques. But for now, you just want to get an overall idea of whether your idea is on the right financial path. If you frequently utilize this method to test the business viability of ideas, you may find you can get to where you can with the numbers in your head like more experienced innovators and executives. For now, though, work the calculations out on paper. You'll find that once you know the basic formulas, you can run them anywhere. The back of an envelope or napkin is all that is needed to do these calculations. Your goal is to just get a basic idea of whether the idea makes business sense. If you're testing the viability of an employee's idea, you will find it will take about a half hour to an hour to work through the calculations and debrief on your conclusions and any next steps they may need to take on the project. The following steps will help you in determining the business viability of your project:

1. Define what your product is. What problem, need, or want does it address? How does it address it? Describe who the average customer of the product is. What do the customers have in common? That is, what characteristics do the customers share? If you could provide a profile of the average customer, what would it be?

2. How many of these customers are in your reachable market? Your reachable market is the target market you can reasonably market to and service. For a small company, this might be a particular side of town, whereas for a large corporation, it could be a particular part of the world. For example, the local Pita Pit in Muncie, Indiana, considers its reachable market to be local customers who are health conscious and active adults north of the river that runs through town. Roche Applied Sciences, a worldwide manufacturer of medical products, is located in the same part of Indiana as the Pita Pit, but considers its local market to be life scientists in government, private, and university labs in North America. Some companies such as ExxonMobil may even consider the whole world to have reachable customers for its products.

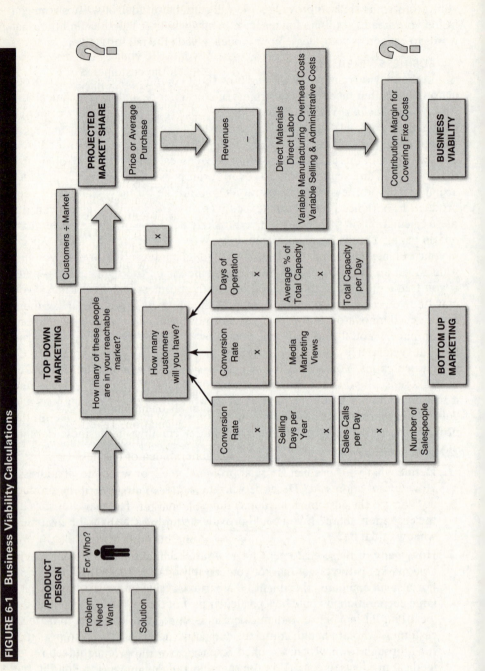

FIGURE 6-1   Business Viability Calculations

3. Once you've determined how many potential customers are in your reachable market, calculate how many of these customers you think you can reasonably convince to buy your product. This is just an estimation. You will do more thorough market research when you write your I Plan. There may be different ways you are going to try to reach the customer. For example, if you utilize a sales force, how many salespeople can you devote to selling the product? How many sale calls can they make in an average day? How many days per year will they try selling the product? Multiply the number of salespeople by the sales calls per day by the number of days the sales force will talk to customers. Now multiply that number by the percentage of sales calls that you reasonably think you can convert into a sale. This is just an educated guess based on past experience, so don't stress over the exactness of your number. If you are using television, newspaper, radio, or Internet marketing, estimate how many of your potential customers see the advertisements and multiply that number by the percentage of people you think will go ahead and make a purchase of your product. If you're offering a service, you can calculate this figure based on how much you can deliver it. This is your total capacity. Estimate what the average percentage of total capacity you will have on an average day. Multiply the total capacity by the average percentage of total capacity by the number of days you can offer the service during the year. For example, a new computer software support service may consist of three people who can potentially make five visits to clients per day. If we assume that they only get two calls per day for the service and that they work 200 days per year, we can estimate that we will have 400 visits per year. There may be some considerations regarding customers being reached by multiple marketing channels or having service contracts that need to be taken into account in your calculation. Take those adjustments into account, and perform the calculations without getting too hung up on small details. The key is to get a general idea of business viability in this exercise.

4. Divide the number of customers you think you can attain by the estimated number of target customers in your reachable market. This is your projected market share, and is a good first check on the business viability of your idea. Is the market share large enough to make the business worthwhile? If not, will you need to hire more sales people to sell the product? Will you have to use more advertising? Would you reasonably be able to do this? These are just a few of the insights you can gain by considering how much of the market you can attain with your idea.

5. After you've estimated your market share, you can examine the economic logic of your idea. What price will you charge for the product? Multiply the price by the number of customers you project for the product. If you think some customers will be repeat customers, make the appropriate adjustment to your calculation. This total gives you your projected revenues for the product.

6. Estimate the cost of goods sold for your product. What will materials cost for the product? How much will it cost for labor used in making the product? What are the variable manufacturing overhead costs? These are the additional costs incurred due to the manufacturing of a product, such as electricity. What are the variable selling and administrative costs incurred because the product is being manufactured? This may be the most difficult calculation of the business viability process. If you have pretty good knowledge of operations, you can probably make a reasonable estimate for cost of goods sold. If you struggle with this calculation, an engineer, cost accountant, or production manager may be able to provide good estimates of these figures. However, for a quick calculation, you can make a ballpark estimate to get a general idea for the viability of an idea.

7. Subtract the cost of goods sold from revenues. The resulting number is the contribution margin for covering fixed costs. This figure gives you an idea of how much the product clears internally after covering its manufacturing costs.

If the contribution margin is small, the product may not make sense for the company to pursue. Don't give up though. This information may simply tell you that you need to tweak some of the product and financial variables. For example, what happens to the revenues and gross margin if you raise price? What are the costs of the product if you use a different material? Establishing business viability is akin to trying to solve a Rubik's Cube. Keep working the variables around until something makes business sense. You may apply design principles again through iteration by tweaking the technical, marketing, and financial components until you have a viable idea. You should probably continue testing business viability throughout the rest of the prototyping stages as well, but meeting the design constraint early in the prototyping process gets you off to a good start.

Once you have developed a rough prototype that appears to be technically feasible and viable from a business standpoint, it's time to develop a more advanced prototype. Again, this will likely not be the final version of your product, but will be another progressive step toward developing an innovation that will be accepted by the marketplace.

STEP 3: CONCEPTUAL PROTOTYPING

THE PURPOSE OF A CONCEPTUAL PROTOTYPE

A conceptual prototype advances the best elements of your previous rough prototype. The rough prototype should have given you a general idea of what the product might end up being, but the conceptual prototype starts to take on more detail of the form, fit, and function of the final design. This does not mean that you have to invest significant amounts of money into prototyping yet. In fact, it doesn't necessarily have to have all the working parts of what you envision the final version being. However, it should start to at least resemble what you think it might become. That is why a conceptual prototype is sometimes called a surface prototype, because on the surface the observer can get a better idea of what the product will look like. When the Palm Pilot was being developed at Handspring Inc., company cofounder Jeff Hawkins carried a conceptual prototype of it in his shirt pocket for weeks to see how it felt. He whittled the prototype out of wood. The dimensions of the wooden Palm Pilot were very similar to the version that went onto the market.[17] Capturing the anticipated look of the product can be further attained by putting together a more realistic version of the product through adding vinyl overlays, paint for the overall appearance, and buttons and accoutrements from other products.

RAPID PROTOTYPING TECHNIQUES

For centuries, prototypes have been carefully built using hand tools and machine tools, a process that requires much skill and time. However, there are many technologies available for *rapid prototyping* (RP) that allow a three-dimensional prototype to be constructed in considerably less time, and without requiring that same high level of skill with hand tools and machine tools. The design information for rapid prototyping is typically created using a computer-aided drafting (CAD) program, often in one that allows the user to create virtual spheres, rectangular prisms, and other solids. These are repositioned and scaled, duplicated and arrayed, squashed, twisted, or folded. Sometimes they are joined together, subtracted from one another, or their interaction is what remains. The resulting digital object is then saved in a format that can be used by the prototyping technology.

Rapid prototyping technologies can be classified as either subtractive, where we cut away unwanted material, or additive, where we build a model, typically by stacking up different layers of materials, each a horizontal cross section. One additive process is Laminated Object Manufacturing (LOM), where one layer of a material is placed on top of another; these may be paper or paperboard with glue on one surface, for instance, each piece the exact shape of a horizontal cross section at a different elevation within the object. This same "slicing" is used for most other additive RP technologies. Stereolithography (SLA), which refers to StereoLithography Apparatus, is a process where photo-curable plastic resin is drawn from a vat to selectively place a thin layer of the liquid down where it is cured by a laser beam, one layer at a time; this polymerizes and solidifies the part, growing it from the bottom up. Another RP additive technology is Fused Deposition Modeling (FDM), where a spaghetti-like strand of material is heated and extruded onto a platform to build the first layer of a product; a second layer is extruded on the first, and so on until the entire object has been built. Solid Object Printing (SOP) is a technique where print heads are used to selectively place material. In some instances, we can use a plaster-like powder and have a colored or clear binder agent printed on a thin layer of the powder, on which is wiped the next layer of the powder until the entire part is built. In other instances, we can have the built material itself, sometimes a wax, placed down by the same mechanism seen in some printers. Selective Laser Sintering (SLS) uses a laser to make certain areas of powder, often plastic or metal powder, stick together. Each of these and the other technologies not mentioned have specific advantages and disadvantages. In general, while the specialized materials are somewhat costly, prices for rapid prototyping machines have decreased in some instances as the technology has advanced.

In addition to 3D additive RP technologies, there are subtractive technologies. Some of these are primarily two-dimensional, while others are 3D. Two-dimensional subtractive technologies cut out wanted areas from sheet stock according to digital information. These include lasers, plasma arc cutters, electrical discharge machine, routers, milling machines, and water jets. For some systems, a programming language known as G-code is used to tell a *Computer Numerically Controlled* (CNC) machine to turn on, where to cut, and how fast to cut. In other instances, specialized computer interfaces are used, and some of these are as easy as sending data to a printer. Cutting out parts from a flat sheet is generally a two-axis system. Full movement to cut shapes through all axes is possible on a three-axis system, and it is even possible to have a four-axis system (where it is possible not only to machine along paths for curves generated in the x, y, and z axes, but to add a different motion, such as a turntable, which is considered a different degree of freedom, even though the object really only exists in 3D space), or a five-axis one. Lathes are also used to create parts with circular cross sections.

CNC machines build prototypes from images captured with computer-assisted design (CAD) programs or machine languages such as G-code. A G-code program may appear intimidating to the untrained eye, but with a little training the fundamentals of the language can be quickly picked up. Although there is a bit of a learning curve to the programs, the technology is becoming increasingly easy to use. There are computer-aided manufacturing (CAM) systems that let you generate a complex G-code program by starting with a CAD drawing and using the features of that drawing to create tool paths. If you are interested in learning machine languages and running rapid prototyping equipment, visit your local university or community college. They likely provide courses on how to write milling programs and run the machinery. A short programming course, consisting of 10 hours of lab time along with 25 hours of training in a machine shop, can make one proficient enough to start building prototypes. You will need to devote an additional five hours per week at home writing programs to run in the shop. A helpful feature of modern prototyping software is that you can write the program in Microsoft Word and save it to a flash drive that you can bring later to a programming lab. You can then verify that you wrote a good program to build your prototype by testing it in a virtual milling machine on the computer screen. The screen will show a digital version of your part and the tool that will be used to cut out shapes for your prototype. When you activate the program, you will see how the cutting tool would operate in the real world on your object. The verifying program lets you know if your program will be successful in the machine shop. Fortunately for the novice prototyper, the programming is becoming much easier as NC code is increasingly generated by using CAM systems.

Even if you do not learn how to do rapid prototyping yourself, a basic understanding of the process may help you to get a prototype made. Knowing the different processes and machines will enable you to approach the appropriate technology experts who can build your prototype. You will also have a better idea as to the costs and time involved in the process. Still, if you wish to advance your design skills and become more innovative in your company, we encourage you to learn rapid prototyping. As the rapid prototyping technologies become more available and easy to use and as design becomes a more-common business practice, managers may use prototyping machines in the future like they do LaserJet printers today. Like any technology movement, the spoils will go to those who adopt the new ways sooner.

THE THREE DIMENSIONS OF A GOOD PROTOTYPE

Now that you have a more refined prototype, you will be able to receive even better feedback on whether your idea is hitting the mark, and how it might really work. Be open to the feedback and make changes as needed. Even though you're much further along in the design process, it's okay to continue making changes. Use simulations when you can, but also build a prototype at an intermediary phase of your design, if it is helpful. Often, the purpose of many prototypes is not to present the design to others, but to facilitate gaining needed information. As A. G. Laffley, chairman and CEO of Proctor and Gamble, tells his employees, "The essence of prototyping is try and try again, iterate and reiterate. The key is not to seek perfection at any single step, but, through trial and error, to get a little improvement all along the way. Learn; get closer; learn more; get a little closer. And continually build on the insights of the user."[18] He adds, "Prototyping is the process of finding mistakes, and of adding value, so don't worry about perfection….the key is to get the ideas out there in tangible form; the more people are comfortable with this show-and-tell, the more ideas that will be generated, which is the point."[19]

As you build more advanced prototypes, you will be judged on higher standards of quality. The three criteria that determine the quality of a prototype are functionality, expressivity, and credibility. Functionality is met if the product is able to do what the customer expects of it. The product "must be able to function as a useful, effective and also perhaps a desirable object."[20] For example, carabiners are very useful tools for rock climber to hook their ropes through. They trust that the carabiner will not break if they fall off the side of a mountain. Expressivity means that the product looks like what the customer expects it. It can be original, but it must not be too far away from the norm or else customers may be confused by its appearance. If a customer has to ask, "What is it?" you're probably missing the mark in your design. Regarding the carabiner example, climbers want to know that their equipment meets traditional standards. With their lives depending on their ropes, harnesses, and carabiners, they do not want to take a chance on using equipment that looks too experimental or unreliable. Credibility means there is a seamless interaction between the product and the customer. The product is reliable, and the user can get to the point where they use it without thinking. When a skilled climber reaches a point where they want to secure the rope, they can subconsciously reach down for a carabiner and attach it to bolts in the side of the rock. If a climbing aficionado wanted to design a new carabiner, they would want to take functionality, expressivity, and credibility into account. You will want to take the same approach as you design your prototype.

MANUFACTURABILITY

Manufacturability of the product is also worth exploring. The best design is a collaborative process between the designer, manufacturers, and technicians. Materials and production processes are very important elements of manufacturability. Material requirements include hardness, which is the material's resistance to surface penetration (or local plastic deformation); toughness, which is the material's ability to absorb energy without breaking; elasticity, which is the ability of a material to spring back to its original shape after being subjected to force; plasticity, which is the ability to permanently take on a new shape after being subjected to a force; brittleness, which is the likeliness a material will break; ductility, which is the ability of a material to bend, stretch, or twist without breaking; strength, which is the ability to withstand a force without changing shape or breaking; tension , which is the pulling force a material can withstand from both ends; compression, which is how much a material can withstand pushing or squeezing; torsion, which is the degree of twisting the material utilizes; and shear, which is the amount of force that splits a material.[21] Manufacturing considerations include the volume of production that can be undertaken in a batch, material costs, the speed of production, and the manufacturing applications that will be utilized to build the product.[22] Information on materials to be used and manufacturing processes to be applied will give you a better idea about the costs and requirements that need to be met to build your product.

STEP 4: WORKING PROTOTYPE

THE PURPOSE OF A WORKING PROTOTYPE

Now that you have decided what the product will look like and what its function is, it's time to build a working version of it. Depending on the complexity of the product and your experience, you may need to enlist help from engineers and craftsmen to help you develop a working model of your idea. A corporate sponsor inside the company may be needed now to help you get the expertise and money needed to build a working prototype. Again, the working prototype is probably not the final version of the idea, but it is very close to what will go into production. A working prototype doesn't necessarily have to look like the final version, but it has to successfully demonstrate the principle of the product.[23] Most of the bugs need to be worked out, and it needs to be easy to use.

BUILDING A WORKING PROTOTYPE

Although a working prototype will be more sophisticated than a conceptual prototype, it doesn't have to cost a lot of money to build. *Wired Magazine* provided its favorite examples of iconic working prototypes of famous products. They aren't the most polished objects, but they worked. Examples included the Super Soaker squirt gun and the Apple I computer. The Super Soaker was built with an air pump, a series of check valves, PVC pipes, plastic tubing, and a 2-liter soda bottle. The Apple I consisted of a motherboard and keyboard attached to plywood.[24] The concepts worked. The Super Soaker tallied over $200 million in sales, and the Apple I provided the technical foundation for Steve Jobs and Steve Wozniak to revolutionize the computer industry. As these iconic models demonstrate, the main focus of the working prototype is demonstrating how the product gets the job done.

You may find toys in your attic that can be helpful in building prototypes. K'Nex, Legos, and Erector sets are easy, inexpensive materials that have been used by many inventors and engineers to address design issues. If you've been to the EPCOT theme park at Walt Disney World, you've probably rode the extremely popular ride Soarin' Over California. The ride lifts guests' seats into the air and gives them the sensation of flying by placing them in front of an IMAX-sized screen. Wind blows through the hair and the smell of pine needles waft through the air to add to the effect. The ride runs at 100 percent capacity from the moment the park opens to the minute it closes. EPCOT sometimes even opens a half hour early to allow guests the chance to get in the line queues early to get a ticket for the ride. What you probably didn't know was that an Erector set is responsible for overcoming its design challenges. While IMAX theatres exist in most major cities, the moviegoer always remains seated on the ground. But not at a Disney park. Walt Disney Imagineering had to devise a way to create the sensation of flying. Imagineer Mark Sumner figured it out. He used an Erector set to design the basic seat and lift mechanism. A cantilever system hoists the guests off the floor and into the air. Guests "ooh" and "ah" as they sail over California's landmarks. It's Disney's most popular ride, but it never would have been built if Sumner had not pulled out his Erector set and experimented with the ride mechanics.

MACHINE PRINCIPLES

A basic understanding of machines may come in handy as you develop prototypes. The Naval Education and Training Program Development Center defines a machine as "any device that helps you to do the work. We use machines to transform energy. Another use is to multiply force. Machines may also be used to multiply speed. There are only six simple machines: the lever, block, wheel and axle, inclined plane, screw, and gear. When you are familiar with the principles of these simple machines, you can work on better understanding the operation of complex machines. Complex machines are merely combinations of two or more simple machines."[25] A little understanding of technology, machinery, and power can provide you with a toolkit to better move an idea further. Of course, you will want to work with technical experts, and you will have a better interaction with them if you understand some basics about machinery.

PRESENTATION PROTOTYPING

After you build a successful working prototype, you may decide to produce a presentation prototype that you can show to attract your first customers. A presentation prototype is a selling tool to show potential customers what the product will look like and how it will function. It may not be entirely the same as the product sold, but it will be a close facsimile. When Altair Product Design conceived a bus that would revolutionize public transportation, it decided it had to make a believable prototype to convince government officials that the bus was worth purchasing. The company imagined building a bus that would be to public transformation what a Frank Gehry building is to architecture. The company utilized CAD drawings for demonstrating how the innovative hybrid power train system would work inside a novel bus frame. Altair received positive response from a few potential customers, but company chairman James R. Scapa decided that because of the extreme innovativeness of the product, it would need to be experienced firsthand to win more customers over to the new concept. He told his engineering team to "get physical and get physical fast."[26] So instead of going to customers with CAD drawings and 1:10-scale models, Altair built a bus around an inexpensive aluminum bus frame. Transit buses are made out of stainless steel to endure the wear and tear accumulated over an average 20-year life span, but building the demonstration bus out of steel would have been prohibitively costly. Also, by actually building a less costly version of the bus, Altair was able to more easily identify potential structural flaws in the design. Altair would not sell the aluminum bus on the market, but it proved helpful in selling the product concept to venture capitalists and government officials.

Now that we've covered prototyping, the next step is to manufacture the product. Manufacturing is included as a step in prototyping because it should always be considered in the design process. Keeping the manufacturing end in mind will help you as you design your prototype. The next section will provide an overview of common manufacturing techniques. There are many techniques available, but some of the most common techniques utilized in going from prototype to sellable product are covered.

STEP 5: MANUFACTURING PROCESSES

MANUFACTURING PREPARATIONS

Once the prototype has been approved, it's time to manufacture it. Production managers and shop operators are given guidance on what is to be built. Working drawings are provided to show all the details a particular part must embody so that it can be properly manufactured. Shape, dimensions and sizes, locations of holes and bends, and special details are provided in the drawings. Special instructions on materials and surface finish may be included in the detail drawing as well. Assembly drawings show where the parts go and how they fit together. The picture looks like the object that has been photographed a millisecond after exploding. All the parts of the product are separate in the drawing but very close to each other. This depiction of the product allows you to see every part on its own while also having an idea where it fits into the design. If electrical and hydraulic systems are used, schematic drawings may be used as well. It is important that the production line or machine shop have detailed drawings so that they can plan the most efficient production run of the product.[27]

TOOLING UP

If your product has a unique shape, tools and equipment may need to be prepared to manufacture the object. This process is called "*tooling up*." A common practice is to make a mold of the final prototype. Silicone (or sometimes wax) is wrapped around the object to attain its shape. Then, the silicone is pulled away from the object and used to create a mold. Injection molding can now take place as plastic pellets are melted into liquid form and injected into the mold under pressure. Sometimes production of approximately 20 is run to determine if it looks good to move forward with a full run. With this inexpensive mold, changes can still be made before investing in a full run. If the results look good, a metal mold is typically produced to make a full run of the object. Metal molds are not only more costly, but also stronger and can hold up for repeatable, long production runs. A strong metal mold can stamp out a large number of products during a milling cycle. Another popular method is known as blow molding in which plastic is blown into a mold and expanded to match the mold's shape. Hollow containers, such as shampoo bottles, are commonly made in this fashion. There are many other production techniques, but these two are very common in machine shops that specialize in designing unique products.[28] For further guidance on manufacturing issues, consult experts in manufacturing technology, production operations, and management science.

THE EMERGENCE OF THE D.I.Y. MOVEMENT

In 1977, Ken Olsen, computer pioneer and founder of Digital Equipment Corporation, said to an audience at the World Future Society that "There is no reason for any individual to have a computer in his house."[29] At that time, the technology paradigm in the industry was large mainframe computers, and they were only used by large organizations like the military and Fortune 500 companies. However, in areas like Cupertino, California, where a large number of engineers and technologists lived, an underground movement was taking place. Electrical hobbyists, including Apple founders Steve Jobs and Steve Wozniak, were building and selling computer kits. The kits were very basic. The customers had to add their own case, keyboard, and video display, but with a little handiwork the setup worked. It was the start of the computer revolution. As more people bought computers for personal use, entrepreneurs began to enter the market offering better hardware and software. Many of the hobbyists who had bought the first kits rode the wave of growth to start computer-related companies of their own.

The 1970s and 1980s were a digital renaissance. More powerful computers needed advanced chips and circuitry. Better chips and circuitry allowed programmers to create more advanced software. Prices were affordable enough that families and small businesses could buy a personal computer for their desks. And more importantly, customers didn't have to be expert programmers to operate the machines. The diffusion of computer technology into everyday life and business operations transformed society. The computer revolution was complete. Today nearly anyone who wants a computer has one, and prosperity has increased around the world.

Started during an era of stagflation and cynicism, the digital movement brought us out of the 1970s analog world and into a new one where people all over the world could communicate with each other, children could learn their ABCs playing games, and businesses could track their financial performance with spreadsheets. It's hard to find an area of life where computers are absent today. Innovation and technology have that effect on societies and economies. A successful product movement brings an influx of new needs and wants to satisfy a growing group of customers.

To many people, the early part of the twenty-first century is reminiscent of the 1970s. There has been much economic unrest. Trust in politicians is at an all-time low. Financial scandals and mismanagement have decimated the investment fabric of commerce. Banks have tightened up credit. It's no wonder so many people are pessimistic about the future. Are there any technological movements under way that might bring the same wave of innovation and entrepreneurial rejuvenation that computers did 30 years ago? We believe there is. Green technology is one field that is receiving increasing attention by government, corporations, and citizens. Innovations in new materials, manufacturing processes, and business models will support the formation of new companies and jobs in green industries. The green revolution is still in its infancy, but every industry that has transformed society has gone through the same growing pains. By all indications, the green movement will become an everyday reality in our lives like computers are now. But there is another technical revolution that is taking place in garages and workshops around the world that is not receiving as much coverage: the *D.I.Y.* movement.

D.I.Y. stands for Do It Yourself, and it is increasingly becoming an ethic that is filtering into all areas of life. You can see it on your television set. The Food Network teaches viewers how to prepare four-star meals in their own kitchens. HGTV shows homeowners what materials to buy at their local hardware store, how to tear down a wall, and what they need to do to renovate their bathroom. There is another D.I.Y. presence that is growing in popularity on television, too: garage laboratories and workshops. Evidenced in such shows as Mythbusters, Robot Wars, Everyday Edisons, American Chopper, and Monster Garage, people of all ages are starting to take interest in using their hands for purposes others than tapping on a keyboard. They're getting them dirty again, working with machines, cars, and, most recently, manufacturing. You might respond to this trend with a bit of a surprise. Manufacturing? In a garage? Isn't manufacturing only done by large companies that have the money to buy millions of dollars of equipment and organize $100,000 production runs? Within the point of view of the industrial economy, the answer would be yes. But within the point of view of the emerging *creative economy*, the answer is no.

A revolution is taking place in D.I.Y. manufacturing, similar to the one that took place in the 1970s with computers. Before desktop publishing, only newspapers, advertising agencies, and book companies provided printed materials. Most people didn't have the equipment or expertise to design layouts and produce high-quality print products. Personal computers, publishing software, and printers changed all that by turning every desk into its own printing press. A new movement is under way in garages across the country that could be called "desktop manufacturing."

Desktop manufacturing enables you to take an idea and, with a moderate investment in machinery, prototype a fairly sophisticated model in your home or office. With free open-source design programs like Blender and Google SketchUp, home-based designers can transmit their ideas to 3D printers to be built. 3D printers are mini CNC rapid prototyping machines that allow you to make models of products you have in mind. The machines operate on the same model as the CNC devices described earlier in this chapter, but on a smaller scale. It's called *3D printing* because it's similar in concept to a laser printer. Whereas a laser printer prints on paper, a 3D printer lays down warm layers of acrylonitrile butadiene styrene (ABS) plastic that harden as it cools. ABS has the same texture and strength as a LEGO block. In effect, the mini CNC machine prints your prototype.

Companies such as MakerBot Industries are manufacturing D.I.Y. rapid prototyping kits that hobbyists can buy through the mail and assemble at home for less than $1000. The kits are fairly easy to put together, requiring only minor soldering on noncritical parts in the machine. The parts are even labeled and step-by-step instructions are provided for constructing the 3D printer. Once the machine is assembled, you can send designs to the machine. Sample designs can be downloaded from open-source websites, which can be used to test the performance of the 3D printer as well as for making interesting objects for personal use. The first MakerBot machine was called the Cupcake CNC because the machine if fairly small compared to its industrial cousins. The machine is gaining a lot of interest among hobbyists and amateur designers because with a little practice on the 3D printers, anyone can learn to prototype products. Skills learned on the home-based 3D printers are transferable to the larger versions found inside industrial shops and larger design firms.

If there was ever a time to learn how to design and prototype, it is today. Companies are embracing design, and prototyping technologies are becoming easier to use, less expensive, and more available. If you have an interest in design and innovation, take classes, study online, or build your own workshop in your garage. You will bring a skill set to your company that will be much appreciated. It won't be long before desktop manufacturing will be available to every garage. First movers in this technology may be rewarded with riding a wave of opportunity and prosperity like computer aficionados in the 1970s. As the home prototyping machines increase in size and capability and become lower in price, we expect the personal manufacturing movement to accelerate. The computer industry provides us good insight into how the D.I.Y. revolution may take place. There is a time in an industry when only experts can participate in a field. The economics of scale and the complexity of technology make it hard for domain outsiders to be involved in the subject. However, when innovators find ways to provide kit models for the interested hobbyist, a new industry begins to grow. Those who are in the kit stage of an industry have the opportunity to learn how the machinery works at a basic level, and as the underground movement catches steam and a market evolves, more technology becomes available. Innovators ride the wave of technological advancement and become leaders when the movement spreads through society. For example, Steve Jobs is still a leading innovator of hardware today, as is Bill Gates in software. Garages are where great companies like Harley-Davidson, Hewlett-Packard, and the Walt Disney Company were founded. Will another round of great companies be started in garages around the world in the twenty-first century? Bill Gates thinks so. When the business titan was asked what he feared most, he said, "I fear someone in a garage who is devising something completely new."[30] Is your company prepared for the next innovation revolution taking place in garages all around the world? Are your executives aware of the design movement going on among everyday people? These are important questions that every firm must address if they are to keep up with the technology trends on the horizon.

PROTOTYPING COMMODITIES, SERVICES, EXPERIENCES, AND TRANSFORMATIONS

This chapter has focused primarily on prototyping products, but the principles of design can also be employed to prototype other economic deliverables. In Chapter 4, we discussed how Pine and Gilmore recognized five economic deliverables: *commodities*, products, services, experiences, and transformations. In the following section, we discuss how a manager can prototype the other economic offerings. Anything that can be sold can be improved with design.

COMMODITY PROTOTYPING

Commodities are resources that are obtained from the natural world, and are typically utilized to manufacture products. Commodities are, thus, the ingredients of the products we use every day. Innovation can occur in commodities when companies find new uses for the materials they have. Koch Industries is one of the largest privately owned corporations in the United States. The company's main source of revenues comes from using its materials and commodities in new product lines. This type of business may not receive as much press as iPods or smartphones, but it's big business. It is estimated that Koch brings in $100 billion per year. Much of this is due to their innovation. A recent example of design success is the introduction of three-ply toilet tissue by their Georgia Pacific division. Quilted Northern Ultra Plush toilet tissue was a huge success in its first year, netting $135 million in sales. Ultra Plush was a successful proof of concept for utilizing three-ply tissue paper in a new range of products. As a result, the company is investing $500 million to advance the proprietary tissue-making technology into other products.[31]

MBA Polymers, based in Richmond, California, is another company that has prospered by being a materials innovator. Looking for a way to help improve the environment, Michael Biddle built a recycling plant in his two-car garage, selling recycled plastic taken from junked electronics and automobiles. Now MBA Polymers is the world's most advanced recycler of plastics used in durable goods. Biddle is a business owner who started out with little more than a great idea. Designing new technologies and processes to convert junk into useable commodities showed what is possible with grit, creativity, and passion. Biddle says "If you do something you love and you do something that makes a difference you will attract around you other people who will share your vision, and that is the secret to success."[32] Koch Industries and MBA Polymers demonstrate that design can be applied through a wide range of products.

SERVICE PROTOTYPING

Service-based businesses provide specific tasks customers want done but don't want to do themselves. Lance A. Bettencourt's advice for true service innovation is to "shift the focus away from the service solution and back to the customer. Rather than asking, 'How are we doing?' a company must ask, 'How is the customer doing?' "[33] Therefore, good service innovation requires empathy. The service provider must be in tune with the deep, and sometimes unspoken, needs of the customer. Pollster Frank Lutz gives us some insight into what people may want in service innovation. In his book, *What Americans Really Want…Really,* he pinpoints five lifestyle attributes that really matter to Americans:

1. More money: Lutz found that products and services that help people make money reduces anxiety for women and provides a greater sense of freedom to men. If you can tie your service to showing how there is a financial benefit for using it or how it helps the customer making money, it will be embraced by the average American.

2. Fewer hassles: Americans always have a lot of responsibilities and perform many roles and duties. Services that make life easier are embraced.

3. More time: People's busy lives are making life more stressful than ever. Lutz said that when people make more money they are afforded the luxury of being able to pay others to perform annoying duties. Time is then freed up time to pursue things that are more satisfying.

4. More choices: Consumers like to have choices when they buy something. They also want to customize their purchases. One of the reasons Apple is so popular is their customers can buy movies, music, and books wherever and whenever they want. Instead of driving to multiple locations, they can peruse Apple iTunes and iBookstore at their convenience, and select the exact offerings they want.

5. No worries: This term is becoming increasingly popular in modern conversations. It roughly translates into meaning you don't have to worry about a disaster happening if you buy the service. Easing anxiety is important to Americans today. Fed Ex's slogan, "When it absolutely, positively has to get there overnight" delivers on meeting this want by today's consumer. Fed Ex customers pay a premium on deliveries for the assurance that a package will reach who it is supposed to when it is supposed to.

Two interesting examples of *service design* that encapsulate what Bettencourt and Lutz discuss come from two industries that most people would not think of when design is mentioned: banking and fast food.

Bank of America has embraced design principles to enhance service at its retail branches. It utilizes experiments to test ideas for improving customer interactions. With 4,500 banking centers in 21 states, it would be very risky to design wholesale changes in the system without first testing out the concepts. In 1999, then CEO Kenneth Lewis oversaw the creation of the Innovation & Development (I&D) Team. The I&D Team ran many of its experiments by reconfiguring 20 branches in Atlanta. Stefan Thomke reported in the *Harvard Business Review* that:

> Five branches were redesigned as 'express centers,' efficient, modernistic buildings where consumer could quickly perform routine transactions such as deposits and withdrawals. Five were turned into 'financial centers,' spacious, relaxed outlets where customers would have access to the trained staff and advanced technologies required for sophisticated services such as stock trading and portfolio management. The remaining ten branches were configured as 'traditional centers,' familiar-looking branches that provided conventional banking services, though often supported by new technologies and redesigned processes.[34]

The company then went through a five-step process to carefully design how the centers would look and work. Once an idea was approved for testing, a prototype branch at the company's headquarters in Charlotte, North Carolina, would be configured where team members could design, rehearse, and measure each step of the experiment. Then when the prototype seemed to work well, it was transferred to experimental sites. Thomke said the principles of design and prototyping were utilized extensively in the service innovations: "By the time an experiment was rolled out in one of the Atlanta branches, most of the kinks had been worked out. The use of the prototype center reflects an important tenet of service experiments: Design and production problems should be worked out offline, in a lab setting without customers, before the service delivery is tested in a live environment."[35] When the new service design worked in its live settings in Atlanta, the innovation was passed along to its other branches across the country.

Another company that has undergone a $2.4 billion design makeover is McDonald's. Ray Kroc' converted a hamburger stand into a multinational food conglomerate by optimizing the burger business to a point never before seen in the food industry. At the end of the twentieth century, the only innovations that were taking place were on the menu. The company needed to find a way to grow sales beyond opening new stores and offering new food. It needed to create a new way of delivering its service. Enter Denis Weil, VP of concept and design for McDonald's. Weil utilized design principles to overhaul the business. He's done it very well. Tim Brown, IDEO's CEO, paid Weil a strong compliment when he said, "There is a mythology that design is a glamorous, personality-led activity. Denis really represents that you don't have to wear a black turtleneck to do it. McDonald's has become one of the few companies that does design management well." How did the company do it? Similar to Bank of America's approach, McDonald's built a 250,000 square foot warehouse in Chicago that houses its Innovation Center. The facility houses three restaurant facsimiles where it can test concepts and experiment. Different concepts are incorporated into the models with target customers interacting with the designs. For example, a mother and son may try to operate a self-order kiosk instead of talking to a person at the counter. Ideas that receive enthusiastic response from customers are brought to stores in the real world. McDonald's president Don Thompson says the company is embracing design to revolutionize the fast-food industry because, "If you have a restaurant that is appealing, contemporary, and relevant, the food tastes better." To this end, the company is using design to transform the restaurants into a new format. Weil describes the new restaurant concept as "a community center. The restaurant in Oak Brook, for example, has been divided into four seating zones, each designed for a different activity—chilling out, working, casual dining, and group events."[36] The new service design has required the company to construct new buildings with chic looks. But customers in the drive through haven't been forgotten about during the design process. Utilizing insights about queuing behavior and information technology, new design in drive-throughs has created a more convenient and fast service. Double customer lanes help process more cars. Many McDonald's stores now utilize automatic salutations and take orders at call centers in India. Automated soda machines make the drinks. Drive-through attendants are freed from the tasks of taking orders and making drinks, and can better focus on customer service. This innovation might appear to have a minimal impact on performance. However, utilizing the redesigned drive-through approach has helped McDonald's to become friendlier and more efficient, two key drivers of customer satisfaction in the fast-food industry. McDonald's is an excellent example of how any service can be improved by understanding and applying the principles of design.

EXPERIENCE PROTOTYPING

Experiences are memorable encounters a company provides to its customers. Perhaps the best company at prototyping experiences is the Walt Disney Company. As we've discussed previously, Walt Disney Imagineering is an amazing corporate unit that dreams up the most original and fun experiences in the theme park industry. They do this through a time-tested design process in which they are given a general project to work on with the executive team. For example, after the company had garnered tremendous success with its Typhoon Lagoon water park at Walt Disney World, it decided to open a second location at the Orlando site. The Imagineers were given the challenge of designing a water park that was different from its predecessor. They let their minds run free and drew many concepts, but none of them caught fire inside the company. Then one day Eric Jacobson looked at the snow dome collection in his office, picked one up, and said, "Too bad we can't make a park out of one of these." Another Imagineer said, "Why not?" and the team began to tinker with the idea of a snowy ski resort in Orlando, Florida. The concept of Blizzard Beach Water Adventure Park was born.[37]

Kevin Lansberry, Senior Vice President of World Wide Travel Operations at Disney, was in the concept pitch meetings for Blizzard Beach and said, "You get this concept shown to you for a snow themed water park in the middle of Florida, and it seems crazy. But then you think about their track record and the many great experiences that the parks have, and you give them the go ahead to take it a little further. The leadership team provides feedback and the Imagineering team advances the design and builds models of the concepts. The concept helps set the feel and back story for the attractions. Every Disney attraction, restaurant, and hotel has a back story that provides a reason for why the attraction is there, and the esthetic details and cast member attire and behavior inside that park are kept consistent with that theme."[38]

The models give the executive team a better understanding of what the attraction can be. The reality of the project's construction costs and timeline affects the design objectives given to the Imagineering team. Typically, there are many adjustments made to the models until they are given the go-ahead to move further in the design process. Once a model is approved, conceptual and working prototypes are made if new ride technology is being developed. All the bugs need to be worked out before a ride is built. Once it seems to work and the Imagineers have gained proof of concept the actual construction takes place. Disney will often use concepts and technologies from past rides as proofs of concept to develop more thrilling rides in other parks. For example, the widely popular ride Test Track at EPCOT places the guest in a sports car that undergoes various road tests. The apex of the experience is when the car leaves the ride building and hits a test track, whips around, turns and hits a top speed of 60 miles per hour down a long straightaway. During this stage of the ride, the car is actually travelling over the EPCOT business headquarters and parking lot, but the guests don't seem to mind because they are flying down a track screaming at the top of their lungs. As a proven concept, Disney is now using the same format to build Cars Land, a new attraction at Disney California Adventure in Anaheim. Cars Land will utilize the Test Track technology, but instead of racing over a parking lot, the ride will take guests through a re-creation of the Southwest landscape which is portrayed in the movie *Cars*. It promises to be the best in both thrills and themes.

Another technique Disney uses to prototype experiences is 3D animation. By creating a virtual world based on the experience you want to put the customer in, you can experiment with different layouts and have the customers "move" through the environment by using their computer mouse. The technology has become so advanced that many programs adhere to the laws of physics and show what happens if different weather conditions or activities take place in the built environment. Designers can manipulate the layout at will to test customer reactions to the designs. Basic 3D software is not costly, but the more advanced programs may require machine language knowledge and animation training to use them to full effect. This technology is now available for any company to use.

TRANSFORMATION PROTOTYPING

Transformations are experiences that help customers realize their aspirations and dreams. In a transformation, the customer is the product. One significant area of society that is focused on transformation is religion, and one of its most successful practitioners is Rick Warren. Rick Warren runs a very successful ministry because he utilized the principles of design and innovation to build his following. When he was in seminary, he attended a conference conducted by the popular but controversial pastor Robert Schuller. Schuller was an innovator himself. When most churches were competing among themselves for members, Schuller targeted non-churchgoers as his audience. He developed messages that were appealing and delivered his sermons at a rented drive-in theatre. Schuller would stand atop the concession stand on Sunday mornings and deliver sermons to the congregation who were sitting in their cars and listening over the window-mounted speakers. He designed church services to be relaxing, easy to attend, and comfortable. It worked, and his popularity grew. In 1977, when his congregation reached 10,000, he built a $16 million mirrored-glass-and-steel church called the Crystal Cathedral. To keep with his church's traditions, the walls were designed so that people could still choose to sit in their cars and see the sermon from the parking lot if they wanted. Schuller enjoyed immense popularity over the ensuing decades.

Rick Warren was impressed by Schuller's methods and wanted to take a similar approach after he graduated from seminary. He was a good student in seminary and was very motivated to build a successful church. He studied the U.S. Census, along with other demographic data, and saw that Orange County, California, was the fastest-growing area of the United States at that time. And the fast-growing part of Orange County was Saddleback Valley. He knew that this was where he should build his church. The Southern Baptist home office granted him the right to build his church there, and he began to plan how he would make it successful. Following Schuller's methods, he targeted non-churchgoers to be his congregation. To better understand the local market, he went from door to door surveying residents in the area. He first asked if they went to church. If they said "yes," he moved onto the next house. But if someone said no, he then asked them "why not?" He also asked the person what they didn't like about church and what an ideal church would be like to draw them in. After amassing a good database of customer information, he sifted through the data to recognize trends and profiles. He then crafted sermons and practices that would appeal to this target market. But before he opened the church, he prototyped the sermons by giving rehearsal services at a local high school. Warren mailed 15,000 letters inviting people from his database to the rehearsal. Sixty people showed up, and the service was a success. With positive feedback, Warren used the basic approach from that prototype to serve as his road map as he built the church. It worked. Today Saddleback Church has 20,000 members.[39]

While you may not have plans to lead a 20,000-member church, your business may be involved in having a substantial impact on people's lives. Prototyping your deliverables is a good practice to use. For example, if you run an executive coaching firm and have new instruments for assessing different leadership traits, ask some of your colleagues or clients if they would take the survey and give you feedback. When the survey is receiving enthusiastic comments and giving people valuable insights, start to include it as part of your paid practice. If part of your job is to give public talks and promote ideas, offer to give the talk for free to a small group outside of your traditional venues. This is what stand-up comedians do to hone their acts. In the book *Talent is Overrated,* Geoff Colvin chronicles how Chris Rock works on a new act in small comedy clubs for months before he performs it in front of a large audience or on television.[40] Rock's flawless delivery on the big stage comes from ongoing practice and refinement in the small clubs spread across the country. If you are in the transformation business, you can take the same approach to your written materials, workshops, and talks.

Summary

This chapter focused on how to get products made. Technology and engineering were covered to assist the reader with gaining a basic technical literacy. The most common disciplines of engineering were explained. Prototyping was discussed in depth. Five steps for prototyping were given. The emergence of the Do It Yourself movement was covered. Guidelines for prototyping commodities, services, experiences, and transformations were also provided. Applying all these design principles and guidelines will help the innovation process become more successful. Good design encompasses technical feasibility, economic viability, and consumer desirability. Meeting these three constraints in the design process will also make it easier when you write an I Plan. The odds of successful innovation go up with good design, and better design, leads to more innovative achievement. This combination of skills will become more important as the marketplace becomes increasingly competitive.

INNOVATION-IN-ACTION

Unleashed Designers Gone Astray

In 2004, LEGO, the company behind the internationally successful and imagination-driving toy bricks, was struggling. Surprisingly, design, its prime competitive advantage, was the root of its problems.

The problems began in the late 1990s. Hoping to extend the LEGO brand, executives promoted new product development that went beyond LEGO's traditional field of play and into a field already occupied by many other competitors. In 2002, for example, the company launched the "Galidor" toy line, which featured action figures and a concurrent Saturday morning cartoon. "Galidor" was a bold departure from LEGO's traditional lines, but it was also significantly similar to what competitors were already doing or had already done. In effect, it just was not LEGO.

Even in its core business, LEGO was struggling. For a while, managers had let designers run free with their ideas. Naturally, designers had seized upon that creative freedom, crafting imaginative but complex models and driving the number of individual LEGO components from 7,000 to 12,400 in just seven years. Unfortunately, the adult designers liked the ideas a lot more than kids. As a result, the uninhibited creative freedom resulted in increased supply costs and decreased sales. The "City" line, once a strength that had generated 13 percent of the company's total revenue, accounted for a negligible 3 percent.

Blame was correctly placed at the feet of the managers, not the designers. Managers' assumption that LEGO would thrive by allowing its designers to operate without constraints was incorrect. It turns out that designers operate better with constraints than without.

Accordingly, LEGO reinstituted constraints on its designers. LEGO put each individual designer's request for components to a vote among all of its designers, with only the top vote-getters winning approval. LEGO also eliminated more than 5,000 rarely used pieces. It also required that designers work directly with marketing managers and manufacturing personnel when designing. The marketers brought designers information on the kinds of components kids wanted and the manufacturing personnel brought an understanding regarding feasibility of production.

In the end, LEGO rediscovered its "mojo." And, by 2008, "City" was back on top, accounting for 20 percent of the company's revenue. The company learned that management of innovation was an essential ingredient of success.

Source: Based on: http://www.businessweek.com/innovate/content/jul2010/id20100722_781838. htm, Accessed on January 10, 2011

Key Terms

3D printing
Business viability
Chemical engineering
Civil engineering
Commodities
Computer Numerically Controlled
(CNC)
Conceptual prototype
Creative economy
D.I.Y.
Drawings
Electrical engineering
Engineering

Industrial design
Industrial engineering
Manufacturability
Mechanical engineering
Model building
Presentation prototype
Rapid prototyping
Service design
Sketches
Technical drawing
Tooling up
Transformation
Work

Discussion Questions

1. Explain the profession of engineering.
2. What structural shift is taking place in today's economy?
3. What role will design play in this economic shift?
4. What basic approaches do engineers apply to problems?
5. What is industrial design?
6. How would you make a model of an idea?
7. What calculations can you perform to get a sense of the business viability of an idea?
8. What is conceptual prototyping?
9. How is rapid prototyping improving the design process?
10. What are the three dimensions of a good prototype?
11. When would you use a presentation prototype?
12 Why is the D.I.Y. movement changing the world?
13. How can design help create experience innovations?
14. How can design help create transformation innovations?
15. What impact do you foresee more widespread design will have on the world?

Endnotes

1. http://www.ted.com/speakers/woody_norris.html
2. Ridley, M. 2010. *The Rational Optimist: How Prosperity Evolves.* New York: Harper Collins Publishers.
3. Florida, R. L. 2002. *The Rise of Creative Class: And How It's Transforming Work, Leisure, Community and Everyday Life.* New York: Basic Books.
4. Pink, D. H. 2005. *A Whole New Mind: Moving from the Information Age to the Conceptual Age.* New York: Riverhead Books.
5. http://www.usatoday.com/money/economy/2010-09-13-buffett-ballmer-immelt_N.htm

6. Furnas, C. C. & McCarthy, J. 1966. *The Engineer.* New York: Time-Life Books.
7. Ibid.
8. Brockman J. B. 2009. *Introduction to Engineering: Modeling and Problem Solving.* New York: John Wiley & Sons, Inc.
9. Oakes, W., Leone, L. & Gunn, C. 2003. *Engineering Your Future.* Wildwood, MO: Great Lakes Press, Inc.
10. www.bls.gov/oco/ocos027.htm
11. Wright, P. 1987. *Spycatcher: A Candid Autobiography of a Senior Intelligence Officer.* New York: Viking Adult.
12. Aspelund, K. 2006. *The Design Process.* New York: Fairchild Publications, Inc.
13. Ibid.
14. Kelley, T. & Littman, J. 2005 *The Ten Faces of Innovation: IDEO's Strategies for Beating the Devil's Advocate & Driving Creativity Throughout Your Organization.* New York: Random House, Inc.
15. Ibid.
16. Sutherland, M. 1999. *Model Making: A Basic Guide.* New York: W.W. Norton & Company, Inc.
17. Lynn, G. S. & Reilly, R. R. 2002. *Blockbusters: The Five Keys to Developing Great New Products.* New York: Harper Collins Publishers.
18. Lafley, A. G. & Charan, R. 2008. *The Game Changer: How You Can Drive Revenue and Profit Growth with Innovation.* New York: Random House.
19. Ibid.
20. Rusten, G. & Bryson, J. 2010. *Industrial Design, Competition, and Globalization.* New York: Palgrave Macmillan.
21. Rogers, G., Wright, M. & Yates, B. 2010. *Gateway to Engineering.* Clifton Park, NY: Delmar, Cengage Learning.
22. Central Saint Martins College of Art & Design. 2007. *Making It.* London, UK: Laurence King Publishing, Ltd.
23. Kivenson, G. 1977. *The Art and Science of Inventing.* New York: Van Nostrand Reinhold Company.
24. Leckart, S. 2010. "Original Models: A Look At Iconic Tech Prototypes," *Wired Magazine,* August 11.
25. Naval Education and Training Program. 2008. "Basic Machines and How They Work," www.bnpublishing.net, August 22.
26. Vasilash, G. S. 2010. "Developing a Better Bus." *Time Compression Magazine,* August 26: 12.
27. Brusic, S. A., Fales, J. F. & Kuetemeyer, V. F. 1999. *Technology: Today and Tomorrow.* New York: Glenco McGraw-Hill.
28. Rogers, G., Wright, M. & Yates, B. 2010. *Gateway to Engineering.* Clifton Park, NY: Delmar, Cengage Learning.
29. Jonathon, G. 1999. *Bill Gates: The Path to the Future.* New York: Avon Books.
30. Auletta, K. 2009. *Googled: The End of the World As We Know It.* New York: Penguin Group.
31. http://www.kochind.com/files/DiscoveryApril2010.pdf
32. http://www.bsu.edu/news/article/0,1370,--50891,00.html
33. Betterncourt, l. 2010. *Service Innovation: How To Go from Customer Needs to Breakthrough Services.* New York: McGraw-Hill Companies, Inc.
34. Thomke, S. April 2003. R & D comes to service, *Harvard Business Review* 81 (4): 70–79.

35. Ibid.
36. Paynter, B. October 2010. "Super Style Me." *Fast Company*, 106
37. Sklar, M. 2010. *Walt Disney: Imagineering.* New York: Disney Enterprises, Inc.
38. Goldsby, M. G. (July 2010). Personal interview.
39. Sheler, J. 2009. *Prophet of Purpose: The Life of Rick Warren.* New York: Random House.
40. Colvin, G. 2008. *Talent is Overrated: What Really Separates World-class Performers from Everybody Else.* New York: Penguin Group.

PART 4

ORGANIZATIONAL INNOVATION
(I-TEAMS)

CHAPTER 7

AUDITING ORGANIZATIONAL INNOVATION

INTRODUCTION

The culture of an organization can be defined in several ways. According to Deal and Kennedy (2000), some of the best definitions of culture include:

- It is made up of the values, beliefs, assumptions, behavioral norms, artifacts, and patterns of behavior.
- A social energy that moves members to act.
- It is a unifying theme that provides meaning, direction, and mobilization for organization members.
- It functions as an organizational control mechanism, informally approving or prohibiting behavior.[1]

These definitions also apply to an innovative organizational culture. In order to strongly support a successful innovative strategy, there is the need for a focus on issues such as risk, reward, and managerial support. For this reason, we are offering unique tools for assessing entrepreneurial and innovative cultures.

ASSESSING INNOVATION IN ORGANIZATIONS

The existence of particular methods for assessing innovative culture has many uses. First, they will serve as a baseline for any organizational change efforts. Second, an assessment instrument can help key into problem points. Specifically, it can help identify the particular organizational factors that may be serving as barriers to innovative activity. Once key problem areas are identified, change will successfully result in an improved culture.

Finally, an assessment instrument can help involve organizational members in the change process. The identification of employee perceptions is integral to the overall change process. There are numerous ways which could be used to assess a firm's innovative culture, each with its own advantages and disadvantages.

The critical nature of innovation and creativity as an important element of entrepreneurship points to the importance of being able to assess the level of innovative factors that exist in the organization. There are three methods which will be discussed here. For clarification purposes, we are separating them into two focus areas: entrepreneurial readiness and innovative readiness.

Entrepreneurial Readiness in Organizations

The Organizational Metaphor

Innovative Readiness in Organizations

Organizational Assessment of Innovation and Creativity
The Corporate Entrepreneurial Assessment Instrument (CEAI)

ENTREPRENEURIAL READINESS

Researchers Morris, Kuratko, and Covin (2011) compared traditional and entrepreneurial cultures. This comparison suggests that companies with entrepreneurial cultures stress such activities as an immediate exchange of ideas, face-to-face interactions, ideas over hierarchy or status, "hard driving" method of operation, and a joy of discovery.[2] As discussed in Chapter 2, research conducted by the authors agrees with Morris et al. (2011) and suggests five factors that foster an entrepreneurial culture. These factors include management support, autonomy, rewards/reinforcement, allocation of time, and organizational boundaries.[3]

THE ORGANIZATIONAL METAPHOR

The *organizational metaphor* assesses a firm's entrepreneurial culture in an informal, nonthreatening way.[4] Besides serving as an assessment method, it also serves as an icebreaker and a way to open creative channels within groups of individuals. A review of the steps described in Table 7.1 shows how participants are asked to take factors of organizational life and translate them into metaphorical images. This allows employees to describe aspects of the firm that are not always positive in a way that is nonthreatening and humorous.

Several examples of images generated by previous training teams are presented in Figure 7.1. These are some common themes that are often depicted in these exercises. For example, in this figure Part A shows a two-headed creature. Groups tend to draw this metaphor when employees perceive that their firm is

TABLE 7-1	Organizational Metaphor
Purpose:	This exercise evokes a description of your organization from a dynamic living organism perspective.
Goal:	To draw an animal that best represents our organization—real or imaginary.
Instructions:	In your group, reach some agreement with answers to the following questions or statements. The answers must be represented on the drawing....no words are allowed!!

1. What animal (real or imaginary) really depicts the organization today?
2. Describe this animal in detail.
3. Is it male, female, neither, both?
4. Describe its temperament—gentle, domestic, wild, unpredictable.
5. What are its feeding habits, living routines, and other habits?
6. Describe its environment; how it succeeds in competition for food?
7. What are its strengths, weaknesses, vulnerabilities?
8. How does it relate to the internal systems which comprise it? Does it use its organs for functions to its advantage or cause harm to it?
9. How would you adapt or change the animal if you had the power to do so and why? (to be explained after the drawing is completed)

moving in two different directions at the same time. Part B depicts a creature with many legs and arms (somewhat similar to an octopus). This metaphor usually reflects a feeling that the firm has many uncoordinated activities that distract the organization from its main purpose. Finally, Part C shows a metaphor where a large lumbering creature (somewhat similar to an elephant) who has one leg chained down. This metaphor generally describes a firm which is slow to respond to changes in the environment and often burdened by a long tradition of red tape and bureaucracy.

While certainly not a systematic assessment of the firm, the organizational metaphor does provide an in-depth view of culture from the perspective of the firm as a living environment. The facilitator's role in this process is to provide participants with an open atmosphere where all comments are accepted in the light of friendly intercourse yet sincere concern for the organization. As suggested earlier, it is a way for individuals to be comfortable and open with each other.

The metaphor process also meshes well with the notion of creativity which is addressed in the training process to be discussed later. Participants usually respond well and the process sets the stage and tone for thinking creatively.

The final benefit of the organizational metaphor is that it primes participants for the more systematic assessment that follows. The metaphor exercise highlights the attributes of the organization that makes up the factors in the survey instrument (the CEAI) which is completed later.

FIGURE 7-1 Organizational Metaphors

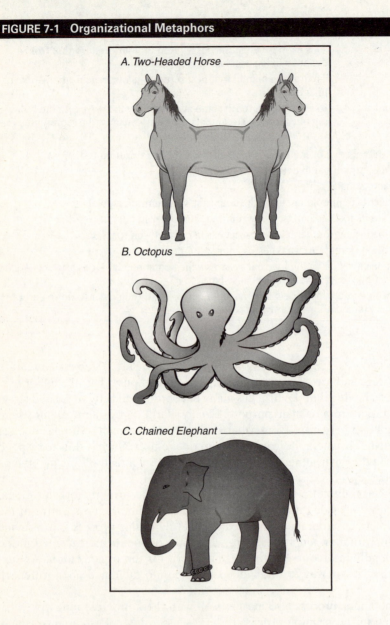

A. Two-Headed Horse

B. Octopus

C. Chained Elephant

INNOVATION READINESS

One of the best ways to raise a good discussion about a firm's "innovative readiness" is to fill out the following questionnaire, called the *Organizational Assessment of Innovation and Creativity*. Just follow the instructions and when you are finished you will be given further instructions on how to score the questionnaire.

ORGANIZATIONAL ASSESSMENT OF INNOVATION & C

In my organization:

Score:

1. People take the time to develop creative ideas and new practices.
2. A lot of time is available to spend on innovation.
3. People are rewarded for innovative thinking even if it doesn't result in an immediate payoff.
4. We don't have time to be creative or innovative.
5. People are encouraged to attend seminars, workshops, and conferences outside the organization.
6. There is plenty of opportunity for training on, and application of, creativity and innovation skills and processes.
7. There are opportunities to get resources (e.g., money, staff help, work time) to support innovative projects.
8. Employees are encouraged to spend time talking with each other about their creative and innovative ideas.
9. We are encouraged to stay in touch with colleagues in other organizations in order to stay abreast of new developments.
10. Most employees have appropriate freedom and discretion to try new approaches or to improve old ones.
11. People who are more creative and innovative are given more responsibility.
12. People who spend time coming up with new and innovative ideas are seen as wasting valuable time that could be used to get their regular work done.
13. We have so much work to do there is little time to be creative or innovative.
14. People aren't encouraged to use their creativity.
15. While we do a good job of reworking and improving past practices, we don't try many really new things.
16. When suggestions for new and innovative ideas are made, they are usually shot down pretty quickly.
17. Most people believe innovative thinking takes too much time to be Worthwhile.
18. People get blamed for being associated with something new that failed.
19. Managers drag their feet on new innovative projects for fear of being associated with a failure and thus limiting their careers.
20. Cross-functional teams routinely work together very effectively, putting the overall goals of the project ahead of their own personal and departmental objectives

In my organization, senior management:

Score:

1. Drives innovation and expects everyone to join in
2. Sends a clear message that the organization is committed to innovation
3. Executes the same innovative behaviors they expect of others
4. Has clearly articulated the goals and strategies of the organization to all employees
5. Acts on innovative ideas regularly

6. Has included clear innovative performance goals in our strategic plan and how we will achieve them

7. Welcomes employees' unsolicited ideas on new ways to do things

In my organization, employees are expected to:

Score:

1. Get their routine work done first and foremost, always before pursuing new developments

2. Bring their new and innovative ideas forward

3. Try new ways for solving problems

4. Share their ideas with others so they can be developed further

5. Leave creative and innovative thinking to those who are hired for it

6. Follow closely the work policies and procedures laid out for them and not stray from them

SCORING INSTRUCTIONS

There are certain items in the questionnaire, whose scores must be reversed. These are the following:

In the first section, called "In my organization," the scores for statements 4, 12, 13, 14, 15, 16, 17, 18, and 19 must be reversed. For example, if you gave statement 4 (we don't have time to be creative or innovative), a score of "2," you must reverse this to become a score of "8." If you scored it "6," you must reverse it to a score of "4."

In the second section, entitled "In my organization, senior management:" none of the seven items are reversed.

In the third section, entitled "In my organization, employees are expected to:" the scores for statements 5 (leave creative and innovative thinking to those who are hired for it) and 6 (follow closely the work policies and procedures laid out for them and not stray from them) must be reversed prior to totaling.

Once you have made these reversals, simply add up the scores to create a grand total of the three sections.

HOW TO INTERPRET THE SCORES

The highest possible overall score combining the three sections is 297. The lowest possible overall score is 33. If you scored your organization 200 or higher, you probably have a very entrepreneurial culture. If you scored 99 or lower, you probably have a culture that discourages entrepreneurship. If your score is somewhere between 100 and 199, your entrepreneurial culture is somewhere between very strong and very weak, with room for improvement.

HOW TO BENEFIT FROM THIS QUESTIONNAIRE

The way to achieve maximum benefit from this questionnaire is to discuss your scores with others in your organization. See if your perceptions are similar or different from others. Discuss the strong points of your culture, and the weak points. Create suggestions for improving on the weak points and building on the strong points to create a stronger entrepreneurial culture in your organization.

CORPORATE ENTREPRENEURIAL ASSESSMENT INSTRUMENT

Another assessment instrument that has proven successful in research circles is the *Corporate Entrepreneurial Assessment Instrument* (CEAI) developed by Donald F. Kuratko at Indiana University and Jeffrey S. Hornsby at Kansas State University. It is one of the few research-based surveys that attempts to measure the innovative readiness within an organization. While the instrument has been through a number of iterations since its first publication (Kuratko, Montagno & Hornsby, 1990),[5] the development of the survey items are extensively based on the research and writings to date (Hornsby, Kuratko & Zahra, 2002; Hornsby, Kuratko, Shepherd, & Bott, 2009).[6] The remainder of this section will provide a summary of the literature used to support item development, describe how the instrument was empirically derived, and outline the steps necessary to utilize the instrument for assessing innovative culture within organization.

RESEARCH ON ORGANIZATIONAL ELEMENTS FOR INNOVATION

Research has examined the organizational elements that affect (either by promoting or impeding) the breadth and depth of entrepreneurial (innovative) actions that are taken within the firm at a point in time to pursue corporate entrepreneurship (Zahra, 1991; Zahra & Covin, 1995; Zahra, Nielsen & Bogner, 1999).[7] This research has studied different internal organizational factors, including the firm's incentive and control systems (Sathe, 1985), culture (Brazeal, 1993; Hisrich & Peters, 1986; Kanter, 1985),[8] organizational structure (Covin & Slevin, 1991; Dess et al., 1999; Naman & Slevin, 1993),[9] and managerial support (Kuratko, Hornsby, Naffziger & Montagno, 1993; Stevenson & Jarillo, 1990).[10] Because they affect the nature of the firm's internal environment, these factors, both individually and in combination, are recognized as internal elements of the innovative behavior on which corporate innovation is built. An internal environment supportive of innovation tends to have strong elements of innovative behavior, while an environment that dismisses innovation and its importance yields weak elements of innovative behavior (Hornsby, Kuratko & Zahra, 2002).[11]

Other research has contributed to our understanding of the organizational elements of innovative behavior. Miller (1983),[12] for example, correlated several macro-level variables (e.g., company type, environment, structure, and decision making) with the intensity of entrepreneurial activity. Quinn (1985)[13] identified several actions large corporations can take to develop the right "atmosphere" for entrepreneurial behavior to flourish. Some of these actions are oriented to changing the firm's structure in ways that will facilitate innovation. Souder (1981)[14] found a positive relationship between six management practices and performance for 100 new ventures in 17 organizations. Fry (1987) and Kanter (1985)[15] also identified a set of factors that were associated with successful corporate innovation, while Schuler (1986)[16] outlined essential structural practices that firms need to use to facilitate entrepreneurial (innovative) actions.

Burgelman (1983 a & b) argued that corporate innovation (entrepreneurship) can take two primary forms—autonomous strategic behavior and induced strategic behavior. As an organizational antecedent, induced strategic behavior is a top-down process in which the firm's current strategy and structure shape the entrepreneurial actions taken to develop product, process, and administrative innovations. Autonomous strategic behavior is a bottom-up process in which product champions pursue new ideas, often through a political process, by means of which they develop and coordinate activities associated with an innovation until it achieves success. A top-level managerial decision to encourage risk taking and not to punish failure is a strong antecedent of autonomous strategic behavior on the part of managers' behavior as well as others' in the firm. An important contribution of Burgelman's (1983 a & b; 1984)[17] work is the recognition of the effect of the firm's culture, strategy, and structure as antecedents of autonomous strategic behavior—behavior that is grounded in innovative actions. Other research (e.g., Floyd & Wooldridge, 1990, 1992, 1994)[18] has recognized the importance of managers in enhancing and cultivating autonomous strategic behavior. Thus, top-level managers should verify that organizational antecedents are in place that will elicit and support value-creating entrepreneurial behavior (in the form of autonomous strategic behavior) on the part of managers. See Table 7-2 for a compilation of the research that fostered the key elements.

TABLE 7-2 Research on Organizational Elements for Innovation

Factor	Research Citations
Rewards/ Reinforcement	Kanter, 1985; Sathe, 1985; Block & Ornati, 1987; Fry, 1987; Sykes, 1992; Barringer & Milkovich, 1998; and Kuratko, Ireland & Hornsby, 2001; Kuratko, Hornsby & Goldsby, 2004; Ireland, Kuratko & Morris, 2006a, b; Hornsby, Kuratko, Shepherd & Bott, 2009.
Top Management Support	Quinn, 1985; Hisrich & Peters, 1986; MacMillan, Block & Narasimha, 1986; Sathe, 1989; Sykes & Block, 1989; Stevenson & Jarillo, 1990; Damanpour, 1991; Kuratko, et al, 1993; Pearce, Kramer & Robbins, 1997; Antoncic & Hisrich, 2001; and Kuratko, et al., 2001; Kuratko, Ireland, Covin & Hornsby, 2005; Hornsby, Kuratko, Shepherd & Bott, 2009; Ireland, Covin & Kuratko, 2009.
Resources/Time Availability	Kanter, 1985; Sathe, 1985; Burgelman & Sayles, 1986; Hisrich & Peters, 1986; Sykes, 1986; Sykes & Block, 1989; Damanpour, 1991; Stopford & Baden-Fuller, 1994; Slevin & Covin, 1997; Kuratko, Hornsby & Goldsby, 2007; Hornsby, Kuratko, Shepherd & Bott, 2009; Ireland, Covin & Kuratko, 2009.
Organizational Boundaries	Hisrich & Peters, 1986; Schuler, 1986; Sykes & Block, 1989; Guth & Ginsberg, 1990; Covin & Slevin, 1991; Damanpour, 1991; Zahra, 1991; Brazeal, 1993; Hornsby, et al, 1993; Hornsby et al, 1999; Antoncic & Hisrich, 2001; Hornsby et al, 2002; Hornsby, Kuratko, Shepherd & Bott, 2009.
Work Discretion (Autonomy)	Burgelman, 1983, 1984; Kanter, 1985; Quinn, 1985; Sathe, 1985; MacMillan, Block & Narasimha, 1986; Ellis & Taylor, 1988; Sathe, 1989; Sykes & Block, 1989; Stopford & Baden-Fuller, 1994; Hornsby et al, 1999; and Hornsby et al, 2002; Hornsby, Kuratko, Shepherd & Bott, 2009.

Note: References for the citations in Table 7-2:

Antonic, B. & Hisrich, R. D. 2001. Intrapreneurship: Constructive refinement and cross-cultural validation, *Journal of Business Venturing* 16: 495–527.

Barringer, M. W. & Milkovich, G. T. 1998. A theoretical exploration of the adoption and design of flexible benefit plans: A case of human resource innovation, *Academy of Management Review* 23: 305–324.

Block, Z. & Ornati, O.A. 1987. Compensating corporate venture managers, *Journal of Business Venturing* 2: 41–51.

Brazeal, D. V. 1993. Organizing for internally developed corporate ventures, *Journal of Business Venturing* 8: 75–90.

Burgelman, R. A. 1983(a). A process model of internal corporate venturing in the diversified major firm, *Administrative Science Quarterly* 28: 223–244.

Burgelman, R. A. 1983(b). Corporate entrepreneurship and strategic management: Insights from a process study, *Management Science* 23: 1349–1363.

Burgelman, R. & Sayles, L. 1986. *Inside corporate innovation: Strategy, structure, and managerial skills.* New York: The Free Press.

Burgelman, R. A. 1984. Designs for corporate entrepreneurship in established firms, *California Management Review* 26 (3): 154–166.

Burgelman, R. A. 1994. Fading memories: A process theory of strategic business exit in dynamic environments, *Administrative Science Quarterly* 39: 24–57.

Covin, J. G. & Slevin, D. P. 1991. A conceptual model of entrepreneurship as firm behavior, *Entrepreneurship Theory and Practice* 16 (1): 7–25.

Damanpour, F. 1991. Organizational innovation: A meta-analysis of effects of determinant and moderators, *Academy of Management Journal* 34: 355–390.

Ellis, R. J. & Taylor, N. T. 1988. Success and failure in internal venture strategy: An exploratory study. Frontiers of Entrepreneurship Research. Wellesley, MA: Babson College.

Fry, A. 1987. The Post-it-Note: An intrapreneurial success, *SAM Advanced Management Journal* 52 (3): 4–9.

Guth, W. D. & Ginsberg, A. 1990. Corporate entrepreneurship, *Strategic Management Journal* 11 (Special Issue): 5–15.

Hisrich, R. D. & Peters, M. P. 1986. Establishing a new business venture unit within a firm, *Journal of Business Venturing* 1: 307–322.

Hitt, M. A., Ireland, R. D., Camp, S. M. & Sexton, D. L. 2001. Strategic entrepreneurship: Entrepreneurial strategies for wealth creation, *Strategic Management Journal* 22 (Special Issue): 479–491.

Hornsby, J.S., Naffziger, D.W., Kuratko, D.F. & Montagno, R.V. 1993. An interactive model of the corporate entrepreneurship process, *Entrepreneurship Theory and Practice,* 17 (2): 29–37.

Hornsby, J. S., Kuratko, D. F. & Montagno, R. V. 1999. Perception of internal factors for corporate entrepreneurship: A comparison of Canadian and U.S. managers, *Entrepreneurship Theory and Practice* 24 (2): 9–24.

Hornsby, J. S., Kuratko, D. F., & Zahra, S. A. 2002. Middle managers' perception of the internal environment for corporate entrepreneurship: Assessing a measurement scale, *Journal of Business Venturing* 17: 49–63.

Hornsby, J. S., Kuratko, D. F., Shepherd, D. A., & Bott, J. P. 2009. Managers' Corporate Entrepreneurial Actions: Examining Perception and Position, *Journal of Business Venturing* 24 (3): 236–247

Ireland, R. D., Covin, J. G., & Kuratko, D. F. 2009. Conceptualizing Corporate Entrepreneurship Strategy, *Entrepreneurship Theory and Practice*, 33 (1): 19–46;

Ireland, R. D., Kuratko, D. F., & Morris, M. H., 2006a. A health audit for corporate entrepreneurship: Innovation at all levels—Part I, *Journal of Business Strategy* 27 (1): 10–17.

Ireland, R. D., Kuratko, D. F., & Morris, M. H., 2006b. A health audit for corporate entrepreneurship: Innovation at all levels—Part 2, *Journal of Business Strategy* 27 (2): 21–30.

Kanter, R. M. 1985. Supporting innovation and venture development in established companies, *Journal of Business Venturing* 1: 47–60.

Kuratko, D. F., Hornsby, J. S., Naffziger, D. W. & Montagno, R. V. 1993. Implementing entrepreneurial thinking in established organizations, *SAM Advanced Management Journal* 58 (1): 28–33.

Kuratko, D. F., Ireland, R. D. & Hornsby, J. S. 2001. Improving firm performance through entrepreneurial actions: Acordia's corporate entrepreneurship strategy, *Academy of Management Executive* 16 (4): 60–71.

Kuratko, D. F., Ireland, R. D., Covin, J. G. & Hornsby, J. S. 2005. A model of middle-level managers' entrepreneurial behavior, *Entrepreneurship Theory and Practice* 29 (6): 699–716.

Kuratko, D. F., Hornsby, J. S. & Goldsby, M.G. 2004. Sustaining corporate entrepreneurship: A proposed model of perceived implementation/outcome comparisons at the organizational and individual levels, *International Journal of Entrepreneurship and Innovation* 5 (2): 77–89.

Kuratko, D. F., Hornsby, J. S., & Goldsby, M. G. 2007. The relationship of stakeholder salience, organizational posture, and entrepreneurial intensity to corporate entrepreneurship, *Journal of Leadership and Organizational Studies* 13(4): 56–72; MacMillan, I. C., Block, Z. & Narasimha, P.N. Subba. 1986. Corporate venturing: Alternatives, obstacles encountered, and experience effects, *Journal of Business Venturing* 1: 177–191.

Pearce, J. A., Kramer, T. R. & Robbins, D. K. 1997. Effects of managers' entrepreneurial behavior on subordinates, *Journal of Business Venturing* 12: 147–160.

Quinn, J. B. 1985. Managing innovation: Controlled Chaos, *Harvard Business Review* 63 (3): 73–84.

Sathe, V. 1989. Fostering entrepreneurship in large diversified firm, *Organizational Dynamics* 18 (1): 20–32.

Sathe, V. 1985. Managing an entrepreneurial dilemma: Nurturing entrepreneurship and control in large corporations. In *Frontiers of Entrepreneurship Research* (pp. 636–656). Wellesley, MA: Babson College.

Schuler, R. S. 1986. Fostering and facilitating entrepreneurship in organizations: Implications for organization structure and human resource management practices, *Human Resource Management* 25: 607–629.

Slevin, D. P. & Covin, J. G. 1997. Time, growth, complexity, and transitions: Entrepreneurial challenges for the future, *Entrepreneurship Theory and Practice* 22: 43–68.

Stevenson, H. H. & Jarillo, J. C. 1990. A paradigm of entrepreneurship: Entrepreneurial management, *Strategic Management Journal* 11 (Special Issue): 17–27.

Stopford, J. M. & Baden-Fuller, C. W. F. 1994. Creating corporate entrepreneurship, *Strategic Management Journal* 15: 521–536.

Sykes, H. B. 1992. Incentive compensation for corporate venture personnel, *Journal of Business Venturing* 7: 253–265.

Sykes, H. B. 1986. The anatomy of a corporate venturing program, *Journal of Business Venturing* 1: 275–293.

Sykes, H. B. & Block, Z. 1989. Corporate venturing obstacles: Sources and solutions, *Journal of Business Venturing* 4: 159–167.

Zahra, S. A. 1991. Predictors and financial outcomes of corporate entrepreneurship: An exploratory study, *Journal of Business Venturing* 6: 259–286.

While the literature illustrates a wide variety of entrepreneurial factors, there are a few elements that are consistent throughout the writings in this field. One is the appropriate use of rewards. Theorists stress that any reward system, in order to be effective, must consider goals, feedback, emphasis on individual responsibility, and rewards based on results. A second element is management support, which relates to willingness of managers to facilitate innovation projects. Resources (while include time) and their availability are a third element recognized in many of the writings. Employees must perceive the availability of resources for innovative activities. A fourth consistent element is organizational structure, which is identified in various ways yet always appears as an essential factor. Finally, risk taking appears as a consistent element in that employees and management must have a willingness to take a risk and have a tolerance for failure should it occur.

Much of our understanding of the impact of organizational architecture on individual-level innovative behavior is based on the empirical research of Kuratko and his colleagues (Kuratko, Montagno & Hornsby, 1990; Hornsby, Kuratko & Montagno, 1999; Hornsby, Kuratko & Zahra, 2002; Kuratko, Ireland, Covin & Hornsby, 2005; Hornsby, Kuratko, Shepherd & Bott, 2009).[19] In the Kuratko et al. (1990) study, results from factor analysis showed that what had been theoretically argued and hypothesized to be five conceptually distinct factors that would elicit and support innovative behavior on the part of first- and middle-level managers (top management support for CE, reward and resource availability, organizational structure and boundaries, risk taking, and time availability) were actually only three in number. More specifically, based on how items loaded, they concluded that three factors—management support, organizational structure, and reward and resource availability—were important influences on the development of an organizational climate in which innovative behavior on the part of first- and middle-level managers could be expected. Although this study's results did not support the hypothesized five-factor model, the findings established the multidimensionality of antecedents of managers' innovative behavior.[20]

To extend this earlier work, Hornsby et al. (1999) conducted an empirical study designed to explore the effect of organizational culture on innovative behavior in a sample of Canadian and U.S. firms. In particular, Hornsby et al. (1999) wanted to determine if organizational culture creates variance in innovative behavior on the part of Canadian and U.S. managers. The results based on data collected from all levels of management showed no significant differences between Canadian and U.S. managers' perceptions of the importance of five factors—management support, work discretion, rewards/reinforcement, time availability, and organizational boundaries—as antecedents to their innovative behavior.[21] These findings partially validate those reported by Kuratko et al. (1990) and extend the importance of organizational antecedents of managers' innovative behavior into companies based in a second (albeit similar) national culture.

Hornsby et al. (2002)[22] developed the Corporate Entrepreneurship Assessment Instrument to partially replicate and disentangle previously reported findings. The instrument featured 48 Likert-style questions that were used to assess antecedents of innovative behavior. In this study, only middle-level managers, from both Canada and the United States, were surveyed. Results from factor analyses suggested that there are five stable antecedents of middle-level managers' entrepreneurial behavior:

1. *management support* (the willingness of top-level managers to facilitate and promote innovative behavior, including championing of innovative ideas and providing necessary resources),

2. *work discretion/autonomy* (top-level managers' commitment to tolerate failure, provide decision-making latitude and freedom from excessive oversight, and delegate authority and responsibility),

3. *rewards/reinforcement* (development and use of systems that reward based on performance, highlight significant achievements, and encourage pursuit of challenging work),

4. *time availability* (evaluating workloads to assure time to pursue innovations and structuring jobs to support efforts to achieve short- and long-term organizational goals), and

5. *organizational boundaries* (precise explanations of outcomes expected from organizational work and development of mechanisms for evaluating, selecting, and using innovations).

Numerous studies have been conducted by the authors to assess the reliability and validity of the CEAI. Research has established that the extent to which these factors are used may be assessed using a reliable (Rutherford & Holt, 2007)[23] and valid (Holt, Rutherford & Clohessy (2007)[24] measure—the Corporate Entrepreneurship Assessment Instrument.

USING THE CEAI FOR INNOVATIVE READINESS

When interpreting the results of the CEAI, keep in mind that higher scores on the CEAI factors are related to increased entrepreneurial (innovative) activity. With this in mind, the application of the instrument in an organization could also serve to point out problem areas for further attention by upper management. The CEAI is intended for those employees in managerial, professional, and technical positions. While the CEAI could be used for operational workers, most organizations have not given those workers the mandate to act in an innovative manner. The specific steps for using the CEAI are described below.

Step 1: Distributing the Survey Instrument: Depending on the size of your organization all managers can be surveyed or a random sampling of managers can be utilized.

Step 2: Individual Scoring: In order to provide immediate feedback to the employee regarding his or her perceptions of the firm's innovative culture, each participant should be allowed to score the survey. Each scale in the assessment questionnaire has its own scoring box where employees can put in their answers and calculate an average score for each scale. Items 21, 36, 39, 40, and 46 are reverse-scored in order to prevent a response set in the positive direction.

Step 3: Organizational Scoring: In order for the firm to assess their overall innovative culture, each participant's scoring sheets should be collected. However, it is extremely important that all information be kept confidential since some of the items are somewhat sensitive regarding the employees' feelings concerning management. The organization's score on each scale is simply calculated by averaging respondent scores. Each employee's scores should be verified before these calculations take place.

Step 4: Interpreting the Scores: The highest score possible for any scale is a 5 and the lowest is a 1. Since the scores are based on averaging across employees it is virtually impossible for the organization to score a perfect 1 or 5 on any scale. In general, the higher the score, the more the organization's culture supports these types of activities.

Step 5: Improving Your Innovative Culture: This step is optional but may help managers take active steps toward improving the firm's innovative (entrepreneurial) culture. Each manager or group of managers could brainstorm and identify one to three suggestions that could improve the organization's scores in problem areas.

CEAI ASSESSMENT

CORPORATE ENTREPRENEURSHIP ASSESSMENT INSTRUMENT

We are interested in learning about how you perceive your workplace and organization. Please read the following items. On the line to the left of each item, please indicate how much you agree or disagree with each of the statements. If you strongly agree, write the number "5." If you strongly disagree, write the number "1." There are no right or wrong answers to these questions so please be as honest and thoughtful as possible in your responses. All responses will be kept strictly confidential. Thank you for your cooperation.

5—Strongly Agree   4—Agree   3—Not Sure   2—Disagree
1—Strongly Disagree

Section 1: Management Support for Corporate Entrepreneurship

1. My organization is quick to use improved work methods.
2. My organization is quick to use improved work methods that are developed by workers.
3. In my organization, developing one's own ideas is encouraged for the improvement of the corporation.
4. Upper management is aware and very receptive to my ideas and suggestions.
5. A promotion usually follows from the development of new and innovative ideas.
6. Those employees who come up with innovative ideas on their own often receive management encouragement for their activities.
7. The "doers on projects" are allowed to make decisions without going through elaborate justification and approval procedures.
8. Senior managers encourage innovators to bend rules and rigid procedures in order to keep promising ideas on track.

9. Many top managers have been known for their experience with the innovation process.

10. Money is often available to get new project ideas off the ground.

11. Individuals with successful innovative projects receive additional rewards and compensation beyond the standard reward system for their ideas and efforts.

12. There are several options within the organization for individuals to get financial support for their innovative projects and ideas.

13. People are often encouraged to take calculated risks with ideas around here.

14. Individuals risk takers are often recognized for their willingness to champion new projects, whether eventually successful or not.

15. The term *risk taker* is considered a positive attribute for people in my work area.

16. This organization supports many small and experimental projects, realizing that some will undoubtedly fail.

17. An employee with a good idea is often given free time to develop that idea.

18. There is considerable desire among people in the organization for generating new ideas without regard for crossing departmental or functional boundaries.

19. People are encouraged to talk to employees in other departments of this organization.

Section 2: Work Discretion

20. I feel that I am my own boss and do not have to double-check all of my decisions with someone else.

21. |Harsh criticism and punishment result from mistakes made on the job.

22. This organization provides the chance to be creative and try my own methods of doing the job.

23. This organization provides the freedom to use my own judgment.

24. This organization provides the chance to do something that makes use of my abilities.

25. I have the freedom to decide what I do on my job.

26. It is basically my own responsibility to decide how my job gets done.

27. I almost always get to decide what I do on my job.

28. I have much autonomy on my job and am left on my own to do my own work.

29. I seldom have to follow the same work methods or steps for doing my major tasks from day to day.

Section 3: Rewards/Reinforcement

30. My manager helps me get my work done by removing obstacles and roadblocks.

31. The rewards I receive are dependent upon my work on the job.

32. My supervisor will increase my job responsibilities if I am performing well in my job.

33. My supervisor will give me special recognition if my work performance is especially good.

34. My manager would tell his/her boss if my work was outstanding.

35. There is a lot of challenge in my job.

Section 4: Time Availability

36. During the past three months, my workload kept me from spending time on developing new ideas.

37. I always seem to have plenty of time to get everything done.

38. I have just the right amount of time and workload to do everything well.

39. My job is structured so that I have very little time to think about wider organizational problems.

40. I feel that I am always working with time constraints on my job.

41. My coworkers and I always find time for long-term problem solving.

Section 5: Organizational Boundaries

42. In the past three months, I have always followed standard operating procedures or practices to do my major tasks.

43. There are many written rules and procedures that exist for doing my major tasks.

44. On my job I have do doubt of what is expected of me.

45. There is little uncertainty in my job.

46. During the past year, my immediate supervisor discussed by work performance with me frequently.

47. My job description clearly specifies that standards of performance on which my job is evaluated.

48. I clearly know what level of work performance is expected from me in terms of amount, quality, and timelines of output.

Scoring Scales

Scale 1: Management Support for Entrepreneurship

Statement

1	1	2	3	4	5
2	1	2	3	4	5
3	1	2	3	4	5
4	1	2	3	4	5
5	1	2	3	4	5
6	1	2	3	4	5
7	1	2	3	4	5
8	1	2	3	4	5
9	1	2	3	4	5
10	1	2	3	4	5
11	1	2	3	4	5
12	1	2	3	4	5
13	1	2	3	4	5
14	1	2	3	4	5

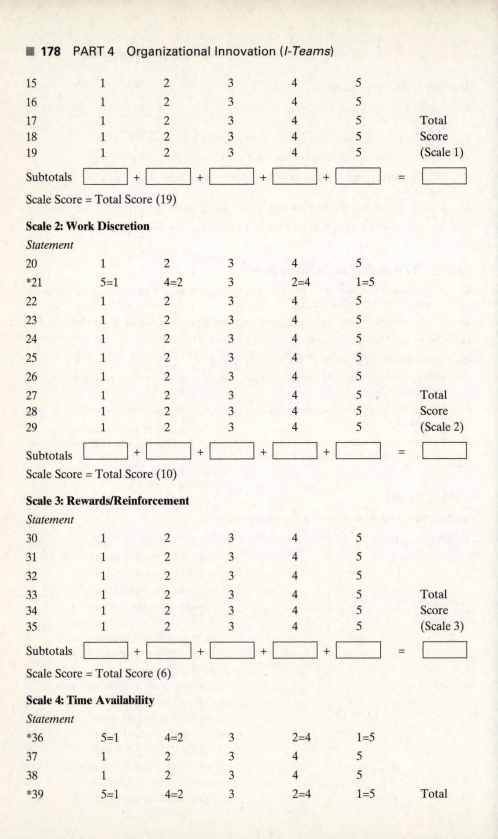

15	1	2	3	4	5	
16	1	2	3	4	5	
17	1	2	3	4	5	Total
18	1	2	3	4	5	Score
19	1	2	3	4	5	(Scale 1)

Subtotals [   ] + [   ] + [   ] + [   ] + [   ] = [   ]

Scale Score = Total Score (19)

Scale 2: Work Discretion

Statement

20	1	2	3	4	5	
*21	5=1	4=2	3	2=4	1=5	
22	1	2	3	4	5	
23	1	2	3	4	5	
24	1	2	3	4	5	
25	1	2	3	4	5	
26	1	2	3	4	5	
27	1	2	3	4	5	Total
28	1	2	3	4	5	Score
29	1	2	3	4	5	(Scale 2)

Subtotals [   ] + [   ] + [   ] + [   ] + [   ] = [   ]

Scale Score = Total Score (10)

Scale 3: Rewards/Reinforcement

Statement

30	1	2	3	4	5	
31	1	2	3	4	5	
32	1	2	3	4	5	
33	1	2	3	4	5	Total
34	1	2	3	4	5	Score
35	1	2	3	4	5	(Scale 3)

Subtotals [   ] + [   ] + [   ] + [   ] + [   ] = [   ]

Scale Score = Total Score (6)

Scale 4: Time Availability

Statement

*36	5=1	4=2	3	2=4	1=5	
37	1	2	3	4	5	
38	1	2	3	4	5	
*39	5=1	4=2	3	2=4	1=5	Total

*40	5=1	4=2	3	2=4	1=5	Score
41	1	2	3	4	5	(Scale 4)

Subtotals [   ] + [   ] + [   ] + [   ] + [   ] = [   ]

Scale Score = Total Score (6)

Scale 5: Organizational Boundaries

Statement

*42	5=1	4=2	3	2=4	1=5	
*43	5=1	4=2	3	2=4	1=5	
*44	5=1	4=2	3	2=4	1=5	
*45	5=1	4=2	3	2=4	1=5	
46	1	2	3	4	5	Total
*47	5=1	4=2	3	2=4	1=5	Score
*48	5=1	4=2	3	2=4	1=5	(Scale 5)

Subtotals [   ] + [   ] + [   ] + [   ] + [   ] = [   ]

Scale Score = Total Score (7)

*Item 21 revised scores.
*Items 36, 39, 40 are revised scores
*Items 42, 43, 44 , 45, 47, and 48 are revised scores
Source: CEAI is adapted from original work done by D. F. Kuratko, R. M. Montagno, and J. S. Hornsby, 1990. "Developing an Entrepreneurial Assessment Instrument for an Effective Corporate Entrepreneurial Environment," *Strategic Management Journal*, 11: 49–58; and J. S. Hornsby, D. F. Kuratko, and S. A. Zahra, "Middle Managers' Perception of the Internal Environment for Corporate Entrepreneurship: Assessing a Measurement Scale," *Journal of Business Venturing*, 17, 2002: 49–63.

Essentially concerned with a firm's "innovative readiness," the CEAI can significantly benefit organizations as managers search for ways to initiate innovation inside the organization. For managers, the CEAI provides an indication of a firm's likelihood of being able to successfully implement an innovation strategy. It highlights areas of the work environment that should be the focus of ongoing development efforts. Furthermore, the CEAI can be used as an assessment tool for evaluating corporate training needs in entrepreneurship and innovation. Determining these training needs can set the stage for improving managers' skills and increasing their sensitivity to the challenges of prioritizing and supporting corporate innovation activity. Beyond this, the CEAI can be used at different points in time to measure the actual change in perceptions by managers within the organization. Perceptions are critical to the reality that exists in the organization.

The perception of managers at the executive, middle, and operating levels regarding the role of innovation within the firm and what the firm is explicitly doing to reinforce innovative behavior is critical. Managers are most likely to engage in innovative behavior when the organizational antecedents to that behavior are well designed and they are aware of their existence.[25]Individuals assess their innovative capacities in reference to what they perceive to be a set of organizational resources, opportunities, and obstacles related to innovative activity. Determining that the value of innovative behavior exceeds that of other behaviors leads managers to champion, synthesize, facilitate, and implement innovative behavior.

IMPROVING YOUR FIRM'S INNOVATIVE READINESS

Once the scores of the CEAI have been calculated for the organization as a whole, teams can be formulated to outline suggestions for improvements on each of the dimensions. Teams can use the following template for identifying one to three suggestions that could lead to higher scores on the five innovation factors.

I. Management Support for Entrepreneurship

    1.

    _____

    2.

    _____

    3.

    _____

II. Work Discretion

    1.

    _____

    2.

    _____

    3.

    _____

III. Rewards/Reinforcement

    1.

    _____

    2.

    _____

    3.

    _____.

IV. Time Availability

    1.

    _____

    2.

    _____

    3.

    _____

V. Organizational Boundaries

1.
_____

2.
_____

3.
_____

A full discussion of these suggestions and how they might improve the specific element in the organization is another critical step in establishing employee support for the innovative strategy. It also enhances employees' perceptions of the commitment that management displays toward the effective implementation of innovative actions.

DIAGNOSING THE INTERNAL "READINESS" FOR CORPORATE INNOVATION

Completing the Corporate Entrepreneurial Assessment Instrument is an excellent diagnostic tool used to assess, evaluate, and manage the firm's internal work environment in ways that support innovative behavior. When using the CEAI to inventory the firm's current situation regarding innovation, managers identify parts of the firm's structure, control systems, human resource management systems, and culture that inhibit and parts that facilitate entrepreneurial (innovative) behavior as the foundation for successfully implementing a corporate innovation strategy.

The CEAI instrument consists of 48 Likert-style questions. The instrument has been shown to be psychometrically sound as a viable means for assessing areas requiring attention and improvement in order to reach the goals sought when using a corporate innovative strategy. The instrument can be used to develop a profile of a firm across the dimensions and internal climate variables that we discussed earlier. Low scores in an area of the CEAI suggest the need for training and development activities to enhance the firm's readiness for innovative behavior.

The CEAI can significantly benefit organizations and is of value to managers seeking to develop a corporate innovation strategy. Why? Because the instrument provides an indication of a firm's likelihood of being able to successfully implement an innovation strategy. It highlights areas of the internal work environment that should be the focus of ongoing design and development efforts. Further, the CEAI can be used as an assessment tool for evaluating corporate training needs with respect to entrepreneurship and innovation. Determining these training needs sets the stage for improving managers' skills and increasing their sensitivity to the challenges of eliciting and then supporting innovative behavior.

Managers and employees across a firm are most likely to engage in innovative behavior when the organizational antecedents to that behavior are well designed and are widely known and accepted. Individuals assess their innovative capacities in reference to what they perceive to be a set of organizational resources, opportunities, and obstacles related to innovative activity. Determining that the value of innovative behavior exceeds that of other organizational behaviors causes managers to continuously champion, facilitate, and nurture innovative behavior.

CREATE AN UNDERSTANDING OF THE CORPORATE INNOVATION PROCESSES

Having assessed the degree to which its internal work environment supports innovation and the innovative behavior, the next step in the innovation audit determines the degree to which a corporate innovation strategy and innovative behavior are understood and accepted by the employees. A corporate innovation strategy is successfully implemented only when all affected individuals are committed to it. Of course, commitment to any strategy increases when those involved with and affected by a strategy are fully aware of the outcomes being sought by using that strategy. The readiness of each employee to display innovative behavior should be realistically assessed. Actions to enhance innovative skills of employees should then be set into motion. These commitments and processes help to shape a common vision around the importance of an innovative strategy and the innovative behavior that is critical to its successful use.

Our experience suggests that firms should develop a program with the purpose of helping all parties who will be affected by an innovative strategy to understand the value of the innovative behavior that the firm is requesting of them as the foundation for a successful corporate innovation strategy. To illustrate how this can be accomplished, we outline the elements of this type of training program.

A CORPORATE INNOVATION EMPLOYEE DEVELOPMENT PROGRAM.

1. *Introduction to Corporate Innovation*—A review of managerial and organizational behavior concepts, definitions of corporate innovation and a corporate innovation strategy, examination of the innovation in established companies, and a review of several innovative cases.
2. *Innovative Breakthroughs*—An overview of innovative breakthroughs in the company and in other organizations. Best practices in terms of highly innovative initiatives can be reviewed. This challenges participants to think innovatively and emphasizes the need to take risk and be proactive in order to do so. Importantly, employees must be given a reference point in terms of the types of innovative behaviors that are expected of them.
3. *Creative Thinking*—The process of thinking creatively is foreign to those working in firms that have not attempted to implement an innovative strategy. Misconceptions about thinking creatively should be reviewed and a discussion of the most common creativity inhibitors should be presented and evaluated. After completing a creativity inventory, participants engage in several exercises to facilitate their own creative thinking.

4. *Innovation Development Process*—Participants should generate a set of specific ideas on which they would like to work. Issues of strategic fit can be examined, together with a review of the types of criteria the organization uses to evaluate new concepts. Additionally, participants can identify the resources they will require to complete their projects.

5. *Barriers, Facilitators, and Triggers to Innovative Thinking*—Culture factors from the CEAI are reviewed. This is done to discuss the most common barriers to innovative behavior. This effort includes examining a number of aspects of the firm's culture, including structural barriers and facilitators. Specific types of internal and external triggers for different forms of innovation can be explored. Participants can complete exercises that will help them deal with barriers in their internal work environment. In addition, video case histories are shown to describe the innovative behaviors of innovators in companies similar to the participants' firm that have positively contributed to implementing innovative strategies. Time in this module might be devoted to strategies for soliciting sponsors and leveraging internal corporate resources. In addition, it is important here to review the firm's structure, control systems, and human resource management system to verify that each is oriented toward facilitating innovative behavior.

6. *Innovation Planning*—After participants examine several aspects of facilitators and barriers to behaving innovatively in their organization, groups are asked to begin the process of completing an innovation plan. The plan includes setting goals, establishing a work team, assessing current conditions, and developing a step-by-step timetable for project completion and evaluation.

FINAL THOUGHTS

Finally, we should note that experience suggests to us that the type of program we are outlining here should be ongoing in nature. As new innovative opportunities surface in a firm's external environment, as the internal work environment changes simply from being used, and as new employees join the organization, it is appropriate for those from whom innovative behavior is expected to work together to find the best ways to proceed to implement a corporate innovation strategy . In this sense, efforts to successfully engage in corporate innovation must themselves be entrepreneurial—changing in response to ever-changing conditions in the firm's internal and external environments.[26]

The innovative audit can be used by firms competing in all types of industries as well as by not-for-profit organizations. In all instances, the audit provides insights to an organization's decision makers about the three core issues we are describing. These insights are very helpful to firms interested in understanding what can be done to improve their ability to compete in today's complex, rapidly changing competitive environments. In many instances, decision makers believe that innovation is a path to improved performance.

Summary

Innovation and creativity are important elements of entrepreneurship; however, being able to assess the level of innovative factors which exist in the organization is critical for any sustained activity. There are three methods which we discussed in this chapter. For clarification purposes, we separated them into two focus areas: entrepreneurial readiness and innovative readiness. With the *Entrepreneurial Readiness in Organizations* we introduced "The Organizational Metaphor." Then for the *Innovative Readiness in Organizations* segment we introduced the following two instruments: "Organizational Assessment of Innovation and Creativity" and "The Corporate Entrepreneurial Assessment Instrument." It is through the use of these instruments that an organization can begin to audit its entrepreneurial and innovative readiness.

INNOVATION-IN-ACTION

Measuring Innovation From The Executive Point of View

In a recent McKinsey Global Survey, over 800 senior executives were asked which types of innovations their companies pursue and measure, what metrics they have used, as well as their satisfaction with those metrics.

In general, 65 percent of those responding said that measuring innovation was one of their top three priorities. Companies reporting the highest contribution to growth from their innovation projects were more interested in measuring their innovations and used metrics across the whole innovation process (including inputs, process, and outcomes). They were also more satisfied than others with the ability of such metrics to help their organizations do everything from developing individual performance incentives, improving innovation performance, and communicating with investors. Companies seem to rely on metrics for outputs more than for inputs, so they aren't assessing the whole process of innovation. Forty-five percent don't track the relationship between spending on innovation and shareholder value. Moreover, although many companies are satisfied with their use of innovation metrics in general, far fewer are satisfied with specific uses, such as aligning individual performance incentives.

Some specific interesting findings included: executives focused on a few simple outcome metrics than input metrics or performance metrics, such as time to market or time to breakeven;

where innovation is the most important strategic priority, the top three metrics are customer satisfaction, the number of ideas in the pipeline, and R&D spending as a percentage of sales;

while companies typically benchmark their performance in most areas relative to that of their peers, many companies don't do so with innovation metrics; and over 50 percent of companies believe they are spending about the right amount on innovation.

Successful Innovative Companies

The most successful innovative companies tend to measure their innovations as a portfolio and are more likely to pursue and measure all types of innovation with the goal of a balanced portfolio. These high-performing organizations use only one more metric than other respondents.

They are likelier to use metrics across the whole innovation process, such as assessing the number of people actively devoted to innovation, the number of new ideas sourced from outside the organization, and the percentage of innovations that meet their development schedules. Innovative companies also track the financial returns from innovation in general and customer satisfaction with specific innovations. These firms are satisfied with their use of metrics across a wide range of activities, including allocating resources, aligning metrics with individual performance incentives, and communicating with investors.

Source: Based on: "Assessing Innovation Metrics: McKinsey Global Survey Results," mckinseyquarterly.com/McKinsey_Global_Survey_Results_Assessing_innovation_metrics_2243. Accessed on January 20, 2011.

Key Terms

Barriers, Facilitators, and Triggers to Innovative Thinking
Corporate Entrepreneurial Assessment Instrument
Creative Thinking
Entrepreneurial Readiness
Innovation Development Process
Innovation Planning
Innovative Breakthroughs

Innovative Readiness
Management support
Organizational Assessment of Innovation and Creativity
Organizational boundaries
Organizational metaphor
Rewards/reinforcement
Time availability
Work discretion/autonomy

Discussion Questions

1. Briefly describe what is meant by "culture."
2. What is the concept of assessment of entrepreneurial readiness?
3. What is the organizational metaphor? Describe some of the results.
4. How can innovative readiness in an organization be assessed?
5. Describe the "Organizational Assessment of Innovation & Creativity."
6. How do you interpret the scores from that instrument (in Question 5)?
7. What does CEAI represent?
8. Outline the factors that are identified in the CEAI.
9. How would you use the CEAI in your organization? Be specific in your answer.
10. What is the overall value of assessing the organization for innovative readiness?

Endnotes

1. Deal, T. & Kennedy, A. 2000. *Corporate Cultures.* Reading, MA: Perseus Publishing.
2. Morris, M. H., Kuratko, D. F. & Covin, J. G. 2011. *Corporate Entrepreneurship & Innovation*, 3rd ed. Mason, OH: Cengage/SouthWestern Publishers.
3. Ibid.
4. The Organizational Metaphor was developed by the authors.
5. Kuratko, D. F., Montagno, R.V. & Hornsby, J. S., 1990. Developing an intrapreneurial assessment instrument for an effective corporate entrepreneurial environment, *Strategic Management Journal* 11, Summer: 49–58.
6. Hornsby, J. S., Kuratko, D. F. & Zahra, S. A., 2002. Middle managers' perception of the internal environment for corporate entrepreneurship: Assessing a measurement scale, *Journal of Business Venturing* 17 (3): 253–273; Hornsby, J. S., Kuratko, D. F., Shepherd, D. A. & Bott, J. P. 2009. Managers' corporate entrepreneurial actions: Examining perception and position, *Journal of Business Venturing* 24 (3): 236–247.
7. Zahra, S. A. 1991. Predictors and financial outcomes of corporate entrepreneurship: An exploratory study, *Journal of Business Venturing* 6: 259–285; Zahra, S. A. & Bogner, W. C. 2000. Technology strategy and software new ventures' performance: Exploring the moderating effect of the competitive environment, *Journal of Business Venturing* 15 (2): 135–173; and Zahra, S. A. & Covin, J. G. 1995. Contextual influences on the corporate entrepreneurship performance relationship: A longitudinal analysis, *Journal of Business Venturing* 10: 43–58.
8. Sathe, V. 1985. Managing an entrepreneurial dilemma: Nurturing entrepreneurship and control in large corporations. In *Frontiers of Entrepreneurship Research* (pp. 636–656), Wellesley, MA: Babson College; Hisrich, R. D. & Peters, M. P. 1986. Establishing a new business venture unit within a firm, *Journal of Business Venturing* 1: 307–322; Brazeal, D. V. 1993. Organizing for internally developed corporate ventures, *Journal of Business Venturing* 8: 75–90; Kanter, R. M. 1985. Supporting innovation and venture development in established companies, *Journal of Business Venturing* 1: 47–60.
9. Covin, J. G. & Slevin, D. P. 1991. A conceptual model of entrepreneurship as firm behavior, *Entrepreneurship Theory and Practice* 16 (1): 7–25; Dess, G. G., Lumpkin, G. T. & McGee, J. E. 1999. Linking corporate entrepreneurship to strategy, structure, and process: Suggested research directions, *Entrepreneurship Theory & Practice* 23 (3): 85–102; Naman, J. & Slevin, D. 1993. Entrepreneurship and the concept of fit: A model and empirical tests, *Strategic Management Journal* 14: 137–153.
10. Kuratko, D. F., Hornsby, J. S., Naffziger, D.W. & Montagno, R. V. 1993. Implementing entrepreneurial thinking in established organizations, *SAM Advanced Management Journal* 58 (1): 28–33; Stevenson, H. H. & Jarillo, J. C. 1990. A paradigm of entrepreneurship: Entrepreneurial management, *Strategic Management Journal* 11 (Special Issue): 17–27.
11. Hornsby, J. S., Kuratko, D. F. & Zahra, S. A. 2002. Middle managers'perception of the internal environment for corporate entrepreneurship: Assessing a Measurement Scale, *Journal of Business Venturing* 17 (3): 253–273.
12. Miller, D. 1983. The correlates of entrepreneurship in three types of firms, *Management Science* 27: 770–791.

13. Quinn, J. B. 1985. Managing innovation: Controlled Chaos, *Harvard Business Review* 63 (3): 73–84.
14. Souder, W. 1981. Encouraging entrepreneurship in large corporations, *Research Management* 24 (3): 18–22.
15. Fry, A. 1987. The post-it-note: An intrapreneurial success, *SAM Advanced Management Journal* 52 (3): 4–9; Kanter, R. M. 1985. Supporting innovation and venture development in established companies, *Journal of Business Venturing* 1: 47–60.
16. Schuler, R. S. 1986. Fostering and facilitating entrepreneurship in organizations: Implications for organization structure and human resource management practices, *Human Resource Management* 25: 607–629.
17. Burgelman, R. A. 1983(a). A process model of internal corporate venturing in the diversified major firm, *Administrative Science Quarterly* 28: 223–244; Burgelman, R. A. 1983(b). Corporate entrepreneurship and strategic management: Insights from a process study, *Management Science* 23: 1349–1363; Burgelman, R. A. 1984. Designs for corporate entrepreneurship in established firms, *California Management Review* 26 (3): 154–166.
18. Floyd, S. W. & Wooldridge, B. 1990. The Strategy Process, middle management involvement, and organizational performance, *Strategic Management Journal* 11: 231–242; Floyd, S. W. & Wooldridge, B. 1992. Middle management involvement in strategy and its association with strategic type, *Strategic Management Journal* 13: 53–168; Floyd, S. W. & Wooldridge, B. 1994. Dinosaurs or dynamos? Recognizing middle management's strategic role, *Academy of Management Executive* 8 (4): 47–57.
19. Kuratko, D. F., Monagno, R. V. & Hornsby, J. S. 1990. Developing an intrapreneurial assessment instrument for an effective corporate entrepreneurialenvironment, *Strategic Management Journal* 11, Summer: 49–58; Hornsby, J. S., Kuratko, D. F. & Montagno, R. V. 1999. Perception of internal factors for corporate entrepreneurship: A comparison of Canadian and U.S. managers, *Entrepreneurship Theory and Practice* 24 (2): 9–24; Hornsby, J. S., Kuratko, D. F. & Zahra, S. A. 2002. Middle managers' perception of the internal environment for corporate entrepreneurship: Assessing a measurement scale, *Journal of Business Venturing* 17: 49–63; Kuratko, D.F., Ireland, R. D., Covin, J. G. & Hornsby, J. S. 2005. A model of middle-level managers' entrepreneurial behavior, *Entrepreneurship Theory and Practice* 29 (6): 699–716; Hornsby, J. S., Kuratko, D. F., Shepherd, D. A., Bott, J. P. 2009. Managers' corporate entrepreneurial actions: Examining perception and position, *Journal of BusinessVenturing* 24 (3): 236–247.
20. Kuratko, D. F., Monagno, R. V. & Hornsby, J. S. 1990. Developing an intrapreneurial assessment instrument for an effective corporate entrepreneurial environment, *Strategic Management Journal* 11, Summer: 49–58.
21. Hornsby, J. S., Kuratko, D. F. & Montagno, R. V. 1999. Perception of internal factors for corporate entrepreneurship: A comparison of Canadian and U.S. managers, *Entrepreneurship Theory and Practice* 24 (2): 9–24.
22. Hornsby, J. S., Kuratko, D. F. & Zahra, S. A. 2002. Middle managers' perception of the internal environment for corporate entrepreneurship: Assessing a measurement scale, *Journal of Business Venturing* 17: 49–63.
23. Rutherford, M. W. & Holt, D. T. 2007. Corporate entrepreneurship: An empirical look at the innovativeness dimension and its antecedents, *Journal of Organizational Change Management* 20 (3): 429–446.

24. Holt, D. T., Rutherford, M. W. & Clohessy, G. R. 2007. Corporate Entrepreneurship: An empirical look at individual characteristics, context, and process, *Journal of Leadership and Organizational Studies* 13 (4): 40–54.
25. Morris, M. H., Kuratko, D. F. & Covin, J. G. 2011. *Corporate Entrepreneurship & Innovation*, 3rd ed. Mason, OH: Cengage/SouthWestern Publishers.
26. Ireland, R. D., Kuratko, D. F. & Morris, M. H. 2006. A Health audit for corporate entrepreneurship: Innovation at all levels—Part 2, *Journal of Business Strategy* 27 (2): 21–30; Ireland, R. D., Kuratko, D. F. & Morris, M. H. 2006. A health audit for corporate entrepreneurship: Innovation at all levels—Part I, *Journal of Business Strategy* 27 (1): 10–17.

8

HUMAN RESOURCE MANAGEMENT IN CORPORATE INNOVATION

INTRODUCTION

As we have discussed in previous chapters, creative, innovative, and entrepreneurial behaviors are rapidly becoming desired attributes in organizations as they face economic uncertainty, international competition, and technological advances. As Hamel suggests, "In these suddenly sober times, the inescapable imperative for every organization must be to make innovation an all-the-time, everywhere capability."[1] Zahra, Kuratko, and Jennings noted that

> Some of the world's best-known companies had to endure a painful transformation to become more entrepreneurial. They had to endure years of reorganization, downsizing, and restructuring. These changes altered the identity or culture of these firms, infusing a new innovative spirit throughout their operations…change, innovation, and entrepreneurship became highly regarded words.[2]

Furthermore, Dess, Lumpkin, and McGee noted that "Virtually all organizations—new startups, major corporations, and alliances among global partners—are striving to exploit product-market opportunities through innovative and proactive behavior"[3]—the type of behavior that is called for by innovation and entrepreneurship. We have been focused on finding ways to create and facilitate this innovative behavior throughout our chapters. However, what human resource practices help initiate and sustain this type of behavior? The goal of this chapter is to discuss the important human resource management (HRM) elements necessary for initiating and sustaining innovative behavior.

In this chapter we will first outline a model of the critical organizational characteristics involved with HRM. Next, each element of the model is discussed. Finally, we present some conclusions about applying the model for increasing desired innovative behaviors.

AN ORGANIZATIONAL INNOVATION CHARACTERISTICS MODEL

In order for an organization to achieve an innovation ideology, it must focus on the organizational factors that have been successfully linked to increasing innovativeness. The model in Figure 8-1 depicts many of the critical elements for altering the human, structural, and cultural/environmental variables necessary for implementing the innovation required. The model suggests that creating a *high-performance work system (HPWS)* and effective human resource management practices play a mediating role between critical antecedents or an innovative environment and actual changes in the *entrepreneurial orientation* of the organization. The model also suggests that organizational level plays a key role in creating an innovative organizational posture. Specifically, the model makes the following assertions:

- *Environmental antecedents*, including top management support, rewards/ reinforcement, autonomy/discretion, *time availability*, and organizational boundaries, impact the human resource practices of an organization. The concept of *high-performance work systems* is utilized to highlight the critical organizational and human resource practices necessary to initiate innovative and entrepreneurial behavior. The environmental antecedents are necessary for creating HPWS.

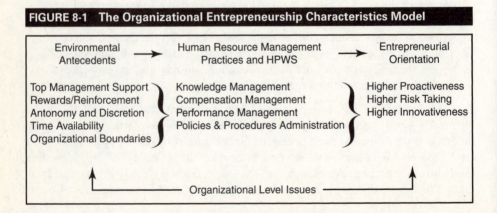

FIGURE 8-1 The Organizational Entrepreneurship Characteristics Model

Environmental Antecedents → Human Resource Management Practices and HPWS → Entrepreneurial Orientation

Top Management Support
Rewards/Reinforcement
Antonomy and Discretion
Time Availability
Organizational Boundaries

Knowledge Management
Compensation Management
Performance Management
Policies & Procedures Administration

Higher Proactiveness
Higher Risk Taking
Higher Innovativeness

Organizational Level Issues

- HPWS leads to an organizational entrepreneurial orientation causing increased proactiveness, risk taking, and innovative behaviors.
- The link between the environment, human resource practices, and entrepreneurial orientation is moderated by the level of the person(s) in the organization and the type of job(s) performed.

ENVIRONMENTAL ANTECEDENTS FOR INNOVATION

Corporate innovation occurs when the organization strives to…"exploit product-market opportunities through innovative and proactive behavior."[4] An effective corporate innovation strategy facilitates the firm's efforts to exploit its current competitive advantages and explore the opportunities and the competencies required to successfully pursue them.[5] Some firms foster an environment that is more entrepreneurially intense than others.[6] As we presented in Chapter 7, assessing an innovative (entrepreneurial) environment has become an important element for successfully implementing a corporate innovation strategy. An organizational change effort, such as implementing an innovation strategy, requires an analysis of the current environment or state of readiness/antecedents for encouraging proactive corporate innovative behavior. In Chapter 7 we introduced one instrument that has been utilized to assess environmental issues related to implementing a corporate innovation strategy: the *Corporate Entrepreneurship Assessment Instrument (CEAI)*. Researchers Donald F. Kuratko and Jeffrey S. Hornsby developed the 48-item CEAI to assess the innovative readiness of an organization[7]. Reviewing from Chapter 7, there are five stable antecedents or elements of managers' innovative actions:

1. Top Management Support—The willingness of top-level managers to facilitate and promote innovative behavior, including the championing of innovative ideas and providing the resources people require to take innovative actions.
2. Work Discretion/Autonomy—Top-level managers' commitment to tolerate failure, provide decision-making latitude and freedom from excessive oversight, and delegate authority and responsibility to managers.
3. Rewards/Reinforcement—Developing and using systems that reward employees based on performance, highlighting significant achievements, and encouraging the pursuit of challenging work.
4. Resource Availability—Evaluating workloads to ensure that individuals and groups have the time needed to pursue innovations and that their jobs are structured in ways that support efforts to achieve short- and long-term organizational goals.
5. Organizational Boundaries—Precise explanations of outcomes expected from organizational work and development of mechanisms for evaluating, selecting, and using innovations.

While the antecedents to entrepreneurship and innovation continue to be identified and tested, their impact on organizational behavior, especially in the development of effective human resource practices and work systems, should also be discussed. Current human resource systems may not foster the desired innovative and entrepreneurial outcomes because they reinforce standardization, rigidity, and inflexibility instead of promoting creativity, empowerment, and intrinsic motivation. The following section describes the human resource management practices and high-performance work systems that are necessary for an organization to foster innovation.

HUMAN RESOURCE MANAGEMENT AND HIGH-PERFORMANCE WORK SYSTEMS

The model in Figure 8-1 proposes that the environmental antecedents impact the development and management of human resources in an innovative organization. A firm's human resources are seen as particularly important for providing a sustained competitive advantage and play an essential role in a firm's ability to be entrepreneurial.[8] Human resource practices that impact creativity, innovation, and entrepreneurship can be categorized as part of a high-performance work system. Bohlander and Snell suggest that HPWS is a result of "a specific combination of HR practices, work structures, and processes that maximizes employee knowledge, skill, commitment and flexibility."[9] Nadler, Gerstein, and Shaw define HPWS as:

> an organizational architecture that brings together work, people, technology and information in a manner that optimizes the congruence of fit among them in order to produce high performance in terms of the effective response to customer requirements and other environmental demands and opportunities.[10]

Nadler et al. identified ten important principles for designing an effective HPWS. Table 8-1 includes a complete list of these principles. They center on the importance of human resource practices design, empowerment, culture, and accountability.

Specifically, they argued that "[The] key to maintaining this flexible architecture is having clear design intent. If the purpose of the original design—to enhance speed, accountability, customer focus, technological innovation, flattened hierarchy, or whatever—is explicitly articulated, then there are clear boundaries for adding, deleting, or rearranging design elements."[11] In the case of facilitating innovation and entrepreneurship, the key is to strategically foster innovative behavior by designing human resource systems that support and incentivize this type of behavior.

Beugelsdijk studied the impact of changing six human resource practices on incremental and radical innovations. *Incremental innovation* focuses on smaller process improvements and changes and *radical innovation* includes major product or process changes or new product development. In a study of 988 Dutch firms, he found that firms with decentralized organizational structures and a

TABLE 8-1   Ten Principles for Design of HPWS

1. Start the design of work processes by focusing on customer requirements.
2. Design work around self-managed teams working on complete processes.
3. Provide clear direction, goals, and measures of performance.
4. Variances should be detected and controlled at the source.
5. Link social and technical systems.
6. Ensure continuous flow of information.
7. Enrich jobs to increase motivation and enhance flexibility in assigning work and solving problems.
8. Human resource practices must complement the empowerment of teams and individuals.
9. The management structure, culture, and processes must embrace HPWS design.
10. The organization must restructure to meet competitive conditions.

Source: Based on Nadler, D. A., Tushman, M. L. & Nadler, M. B. 1997. *Competing by Design: The Power of Organizational Architecture.* New York: Oxford University Press, 147–153

focus on employee empowerment, as reflected in the use of task autonomy and flexible working hours, generated more product innovations. He also found that performance-based pay and training and development were positively associated with incremental innovation, but not with radical innovation.[12]

Four of the key human resource practices that create a HPWS are *performance management, knowledge management, compensation and incentives management*, and policies and procedures administration. Each of these practices is described below.

PERFORMANCE MANAGEMENT

The first component of creating a HPWS is the concept of performance management, especially as it relates to the empowerment of employees. Providing an increased opportunity to participate in decisions is critical to creating an entrepreneurial orientation. This process is considered to be one of the key elements of an HPWS because it allows the employees to make decisions that affect their immediate environment, which in turn affect the entire organization. This empowerment leads to more work commitment and better organizational citizenship. According to Hayton and Kelley,[13] corporate entrepreneurship (CE) is promoted by the simultaneous presence of competency in the four roles of innovating, brokering, championing, and sponsoring. In order to foster corporate innovative activity, employee-development activities focused on developing these competencies should be a central focus of a corporate innovation strategy. Additionally, employee feedback systems should focus on progress in developing or overcoming weaknesses in these competencies.

KNOWLEDGE MANAGEMENT

The second component of creating an HPWS is knowledge management. Knowledge management includes attracting, retaining, and developing individuals with the knowledge, skills, and abilities to meet the goals of the organization. Effective selection of individuals who have the ability or inclination to behave innovatively is important. Also, training and development provides employees with the necessary skills to perform their jobs in a more effective manner as well as the opportunity to assume greater responsibility within an organization. Traditional selection and employee-development procedures may not always be productive when it comes to hiring and developing innovative employees. Typical procedures tend to identify individuals that adhere to policies and procedures, follow instruction, and work toward fitting into a company profile in their development activities so they can be labeled "key talent" in the organizational succession chart. Very little empirical research exists to help us better understand the requirements for, and the impact of, directly seeking creative and innovative employees. However, there is ample discussion in the applied literature on some recommendations to attract, retain, and develop these types of individuals.

Mercer makes several recommendations for hiring creative and innovative employees. He suggests that we should test individuals to assess their motivation to do creative work and their flexibility in following rules and procedures. He utilizes the Abilities & Behavior Forecaster™ Test to assess these scores and suggests that creative people will score high on motivation and low on following rules and procedures. Mercer also suggests that you should assess your current successful employees to establish a benchmark for creative need for hiring new employees. Some of the benchmarking results that he found for creative jobs include artists, supply-chain managers, directors, and administrative assistants. Jobs with low creativity scores included accountants, customer-service representatives, regional managers, sales representatives, and convenience-store managers. Mercer cautions overgeneralizing and encourages organizations to determine their own benchmarks for creative need. He warns of mismatching employees by putting creative individuals in noncreative roles (or vice versa) and of the frustration and retention issues that could result. If you are not going to utilize a preemployment test, Mercer recommends restructuring interview questions to ask applicants to describe past creative work experiences, especially in relation to actual problem-solving situations. You should especially avoid yes/no questions and let the applicant tell their story.[14]

Buxton suggests that it is critical to consider the role of teams when staffing for innovation. He suggests several rules of thumb that he believes help build effective, cross-disciplinary innovation teams:

- You need people who fill in the gaps that you have in your own and other existing team members' skill sets as you build up competence in your specialty.
- Test for both breadth of literacy and deep competence. You do not need "jacks-of-all-trades."

- Identify the core competencies needed for a team. List them on a bunch of Post-it notes, and have each person on the team write the name of the "go-to" person on the team who has the most depth in that area. If you lack depth in any specified core competency, you should work to find people that can fill the gap.

- You need to hire I-shaped individuals who can think both pragmatically and abstractly.

- Hire people who do not require predictability and stability in order to be effective. Individuals who can continually reconfigure will be more effective in innovative environments.

- Hire people with strong interpersonal skills. Communication and conflict resolutions skills are critical in innovation team environments.[15]

(For more insights on hiring innovative talent see Table 8-2.)

TABLE 8-2   18 Recommendations for Hiring and Retaining Innovative Talent

1. **Make hiring innovators a primary goal.** Set as one of your primary goals and metrics the increased hiring of more innovative individuals.

2. **Realize the current system may be broken.** Your current system probably restricts the hiring of innovators. Look at every phase of the hiring process to see where nontraditional, diverse, and/or innovative individuals are most likely to be screened out, overlooked, or discouraged.

3. **Develop a hiring plan for innovators.** Prioritize your jobs and business units to make sure that your limited resources and time are directed toward those jobs that, when filled with innovators, have the most business impact.

4. **Create your brand recognition.** Don't expect to have any success in hiring innovative people if you don't make an effort to spread the word by writing and speaking about how your firm desires innovators and, more important, provides them with opportunities to continually innovate and take risks.

5. **Encourage external hiring.** If your organization is currently conservative and scores low on the risk-taking scale, you might find hiring external innovators a lot easier than transforming current risk-adverse employees.

6. **Position descriptions.** Most position descriptions don't mention the need for innovation at all. If you expect to be successful, the desire for innovation must be part of every relevant job description and assessing the need for innovation should be part of every job analysis.

7. **Postings.** Innovation must be part of every job announcement, recruitment ad, and recruiting brochure. Clearly differentiate how your jobs allow individuals more freedom to innovate and take risks than other firms.

continued

8. **Referral focus.** Nothing improves the recruiting of any targeted group better than specifically asking your employees to be on the lookout for referrals who have those skills or characteristics.

9. **Initial resume screening.** The initial screening process for resumes is usually a primary barrier to innovation. Redesign your system so that it includes options for accepting out-of-the-box resume formats and content. It is a fact that some innovative people refuse to produce standard resumes.

10. **The interview.** After resume screening, the interview is a second weak link in hiring innovators. The interview, and in fact the entire assessment process, must be redesigned so that it is tolerant and inclusive (i.e., expect some craziness) if you expect to get a single innovative person hired.

11. **Simulations and creativity assessments.** Whether an online prescreening tool or verbal scenario provided during the interview process, simulations are an effective tool that can excite as well as assess potential applicants.

12. **Contests.** Because most interview formats do not assess the candidate's ability to innovate, recruiting needs to consider contests as a supplement to help identify those that offer innovative ideas and approaches to the problems faced by the company.

13. **Improve the candidate experience.** Most hiring processes are just plain ugly when it comes to customer service and providing a great candidate experience. That weakness becomes critical when you're attempting to hire innovative individuals because they are almost always in high demand. Being in high demand means that they have many options and as a result, they're less tolerant of being treated poorly during any hiring process.

14. **The corporate website.** Almost all candidates, innovative or not, will test the validity of what they have heard by visiting your corporate website. If the message they get there differs from what they've heard, you will lose them in an instant.

15. **Target "magnet" hires.** An effective way of attracting innovators is having the recruiting team specifically identify and target well-known individuals who are known for their innovation.

16. **Follow through with orientation.** Even after they accept your offer, the need to reinforce your message is critical. As part of the orientation process, emphasize the importance of innovation in your organization, educate the new hire on how and where to report ideas, and share how innovation is rewarded.

17. **Follow up with retention.** Even though recruiting doesn't control retention, it is in their best interest to work with retention program managers to ensure that new hires don't immediately exit out the backdoor.

18. **Improve with metrics.** No matter how well your system is designed, it's critical that you track your success and failures in hiring innovative individuals.

Source: Adapted from: *ERE.Net.* "18 Things Recruiters Can Do To Hire More Innovative People," by Dr. John Sullivan, October 16, 2006, http://www.ere.net/2006/10/16/18-things-recruiters-can-do-to-hire-more-innovative-people/

COMPENSATION AND INCENTIVES MANAGEMENT

The third component in creating a HPWS is employee compensation and incentives. The two previous elements help to prepare employees and organizations for successful HPWS implementation and operation, but without effective compensation management, the system will most likely fail. Organizations need to find a way to link pay with performance in order to incentivize employees to focus "on outcomes that are beneficial to themselves and the organization as a whole."[16] Incentives can take many forms, with some examples being stock options and other equity plans, profit-sharing plans, pay raises, bonuses for meeting performance targets, and other monetary incentives. In addition, incentives can take the form of nonmonetary options such as time off, flextime, autonomy, group lunches, and other special employee benefits. In terms of innovation and entrepreneurship, the types of incentives should vary based on the need for incremental or radical innovations. Incremental innovations may be more suited to more traditional incentives, including intrinsic rewards (flextime, autonomy, etc.) and extrinsic rewards (bonuses, merit increases, profit sharing, etc.). However, more radical innovations may require more substantial forms of incentives that are often more difficult to administer and tend to foster apprehension from top management. These incentives include organizational equity in the form of stock, stock options, or even large equity stakes in venture spin-offs. Sjoerd Beugelsdijk affirmed this in a study of Dutch firms and found that incremental innovations are relatively easier to motivate with traditional HR practices but the ability to motivate radical innovations is much more limited because more sophisticated reward systems are not available.

Since many innovation and CE endeavors are conducted in team-based situations, the use of compensation and incentive programs becomes more complex given the team dynamics. The organization is faced with many tough decisions. First, do you compensate at the team level or individual level? More specifically, is your firm up to the challenge of team-based compensation? If so, how do you measure performance and are you prepared for the internal team dynamics that result from shared accountability? Second, what behavior are you trying to reinforce with the team-based compensation? Third, how do you measure team performance? Finally, what incentives do you utilize in the compensation program?

In a study of CE in Israeli defense firms, Lerner, Azulay, and Tishler confirmed the importance of building effective entrepreneurship-oriented compensation programs. The findings of their research suggest that management should not only call for compensation for entrepreneurs, but should also make sure that the system they choose is important and acceptable to the entrepreneurs. Their results show that there is a large gap between the perception of the desired compensation incentives by corporate entrepreneurs and the ones actually practiced by the enterprise. They also found that even when more desirable compensation programs were utilized, many of the corporate entrepreneur respondents were not aware of it.[17]

Whether you utilize individual or team-based compensation programs for incentivizing innovative and entrepreneurial behavior, the design of the program should include the following elements:

- Top management must make entrepreneurship and innovation a strategic initiative for the organization and be willing to alter its traditional culture.
- Top management must provide support for the compensation program so that employees trust the behavior–reward linkage.
- The psychological and behavioral consequences of the incentive structure need to be tailored to the workforce and not haphazardly adopted from external sources.
- Employee feedback should be systematically built in to the assessment of the incentive compensation program.

POLICIES AND PROCEDURES ADMINISTRATION

The administration of *organizational policies* and procedures also impacts the creation of a high-performance work system. Organizations who focus on policies that create boundaries and overly regulate behavior will limit innovative and entrepreneurial behavior. Traditional human resource practices such as creating job descriptions, policy manuals, safety manuals, and operating standards can inhibit desired behavior. Also, a manager's rigid enforcement of policies can also have unwanted effects on employee behavior. While some of these are necessary and important to the operation of the organization (especially those legally required), these traditional practices may also inhibit the creativity and innovative behavior desired when implementing a corporate innovative strategy. Hayton[18] suggests that human resource management practices fall into two categories: traditional HR practices and discretionary HRM. The traditional practices focus upon "clearly defining jobs in terms of their tasks, duties, and responsibilities; carefully structuring equitable rewards for those jobs; and monitoring individual performance." He hypothesizes that these practices are incongruent with the creativity and risk taking required for innovation and entrepreneurship.

Discretionary HRM practices, on the other hand, focus on the discretionary performance of employees by offering incentives and mechanisms for exchanging knowledge and encouraging organizational learning. In a study of 99 small-to-medium enterprises, Hayton found that discretionary HR practices, specifically discretionary behavior, knowledge sharing, and organizational learning, were positively associated with innovative performance and activity. He also found that strategic human capital management enhanced the relationship between discretionary HRM practices and innovative behavior. Also, he found that the positive relationship was strongest in high-technology industries.

ENTREPRENEURIAL ORIENTATION

According to Figure 8-1 cited earlier, organizational *entrepreneurial orientation (EO)* is the result of effective organizational practices related to attending to the antecedents necessary to implement a CE strategy and practicing relevant HRM for innovation. EO is an organizational state or quality that's defined in terms of several behavioral dimensions. Based on the pioneering work of Miller,[19] Covin and Slevin defined EO as implying the presence of organizational behavior reflecting risk taking, innovativeness, and proactiveness.[20] The three main EO attributes are defined below.

INNOVATION

According to Lumpkin and Dess, an entrepreneurial innovation can be defined as the "willingness to support creativity and experimentation in introducing new products/services."[21] Covin and Miles suggested that innovation was the single most critical factor in defining CE. They argued that after considering "the various dimensions of firm-level entrepreneurial orientation identified in the literature…innovation, broadly defined, is the single common theme underlying all forms of corporate entrepreneurship."[22] All the other dimensions were simply correlates of innovation. Covin and Miles concluded that "without innovation there is no corporate entrepreneurship regardless of the presence of these other dimensions."[23]

RISK TAKING

Risk taking has long been conceptually associated with entrepreneurship. Many definitions of entrepreneurship focus on the willingness of entrepreneurs to engage in calculated risks. Interestingly, entrepreneurs may not view themselves as risk takers. Busenitz argued that entrepreneurs tend to view situations more favorably than nonentrepreneurs, even when they are more risky.[24]

PROACTIVENESS

The concept of proactiveness has received less attention from entrepreneurial scholars[25] (Weaver, 2002). It has been defined as…"an opportunity-seeking, forward-looking perspective characterized by the introduction of new products and services ahead of the competition and acting in anticipation of future demand."[26]

At least three models suggested by Covin and Slevin,[27] Lumpkin and Dess,[28] and Ireland, Covin, and Kuratko[29] incorporate the antecedents and/or consequences of the organizational-level phenomenon of EO. The "Ireland, Covin, and Kuratko" model of a corporate entrepreneurship strategy differs in four ways from other models—(1) by conceptualizing EO as an organizational state, (2) by specifying organizational locations from which innovative behavior may emerge, (3) by specifying a "philosophical" component of a CE strategy, and

(4) by specifying that organizations can pursue innovation as a separate and identifiable strategy. It is our contention that human resource practices, as described earlier, play a major role in the execution of an innovative strategy that can lead to EO. The human resource practices that create a HPWS facilitate the execution of such a strategy.

Many studies confirm the positive correlation between EO and organizational performance. Rauch et al. observed that the Covin and Slevin EO scale possesses a positive and moderately large correlation with performance ($r = .235$). Rauch and colleagues equate the strength of the EO–performance relationship to that of taking a "sleeping pill and having a better night's sleep." [30] Some of the areas of performance often linked to EO include financial indicators such as growth, sales, and profit. Nonfinancial measures include the number of ideas implemented and satisfaction.

ORGANIZATIONAL-LEVEL ISSUES

It is well documented in the conceptual literature that managers at all structural levels have critical strategic roles to fulfill for the organization to be successful.[31] According to Floyd and Lane, senior-, middle-, and first-level managers have distinct responsibilities with respect to each subprocess. *Senior-level managers* have ratifying, recognizing, and directing roles which, in turn, are associated with particular managerial actions.[32] In examining the role of middle-level managers, Kuratko, Ireland, Covin, and Hornsby contend that *middle-level managers* endorse, refine, and shepherd entrepreneurial opportunities and identify, acquire, and deploy resources needed to pursue those opportunities, whereas *first-level managers* have experimenting roles corresponding to the competence-definition subprocess, adjusting roles corresponding to the competence-modification subprocess, and conforming roles corresponding to the competence-deployment subprocess.[33] Thus, organizations pursuing corporate innovative strategies likely exhibit a cascading, yet integrated, set of innovative actions at the senior, middle, and first levels of management. At the senior level, managers act in concert with others throughout the firm to identify effective means through which new businesses can be created or existing ones reconfigured.

Corporate innovation is pursued in light of environmental opportunities and threats, with the purpose of creating a more effective alignment between the company and conditions in its external environment. The innovative actions expected of middle-level managers are framed around the need for this group to propose and interpret innovative opportunities that might create new business for the firm or increase the firm's competitiveness in current business domains. First-line managers exhibit the "experimenting" role as they surface the operational ideas for innovative improvements. An important interpretation of Burgelman's work has been the belief that managers would surface ideas for innovative actions from every level of management, especially the first-line and middle levels. Therefore, managers across levels are jointly responsible for their organization's innovative actions.[34] Based on the different roles of the different levels of management highlighted above, it can be contended that mangers at different levels have different perceptions of the feasibility and/or desirability of these organizational factors for promoting innovative action.

Top-management support refers to the extent to which one perceives that top managers support, facilitate, and promote innovative behavior; including the championing of innovative ideas and providing the resources people require to take innovative actions. Recent research suggests that top-management support has been found to have a positive relationship with an organization's innovative outcomes.[35] Managers differ in their structural ability to use top-management support as a resource for innovative action. The more senior a manager is, the closer he or she is to top management. This closeness enables greater awareness of the nature of that support.[36] For example, more senior managers are likely to better know the bounds of top-management support and thereby can utilize them by pushing it to the fullest. While first-line managers may be aware of top-management support, they do not have the structural "proximity" to have a fine-grained knowledge of the nature of that support.[37] First-line managers are likely to be more cautious in how they choose to use top-management support for their innovative activities.

Work discretion refers to the extent to which one perceives that the organization tolerates failure, provides decision-making latitude and freedom from excessive oversight, and delegates authority and responsibility to lower-level managers and workers.[38] Often innovative outcomes arise from those that have work discretion for innovative experimentation.[39] Managers likely use their work discretion to enhance performance on salient tasks, and task salience differs across managerial level. First-line managers are focused on managing and instructing others to more efficiently perform their tasks, middle-level managers are focused on how to link groups, and senior managers are focused on scanning the environment for opportunities and threats. Innovative actions are more likely to arise from scanning the external and internal environments than focusing attention more narrowly on efficiency.[40] Therefore, more senior managers are better able to use work discretion to generate innovative outcomes.

Rewards and reinforcement refers to the extent to which one perceives that the organization uses systems that reward based on innovative activity and success.[41] Rewards have been found to be positively related to entrepreneurial activity.[42] However, unlike the signals of top-management support for which senior managers can more fully appreciate, these signals from rewards and reinforcement are typically less ambiguous. Such rewards and reinforcement are likely to have a more positive influence on lower-level managers because, as Hayton argued, these lower-level managers are more risk averse and such rewards likely help overcome that aversion.[43]

Time availability for managers has also been found to be an important resource for generating innovative outcomes.[44] Similar to work discretion, managers are expected to invest "slack" time on those tasks most salient given their roles and responsibilities. The most salient tasks for first-line managers is narrower in scope and centers more on adjusting and conforming activities (and often focused on efficiency), whereas the more salient tasks of senior managers are broader, allowing them to scan more broadly the organization and the external environment.[45] These broader scanning activities are more likely to generate innovative ideas by scanning the environment and recognizing opportunities.[46] Therefore, more senior managers are better able to use time as a resource to generate innovative activities than are first-line managers.

Finally, flexible organizational boundaries are useful in promoting innovative activity because they enhance the flow of information between the external environment and the organization and between departments/divisions within the organization.[47] More senior managers are better structurally positioned to access and use this information, given their attention is already broadly allocated across the organization and the external environment. First-line managers also benefit from these permeable boundaries but, given the structural position, they interact across fewer boundaries due to their narrow job focus and therefore benefit less from boundary permeability.[48]

In a recent study on organizational-level effects on corporate innovative behavior, Hornsby, Kuratko, Shepherd, and Bott found support for many of the relationships suggested earlier. They found that managerial level moderated the relationship between top-management support and the number of ideas implemented and moderated the relationship between work discretion and the number of ideas implemented. Managers at higher levels were better able to make the most of top-management support and of work discretion. These findings have important implications for innovation and CE. First, under high levels of perceived managerial support, senior and middle managers, by virtue of their higher-ranking positions, were more likely to implement innovative ideas. First-level managers, however, were relatively unlikely to see their ideas implemented or make unofficial improvements, regardless of the level of managerial support.[49]

Second, the nature of the interaction indicates that there was a positive relationship between work discretion and number of ideas implemented for senior and middle-level managers; however, for first-level managers, this relationship was negative. These results indicate that work discretion only results in increased innovative actions (in the form of number of ideas implemented) for senior and middle-level managers, or those individuals with the experience and personal discipline likely necessary to support autonomy and discretion. An explanation for this finding may be that these lower-level managers, even though they perceived an environment of work discretion, did not see the link between it and their own activities. Garvin and Levesque refer to this as the "two cultures problem" where organizations traditionally focus on incremental improvement through a focus on stability and efficiency.[50] Corporate innovation requires a "melding" of cultures. If the CE strategy has not been integrated down into lower levels of management, an increased focus on traditional practices could result when a lower manager has more discretion and autonomy. Also, specific control systems that exist in the organization, especially managerial flexibility, may lead the lower-level managers to perceive the need to spend more time on standard procedures and activities and not engage in more innovative behavior.[51]

Summary

Human resource practices, especially the organizational architecture that creates a high-performance work system, are a critical mediating factor between innovative environments and strategy and actual entrepreneurial and innovative behavior. The relationships between the elements shown in Figure 8-1 are complex and their linkages are in need of much more research.[52] The more we understand the organizational architecture for an innovative strategy, the more successful firms will be with future corporate innovation efforts. Research also suggests that issues such as management level can moderate the relationships. It seems clear that senior or top management plays a major strategic role in fostering corporate entrepreneurship and innovation. Furthermore, middle and frontline managers also need to facilitate and encourage innovative activity. Table 8-3 summarizes some of the major activities that managers should initiate if they want an entrepreneurial or innovative organization.

TABLE 8-3 Tips for Fostering Innovation

1. Have leaders and managers discuss their definition of *innovation.*
2. Treat innovation as a key source of strategic growth.
3. Have managers sign a "Declaration of Innovation."
4. Work with leaders to identify barriers to innovation.
5. Have managers share ideas and critique in a nonthreatening way.
6. Make innovation fun.
7. Publicize successfully implemented ideas.
8. Establish rewards for successful idea sharing and innovation.
9. Utilize cross-functional involvement to gain buy-in from various departments.

Source: Based on: Kathy, G. 2009. "Motivating Innovation," *HRMagazine,* 54: 30–35

INNOVATION-IN-ACTION

How Innovation Changed Kia

Some observers would say the most impressive introduction at the 2010 New York International Auto Show was the 2011 Kia Optima. Yes, you read that correctly—Kia.

Kia Motors Corporation, the second-largest Korean car company, has been around since 1944 and sold vehicles in the United States since 1994. The Kia brand has been historically associated with the word "cheap." Kia's value proposition has been its price point, not fashionable styling. A 2010 Optima, for example, was priced about $1600 less than a Toyota Camry, but was rather unremarkable otherwise.

Kia's repositioning did not happen overnight. In 2005, while struggling with sagging sales and sinking profits, Kia identified design as its "core future growth engine." The next year, Kia hired Peter Schreyer, an award-winning auto designer who had previously worked at Audi and Volkswagen, as Chief Design Officer.

At the time of his arrival at Kia, Schreyer recognized that the design of Kia cars was very "neutral." Kia was "just another Asian carmaker" and observers would have struggled to determine whether a Kia vehicle was Korean or Japanese. Schreyer believed that it was important that observers recognize a Kia at first sight. Since his arrival, Schreyer has managed design activities at Kia's design centers, located in Frankfurt, Los Angeles, Tokyo, and Korea, with the goal of creating the unexpected. Schreyer's vision was that Kia be known more for visual appeal than its tradition of cheap cars.

The first notion of what the redesigned Kia lineup might look like appeared at the 2007 Frankfurt Motor Show, when the company unveiled the Kia concept vehicle, which featured a new corporate grille intended to create a recognizable face for the brand. The grille, dubbed the "Tiger Nose," will ultimately be incorporated into all Kia models.

The 2011 Optima possesses several features generally new to Kia, including coupe-like profiling and cockpit-style instrumentation. The car has already won multiple awards, including Cars.com's "Best of 2011" award. Schreyer understands that placing a premium on design should allow Kia to generate higher margins through charging higher prices. That is, better design means greater profits.

Since Schreyer's arrival (and before sales of the 2011 Optima began), Kia's profits have surged to record levels and show no signs of slowing down. And, if the projections are correct, the new Optima will help Kia boost global sales by about 27 percent, which is a pretty big return for a mere shift of focus.

Source: Adapted from: http://www.caradvice.com.au/60510/interview-with-head-of-design-at-kia-peter-schreyer/; http://www.businessweek.com/magazine/content/10_23/b4181020680640.htmWebsites accessed: January 13, 2011.

Key Terms

Corporate entrepreneurship
Compensation and incentives
Entrepreneurial orientation
Environmental antecedents
First-level managers
High-performance work systems
Incremental innovation
Knowledge management
Middle-level managers
Organizational boundaries

Organizational policies
Performance management
Radical innovation
Resource availability
Rewards and reinforcement
Senior-level managers
Time availability
Top-management support
Work discretion

Discussion Questions

1. What are the antecedents to corporate entrepreneurship and innovation?
2. Why is top-management support so important to the implementation of corporate entrepreneurship?
3. How can you create a high-performance work system?
4. What are the important human resource elements of a high-performance work system?
5. What are the critical elements of an organizational entrepreneurial orientation?
6. Describe the role of senior, middle-level, and frontline managers in the corporate entrepreneurship process?
7. What role should managers play in the creation of high-performance work systems?

Endnotes

1. Hamel, G. 2000. *Leading the Revolution.* Boston, MA: Harvard Business School Press, 15.
2. Zahra, S. A., Kuratko, D. F. & Jennings, D. F. 1999. Entrepreneurship and the acquisition of dynamic organizational capabilities, *Entrepreneurship Theory and Practice* 24: 5–10.
3. Dess, G. G., Lumpkin, G. T. & McGee, J. E. 1999. Linking corporate entrepreneurship to strategy, structure, and process: Suggested research directions, *Entrepreneurship Theory & Practice* 23: 85–102.
4. Ibid, p. 85.
5. Covin, J. G. & Miles, M. P. 1999. Corporate entrepreneurship and the pursuit of competitive advantage, *Entrepreneurship: Theory and Practice* 23: 47–63.
6. Morris, M., Kuratko, D. & Covin, J. 2008. *Corporate entrepreneurship & innovation: Entrepreneurial development within organizations.* Mason, OH: Thomson Southwestern.
7. Hornsby, J. S., Kuratko, D. F. & Zahra, S. A. 2002. Middle managers' perception of the internal environment for corporate entrepreneurship: Assessing a measurement scale, *Journal of Business Venturing* 17: 253–273. Kuratko, D. F., Montagno, R. V.

& Hornsby, J. S., 1990. Developing an intrapreneurial assessment instrument for an effective corporate entrepreneurial environment, *Strategic Management Journal* 11, Summer: 49–58; Hornsby, J. S., Kuratko, D. F. & Montagno, R. V. 1999. Perception of internal factors for corporate entrepreneurship: A comparison of Canadian and U.S. managers, *Entrepreneurship Theory and Practice* 24 (2): 9–24; Kuratko, D. F., Ireland, R. D,, Covin, J. G. & Hornsby, J. S. 2005. A model of middle-level managers' entrepreneurial behavior, *Entrepreneurship Theory and Practice* 29 (6): 699–716.

8. Wiklund, J. & Shepherd, D. 2003. Knowledge-based resources, entrepreneurial orientation, and the performance of small and medium-sized businesses, *Strategic Management Journal* 24: 1307–1319.

9. Bohlander, G. & Snell, S. 2004. *Managing Human Resources.* Cincinnati, OH: South-Western, 690.

10. Nadler, D., Gerstein, S. & Shaw, R. 1992. *Organizational Architecture: Designs for Changing Organizations.* San Francisco, CA: Josey-Bass, 118.

11. Ibid, p. 121.

12. Beugelsdijk, S. 2008. Strategic human resource practices and product innovation, *Organization Studies* 29: 821–827.

13. Hayton, J. & Kelley, D. 2006. A competency-based framework for promoting corporate entrepreneurship, *Human Resource Management* 45: 407–427.

14. Mercer, M. "Hiring creative employees: Using benchmark testing," Accessed on September 29, 2010, http://www.sideroad.com/Management/hiring-creative-employees.html.

15. Buxton, B. 2009. *BusinessWeek Online*, Accessed on July 14, 2009, http://www.businessweek.com/innovate/content/jul2009/id20090713%5f33

16. Bohlander & Snell, *Managing Human Resources*, p. 698.

17. Lerner, M., Azulay, I. & Tishler, A. 2009. The role of compensation methods in corporate entrepreneurship, *International Studies of Management and Organization* 39: 53–81.

18. Hayton, J. 2003. Strategic human capital management in SMEs: An empirical study of entrepreneurial performance, *Human Resource Management* 42: 375–391.

19. Miller. D. 1983. The correlates of entrepreneurship in three types of firms, *Management Science* 297: 770–791.

20. Covin, J. G. & Slevin, D. P. 1989. Strategic management of small firms in hostile and benign environments, *Strategic Management Journal* 10: 75–87.

21. Lumpkin. G. T. & Dess. G. G. 2001. Linking two dimensions of entrepreneurial orientation to firm performance: The moderating role of environment and industry life cycle, *Journal of Business Venturing* 16: p. 431.

22. Covin, J. G. & Miles, M. P. 1999. Corporate entrepreneurship and the pursuit of competitive advantage, *Entrepreneurship: Theory and Practice* 23: 47.

23. Ibid, p. 49.

24. Busenitz, L. W. 1999. Entrepreneurial risk and strategic decision making: It's a matter of perspective, *Journal of Applied Behavioral Science* 35: 325–340.

25. Marino, L., Strandholm, K., Steensma, H. K. & Weaver, K. M. 2002. Assessing the psychometric properties of the entrepreneurial orientation scale: A multi-country analysis, *Entrepreneurship Theory and Practice* 26: 71–94; Weaver, K. M, Dickson, M. P., Gibson, B. & Turner, A. 2002. Being uncertain: The relationship between entrepreneurial orientation and environmental uncertainty: A multi-country SME analysis, *Journal of Enterprising Culture* 10: 87–105.

26. Rauch. A., Wiklund. J., Lumpkin. G. T. & Frese. M. 2009. Entrepreneurial orientation and business performance: an assessment of past research and suggestions for
the future, *Entrepreneurship: Theory and Practice* 3: 761–787.

27. Covin, J. G. & Slevin, D. P. 1991. A conceptual model of entrepreneurship as firm
behavior, *Entrepreneurship Theory and Practice* 16: 7–25.

28. Lumpkin. G. T., Dess. G. G. 1996. Clarifying the entrepreneurial orientation
construct and linking it to performance, *Academy of Management Review* 211:
135–172.

29. Ireland. R. D., Covin. J. G. & Kuratko. D. F. 2009. Conceptualizing corporate entrepreneurship strategy, *Entrepreneurship Theory and Practice* 331: 19–46.

30. Rauch, A., Wiklund, J., Lumpkin, G. T. & Frese, M. 2009. Entrepreneurial orientation and business performance: An assessment of past research and suggestions for
the future, *Entrepreneurship Theory and Practice* 33: 761–787.

31. Ireland, R. D., Hitt, M. A. & Vaidyanath, D. 2002. Strategic alliances as a pathway
to competitive success, *Journal of Management* 28: 413–446.

32. Floyd, S. & Lane, P. 2000. Strategizing throughout the organization: Managing role
conflict in strategic renewal, *Academy of Management Review* 25: 154–177.

33. Kuratko, D. F., Ireland, R. D., Covin, J. G. & Hornsby, J. S. 2005. A model of middle-level managers' entrepreneurial behavior, *Entrepreneurship Theory & Practice*
29: 699–716.

34. Burgelman, R. A. 1983. Corporate entrepreneurship and strategic management:
Insights from a process study, *Management Science* 23: 1349–1363. Burgelman, R. A.
1984. Designs for corporate entrepreneurship in established firms, *California Management Review* 26: 154–166.

35. Antonic, B. & Hisrich, R. D. 2001. Intrapreneurship: Constructive refinement and
cross- cultural validation, *Journal of Business Venturing* 16: 495–527; Hornsby,
Kuratko. & Zahra, *Journal of Business*, 49–63; Kuratko, D. F, Ireland, R. D. &
Hornsby, J. S. 2001. Improving firm performance through entrepreneurial actions:
Acordia's corporate entrepreneurship strategy, *Academy of Management Executive*
15: 60–71; Lyon, D. W., Lumpkin, G. T. & Dess, G. G., 2000. Enhancing entrepre-
neurial orientation research: Operationalizing and measuring a key strategic deci-
sion making process, *Journal of Management* 26: 1055–1085; Morris, M. H., Kuratko,
D. F. & Covin, J. G. 2008. *Corporate Entrepreneurship & Innovation*. Mason, OH:
Cengage/Southwestern Publishing.

36. Floyd, S. & Lane, P. 2000. Strategizing throughout the organization: Managing role
conflict in strategic renewal, *Academy of Management Review* 25: 154–177.

37. Hales, C. 2005. Rooted in supervision, branching into management: Continuity
and change in the role of first–line manager, *Journal of Management Studies*
42: 471–506.

38. Hornsby, Kuratko & Zahra, Middle managers' perception of the internal environment for corporate entrepreneurship: Assessing a measurement scale, pp. 49–63.

39. Kuratko, D. F, Ireland, R. D. & Hornsby, J. S. 2001. Improving firm performance
through entrepreneurial actions: Acordia's corporate entrepreneurship strategy,
Academy of Management Executive 15: 60–71.

40. Lang, J. R., Calantone, R. J. & Gudmundson, D. 1997. Small firm information seeking as a response to environmental threats and opportunities, *Journal of Small Business Management* 35: 11–23; Beal, R. 2000. Competing effectively: Environmental
scanning, competitive strategy, and organizational performance in small manufacturing firms, *Journal of Small Business Management* 38: 27–47

41. Hornsby, Kuratko & Zahra, Middle managers' perception of the internal environment for corporate entrepreneurship: Assessing a measurement scale, 49–63.

42. Sathe, V. 1989. Fostering entrepreneurship in large diversified firm. *Organizational Dynamics* 18: 20–32; Sykes, H. B. 1986. The anatomy of a corporate venturing program. *Journal of Business Venturing* 1: 275–293; Sykes, H. B., Block, Z., 1989. Corporate venturing obstacles: Sources and solutions. *Journal of Business Venturing* 4: 159–167; Block, Z., Ornati, O. A. 1987. Compensating corporate venture managers. *Journal of Business Venturing* 2: 41–51.

43. Hayton, J. C. 2005. Promoting corporate entrepreneurship through human resource management practices: A review of empirical research, *Human Resource Management Review* 15: 21–41.

44. Sykes, H. B. & Block, Z. 1989. Corporate venturing obstacles: Sources and solutions. *Journal of Business Venturing* 4: 159–167; Stopford, J. M. & Baden-Fuller, C. W. F., 1994. Creating corporate entrepreneurship, *Strategic Management Journal* 15: 521–536; Das, T. K. & Teng, B. S. 1997. Time and entrepreneurial risk behavior, *Entrepreneurship Theory and Practice* 22: 69–88.

45. Floyd, S. & Lane, P. 2000. Strategizing throughout the organization: Managing role conflict in strategic renewal, *Academy of Management Review* 25: 154–177.

46. Shepherd, D. A., McMullen, J. S. & Jennings, P. D. 2007. The formation of opportunity beliefs: Overcoming ignorance and doubt, *Strategic Entrepreneurship Journal* 1: 75–95.

47. Miller, D. J., Fern, M. J. & Cardinal, L. B. 2007. The use of knowledge for technological innovation within diversified firms, *Academy of Management Journal* 50: 307–326.

48. Hales, C. 2005. Rooted in supervision, branching into management: Continuity and change in the role of first—line manager, *Journal of Management Studies* 42: 471–506.

49. Hornsby, J. S., Kuratko, D. F., Shepherd, D. A. & Bott, J. P. 2009. Managers' corporate entrepreneurial actions: Examining perception and position, *Journal of Business Venturing* 24: 236–247.

50. Garvin, D. & Levesque, L. October 2006. Meeting the challenge of corporate entrepreneurship, *Harvard Business Review*, 1–11.

51. Morris, M. H., Allen, J., Schindehutte, M. & Avila, R. 2006. Balanced management control systems as a mechanism for achieving corporate entrepreneurship, *Journal of Managerial Issues* 18: 468–493

52. Rauch, A., Wiklund, J., Lumpkin, G. T. & Frese, M. 2009. Entrepreneurial Orientation and Business Performance: An Assessment of Past Research and Suggestions for the Future, *Entrepreneurship Theory and Practice* 33: 761–787.

TEAM-BASED INNOVATION

INTRODUCTION

Teams are an important component to the success of corporate innovation and entrepreneurship. They are different from groups because they have a common purpose, complementary skills, common goals, and joint accountability.[1] Teams are an integral part of the management process in successful organizations.[2] Utilized effectively, teams enhance performance, quality, efficiency, and innovation.[3] However, few research studies exist that investigate critical issues related to corporate innovation team development. Much of the discussion related to innovation team development borrows heavily from the organizational behavior and human resource management areas where teams have been a popular area of study over the past 30 years. The need to understand the relationship between teams and innovation and entrepreneurship is supported by several research studies that suggest that team-founded new ventures are more successful than individually-founded ventures.[4] Also, current research suggests that team membership and the transition of members on and off the team affect team performance. However, it appears that in many cases teams struggle and often fail due to the collaborative requirements of teams, especially cross-functional teams.[5]

OVERVIEW OF TEAM DEVELOPMENT

The basic tenet of *work teams* is that jobs and organizations should be designed around processes instead of functions and that the basic production unit should be the team and not the individual. Fully mature work teams set their own work goals and perform all the tasks associated with the work process. Teams are formed for synergy—that is, to accomplish more than individuals can accomplish separately. The focus of teams is to improve quantity and/or quality of outputs.

Most employers feel like they can immediately reap the benefits of synergistic teamwork right after employees have been assigned to teams. In general, this notion is wrong because management fails to consider the type of team being implemented (functional versus cross-functional, project versus developmental, permanent versus temporary, and autonomous versus semiautonomous); the need for interpersonal development to enhance team skills in communication, decision making, and conflict resolution; and the team learning curve (the amount of time it takes for a team to become fully functional or productive). For example, many researchers claim that it takes an average of three years for a permanent team to reach its full potential as a team. It is not that the team is performing poorly but it takes time for individuals to feel comfortable in a team-based environment and they need time to improve their interpersonal and technical skills related to the team activities.[6]

The remainder of this chapter will provide an overview of the critical elements related to effective team development. These elements include team structure, stages in team development, person–team fit, interpersonal skills, and management support, including reward systems, information resources, and training and development. Figure 9-1 provides an illustration of the integral

FIGURE 9-1 Critical Elements of Innovation Team Effectiveness

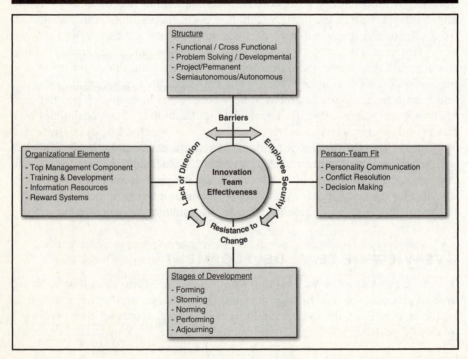

elements for forming and sustaining effective innovation teams along with the barriers that may impede team performance. Some suggestions for implementing teams in your organization are also provided.

LEVELS OF WORK TEAM IMPLEMENTATION AND TYPES OF TEAMS

Innovations can range from the radical (new products and methods) to the incremental (process improvements). The type of problems involved in the innovation effort may necessitate a specific team type or structure. There are a variety of team types; each can vary over several dimensions, including function, purpose, time duration, and leadership. The choice of team type depends on the nature of the organization, the task to be performed, and workforce expertise. Many different types of teams can exist in the same organization. Team type dimensions include:

- **Functionality**
  - *Functional teams*—Team members are from the same work unit.
  - *Cross-functional teams*—Cross-functional teams are comprised of member from different functional units or departments to work on mutual problems. It is also important that these teams have a defined mission. Since these team members are from different functional units, problems related to role conflict can arise since they have to satisfy their line manager as well as team demands.

- **Purpose**
  - *Problem-solving teams*—Team members are focused on specific issues to develop and implement solutions.
  - *Developmental teams*—Team members concentrate on developing new products or systems.

- **Duration**
  - *Project*—The team is created for a specific purpose and is dissolved when the task has been completed. It, generally, is functional in nature and used for problem solving and root cause analysis. It is important for these teams to have a defined mission or objective. Once the objective is completed the team should disband to allow team members to focus on their regular tasks.
  - *Permanent*—Permanent teams have a long-term focus in order to effectively handle major projects or issues. They are generally cross-functional, especially when related to corporate innovation activities.

- **Discretion**
  - *Semiautonomous*—The team has control over enforcing team norms but the manager still has typical human resource authority for selection,

performance assessment, and discipline. This is generally a permanent team with some formal authority structure such as a supervisor or facilitator. It can include manufacturing cells, quality/safety teams, and new venture teams. *Semiautonomous teams* are generally permanent in nature and autonomy increases as the team matures and reaches full performance.

o *Autonomous*—The team has full control over its operations and leadership. This is a permanent team that is totally empowered to make decisions concerning group membership, discipline, scheduling, and so on. These teams are generally used sparingly and found in professional occupations. Some common areas that utilize self-directed *autonomous teams* are research and development, engineering, and venture spin-offs.

In relation to corporate innovation, the type of team needed is related to the form of innovation required. Incremental innovations requiring process improvements would tend to be more functionally based to emphasize problem solving and project orientation since the focus is more on short-term problems. On the other hand, radical innovations focusing on new products and new venture spin-offs would necessitate the need for cross-functionality, developmental emphasis, and a more permanent focus (or at least a long-term focus). However, just as innovation is on a continuum from the incremental to the radical, the appropriate team structure should be selected based on the project confronted by the organization.

Researchers Michael Hyung-Jin Park, Jong Won Lim, and Philip Birnbaum-More studied the effect of multiknowledge (i.e., possessing both marketing and technological knowledge) individuals on performance in cross-functional teams. Their survey of 62 cross-functional teams revealed that the proportion of multiknowledge individuals has an indirect positive effect through information sharing on product innovativeness and a direct positive effect on time efficiency of new product development teams.[7] In further support of the importance of using cross-functional teams for effective problem solving and innovation, researchers Bantel and Jackson investigated the relationship between the social composition (i.e., team size, location, average age, average tenure in the firm, and education level) of top management teams and innovation adoptions in 199 banks. Their results indicate that innovative banks are managed by more educated (based on advanced college degrees) teams who are diverse with respect to their functional areas of expertise.[8]

Another study conducted by Floortje Blindenbach-Driessen and Jan Van Den Ende suggested that we should be cautious in our use of cross-functional teams. A comparison of 135 innovation projects in 96 firms showed that multidisciplinary teams had a lower effect on performance of innovation projects in project-based firms than in other firms. Their explanation for this finding is that collaboration is abundant in project-based firms and that multidisciplinary teams have a limited added effect. However, cross-functional teams enhanced performance in the nonproject-based firms. They further suggest that project-based firms need specialization within their innovation projects instead of collaboration between disciplines and functions.[9]

It is important to realize that an organization should make significant investments in both technical and interpersonal training to help team members maximize their potential as a team and avoid some of the conflicts and pitfalls that hinder team development.

STAGES OF TEAM FORMATION

Borrowing from traditional group behavior research and the formative work conducted by Tuckman,[10] teams appear to go through at least a five-stage process as they mature. This development process occurs for every team but the pace of progression can vary based on the skill level of the team members, team-member experience with teams in the past, and team member interpersonal skills. Initially, Tuckman suggested a four-stage model and then added the fifth stage in 1972. The following stages need to be recognized by the group so that effective strategies for interpersonal development and leadership can be implemented for team growth. Figure 9-2 presents the stages and the issues facing the team when attempting problem solving and innovation.

FORMING STAGE

During the forming stage, team members are on their best behavior. Basic introductions are conducted and team members generally withhold negative opinions about others on the team or the mission of the team. It is important that the team

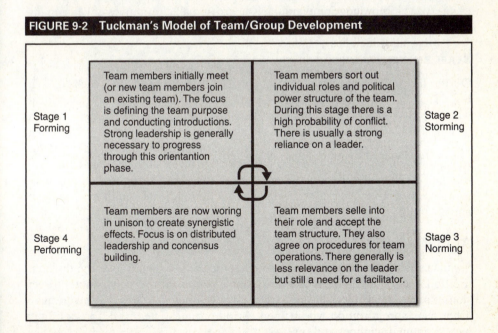

FIGURE 9-2   Tuckman's Model of Team/Group Development

Stage 1 Forming	Team members initially meet (or new team members join an existing team). The focus is defining the team purpose and conducting introductions. Strong leadership is generally necessary to progress through this orientantion phase.	Team members sort out individual roles and political power structure of the team. During this stage there is a high probability of conflict. There is usually a strong reliance on a leader.	Stage 2 Storming
Stage 4 Performing	Team members are now woring in unison to create synergistic effects. Focus is on distributed leadership and concensus building.	Team members selle into their role and accept the team structure. They also agree on procedures for team operations. There generally is less relevance on the leader but still a need for a facilitator.	Stage 3 Norming

facilitator or manager play a directing role and initiate formal introductions and encourage team members to meet each other.

STORMING STAGE

During this stage, team members search out the power and influence relationships in the team. The formal and informal authority relationships are investigated and each member attempts to assess his or her own individual place in the group. Obviously, dysfunctional conflicts can erupt during this stage if the individuals do not have the necessary conflict-resolution skills and if there is not a strong manager or facilitator that can manage the conflict. The conflict, at least initially, may not be bad, but if left to fester, can cause the team to stagnate in the storming stage indefinitely. It is important that the facilitator play a selling role, foster group acceptance, and develop group decision-making procedures and other group rules so that the team can successfully complete the storming stage.

NORMING STAGE

During the norming stage there is an initial integration of team members where there is acceptance by team members of the team's rules of engagement. Each member is relatively satisfied with his or her place in the group and the leadership structure that is running the group. Group members should avoid an environment of false consensus where it appears that the individuals agree because they are too afraid to speak out. Since the team may not have reached a desired level of maturity, the facilitator/manager plays a supporting role and may have to intervene and make sure everyone is heard and all alternatives have been discussed.

PERFORMING STAGE

During this stage, team members become totally integrated and reach full synergy. Team members engage in open, mature communication. Conflicts are dealt with directly and no team member is afraid to speak up. Also, interpersonal and technical skills of each member develop substantially and start to complement the strengths and overcome the weaknesses of other team members. During this stage, the facilitators/managers should back off in terms of their formal authority role and allow the team to function by consensus as much as possible. The manager becomes more of a liaison between other departments, senior management, and the team.

ADJOURNING STAGE

Some teams are permanent in nature in that they hold a specific place in the organizational chart. These types of teams include manufacturing cells, standing decision-making committees, and research and development teams. However, many other teams are formed for a defined period of time. These task forces usually have a defined mission to complete. It is important that these teams recognize

FIGURE 9-3   Team Formation and Performance

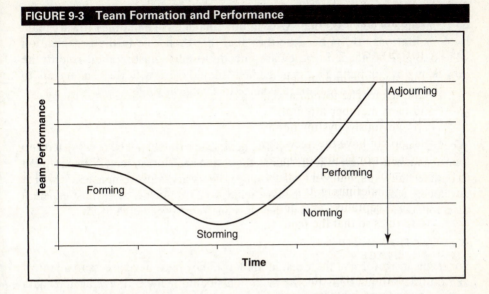

that once the task has been completed and evaluated it is time to move on to other projects. Temporary teams, while important for dealing with unexpected problems, cause stress and role confusion to team members since they hold a formal position in a department (with tasks and responsibilities) along with their obligations to the temporary team mission. The team leader or facilitator plays a delegating role, making sure all team members are invited to lead initiatives and contribute based on their knowledge and experiences.

Given the level of individual and team dynamics at each level of development, team performance generally declines after initial start-up but rebounds as the team progresses through the stages of development. Figure 9-3 describes the team learning curve experienced by teams as they advance through the five stages identified earlier.

KEY OGANZIATIONAL ELEMENTS OF WORK TEAMS

Several elements contribute to the successful implementation of the team concept. The following key organizational elements seem to be ones commonly cited by firms who have successfully implemented work teams. These include management commitment, training and development, information resources, reward systems, conflict resolution, and communication.

MANAGEMENT COMMITMENT

Top-management support is critical to team implementation, especially during the forming and storming stages of development. Since it takes time for the synergistic effects of teams to develop, senior management must be patient and willing to expend the resources it takes to develop the team. Results may not be immediately forthcoming. Also, middle managers sometimes thwart team implementations efforts because they feel that their role in the organization will no longer be needed or they are uncomfortable adjusting their role to the new team environment. Top management should work with these managers to develop them and reduce their resistance to change as well.

TRAINING AND DEVELOPMENT

Whether the team is temporary or permanent, teams should not be constructed and then abandoned. As any other resource, they often need investment. A commitment to both technical and interpersonal training is necessary. Most companies do well at developing technical skills but the cost-minded CFOs often rebel against expenditures for developing soft skills that they "assume" employees already have.

INFORMATION RESOURCES

For teams to perform at their maximum level, they must have access to all information relevant to their specific tasks. This could include financial/sales data and production data. Teams cannot be spoon-fed information. This is especially problematic for cross-functional teams that require team members to gain an integrated understanding of the problem.[11]

REWARD SYSTEMS

This is probably the most difficult component. Many organizations and employees are reluctant to provide rewards on a team basis. Most performance measurement/appraisal systems are set up to measure individual performance and would have to be adapted to capture the nature of team performance.[12] Also, individual apprehension by employees exists when there are some team members that may not be as deserving as others.[13]

PERSON-TEAM FIT: PERSONALITY AND INTERPERSONAL SKILLS

Knowledge of oneself—self-awareness—is essential to one's productive personal and interpersonal functioning and in understanding and empathizing with other people, especially in a team environment. When you are assessing team development issues, such as who to include and what type of interpersonal training is required, problems related to individual personality and communication, conflict resolution, and decision-making skills must be examined.

PERSONALITY

Personality is a stable set of characteristics and tendencies that determine those commonalties and differences in the psychological behavior (thoughts, feelings, and actions) of people. Perhaps the most common personality assessment instrument is the *Myers-Briggs Type Indicator (MBTI)*. This instrument was based on the early work of Carl Jung and developed by the mother–daughter team of Briggs and Myers. Specifically, they suggest the following four continua of traits:

- Extravert (E) or Introvert (I): Where you prefer to focus and where you get your energy.
- Sensing (S) or Intuiting (N): Type of preferred information.
- Thinking (T) or Feeling (F): How you prefer to make decisions.
- Judging (P) or Perceiving (P): How you prefer to cope with the outside world.

These four traits combine to form 16 possible types or preference combinations. Consulting Psychologists Press (CPP), which currently owns the Myers-Briggs Type Indicator, suggests that there are common traits related to an innovative individual. They suggest that people with a preference for Sensing are drawn toward details, specifics, and incremental understanding, whereas people with a preference for Intuition are drawn toward the big picture, patterns, and original ideas. The Sensing tendency to build things incrementally based on experience is about seeking to adapt current realities. In contrast, the Intuition tendency to create the big picture from scratch based on hunches and through discerning underlying patterns is about seeking originality. Your *innovation attitude* is determined by your preference for either Sensing or Intuition in combination with your preference for either Judging or Perceiving.[14]

In general, personality diversity among team members is desired to allow for the sharing of different perspectives. However, individuals who are extreme introverts may find working in the social environment of teams overwhelming. While specific types (e.g., ENTP [entrepreneurial]) may lead to more innovative team members, other types may serve a complementary role that enhances overall team performance. The Myers-Briggs Type Indicator can be purchased from the company Consulting Psychologists Press. You can also find many similar assessments by conducting a Web search. Some of them have a fee and others are free of charge.

COMMUNICATION

One of the hardest challenges for individuals when placed in a team-based environment is to effectively communicate with team members. In traditional organizations, many employees are not expected to communicate their opinions or share their ideas. However, this type of communication is the key to team success. Also, creativity in teams is highly dependent on effective communication.[15] If possible, communication training regarding how to communicate effectively should be conducted prior to team formation and continue on through the team-orientation process.

Two major aspects of communication to focus on for development include self-disclosure and receptivity to feedback. Self-disclosure represents your willingness to express your feelings, opinions, and beliefs, while receptivity to feedback represents your openness to receive feedback from others on your behaviors, opinions, and beliefs. In effect, team members must effectively balance the sharing and receiving of information among each other. High-performing teams are comprised of individuals who are high in both self-disclosure and receptivity to feedback. However, this is a struggle for team members, especially in the early stages of development. Individuals struggle to break out of their traditional guarded posture to practice effective open communication.

CONFLICT RESOLUTION

Conflict is the tension that exists when people or organizations have conflicting and competing goals. An organization's approach to conflict can make it either constructive or destructive. Modern organizations must approach conflict differently. They must realize that conflict in a team-based environment:

- Is natural and often inevitable
- Is a possible motivator for change
- Can result from competition over values, power, or resources
- Can be constructive or destructive
- Can contribute to organizational innovation
- Can be managed to minimize losses and maximize gains for all team members

Most people tend to dislike conflict. We have been taught since early childhood socialization that conflict is bad and should be avoided if possible. However, in many cases, conflict can be a constructive force, especially in an organization that emphasizes innovation and creative problem solving.[16] In general:

Conflict is destructive if it...

- Diverts energy from important tasks and issues
- Produces barriers to cooperation and collaboration
- Decreases productivity
- Deepens differences among parties
- Destroys morale
- Produces negative behavior
- Prevents discussion and confrontation of differences

Conflict is constructive when it...

- Opens an issue to cooperative discussion and debate
- Leads to an innovative solution of a problem
- Leads to a higher level of understanding, communication, and trust
- Helps people to grow personally and apply their new knowledge, skill, and understanding to future situations
- Helps individuals realize the importance of communication

Positive conflict-resolution strategies that result in win–win solutions require open communication and a willingness to negotiate on important issues. There appears to be at least five types of conflict management styles:

- *Forcing*—Assertive and uncooperative behavior where you force your solution on others.
- *Compromising*—Arriving at a middle ground between the parties.
- *Avoiding*—Unassertive and uncooperative behavior where the individual runs from the conflict and those engaged in the conflict.
- *Accommodating*—Cooperative but unassertive behavior characterized by giving in to the other side.
- *Collaborating*—Cooperative and assertive behavior ending in a win–win solution where both sides get what they really need.

While in the short run, any of the styles may be somewhat effective, most team-based situations require at a minimum compromise and at a maximum collaboration in order to be a high-performing team. Forcing, avoiding, and accommodating styles often damage relationships and lead to a lack of team integration. Also, while compromising is an easier alternative since you are essentially dividing the "pie" down the middle, teams or individuals in conflict should attempt a collaborative result where each side negotiates the issue until both sides are satisfied that their critical issues are resolved.

Effective management of conflict comes from the following steps:

1. Identifying and understanding root causes of conflict
2. Recognizing styles of conflict and working toward a collaborative resolution
3. Exploring needs and differences among team members
4. Working toward constructive resolution of the conflict.

What kind of strategies do teams use in situations of conflict and what are the consequences for creativity? Researchers Petra, Goldschmidt, and Meijer analyzed how design teams coped with conflict during idea generation.[17] They found that even in a laboratory environment, design teams encounter a considerable amount of conflict. The high-innovation and high-functionality groups used a more competing and a more compromising style, whereas groups rated low on the same parameters used a more collaborating style. This result seems counterintuitive and contradicts past research. The authors suggest that creative performance in teams is not achieved mainly by agreement but needs cognitive confrontation. However, this finding makes no suggestion for long-term team survival. One possible explanation of these results is that the design project was viewed as short term and temporary, given its experimental nature, so participants may have engaged in behaviors that could be detrimental to long-term team effectiveness.

DECISION MAKING

Decisions by teams have many advantages over those made by individuals. Any one individual may be limited by professional expertise, ability to gather information, and ability to integrate information. In a team environment, individuals bring together a broader base of skills, experience, and expertise. Teams also provide a forum for brainstorming and critical evaluation of alternatives. The following guidelines are helpful when deciding who to include in the *decision-making process*:

- If a high-quality decision is necessary but employee acceptance is not a concern, then include those who are experts in the area.
- If acceptance by employees is necessary but quality of the decision is not an issue, then include representation by those employees affected by the decision.
- If a high-quality decision and employee acceptance are both important, form a team of experts and employee representatives.
- If both decision-making quality and employee acceptance are not important, make the decision yourself.

When making team-based decisions, at least five steps should be followed. It is important to note that many *decision-making processes* are suggested in the literature. Critical elements of an effective decision-making process include problem identification, creative brainstorming, action planning, implementation, and evaluation.

Step 1—Identifying/Defining the Problem
The team members must take the time to assess the major issues. You need to make sure you are getting at the root cause of the problem and not merely addressing symptoms. Some specific issues to address at this stage are:

- Was everyone who might have relevant data represented at the team meeting?
- Were those most directly involved in defining the problem encouraged by the leader and other team members to give information?
- Was everyone asked whether he or she agrees with the final problem statement as written?

Step 2—Solution Generation
Activity at this step requires brainstorming possible alternatives. Some specific rules to follow when brainstorming include:

- No evaluation of any kind is permitted as alternatives are being generated. Individual energy is spent on generating ideas, not defending them.
- The wildest possible ideas are encouraged. It is easier to tighten alternatives up than loosen them.

- The quantity of ideas takes precedence over the quality. Emphasizing quality engenders judgment and evaluation.
- Participants should build on or modify the ideas of others. Poor ideas that are added to or altered often become good ideas.

Some issues to be addressed by team members in this stage include:

- Have all the resources of the team been used to generate ideas?
- Did the leader and other team members take time to encourage those who might be slower at expressing ideas?
- Did the team take time to examine all the ideas and combine them into sets of alternatives?
- Was criticism tactfully discouraged and evaluative comments postponed?

Step 3—Ideas to Action
Once a list of possible solutions have been generated, the team should create an action plan for each of the possible solutions generated. Specifically, the team should assess people, resources (including time), processes, and machinery/equipment involved in the problem. Specific issues to be addressed include…

- Did the team examine the alternatives in terms of human, financial, and other costs associated with each and in terms of new problems that might arise?
- Was the team able to evaluate ideas critically without attacking individual who proposed or supported those ideas?
- Is the chosen solution related to the problem statement and the goals developed earlier?
- Was final consensus reached on a trial solution? If not, was the extent of agreement among team members clearly established?

Step 4—Implementing the Decision
After the team reaches consensus on the best solution, the action plan (completed in Step 3) for that solution must be implemented. Meetings to secure the resources need to be conducted. Also, the team should devise a timeline for full implementation. Issues to be addressed in Step 4 include:

- Did the team identify the various forces that might help or hinder the action being planned?
- Were all team members involved in the discussion, particularly in giving information needed to define actions and ensure that essential steps weren't left out?
- Were all the needed resources for taking the action clearly identified?
- Did each person who accepted responsibility for a task make a clear commitment to carry out that responsibility?

Step 5—Team Decision-Making Evaluation

In order to not repeat mistakes made in the first four decision-making steps, the team should evaluate the effectiveness of their decision-making process. In addition, the team should determine the appropriate criteria to evaluate the success of the decision itself. Some final issues to address include:

- Has the team reviewed the desired outcomes and developed measures to indicate the degree of success achieved?
- Were contingency plans outlined for critical steps so that the overall plan could continue with modifications along the way if necessary?

When it comes to innovation *project teams,* researchers Akgun, Lynn, and Byrne suggest that management should enhance changes in beliefs and routines when facing advances in technological sophistication. They believe that to minimize groupthink, management should break established team mental models and project infrastructures by encouraging new behaviors. They suggest activities such as using a devil's advocate, bringing outsiders into the decision-making process, or training the team on lateral (creative) thinking.[18] Devil's advocates are appointed from within the group to challenge all assumptions and ensure that all possible solutions are considered. Outsiders are experts in the area being addressed who can provide a fresh look to possible alternatives and are not impacted by team conflict or relationships. Lateral or creative thinking involves invoking processes that force team members to continually diverge or brainstorm in an "out of the box" and not rush to quick problem identification or solutions.

As discussed in this section of the chapter, elements related to person–team fit, including personality, communication, conflict resolution, and decision-making styles, are positively related to team effectiveness. One other element, the leader-team fit should also be considered. Researchers Sarin and O'Conner emphasized the impact of team leader characteristics on conflict-resolution behavior, collaboration, and communication patterns of cross-functional new product development teams. They surveyed 246 members of 64 new product development teams and found that leader-participative management style and initiation of goal structure exerted the strongest influence on internal team dynamics. Both participative management and initiation of goal structure had a positive effect on functional conflict resolution, collaboration, and communication quality within the teams studied. They also found that dysfunctional conflict resolution and formal communications were reduced.[19]

COMMMON BARRIERS TO IMPLEMENTATION

Team implementation, as discussed earlier, is a dynamic process requiring organizational commitment. However, there are several barriers that can inhibit team success. These barriers include resistance to change, lack of proper direction, and threats to employee security.

RESISTANCE TO CHANGE

Work teams are not appropriate to all work situations, such as highly specialized functions. Approximately 25–30 percent of workers do not want to be "empowered" through working on teams. Some of the most likely contributors to this resistance include previous bad experiences in team environments, introverted *personality types,* and age of the employees (older workers seem to be more resistant to trying new approaches).

LACK OF PROPER DIRECTION

Teams are often highly motivated but lack clear direction. Since about 70–75 percent of the workforce is not resistant to teams, initially they feel energized or motivated by the notion of this type of structure and the opportunity to be empowered. However, empowerment does not mean abandonment! While the role of the manager changes to more of a facilitator perspective, it should not go away. Someone has to communicate information to the team and facilitate team discussions and other functions. This "leader" must help secure resources and speak for the team to other organizational units.

EMPLOYEE SECURITY

Employees need to trust management in that teams are not being used as a mechanism for downsizing, especially when it comes to their own job. Unions often fear teams, unless they are union based, because they also threaten the collective power of the union process. However, many unionized firms have successfully implemented cross-functional teams comprising of union and nonunion employees. The key to developing employee teams seems to be a common belief in the team's mission and open communication.

CONCLUSION: IMPLEMENTING EFFECTIVE TEAMS

In conclusion, team structures should not be implemented without careful study. Remember, one size does not fit all. Consider your mission, the experience level of your employees, top-management support, and training resources before you implement a team-based strategy. These key steps will help with implementing innovation teams:

- Prepare the organization for the change. Effective teamwork requires trust, effective communication, and viable conflict-resolution strategies. Also, the right people need to be on the team. The right mix of employee skills and experiences, coupled with strong interpersonal skills, will increase team effectiveness. Training and development activities may be required to prepare the organization for effective team implementation and utilization.
- Make sure the appropriate team structure is selected to address the problem at hand. Furthermore, understand that there is a team learning curve

and it can take many months for a team to reach high performance. A good team leader will recognize the stages of team development and lead the team effectively through those stages.

- Be selective when it comes to team leaders. Besides technical experience, utilize effective selection and training practices to find and develop individuals to be effective motivators and communicators.

- Utilize a process for creative or lateral thinking. Typical problem-solving processes often rush to a solution without diverging deeply on what the problem really is and identifying possible solutions.

- Evaluate team effectiveness on a regular basis and seek ways to continuously improve. Table 9-1 contains important questions to consider when evaluating team effectiveness.

TABLE 9-1   Ten Questions to Ask About Your Team

Every organizational intervention or change effort should be monitored and evaluated to assess programmatic strengths and weakness. No change effort is flawless and fine-tuning is often necessary to ensure the continued success of the team implementation effort. Evaluation should take place during implementation as well as when the team effort has been completed and the team is ready to adjourn. The following ten questions are critical to track the success of your firm's efforts in this area:

1. Are the manager/facilitator's expectations clear to everyone?
2. Are members' expectation for each other well communicated? Are individual responsibilities clearly stated?
3. Are you a cohesive and integrated team? Is everyone working toward the same goals?
4. Do members help each other appropriately, giving feedback on how their behavior affects each other's effectiveness? Are members honest with each other?
5. Does the team have all the skills and abilities it needs to do the job?
6. Is each member doing his or her utmost to help you?
7. Does the team communicate well with others?
8. As a group, do you place a high priority on developing each other?
9. Is each member involved in decision making?
10. Are you satisfied as a member of this team?

INNOVATION-IN-ACTION

Creating and Sustaining Hot Spots for Innovation

Hot Spots are the organization phenomena that result from what Linda Gratton refers to as the "twin drivers" of democratic organizational change. These drivers of democratic organizational change and new technologies create the energy that causes business innovation.

According to the developer of the Hot Spot concept, Linda Gratton, "You always know when you are in a Hot Spot… where cooperation flourishes, great energy is created, and innovation, productivity and excitement drive the day." Gratton assesses the necessary ingredients for creating Hot Spot energy and uses the concept of boundary-less cooperation as the fuel for the Hot Spot.

Gratton suggests that Hot Spots' innovation energy comes from people freely combining their insights, wisdom, and intelligence. To create this energy, the following team-building conditions are critical:

1. Having a "cooperative mind-set."
2. Identifying "boundary spanners."
3. Sharing "igniting purpose."
4. Sustaining sufficient "productive capacity."

Dr. Gratton uses the following formula to suggest how these elements fit together to create Hot Spots.

$$\text{Hot Spots} = (\text{Cooperative Mind-Set} \times \text{Boundary Spanning} \times \text{Igniting Purpose}) \times \text{Productive Capacity}$$

Five underlying productive practices—appreciating talent, making commitments, resolving conflicts, synchronizing time, and establishing a rhythm—are necessary to create the conditions for Hot Spots. Gratton also argues that the initial step in creating a Hot Spot is to stop doing things. The old language, practices, and processes of competition must be stopped. Since teams of people working together are responsible for most of the modern innovations, we need a new language and practices that promote cooperation.

Gratton makes several suggestions for improving organizational practices to create and maintain Hot Spots. First, companies need to stop recruiting people who are overly aggressive and could possibly cause deterioration of the democratic organizational norms. Second, companies need to quit reinforcing competitive behavior and recruit talent that focus on relationships and cooperation. Third, while it may be somewhat helpful to benchmark successful practices of other firms, competitive advantage comes from identifying "signature processes" that embody the organization's character. In general, employee development activities should be focused on identifying collaborative ways of working, building relationships, and motivating people. Employees should sense a meaningful purpose, vision, and goals.

Source: Based on Tavis, A. September 2010. "Hot Spots: Why Some Teams, Workplaces, and Organizations Buzz with Energy—And Others Don't." (Book review). Retrieved September 6, 2010, *Entrepreneur.com*: http://www.entrepreneur.com/tradejournals/article/166051344.html

Key Terms

Adjourning stage

Autonomous teams

Cross-functional teams

Decision-making process

Developmental teams

Employee security

Forming stage

Functional teams

Information resources

innovation attitude

Norming stage

Performing stage

Permanent teams

Personality types

Project teams

Resistance to change

Semiautonomous teams

Storming stage

Work teams

Discussion Questions

1. Why are teams so important to the corporate innovation process?
2. Describe the stages of team development. What issues are presented in each stage? How do they relate to innovation?
3. What types of teams would be effective for incremental innovation? Radical innovation?
4. What are the barriers to effective team implementation? How would you overcome these barriers?
5. What are the important steps in a team decision-making or problem-solving process.
6. When is conflict destructive? Constructive?
7. What is the most applicable personality trait for innovation? Why?
8. Why is it important to evaluate team effectiveness? How would you evaluate team effectiveness?

Endnotes

1. Katzenbach, J. & Smith, D. 1993. *The Wisdom of Teams: Creating the High-Performance Organization.* Boston, MA: Harvard Business School Press, 45.
2. Griffin, R. & Moorhead, G. 2010. *Organizational Behavior: Managing People and Organizations*, 9th ed. Cincinnati, OH: South-Western/Cengage Learning, 253.
3. Wellins, R. Byham, W. & Dixon, G. 1994. *Inside Teams.* San Francisco, CA: Jossey-Bass.
4. Gaylen, N. C., Honig, B. & Wiklund, J. 2004. Antecedents, moderators, and performance consequences of membership change in new venture teams, *Journal of Business Venturing* 20: 705–725.
5. Jassawalla, A. R. & Sashittal, H. C. 1999. Building collaborative cross-functional new product teams, *Academy of Management Executive* 13: 50–61.
6. Griffin, R. & Moorhead, G. 2010. *Organizational Behavior: Managing People and Organizations,* 9th ed. Cincinnati, OH: South-Western/Cengage Learning, 253.
7. Hyung-Jin Park, M., Lim, J. W. & Birnbaum-More, P. H. 2009. The effect of multi-knowledge individuals on performance in cross-functional new product development teams, *Journal of Product Innovation Management* 26: 86–96.

8. Bantel, K. A. & Jackson, S. E. 1989. Top management and innovations in banking: Does the composition of the top team make a difference? *Strategic Management Journal* 10: 107–124.

9. Blindenbach-Driessen, F. & Van Den Ende, J. 2010. Innovation practices compared: The example of project-based firms, *Journal of Product Innovation Management* 27: 705–724.

10. Tuckman, B. W. 1965. Developmental sequence in small groups, *Psychological Bulletin* 63: 384–399; Tuckman, B. W. 1972. *Conducting educational research*, 5th ed. New York: Harcourt Brace Jovanovich. (5th ed. 1999 by Wadsworth).

11. Hyatt, D. & Ruddy, T. 1997. An examination of the relationship between work group characteristics and performance: Once more into the breech, *Personnel Psychology* 50: 555.

12. Johnson, S. March–April 1993). Work teams: What's ahead in work design and rewards management. *Compensation and Benefits Management Review* 25 (2): 35–41.

13. McClurg, L. spring. 2001. Team rewards: How far have we come? *Human Resource Management* 40 (1): 73–86.

14. Killen, D. & Williams, G. "Introduction to Type® and Innovation," Consulting Psychologist Press. Accessed on September 8, 2010, http://www.cpp.com/pdfs/6185.pdf.

15. Ward, A. J., Lankau, M. J., Amason, A.C., Sonnenfeld, J. A., & Agle, B.R. (2007). Improving the Performance of Top Management Teams. *MIT Sloan Management Review,* 48(3): 78-91.

16. Carsten, K. January 2008. The virtue and vice of workplace conflict: Food for (pessimistic) thought. *Journal of Organizational Behavior* 29: 5–18.

17. Petra, B., Goldschmidt, G. & Meijer, M. 2010. How does cognitive conflict in design teams support the development of creative ideas? Creativity and Innovation Management 19: 119–133.

18. Akgun, A., Lynn, G. & Byrne, J. 2005. Antecedents and consequences of unlearning in new product development teams. *Journal of Product Innovation Management* 23: 73–88.

19. Sarin, S. & O'Connor, G. C. 2009. First among equals: The effect of team leader characteristics on the internal dynamics of cross-functional product development teams. *Journal of Product Innovation Management* 26: 188–205.

PART 5

IMPLEMENTATION OF INNOVATION
(I-PLANS)

10

INNOVATION TO COMMERCIALIZATION

INTRODUCTION

Robert McKee, a screenwriting coach, once stated: "Persuasion is the center-piece of business activity. Customers must be convinced to buy your company's products or services, employees and colleagues to go along with a new strategic plan or reorganization, investors to buy (or not to sell) your stock, and partners to sign the next deal. But despite the critical importance of persuasion, most executives struggle to communicate, let alone inspire."[1]

Innovations are not successful without commercial appeal. New products and services, no matter how technologically advanced or sophisticated, will not sell without having an authentic connection with the customer. Richard Maxwell and Robert Dickman capture the essence of this condition with their simple observation that "There are two things everyone in business does every day. We all sell something—our products, our services, our skills, our ideas, our **vision** of where our business is going—and we tell stories. We sell things because this is how we as a democratic, capitalist society organize our energy. We tell stories because, as cognitive psychology is continuing to discover, stories are how we as human being organize our minds. If we want to sell something, we have to persuade someone else to buy it."[2] In the previous chapters, we discussed how to develop an innovative product or service. In this chapter, we will provide guidance on how to commercialize your innovation. This chapter opens with a section on how to do market research. Market research will provide the evidence needed to support the potential rewards of your innovation for the company and the customer. This understanding is then used to prepare your selling points. Working with your knowledge of the customer, you will prepare elements of your innovation that your *stakeholders* will be most curious about. You will then be able to craft the story you will tell others about your innovation. The chapter concludes with guidance on how to present this story to others.

MARKET RESEARCH

The contemporary business environment can be characterized in terms of increasing risk, decreased ability to forecast, fluid firm and industry boundaries, a managerial mind-set that must unlearn traditional management *principles,* and new structural forms that not only allow for change, but also help create it. Establishing the viability of an idea is critical when seeking internal or external funding and support. A critical component to establishing idea viability is market research. The following sections describe the critical steps in identifying your market and developing reliable sources of primary and secondary research.

UNDERSTANDING THE REAL POTENTIAL MARKET

A **market** is a group of consumers (potential customers) who have purchasing power and unsatisfied needs. An innovation will only be successful if a market exists for the new product or service. Marketing research involves the gathering of information about a particular market, followed by analysis of that information. The goal of the market research is to identify a potential customer/client base for your innovation. The following actions should be followed:

DEFINE THE RESEARCH PURPOSE AND OBJECTIVES
You need to be able to concretely describe the product or service in some sort of innovation description. Included in this description is an explanation of the specific product or service, identification of the potential customer base, and an analysis of the issues related to where you will do business. This market segmentation process identifies a specific set of characteristics that differentiate one group of consumers from the rest. It is the process of identifying the *niche*! See Appendix A for a detailed example of an innovation description.

SELECT TYPE OF DATA
Before you start the research process, a decision needs to be made with respect to primary and/or secondary data sources. *Primary data* is information you collect yourself using *surveys*, focus groups, and one-on-one interviews. Focus groups are generally utilized for group reactions to product improvements, while surveys and interviews assess widespread interest in the idea and propensity to act in regards to purchasing and/or using the potential product or services. Due to the time-consuming nature of one-on-one interviews, it is recommended that these be utilized when there is need for explanation or language interpretation is required. Primary data is time consuming to collect but it will be current and relevant. *Secondary data* is information that you collect from already published sources such as government reports, chambers of commerce, trade associations, business assistance centers such as the Small Business Development Center (SBDC), and business websites. There are also specific websites that provide

important populations statistics. One of the most popular sites is Maps and Stats. These sites provide *demographic* breakdown based on age, sex, race, location, and household size for stats such as household income. Business information is available not only from some of these sources, but also sources such as the Harris Directory could be useful. The Harris Directory lists company contact information and some basic data for each firm. These sites, like many business directories, charge a subscription fee. Both primary and secondary data sources are valuable. Primary data is not only the most reliable, but it is also the most time consuming and costly. Secondary data can be obtained quickly and many times at no or low cost, but you must assess the relevancy of the data to your market and the currency of the information. It is advisable to utilize as many sources of data, both primary and secondary, and look for consistencies across sources.

THE SURVEY PROCESS

Survey process issues include identifying the survey audience, the number of surveys necessary to represent the population, and the type of surveys to administer. The first issue to address is identifying the survey audience. Your audience is those individuals or businesses who would use your product or service. Specifically, you need to identify who will make the purchasing decision and get him or her to participate.

Next, you need to determine the number of respondents necessary for statistical relevance. The table below provides some guidelines to the number of surveys needed to represent a specific sized population. It is important that you attempt to be as random as possible in survey distribution. In order to accurately approximate the population percentage of those interested in your product or service, it is critical to ensure a cross section of the population is surveyed. For example, if your survey sample is biased toward individuals you think would be interested in your idea, you will overestimate the percentage of the population who would buy your product or service.

Required Samples for Universes of Various Sizes	
Number In the Universe	**Sample Size**
1–55	50
56–63	55
64–70	60
71–77	65
78–87	70
88–99	80
100–115	90
116–138	100
139–153	110
154–180	125

| Required Samples for Universes of Various Sizes ||
Number In the Universe	Sample Size
181–238	150
239–308	175
309–398	200
399–650	250
651–1200	300
1201–2700	350
2701 or more	400

Selecting a survey type is also an important issue. Surveys are usually conducted via in-person interviews, via mail, and on the telephone. Response rates vary from 10–30 percent for mail and up to 70 percent for in-person and telephone approaches. E-mail survey response rates are fractional. In general, most market research surveys are effective when conducted in-person near the site of the possible target market! If you must use mail surveys, make sure the survey is sent to the appropriate person and try to offer some inducement to complete the survey. If the information is valuable, you could promise a copy of the results. You could also offer a gift certificate or have a drawing for a prize for all participants.

CONSTRUCT THE QUESTIONNAIRE

Generally, surveys are comprised of at least four types of questions. The different types include demographic, factual, attitude, and open-ended questions. The following table describes each of the different types of questions. *Two examples of actual surveys can be found at the end of this chapter in Appendix B.*

Common Question Formats

Questions	Description
Demographic Questions	These questions assess data that segments your market on variables such as age, gender, race, business, income, education, and location. The goal of these questions is to describe your client base for business development. Be sure to only ask necessary questions and provide ranges for topics such as individual or business income.
Factual Questions	Include questions concerning previous experience or use. Focus on yes/no questions for actual use and use ranges for amount of usage. It helps to provide ranges instead of asking for exact amounts.
Attitude Questions	Uses rating scale format to assess propensity to act, like/dislike, and importance. This is the most important part of the survey. Rating scales are usually 1 to 5 where 1 is not at all likely and 5 very likely.

Questions	Description
Open-ended Questions	These questions are utilized to initiate comments and wrap-up statements. They are viewed by respondents as time consuming and cause people to refuse or quit the survey without finishing. The resulting data is very hard to analyze and quantify. Many respondents simply ignore them. Only ask them if necessary and put them at the end of the survey. When constructing the survey, it would also be helpful to adhere to the following tips:

TIPS FOR SURVEY DEVELOPMENT

- Make sure each question pertains to a specific objective in line with the purpose of the study.

- Keep each question short and simple. Lengthy or wordy questions often cause confusion.

- Avoid double-barreled items. These are items with conjunctions such as "and," "or," and "but." These items confuse the reader and you do not know which part of the item they are answering.

- Place simple questions first and difficult-to-answer questions later in the questionnaire.

- Avoid leading and biased questions.

- When possible, use scaled questions rather than simple yes/no questions to measure intensity of an attitude or frequency of the experience.

- Make sure the questions assess what you are trying to measure.

- Keep the survey under two pages, if possible. There is an inverse relationship between survey length and quit rate.

- Test face validity on a few people before administering the survey for real. Test for understanding and count the time it takes to complete the survey.

ANALYZE RESULTS AND WRITE REPORT

Typical analyses include averages, frequencies, cross-tabulations, and content-analyzing open-ended questions. Averages and frequencies are fairly straightforward and provide basic descriptive information about each item. Content analysis is a simple count of the number of times a response was given. Perhaps the most useful analysis is the cross-tabulation. This analysis allows you to cross a demographic item with any other item. For instance, you may want to know the difference in willingness to purchase your product or service based on sex, income, location, etc. This type of analysis is essential to identify the actual niche of individuals or businesses that would purchase the product or service. You can use this information to estimate percentages of the population who would purchase and at what price they would purchase the product or service.

Once the analyses are completed, a report should be written summarizing the important findings and interpreting their implications for the viability and feasibility of your idea. This report is often included as part of an innovation plan or feasibility report. Important elements include a statement of support for the product/service; segmentation of the viable market niche; and projection of sales based on likelihood of consumer spending.

Most managers have difficulty preparing and presenting market research and analyses that will convince senior management the innovation's sales estimates are accurate and attainable. The aspects of marketing addressed in this section should aid the manager in developing a comprehensive exposition of the market. With this knowledge, the manager can now begin to concentrate on other areas of interest senior management will have about the innovation. The following section provides guidance on addressing the other elements needed for commercializing your innovation.

PREPARING FOR COMMERCIALIZATION

Many growing companies have interesting and innovative ideas but struggle to bring them to market. A key source of this frustration is the inability to get other needed constituencies to believe in the concept and vision as the manager does. If a manager can clearly convey the concept, vision, and important details, he is much more likely to gain buy-in from needed stakeholders. Unfortunately, many managers attempting entrepreneurial projects have not adequately thought through these concepts or systematically organized them into a compelling narrative. This skill, though overlooked in most business books, may be one of the most distinguishing factors between success and failure in organizations.

An essential challenge during commercialization is explaining why you want to pursue the innovation and how you will do it. Once you have an answer to this question, you will be able to better communicate to others your vision and goals for the company and stakeholders. This preparation will make for better presentations, both formally and informally, to potential investors, loan providers, clients/customers, and employees. By examining these factors, you will also be able to better answer many of the questions you'll face as you try to start up a project. However, these questions can be reexamined and your answers modified as your project grows and evolves. The story of your new idea is one that will be rewritten and retold many times as you face new issues and challenges in your industry, target market, and world. In the following sections, you will learn about elements important to commercializing an innovation.

BUSINESS MODEL

A business model answers the question of how your idea will generate revenue streams for your organization. It is a tool that allows you to explain to stakeholders what you are selling and to whom, and how the product or service will be made and sold. It is critical that all these components of the business model are built from logical and well-supported assumptions about your customers, products, and processes. While simple in concept, it often takes a lot of forethought to decide what you want to do as a corporate innovator. A business model that fits well to an opportunity in the market can lead to a long, profitable track record for a company. For example, Dell's business model has not changed much since its founding in a dorm room at the University of Texas. Specifically, Dell's business model could be summed up as one focused on providing reliable, low-cost computers to small businesses, educational institutions, and homes through direct selling. While the company has scaled operations many times its original size, the standard approach to the market for Dell has not changed much. Future innovations should complement or extend this business model, since the efficient allocation of resources is a critical consideration for Dell's business.

Straying from a business model is a risky move for a company, and should be undertaken with caution. A business model that is not well thought out or suitable for market conditions may even cause a company to fail. There are times where it may make sense to pursue revolutionary innovations, but if it does not strategically fit well into the operations of the company, trouble may follow. The AOL/Time Warner merger is a classic example of an effort to be revolutionary, only to lead to organizational frustration. In 1999, America Online chairman Steve Case was leading a company soaring in the stock market. Looking to capitalize on its market value and build the media company of the future, Case sought content companies that could complement his Internet business. He first approached Michael Eisner of Disney with the idea, but Eisner thought the AOL market valuation didn't accurately reflect reality and was reticent to get involved in such a deal. Case then approached Gerald Levine of Time Warner, and a deal was struck that brought the two companies together. It was bad timing for Time Warner, as soon thereafter the technology bubble burst, bringing its value down with the AOL merger.[3]

To make matters worse, AOL and Time Warner struggled in defining a business model that made the arrangement profitable. Originally, AOL was to provide technological support and Time was to offer content for customers, but the business model's underlying assumptions were faulty and caused the new company to struggle. The merger has led to continuing problems for Time Warner. Had Gerald Levine given more thought to Time Warner's business model, the AOL/Time Warner mess may have been averted.

In considering whether your innovation will gain support from your stakeholders and lead to increased revenues, it is important to consider your company's business model. The first question you must answer in generating the business model is, "What does your company sell?" You should be able to describe the general nature of your company's product/service/experience offerings. You should also understand why these commercial offerings are part of the company's strategy. The second important question to answer is, "Who is your company's customer?" Provide a profile of the average customer your company sells to. The third question is, "How does your company make and sell its products/services/experiences?" And as corollaries to the above questions the following may be asked: Why does your company do it this way? How is your company better than competitors in producing the commercial offering? Why is your company effective in reaching its customers? Having answers to these questions will give you better understanding of how your innovation will aid your company in growing profits rather than leading to market disaster. Taking your answers to the above questions, you can now construct your company's business model. The following approach can be applied:

- Refer to your answers to the questions, "What does your company sell?" "Who is your company 's customer?" and "How does your company make and sell its products/ services/experiences?" and use them to fill in the blanks in the following statement.

- (fill in your company name) sells/provides/offers (fill in your company's product/service/experience) by/through (fill in how your company produces its corporate offerings) and (fill in how your company sells and distributes it) to (fill in your company's customer).

- Circle the action verbs and prepositions that make the most sense in your statement; that is, choose the words that help your business model statement to flow better.

Here's an example of what Harley Davidson's business model might be: "Harley Davidson sells performance motorcycles and related accessories and merchandise through mass customization and franchised dealerships to affluent customers." If you were a manager at Harley and wanted to gain support for your innovation, you would be wise to explain how it fits into the company's current business model and strategy.

You should be able to summarize your company's business model in one statement as well. This statement now allows you to clearly explain how your company makes money and what your company does. With this knowledge, you should now be sure that your innovation fits within that model and be able to explain how it does so to your stakeholders. If your innovation does not fit within that model, you must have good reasons why you still want to pursue it. A better understanding of strategic entrepreneurship can help in making this decision.

VALUE

For a customer to be interested in a new product or service, it must have clear value to them. Value is attained by the customer when they believe the derived *benefits* from the product or service exceed the costs of purchasing it, as depicted in the formula below:

$$\text{Value} = \text{Perceived Benefits} \div \text{Perceived Costs}$$

If the value of an idea is low, then the manager can work on better explaining the benefits of the product or service, or by lowering the costs involved in purchasing and/or using it. For example, the company could lower the price, increase the ease of adoption, and offer incentives for purchasing it.

CREDIBILITY

One of the most important factors executives and other stakeholders consider when deciding the extent of their involvement with a new project is your credibility. Senior managers often have many choices in their company as to who they will invest time and resources in and who will gain their chief support. After all, most businesses are not only economic in nature, but also political. In addition, customers will often base their trust in a brand on their past interactions with a company. Thus, it is important that team members exude a positive image to others who may be critiquing their efforts. It is also vital that the corporate entrepreneur explain why they encompass the qualities of stability, productivity, success, and vision. You should be able to answer questions about what qualities you bring to the project and why you are able to meet the expectations placed on you. You should also be able to do this for each team member, too. The following questions provide guidance in structuring this information:

- What is your educational background?
- What is your employment background?
- What experience do you have inside the company?
- What experience do you have with new product development or start-up situations (either in the past or present)?
- What is the strength of your financial skills?
- What is your marketing/sales background?
- What experience do you have with research and design?
- What experience do you have with production/operations?
- What is your technological background and have you worked in customer support before?
- What is your relationship with the current target market?
- What type of experience do you have in the product domain and content area?
- Do you have an effective network inside the company to get the results you desire for the project? If not, who would be helpful in addressing this need?

You should be able to answer these questions about your prospective team members as well. By collecting profiles on possible teammates and yourself, you will be able to recognize where your team is lacking and know where to shore up the weaknesses. Additionally, you will have information you can use for promoting the capability and strength of your team. With limited resources, senior executives want to know that company money is in good hands and on a project with a high potential for returns.

Customers will also be interested in products developed by a credible team. Some teams are so successful in rolling out innovative products that consumers actually become fans of the I-team. For example, for almost 25 years Apple fans have been attending the weeklong Macworld Expo and Convention. Apple users get sneak peeks at what the company will be bringing to market that year, and can attend seminars on using the company's products. This forum has helped Apple in selling smartphones that now compete with the Blackberry of industry leader RIM. In a very short amount of time, Apple has received considerable traffic on its online App Store, registering 1 billion downloads. Apple fans are willing to cross into new product categories whenever the company unleashes its next innovation. Customers trust the innovative reputation of the engineering and management teams at Apple.[4]

LEGITIMACY

Another factor that will assist you in successfully launching your idea is to provide a sense of meaning to your project. In *Man's Search for Meaning,* Victor Frankl documents his experiences in a Nazi concentration camp. He discovered that the people who survived under the worst imaginable conditions were those who pursued something meaningful in their lives, whether it was looking forward to seeing family again or finishing a project they had started before their encampment. He later applied this thinking to help people find meaning in the regular world. Frankl discovered that when meaning was present, people performed at their best.[5] The same applies in business. You will find that your I-team will be more committed to your project if there is an understood and well-communicated meaning behind it. By sharing this meaning with others, you will gain legitimacy and generate more interest in your project. I-team members will be more motivated to work on it, and others outside the project will be more interested in seeing it be successful if they relate to the purpose and meaning of it. Thus, you should answer the following questions before moving forward on the project:

- Why should this project be in existence?
- What is the compelling reason for working on this project?
- What benefits does this project bring your company?
- What benefits does this project bring your customer?
- What benefits does this project bring members of the I-team?
- Will this project transform your company? If so, how?
- Will this project transform your customer? If so, how?
- Will this project transform members of the I-team? If so, how?
- How will this project make your company better?
- How will this project make your customer better?
- What will we learn from the projects we don't already know?
- What skills will be gained by working on the project?
- What opportunities may arise in the future from working on this project?

LOCATION

Location, location, location. This often-used expression from marketing carries much wisdom. Where you are located is a major implication on all aspects of the project. Therefore, it is important to consider the locations needed for operations and sales in implementing the project. A supply-chain perspective can come in handy in securing these answers. What suppliers will be needed to attain the key resources to build the product or supply the service? How will you provide or sell the product to the end user? Who will help you in getting the product or service to market? Answering these questions will give you more understanding of the complexity and implications of your supply-chain network. Once you have these answers, you can then turn to the following questions:

- Where will the product/service be made?
- What advantages does this location have with regard to access to supplies?
- What disadvantages does this location have with regard to access to supplies?
- What advantages does this location have with regard to labor?
- What disadvantages does this location have with regard to labor?
- What type of facilities will be needed for manufacturing the product/ service?
- What advantages does the manufacturing location have with regard to access to selling/marketing the product/service to customers?
- What type of facility will be needed to sell the product/service?
- What advantage do we have by using our selected suppliers?
- What disadvantages do we have by using our selected suppliers?
- What type of person would be effective in selling to this market?

BUSINESS-LEVEL STRATEGY

Increasingly, businesses are being managed in a considerate fashion recognizing the involved interests of many diverse stakeholders, as opposed to the more traditional view of focusing only on the bottom line. A stakeholder is any group that affects the way a company is run or who is affected by a company's actions, and it is believed by many academics and businesspeople that balancing the interests of many stakeholders lead to higher trust in economic and community relationships and improved image and reputation. Concurrent with this attitude, the most important factor in business is one's reputation; thus, it is essential to manage in a way that develops respect and admiration from the market and society. If that status is tarnished, it is often very hard to regain. Because of the importance of these issues, answering questions regarding your primary stakeholders, *values*, principles, *mission*, and vision is critical. A business-level strategy encompasses your organization's key priorities and helps you in understanding what your organization will try to accomplish.[6] It is important that you align your I-team's stated goals with your company's expectations and gain the support of your key stakeholders. All these factors are tightly interwoven in revealing your philosophy of how a business should be run and the fashion in which an innovation will be implemented. If your innovation does not fit within the overall mission and values of the company, it will be difficult to gain acceptance among senior management and other stakeholders. Therefore, explicitly stating what the organization focuses on and accepts will help you in crafting your *Innovation pitch*. Answering the following questions will assist you in gaining that acceptance:

- Who are your company's key stakeholders?
- What do the key stakeholders expect from your company and why do they hold these views?
- How does your innovation satisfy the expectations of the key stakeholders? How does your innovation satisfy the expectations of senior management?
- Why will your innovation be accepted by the key stakeholders? Why will senior management accept your innovation?
- Values are the ideals that one believes in very strongly and that guide what a person thinks and does. What are the values of senior management? What are the values of your key stakeholders?
- How does your innovation coincide and support those values?
- What will you need to do to gain support of senior management? What will you need to do to gain support of key stakeholders?
- Principles are well-developed rules and codes one uses in conducting his or her daily business. What principles will you operate under in developing and selling your innovation? What principles do you expect your I-team to follow in getting the intended results?

By explaining how your innovation serves the interests of senior management and key stakeholders, alignment of goals will be met for all interested parties. Where there are differences, you will have a better understanding of how to address the gaps. Without understanding the social nature of innovation, you will struggle in bringing your new ideas to market. However, addressing possible criticisms and demonstrating adherence to principles and values will better your chances of having your innovation accepted.

This section provided the preparatory work needed to provide justification for the commercialization of your innovation. In the following section, we examine how to address the customer aspect of the commercialization process in more depth.

MARKETING THE INNOVATION

Many companies make the mistake of going to market with a message that is neither clear nor compelling. Your chief challenge as a corporate innovator is to present the new product or service in attractive enough form to be appreciated by senior management and potential customers. The guidelines in this section will help you in delivering a message that resonates with your upper management and customers.

Taking the information from the previous sections, we can now shape and refine the descriptions of our innovation. After the necessary data and analyses have been compiled, they should be developed into usable information. After all, large quantities of data are merely facts. To be useful, they must be organized into meaningful information. It is at this stage where the I-team really begins to take the idea to the next level by giving semantic structure to the underlying concepts of the innovation. The following method can be very effective in creating a marketing strategy that will be effective with the customer.

CUSTOMER MAPPING

Customer mapping summarizes and simplifies information by providing a pictorial representation of how the value proposition, benefits, *customer outcomes*, and *features* are in alignment. Features will serve to fulfill the value proposition, and the value proposition will deliver benefits to the customer. The following steps can be performed for virtually any product or service in about 20 minutes. You will need easel paper or poster board, a pen or pencil, index cards, and tape for this exercise.

Step 1: Describe the product or service idea you have. The description should be very succinct. For example, in a recent workshop, one participant said she worked for a nonprofit that was focused on healthy lifestyles and that she would like to open an adult playground where grown-ups can act like kids again. The participants can then explain why they came up with this idea. In this particular case, the participant said that for obese people traditional health clubs can be intimidating, and that her idea would make working out more fun. Exercising in a carefree way like kids would change the fundamental nature of the activities. Since burning calories is a key component of fitness, any movement that was done would be more beneficial than staying home and avoiding the gym.

Step 2: What is the value proposition you are offering to the consumer with this product or service? The value proposition succinctly states what the product or service ultimately delivers to the consumer. With regard to the adult playground, it provides adults a way to get some exercise, unwind, socialize, and relieve stress during their busy days.

Step 3: Who is the target market for this idea? For the adult playground, it was overweight adults between the ages of 22 and 50.

Step 4: Provide a product concept combining the product description, value proposition, and target market. In this case, the product concept is "a playground that will offer adults between the ages of 22 and 50 an opportunity to play like children again."

Step 5: Put the product concept on an index card and place it in the middle of a large sheet of paper.

Step 6: Answer the following question as many times as possible, "Why would the target market be interested in this product or service?" This question was posed to the workshop participant as, "Why would overweight adults between the ages of 22 and 50 be interested in a playground just for them?" The answers that were given were: "(1) To relieve stress, (2) For a fun place to go on a date, (3) To have a fun way to get exercise, (4) A chance to do something different, and (5) A chance to relive your childhood."

Step 7: Place each answer on separate index cards and place above the first card. Then draw lines up to each card from the original box.

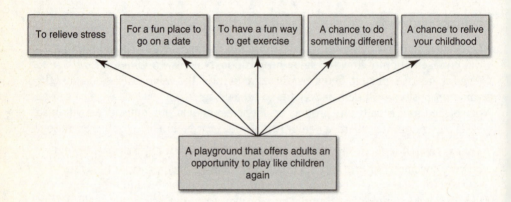

Step 8: Now ask why customers would be interested in the answers to Step 7 and place the new answers to the questions on index cards. So we asked the participant, "Why would these adults be interested in relieving stress, having fun exercise, doing something different, reliving childhood, and having new places for dates?" She responded that "It would provide a different way for adults to get exercise that is more fun and interesting than the traditional gym experience of weightlifting, running on treadmills, and riding stationary bikes. It would also give you a place to look forward to when you're bored with your usual activities." The cards were then placed on the map and logically linked together with arrows. We then asked her what customer outcome these answers would provide: "What outcome would happen if adults had a different way to get exercise that is more fun than a traditional gym?" and "What outcome would happen if you had a workout place that you looked forward to going to?" She replied, "It would increase the number of times I worked out because I'm not intimidated by the surroundings or the people there." It's possible that a participant will have more than one outcome, but in this case workout frequency was the main focus. We then asked why her customers would like this outcome: "Why would adults be interested in getting more workouts in?" She said, "Because it would help people, especially those who struggle with exercise, to become more fit." The map was expanded to the following configuration:

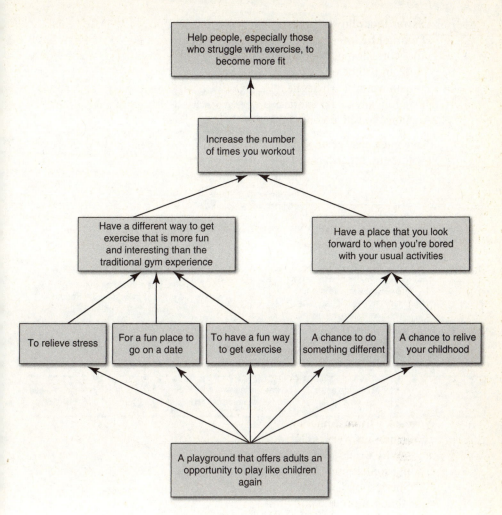

Step 9: Now answer the following question and place the responses on individual index cards, "What features would customers expect this service to have?" or "How could you provide this service to the customer?" The workshop participant stated that there were various ways this could be done, such as building adult versions of traditional playground equipment, providing adult versions of sandboxes where people can gather to socialize, selling adult versions of healthy cafeteria food, and organizing games of dodgeball, flag football, and other childhood hood games. The cards capturing the service features are then placed below the value proposition. In this step, you provide the ways you'll deliver your value proposition.

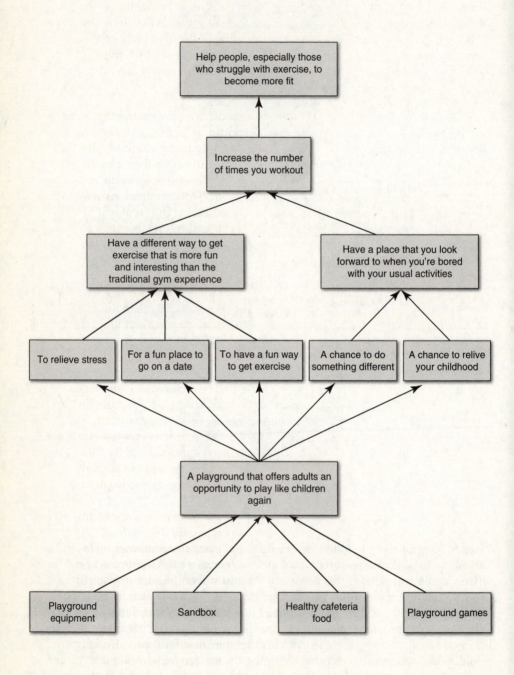

Step 10: Now check the logic of your customer map by asking, "If…will…?" questions. For example, if you offer adult versions of playground equipment, a sandbox, healthy cafeteria food, and playground games, will you be able to provide a playground that will offer adults between the ages of 22 and 50 an opportunity to play like children again? If the answer is yes, then the logic of your service is valid and the connections hold. If there are any links that you do not hold, then modify or drop that link.

Do this for each layer of the map. If you offer a playground that will offer adults between the ages of 22 and 50 an opportunity to play like children again, will this help them to relieve stress, have a fun way to get exercise, give them a chance to do something different, have a chance to relive their childhood, and provide them a fun place to go on a date? If yes, then move up to the next layer.

If you help adults between the ages of 22 and 50 relieve stress, have a fun way to get exercise, and give them a chance to do something different, will they have a different way to get exercise that is more fun and interesting than the traditional gym experience of weights, treadmills, and stationary bikes? If the answer is yes, move to the right side and ask the same type of question. If you give adults between the ages of 22 and 50 a chance to relive their childhoods and have a fun place to go on a date, will they have a place to look forward to when they're bored with their usual activities? If the answer is yes, move up another layer.

If you provide a more fun and interesting place to work out that is not boring, will you help increase the number of times adults between the ages of 22 and 50 work out because they're not intimidated by the setting? If the answer is yes, then move up to the last layer.

If you help adults between the ages of 22 and 50 increase the number of times they work out, will you help them overcome their struggle to become fit? If yes, then you have completed your customer map. If, however, any of the links are questionable, then you may need to modify the map or reexamine some of your answers. For example, maybe younger adults are not intimidated by a traditional gym setting. If so, maybe you need to change the target market to adults between the ages of 35 and 50; or maybe one of the features is too expensive or infeasible in which case you drop it from your plans.

Once you have a map you are satisfied with, draw two lines above and below the value proposition box. Label the middle part *"value proposition,"* the upper layer *"benefits and branding,"* the next layer *"customer outcomes,"* the highest layer *"tagline and customer bliss,"* and the lower part *"service/product features."* The top part of the map provides benefits you will emphasize in your branding and selling points. This will also be helpful as you develop your marketing campaign. The higher up the map, the more you will be able to develop *taglines* and slogans for your company. For example, you could convert "Help people, especially those who struggle with exercise, to become more fit" into "Be a kid again: Smaller and livelier. The Adult Playground is the fun way to fitness." You can now also start thinking about how you would deliver the features in the bottom of the map as well.

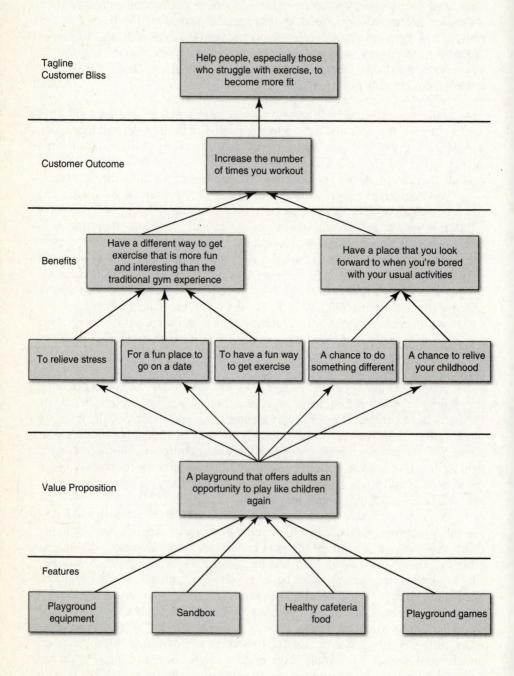

By doing a customer map, you will have a better sense of how to market your idea. You may modify different aspects of the maps, such as changing the product, value proposition, or target market as needed. This becomes your road map for crafting your brand and developing a marketing campaign. The customer map is a visual representation of the elements you will sell to your customers. In the following section, you will learn how to pull those elements out of the map to craft your innovation story for customers.

UTILIZING THE CUSTOMER MAP

An important marketing concept for any business is branding. In a global marketplace, the number of competitors has grown at an astounding rate. With so many choices available to customers, it is important to gain an identity in your market that others recognize and understand as unique and special. For example, in auto insurance, Geico advertises its advantage with regard to cheap and easy products ("I saved a bundle switching to Geico" and "It's so easy even a caveman can do it.") while Allstate advertises its full service approach ("You're in good hands with Allstate"). It's as simple as that, but it does separate the companies from each other. Customers understand the difference. If a company is the same as its competition, its products simply become commodities. In this unfortunate situation, the benefits the product or service provides is seen as easily replaceable. Customer loyalty and emotional attachment to the company is low in this scenario, because in a commoditized market the key source of differentiation is price. While this is sometimes an acceptable strategy, it can be quite risky for an innovative product or service. Ideally, the innovation is offering something never before seen by the target market and is worth paying a higher price for. Therefore, it is wise to create an image and identity that occupies a place in the consumer's mind of distinction in quality, utility, and/or service. People will pay more for products and services when expectations are exceeded or if the goods are seen as having a better, distinctive difference from their competitors' offerings. When this condition has been attained, the company has created more value for the customer. The more value created by the company, the more loyalty and attention the customer will confer in return. Utilizing the customer map from the previous section, you can now answer the following questions in building the brand you will communicate to your customers:

- What is unique about your innovation that will make it attractive to others?
- What is the value proposition you offer the consumer? The value proposition can be found in the middle of your customer map. You can refine the statements on your customer map to better answer these questions as well.
- Why will the customer find your value proposition worthy of their purchase?
- What evidence do you have to support the belief they will purchase what you offer?
- What evidence do you have to convince the customer you can deliver the value proposition?

- What benefits does your product or service offer the consumer? These can be found above the value proposition in your customer map. For the adult playground, the benefits were "(1) To relieve stress, (2) For a fun place to go on a date, (3) To have a fun way to get exercise, (4) A chance to do something different, and (5) A chance to relive your childhood."
- What is the "ultimate bliss" you offer the customer with this product or service? That is, what is the tagline for the product or service? This sentiment will be found at the top of your customer map, and can be modified for the tagline. For example, the workshop participant with the adult playground idea said her tagline would be, "Getting exercise doesn't have to be such a workout anymore."
- What features will you offer your customers that will make the product or service distinctive? This can be found on the customer map below the value proposition. For the workshop participant, the features she wanted to include were "building adult versions of traditional playground equipment, providing adult versions of sandboxes where people can gather to socialize, selling adult versions of healthy cafeteria food, and organizing games of dodgeball, flag football, and other childhood hood games."
- After developing the customer map and answering the above questions, do you believe you have developed a distinctive brand that separates your product or service from your competitors?
- How does the brand fit with your company's current offerings?
- If there is any inconsistency between your innovation's brand and your company's brand, what will you have to do to reconcile the differences?
- What challenges may need to be overcome to develop the features? What could hold you back from developing the features?
- Whose support will you need in overcoming these challenges?
- What evidence can you give these supporters that it is in their best interest to help you overcome these hurdles?
- What can your company learn from meeting these challenges that may be useful in the future?

Table 10.1 provides further considerations you will need to account for in gaining customer acceptance for your innovation.

TABLE 10.1   Perceived Characteristics of the Innovation by the Customer

1. Relative advantage: Is an innovation perceived as better than what has become before it?
2. Compatibility: Is an innovation perceived as being consistent with the existing values, past experiences, and needs of the customers?
3. Complexity: Is an innovation perceived as difficult to understand and use by the customer?
4. Trialability: Can an innovation be used on a limited basis by the potential customer?
5. Observability: Are the benefits of an innovation visible to the potential customer?

Source: Based on: Everett M. Rogers, *Diffusions of Innovation,* 4th edition. New York: The Free Press: 1995, 15–16.

SELLING YOUR INNOVATION STORY

Once an innovation is developed and the marketing strategy determined, the next major challenge is presenting the idea to your key stakeholders. A compelling story will sustain the innovation as it passes different trials both inside and outside the company. In the classic business training video *Everyday Creativity*, National Geographic photographer Dewitt Jones explains how he puts himself in situations to take breathtaking photos. By knowing where to position himself and utilizing his photography skills, he is able to open himself up to photo opportunities. He calls an ideal opportunity situation "the place of most potential."[7] It is your chief task as an innovative manager to explain how your innovation puts your company in the place of most potential. The three key elements that place your innovation in the place of most potential are proving that the right people have produced the right product or service for the right time and place. Evidence that you have found the place of most potential will be based on the degree of innovativeness, profitability, and scalability your idea has. Simply put, will it shake up your market, generate large profits, and have opportunity for further expansion into current and new markets? If you have given serious consideration to all the questions above, you will be in a good position to communicate your idea to any interested party. The following section provides guidelines for developing a business pitch and a presentation to interested stakeholders. This will help you in winning support for the new idea because you will now have a well-developed and tested innovation story to tell. The oral presentation—commonly known as an elevator pitch (because of the analogy of riding an elevator and having only two minutes to get your story told to another person in the elevator)—provides the chance to sell the innovation to senior managers. Imagine a key company figure recognizes you and asks if there is anything you are working on that may interest them. Now's your chance to tell your innovation story. The pitch should be organized, well prepared, interesting, and flexible. You should develop an outline of the significant highlights that will capture the senior manager's interest. Although the outline should be followed, you must also feel free to add or remove certain bits of information as the presentation progresses—a memorized presentation lacks excitement, energy, and interest.

You should use the following steps to prepare your pitch:

1. Know the outline thoroughly.
2. Use keywords in the outline that help recall examples, visual aids, or other details.
3. Rehearse the presentation to get a feel for its length.
4. Be familiar with any equipment you may use if your presentation is given in a scheduled meeting—use your own laptop when possible.
5. The day before a scheduled presentation, practice the complete pitch by moving through each slide.[8]

SUGGESTIONS FOR PRESENTATION

Managers are naturally anxious to tell (and sell) their I-plan. However, if the content is well developed and the delivery practiced, the presentation should go smoothly. In the content of the presentation, it is important to be brief and to the point, to summarize the critical factor or unique "hook" of your innovation up front, and to use no more than 12–15 PowerPoint slides. Following are some key suggestions about the actual delivery of the pitch to senior managers and other key stakeholders:

1. Focus on the problem for which your innovation will be the solution. Senior management wants to know exactly what problem is being solved by your innovation. Pinpoint the target of your solution.

2. Demonstrate the reachable market. Instead of a dramatic potential market, outline the immediate reachable group of customers that will be targeted.

3. Explain the business model. How does this innovation make money for the company? How does it fit within the company's current financial strategies? What is the breakeven point for the innovation? What percentage of total capacity is the breakeven point? Demonstrating a clear method of getting to market and generating profit and growth will allude to a successful beginning and sustainable future for the new product or service.

4. Tout the I-team. Every executive wants to know the skills and abilities of the I-team's capacity for delivering and operationalizing the innovation. Emphasize the experienced people on your I-team as well as any technical advisors who are on board.

5. Explain your metrics. Rather than using generic assumptions such as the famous "1 percent rule" (when someone claims that the company will simply get 1 percent of a huge market with no research to back the claim up), highlight the metrics that were used to calculate the market size and the revenue projections.

6. Motivate the audience. The entire purpose of a presentation is to move the audience to the next step: another meeting to discuss everything in detail. Therefore, you must remember that enthusiasm is hugely important. The senior managers must believe that you are excited before they can be excited.

7. Why *your company* and why *now?* The final point must answer the daunting questions in the minds of the senior managers: Why is this right for the company, and why is this the right time for it to be launched? Be confident in yourself, your I-team, and your company. Always demonstrate a timeline to show the speed with which your I-team plans to roll out the product and how quickly your company can capture a significant portion of the market.

WHAT TO EXPECT

The I-team should realize that the audience reviewing their innovation and listening to their pitch can be conservative and sometimes antagonistic. Innovations bring much uncertainty with them. A large capital investment on an untested innovation brings great risk. Senior managers may pressure the I-team to test their innovation as well as their mettle. Thus, the I-team must expect and prepare for a critical (and sometimes skeptical) audience of executive decision makers. When you make your pitch and submit your I-plan, the executive will listen and then glance at the plan briefly before beginning any initial comments. No matter how good you think your I-plan is, an executive is rarely going to look at it and say, "This is the greatest thing I've ever seen!" Do not expect enthusiastic acceptance or even polite praise. It's highly likely that the remarks will be critical, and even if they aren't, they'll seem that way. Don't panic. Even if it seems like an avalanche of objections, bear in mind that some of the best innovations of all time faced the same opposition. Never expect results in 20 minutes. Each pitch will be a learning experience that will build your confidence for the next one. You should be prepared to handle the questions from the evaluators and learn from their criticism. The senior management team may send you back to the drawing board to rework some of the issues they had problems with. Consider this an opportunity, and rework your innovation where possible. You should never feel defeated but rather make a commitment to bringing innovations to your company, whether it is the present one or another to be developed. Remember that bringing innovations to market is more similar to a marathon than a sprint. The goal is not so much to succeed the *first* time as it is to *succeed.*[9]

Summary

This chapter provided a thorough examination of how to turn your ideas into a compelling story that can be told to senior managers and other key stakeholders to attract their interest and support. Market research provides supporting documentation of customer interest in the innovation. Further sources of information for commercializing your innovation were then covered. The customer mapping approach provided a way to build your brand and craft your marketing messages. Guidelines were then given on how to tell your innovation story.

INNOVATION-IN-ACTION

A Whale of an Idea

Frank Fish, an unassuming biology professor at West Chester University in West Chester, Pennsylvania, was on vacation and enjoying a fine-art sculpture of a humpback whale when the genesis of a business idea was formed.

Fish thought the sculptor had made an error in sculpting bumps along the edges of the whale's flippers. After all, fluid dynamics dictated that the edges should have been smooth. Intrigued, Fish spent decades studying the flippers and how they worked, discovering a few things about fluid dynamics along the way. In 2004, the results of Fish's and his three coauthors' studies were published in *Science, Nature,* and several other publications. The scientific community noticed.

In early 2005, a physics aficionado and entrepreneur by the name of Stephen Dewar met with Fish to learn more about fluid dynamics and humpback whales. Dewar and Fish discussed the potential commercial application of Fish and company's discoveries to the design of airplane wings, boat keels, and turbines.

In late 2005, Dewar and Fish filed patents and, backed by private investors, formed WhalePower, a Toronto company. Knowing that the industry would be hesitant to invest in technology that was a radical departure from conventional wisdom, Fish continued to conduct research. During trials, he discovered that airfoils with his design were up to 13 percent more efficient than smooth-edged airfoils.

Seizing upon the technical term for the "flipper bumps," Fish named the concept Tubercle Technology. Today, WhalePower licenses its Tubercle Technology to the industrial fan industry. And, according to Envira-North Systems, the first company to commercially use industrial fans employing Tubercle Technology, the fans are 25 percent more aerodynamically efficient, consume 20 percent less energy, and create significantly less noise than conventional fans.

WhalePower is growing at double-digit rates and is in the process of negotiating licenses with manufacturers of computers, servers, HVAC units, and other appliances. Fish foresees the use of Tubercle Technology in the wind energy and airline industries.

Source: (Based on: http://inventorspot.com/articles/humpback_whale_inspires_energy_saving_whalepower_tubercle_techno_30079, http://www.entrepreneur.com/article/217520, websites accessed January 10, 2011.

Key Terms

Benefits	Niche
Business model	Pitch
Business-level strategy	Presentation
Credibility	Primary data
Customer mapping	Principles
Customer outcomes	Secondary data
Demographics	Stakeholders
Features	Surveys
Legitimacy	Taglines
Location	Value
Market	Value proposition
Market research	Values
Mission	Vision

Review and Discussion Questions

1. What is the importance of market research?
2. Briefly describe the steps of market research.
3. What are the common question formats for surveys, and why are they used?

4. What is a business model? Why is it important to know your company's business model?
5. How can a manager show credibility to senior management?
6. Why is meaning important in innovative pursuits?
7. What are some factors that must be taken into consideration when selecting a location to produce and sell your product or service?
8. How does a customer perceive value? What can a company do to persuade a customer that an innovation holds value for them?
9. Briefly describe how a customer map is created.
10. How do you prepare your innovation pitch for acceptance by key stakeholders?
11. What are the important steps that must be followed to prepare a successful presentation to key decision makers?
12. What makes for a good innovation presentation?

APPENDIX A

Example of an Innovation Description

A. GENERAL DESCRIPTION OF INNOVATION

Green Fuel Alternatives will be a fuel refinery of soy bio-diesel that will be sold in bulk quantities and to fuel distributors and suppliers in the Midwest. *The Green Fuel Alternatives* refining plant will be built by Renewable Energy Group in the vacant lot of 8101 W. Morris St. in Indianapolis. This location was chosen because of its excellent access to I-465, U.S. Highways 40 and 36, and on-site rail access. This innovation has been named Green Fuel Alternatives so that customers can easily identify what the product is and know that it is beneficial to the environment.

Biofuels have become very popular in the past few years. A growing number of organizations, such as departments of transportation, school corporations, farmers, U.S. state and local governments, and even traditional diesel vehicle drives, are using Biodiesel to meet future sulfur emissions standards (2006 EOA mandate) and become more environmentally responsible. The United States currently imports 58 percent of its oil, with fuel prices continually trending upward. This creates a demand to utilize cheaper and more efficient natural resources to help reduce fuel costs and the dependency on foreign oil. Biodiesel has been tested in labs, and has passed all necessary tests required by the U.S. Environmental Protection Agency (EPA). The American Society for Testing and Materials (ASTM) has even given biodiesel a standard (ASTM D6571) to be used as an acceptable diesel fuel alternative.

Several states around the country, from Main to Washington, have already initiated biodiesel promotion programs. Three examples are the programs in Minnesota, Arkansas, and Texas. The state of Minnesota has mandated the use of B2 (2 percent blend of biodiesel with diesel) in all petroleum diesel consumed in the state by the year 2005 subject to incentive for biodiesel production for the first 5 million gallons up to a period of five years. Texas now provides a net grant of 16.4 cents per gallon to producer of biodiesel for a period of 10 years, but the grant is capped at $3.6 million per plant.[1]

Currently, Green Fuel Alternatives is in the conceptual stage of development because if a biodiesel plant were to be built in Indiana, it would be the first in the state, enabling it to reach northern biodiesel users faster than the competitors. Any Co-op or other fuel distributor that wants to sell biodiesel to its

---

1Frazier, Barnes & Associates. Mississippi Biodiesel Feasibility Study. 2004

customers must currently transport it from Ralston, Iowa, Cincinnati, Ohio, Kentucky, Minnesota, or further away. *Green Fuel Alternatives* will require a 15 million gallon per year (gpy) plant in order to provide enough B100 biodiesel for all of the distributors in Indiana, for some sale outside, and for some private sales. Once the division is started and the refinery is producing a steady amount of fuel, production will reach peak capacity and in the future other plants may need to be constructed in order to provide fuel to other areas of the Midwest. The biodiesel manufactured under the name *Green Fuel Alternatives* is very unique in the fact that it is made from soybean oil only, benefiting local soy biodiesel as well as waste grease and many other types of oils. Green Fuel Alternatives will offer soy biodiesel in an effort to support local farmers and utilize the largest vegetable oil source.

In order to extract the oil from the soybeans, a "cracking" or "crushing" plant is used to heat up the soybeans to a proper temperature in which the soybean oil will come off of the soybeans in a gas form and it will be filtered through a coil to cool it down and revert it to its liquid form. Green Fuel Alternatives will receive its soybean oil from ADM in Frankfort, Indiana. This oil would then be mixed with methanol to create B100 or "neat" biodiesel. B100 biodiesel is essentially 100 percent biodiesel; other blends such as B5 and B20 contain 5 percent and 20 percent biodiesel, respectively, which are the most common blends available. Figure 10.1 *Green Fuel Alternatives* will only manufacture and sell B100 to fuel distributors who will mix blends to satisfy each customer.

The business model for *Green Fuel Alternatives* will be as follows. *Green Fuel Alternatives* will strive to make soy biodiesel more easily accessible in Indiana and strive for a low-cost alternative. We will provide distributors with a quality refined B100 biodiesel that can be easily blended for any diesel fuel application.

FIGURE 10.1   Example of Diagram for Innovation Description

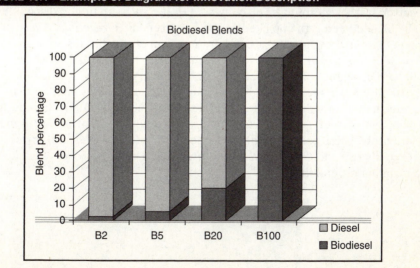

B. PRODUCTS AND SERVICES

Green Fuel Alternatives will provide B100 biodiesel that will be refined by ADM in Frankfort, Indiana, using a "cracking" plant to extract soybean oil feedstock. B100 biodiesel is known as "pure biodiesel" or "neat" because it is 100 percent biodiesel. Some customers prefer B100 because of its increased lubricity and the cleansing characteristics. However, B100 does have trouble in cold weather due to an increased cold flow test and cloud point. Because of this it has become an industry standard when transporting fuel to heat it to avoid gelling in climates below 40 degrees Fahrenheit. The American Society of Testing and Materials has tested biodiesel and uses a standard test for biodiesel called ASTM D 6751.

C. STRATEGY OF DIFFERENTIATION

Green Fuel Alternatives will have a competitive advantage in Indiana compared to other biodiesel providers because current providers are located hundreds of miles away, out-of-state. Green Fuel Alternatives will not be a fuel Co-op distribution center, but a fuel refinery. Currently there are 40 biodiesel providers or fuel Co-ops in Indiana, but they only blend the fuel to make biodiesel and then distribute it to the end user or to a fuel station. *Green Fuel Alternatives* will provide the B100 (100 percent biodiesel) to customers such as Countrymark who will blend it with diesel fuel at its terminals to create a biodiesel blend. Countrymark currently has B100 biodiesel transported in from Iowa, Kentucky, and Ohio, and they simply blend the fuel usually using various methods. Some facilities such as the Countrymark Co-op in Jolietville and Peru, Indiana, use a state-of-the-art direct injection method to blend the biodisel proportionately with petroleum diesel. Currently the B100 fuel is received by these terminals (places where Co-ops pick up fuel to distribute) to be blended and is then picked up for disbursement. *Green Fuel Alternatives* can get fuel to these terminals quicker than competitors because of a convenient location in Indianapolis, Indiana. Because of this, the fuel cooperatives will have constant access to biodiesel. Green Fuel Alternatives will attempt to establish a good relationship with Countrymark and other providers in Indiana and eventually elsewhere that distribute biodiesel. This relationship will enable *Green Fuel Alternatives* to develop long-term contracts with the distributors. These contracts will be a safeguard in case soybean oil prices unexpectedly rise and *Green Fuel Alternatives* has to keep prices at a high level to maintain profitability.

D. KEY DYNAMICS

There are many keys to why biodiesel makes sense:

1. Biodiesel is 100 percent renewable and can be made in the United States, reducing our dependency on foreign oil.
2. Engine life is increased with the use of biodiesel.
3. EPA is requiring the sulfur emissions in 2006 to be reduced from 500 ppm to 15 ppm.
4. Biodiesel has the highest positive energy balance of any renewable fuel to date (3.24 units produced per unit of energy used).
5. Biodiesel can reduce toxic air emissions by as much as 90 percent (B100 compared to petroleum diesel).[2]

2"An Overview of Biodiesel and Petroleum Diesel Life Cycles" U.S. Department of Energy, national Renewable Energy Laboratory (NREL), and the U.S. Department of Agriculture (USDA). May 1998–March 2004.

APPENDIX B

Examples of Market Surveys

EXAMPLE 1: TRAFFIC REPORTING SERVICE FOR CELL PHONES

This survey is being collected to assess the viability of traffic checking services for cellular phones. Your input is critical to assess the feasibility of this idea and will help determine whether future investment and development are warranted. Thank you in advance for completing the survey!

1. **Gender:** Male_____   Female_____

2. **Age:**   ____16–24____25–34____35–44____45–54____55–70

3. **Household Income:** ____under 25,000 ____25,001–45,000 ____45,001–65,000

   ____65,001–85,000 ____85,001–105,000 ____105,001–145,000

   ____145,001–185,000 ____Above 185,001

4. **How long, in miles, is your daily commute roundtrip?**

   ____1–15 ____16–20 ____21–25 ____26–30 ____31–40

   ____41–50 ____51–80 ____over 81

5. **Do you own a cell phone?** ____Yes ____No

6. **Do you have access to the Internet?** ____Yes ____No

7. **Do you ever get stuck in heavy traffic?** ____Yes ____No

8. **Is being stuck in heavy traffic, during rush hour or at other times, a problem for you?** ____Yes ____No

9. **How do you check the status of traffic before beginning your commute?** (please check all that apply)

   ____TV ____Radio ____Internet ____I don't check traffic

   Other (please specify)_____

10. **On a scale of 1 to 5,** 1=not satisfied and 5=completely satisfied, **rate your current traffic-monitoring method listed in question #9.**

    Circle one   1   2   3   4   5

Imagine a service that allows you to check the status of traffic in the Indianapolis area through a website. This service will send you traffic reports according to your commuting route that will alert you of problems **before** you get stuck in traffic. You can choose to have the traffic alerts sent to your e-mail account or sent to your phone as a text message.

11. Would you subscribe to a traffic-alert service that saved you time and frustration on your commute to and from work? ____Yes ____No

12. Which of the methods for traffic monitoring would you be most likely to use? (check all that apply)

____Website ____E-mail ____Phone Messaging

13. In dollars, how much would you be willing to pay on a monthly basis for this service?

____1–6 ____6–12 ____above 12

Thank you for taking the time to fill out this survey.

I greatly appreciate all of your help.

EXAMPLE 2: BUSINESS-TO-BUSINESS SURVEY FOR A VINEYARD

Demographic Information

Name of Business:_____

Your Name:_____

Your Title at Company:_____ (owner, manager, etc.)

Age of Business: ___1–5 years ___6–10 years ___11–20 years ___21 years plus

Number of years you have been with the company _____ Are you the founder?

____Yes ____No

Number of employees in the business_____

Company's Annual Sales:

____less than $500,000 ____$500,001–$1,000,000 ____$1,000,001–$2,000,000

____more than $2,000,000

1. Does the winery use whole grapes in its wine production process? (If no, skip questions 2–4)

____Yes ____No

2a. Approximately how many tons of whole grapes does the winery process annually?

2b. Does this amount fill production to capacity? ____Yes ____No

2c. If no, what factors are limiting from becoming filled to capacity? (Check all that apply)

_____Inadequate space/property

_____Lack of agricultural background

_____Initial cost of setup

_____Labor requirements

_____Time

3a. Do you produce your own grape crop? _____Yes _____No

3b. If so, how many acres are involved in grape production?

_____Less than 25 _____25–50 _____51–75 _____76–100 _____More than 100

3c. What is your approximate cost per acre?

_____Less than $2500 _____$2500–$5000 _____$5001–$7500 _____$7501–$10,000

4. How many suppliers do you currently use to create the desired inventory?

5. What outlets are being used to market the winery's products? (check all that apply)

_____Retail stores _____On-site sales _____Mail order/Internet _____Other wineries

6. How many varieties of grapes does the winery use in its production?

7. When in the year does the company make most of its buying decisions?

_____Spring _____Summer _____Fall _____Winter

8. Please rate the following statements on a scale of 1–5, with 1 representing a total disagreement and 5 representing complete agreement.

Agree	Disagree				
a. I am satisfied with the company's current supply chain.	1	2	3	4	5
b. The company could benefit from having a local grape supplier.	1	2	3	4	5
c. I would like to learn more about using organically grown grapes in my operation.	1	2	3	4	5
d. I would like to diversify the number of products the winery offers.	1	2	3	4	5
e. I am satisfied with the current production output of the winery.	1	2	3	4	5
f. It is important to support local agriculture.	1	2	3	4	5
g. Having a quality product is more important than making a large profit.	1	2	3	4	5

9a. Approximately how many different products does your company currently offer?

9b. Please list those products.

10. On average, how many new products does your company introduce every year?

11. Would you like to know the results of this survey? Yes_____ No_____

Thank you for your cooperation!

Endnotes

1. McKee, R. 2003. Storytelling that moves people, *Harvard Business Review* 81 (6): 51–55.
2. Maxwell, R. & Dickman, R. 2007. *The elements of persuasion.* New York: Collins.
3. Stewart, J. B. 2006. *Disney War.* New York: Simon & Schuster.
4. Campbell, C. Is the iphone killing RIM? *Maclean's* 122 (22): 30–31.
5. Frankl, V. E. 1959. *Man's Search for Meaning.* Boston, MA: Beacon Press.
6. Freeman, R. E. 1984. *Strategic Management: A Stakeholder Approach.* Upper Saddle River, NJ: Pitman Publishing.
7. Jones, D. 2001. *Everyday Creativity.* St Paul, MN: Star Thrower.
8. Kuratko, D. F. 2009. *Entrepreneurship: Theory, Process, Practice.* Mason, OH: Cengage/SouthWestern Publishers.
9. Ibid.

EFFECTIVE INNOVATION PLANS

INTRODUCTION

As we saw in the last chapter, the realization and then preparation of an innovation for commercialization has specific steps. As you develop your business model, conduct market research, and outline your story, each of those elements lays the groundwork for the final innovation plan that you must develop. So the work conducted in the last chapter will now be integrated into the formal elements of an innovation plan.

Planning is essential to the success of any innovative undertaking that you may pursue. Planning is the management key to reducing uncertainty and the risks of change. Although we can never predict the future, planning is a process that allows ventures to stay on track through preparation, expectation, and dedication to the objective. Carefully prepared, these plans are simply the formulation of goals, objectives, and directions for the future of a project. The absence of a plan could mean failure before you even start. In planning, there are critical steps that must not be overlooked. A few of these steps are listed below:

- *Realistic goals must be set*. These goals must be specific, measurable, and set within a time frame.
- All involved managers, employees, and team members must be *committed to the venture* plan.
- *Milestones* must be set for continual and timely evaluation of progress.
- *Obstacles should be anticipated* with flexible provisions for dealing with a bad turn of events.

Alternative strategies must be devised in the event of unforeseen pitfalls.

THE INNOVATION PLAN

DEFINITION

An *Innovation Plan* is the written document that details the proposed innovation and its commercial potential as a venture. It must describe current status, expected needs, and projected results of the new concept.[1] Every aspect of the venture needs to be covered: the project, marketing, research and development, manufacturing, management, critical risks, financing, and milestones or a timetable. A description of all of these facets of the proposed venture is necessary to demonstrate a clear picture of what that venture is, where it is projected to go, and how the innovator proposes it will get there. The innovation plan is the road map for a successful enterprise.[2]

An effective innovation plan will:

- Describe every aspect of a particular innovation;
- Include a marketing plan;
- Clarify and outline financial needs;
- Identify potential obstacles and alternative solutions;
- Establish milestones for continuous and timely evaluation; and
- Serve as a communication tool for all assessment purposes.

PLANNING PITFALLS

Pitfalls in planning are abundant—remember, no one says it's easy! The following section outlines planning pitfalls, indicators, and solutions. Read them carefully before embarking on your plan. The comprehensive innovation plan is useful for existing organizations, not just start-ups. It should be the result of meetings and reflections upon the entire direction of the project. In this manner the innovation plan is a useful tool in business to convey the market feasibility, financial capability, and contingent directions that all interested resource persons in a company wish to see.

TABLE 11-1   Pitfalls in Entrepreneurial Planning (Read carefully before assessing your innovation plan)

Pitfalls	*Indicators*	*Possible Solutions*
1. No Realistic Goals	Lack of time frame to accomplish things Lack of priorities Lack of action steps	*Set up a timetable with specific steps to be accomplished at each elapsed time period.*
2. Failure to Anticipate Issues	No admission of possible Roadblocks No contingency or alternative plans	*List the possible obstacles you face, flaws or weaknesses with alternatives written out that state what you "might have to do."*

Pitfalls	Indicators	Possible Solutions
3. No Commitment or Dedication	Too much procrastination Missed appointments No desire to put up money of your own Project appears to be a hobby or whim for you Appearance of making a fast buck	*Act quickly and be sure to follow-up on all professional appointments. Be ready and willing to demonstrate a financial commitment: "Put your money where your mouth is!"*
4. Lack of Demonstrated Experience (Business or Technical)	No experience in the specific area of your venture Lack of understanding of the industry your venture fits into Failure to convey to others a clear picture of what, how, why your venture works, and who will buy it	*Always explain your experience and background for this venture. If you lack specific knowledge or skills, attempt to get help from those who possess the skills. (Demonstrate a "team" concept of those helping you).*
5. No *Market Niche* (Segment)	Unsure of who will buy your idea No proof of need or desire for your idea Assuming there will be customers or clients just because you think there will be	*Have an established market segment at which you are specifically aiming your venture. Be able to demonstrate why you chose that market and the steps you are taking to prove that there is a need or desire for your idea.*

BENEFITS OF AN INNOVATION PLAN

As we stated in the introduction of this chapter, an innovation plan forces you to plan. All aspects of your innovation idea should be addressed in the plan. You develop and examine operating strategies and expected results. Goals and objectives are quantified so that you can compare forecasts with actual results. This type of planning can help keep you on track.

Other benefits are derived from an innovation plan for both the innovator (and the I-Team) and the executive team that will read it and evaluate the concept. Specifically for the innovator and the I-Team, the following benefits are gained:

- The time, effort, research, and discipline needed to put together a formal innovation plan force the innovator to view the venture critically and objectively.

- The competitive, economic, and financial analyses included in the innovation plan subject the innovator to close scrutiny of his or her assumptions about the concept's success.
- Since all aspects of the innovative concept as a viable venture must be addressed in the plan, the innovator and the I-Team develop and examine operating strategies and expected results for outside evaluators.
- The innovation plan quantifies objectives, providing measurable benchmarks for comparing forecasts with actual results.
- The completed innovation plan provides the innovator and I-Team with a communication tool for the executive team to analyze as well as an operational tool for guiding the new innovation toward success.

The executive team that reads the plan derives the following benefits from the innovation plan:

- The innovation plan provides for the executive team the details of the market potential and plans for securing a share of that market.
- Through prospective financial statements, the innovation plan illustrates the venture's ability to service debt or provide an adequate return on equity.
- The innovation plan identifies critical risks and crucial events with a discussion of contingency plans that provide opportunity for the venture's success.
- By providing a comprehensive overview of the entire operation, the innovation plan gives executives a clear, concise document that contains the necessary information for a thorough business and financial evaluation.
- For an executive team with no prior knowledge of this type of innovation, the innovation plan provides a useful guide for assessing the innovation team (I-Team) and their planning and managerial ability.

To help you prepare an effective innovation plan, we provide in this chapter an innovation plan section that begins with a complete outline of an innovation plan for you to follow. An evaluation segment is then provided so that you can check your work closely before presenting it to others. Self-assessment of your plan is necessary and worthwhile.

The complete innovation plan assessment provided in Table 11-3 offers entrepreneurs an opportunity to self-evaluate the innovation plan as it is developed. Each section is broken down into questions that examine the information needed in that particular segment of the innovation plan. Then the columns are used to evaluate (1) whether the information is in the plan, (2) whether the previous answer is clear, and (3) whether the answer is complete. This gives entrepreneurs the benefit of self-evaluating each segment of their plan before presenting it to financial or professional sources. Before we get to the assessment tool let's examine the major components of an innovation plan.

THE COMPONENTS OF AN INNOVATION PLAN

Readers of an innovation plan expect it to have two important qualities: It must be organized and it must be complete. Also, the innovator should consider who the intended audience is when the plan is presented for funding. Mason and Stark (2004) suggest that most of the research on innovation plans ignore the needs of the different types of funding sources. Their research suggests that innovation plans should be customized based on the following:

- Bankers stress the financial aspects of the plan and place little emphasis on market, innovator, or other issues.

- Equity investors, capital fund managers, venture capital fund managers, and business angels emphasize both market and financial components.[3]

With this in mind, the following list describes the 10 segments that make up a complete and organized innovation plan:

1. *Executive summary*. A short description of the innovation should be the first information the reader encounters. Emphasis should be placed on the unique characteristics of the venture, the major marketing points, and the desired end result. A good summary will guarantee that the rest of the plan will be read.

2. *Descriptions of the innovation*. A more comprehensive account of the innovative concept, including some information about the overall industry. The product or service should be described in terms of its unique value to consumers, with milestones clarified.

3. *Marketing*. The first part is research and analysis. The target market must be identified, with emphasis on who will buy the product or service. Market size and trends must be measured, and the market share must be estimated. In addition, the competition should be studied in considerable detail. The second part is the marketing plan, discussing market strategy, sales and distribution, pricing, advertising, and promotion.

4. *Operations*. The mode of this corporate innovation concept (internal, external, or cooperative) is outlined with its advantages. Operating needs, projected operating costs, and general plans for operations should all be considered in this section. Cost data associated with any of the operation factors should be presented.

5. *Management*. Describe who the management team is since outstanding individuals make the innovation a success. Salaries, employment agreements, stock purchase plans, and ownership levels must be determined. Directors, advisers, and consultants are listed with their potential contribution to the enterprise.

6. *Risks*. Risks should be anticipated and controlled to guarantee in a more successful venture. This analysis uncovers potential problems before they materialize. Advisers and board members can often identify risks and recommend alternative courses of action.

7. *Financial.* Obtaining financing always has depended on fair and reasonable budgeting and forecasting. Pro forma financial statements, such as forecasted statements of earnings, financial position, and cash flows, are presented. These projected statements should represent the financial achievements expected from the business. They also provide a standard against which to measure the actual results of operating the enterprise.

8. *Harvest.* Project a long-term plan for how the innovator(s) will benefit from the success of the venture. Harvest strategies can include selling the business, going public and offering stock, or merging with another business.

9. *Milestone.* Determining the objectives and the timing of their accomplishment. Milestones and deadlines should be established and then monitored while the venture is in progress so they constitute a network of the entire project.

10. *Appendix.* Information not contained in other sections, including names of references and advisers, as well as drawings, documents, agreements, or other materials that support the plan.[4]

PREPARING THE INNOVATION PLAN

Constructing an innovation plan is a challenge because of the great amount of work required to put together the ten components just discussed. After the requisite information is compiled, the package must be assembled in good form. Remember that an innovation plan gives investors their first impression of a company. Therefore, the plan should present a professional image. Form, as well as content, is important. The document should be free of spelling, grammatical, or typographical errors. Perfection should be the norm; anything less is unacceptable. Binding and printing should have a professional appearance. The written plan should not exceed 30 pages (20–25 is ideal). The cover page should be attractive, and it should contain the company name and address. A title page should contain the same information as the front cover, as well as the company's telephone number and the month and year the plan is presented.

The first two pages should contain the executive summary, which explains the company's current status, its products or services, the benefits to customers, *financial forecast* summarized in paragraph form, the venture's objectives in the next few years, the amount of financing needed, and the benefits to investors. This is a lot of information for two pages, but if it is done well, the investor will get a good impression of the venture and will be enticed to read the rest of the plan.

A table of contents should follow the executive summary. Each section of the plan should be listed with the page numbers on which they are found. Obviously, the remaining sections will follow the table of contents. If the last section, the appendix, is too lengthy, it may be necessary to present it is a separate binder in order to keep the plan within the recommended limit of 30 pages. Each of the sections should be written in a simple and straightforward manner. The purpose is to communicate, not dazzle.

An attractive appearance, proper length, an executive summary, a table of contents, and professionalism in grammar, spelling, and typing are important factors in a comprehensive innovation plan. Believe it or not, when reviewed by outside funding sources, these characteristic separate successful plans from failed ones.

Table 11-2 presents some helpful hints for developing the innovation plan.[5]

Finally, a well-written innovation plan is like a work of art: it's visually pleasing and makes a statement without saying a word. Unfortunately, the two are also alike

TABLE 11-2   Helpful Hints for Developing the Innovation Plan

I. Executive Summary

- No more than three pages. This is the most crucial part of your plan because you must capture the reader's interest.
- What, How, Why, Where, etc., must be summarized.
- Complete this part after you have a finished innovation plan.

II. Innovation Description Segment

- Explain your innovation.
- How does it "fit" with the organization?
- The potential of the new innovation should be described clearly.
- Any uniqueness or distinctive features of this innovation should be clearly described.

III. Marketing Segment

- Convince investors that sales projections and competition can be met.
- Use and disclose market studies.
- Identify target market, market position, and market share.
- Evaluate all competition and specifically cover why and how you will be better than your competitors
- Identify all market sources and assistance used for this segment.
- Demonstrate pricing strategy since your price must penetrate and maintain a market share to produce profits. Thus the lowest price is not necessarily the best price.
- Identify your advertising plans with cost estimates to validate proposed strategy.

IV. Operations Segment

- Describe the mode of innovation strategy (internal, external, or cooperative).
- Outline the advantages of selecting this mode of innovation.
- Identify operational needs in terms of facilities or equipment.
- Provide estimates for operating costs.
- Provide general operations description.

V. Management Segment

- Supply resumes of all key people in the management of your venture.
- Carefully describe the legal structure of your venture (sole proprietorship, partnership, or corporation).
- Cover the added assistance (if any) of advisers, consultants, and directors.
- Give information on how and how much everyone is to be compensated.

VI. Financial Segment

- Give actual estimated statements.
- Describe the needed sources for your funds and the uses you intend for the money.
- Develop and present a budget.
- Create stages of financing for purposes of allowing evaluation by investors at various points.

VII. Critical Risks Segment

- Discuss potential risks before investors point them out, e.g.,
  - Price cutting by competitors.
  - Any potentially unfavorable industry-wide trends.
  - Design or manufacturing costs in excess of estimates.
  - Sales projections not achieved.
  - Product development schedule not met.
  - Difficulties or long lead times encountered in the procurement of parts or raw materials.
  - Greater than expected innovation and development costs to stay competitive.
- Provide some alternative courses of action.

VIII. Harvest Strategy Segment

- Outline a plan for the orderly transfer of company assets (ownership).
- Describe the plan for transition of leadership.
- Mention the preparations (insurance, trusts, etc.) needed for continuity of the business.

IX. Milestone Schedule Segment

- Develop a timetable or chart to demonstrate when each phase of the venture is to be completed. This shows the relationship of events and provides a deadline for accomplishment.

X. Appendix or Bibliography

in that they are worth money only if they're good. Following are 10 key questions to consider when you are writing and revising an innovation plan masterpiece.

1. *Is your plan organized so key facts leap out at the reader?* Appearances do count. Your plan is a representation of yourself, so don't expect an unorganized, less-than-acceptable plan to be your vehicle for obtaining funds.

2. *Is your product/service and business mission clear and simple?* Your mission should state very simply the value that you will be providing to your customers. It shouldn't take more than a paragraph.

3. *Where are you really? Are you focused on the right things?* Determine what phase of the business you are really in, focus on the right tasks, and use your resources appropriately.

4. *Who is your customer?* Does the plan describe the business's ideal customers and how you will reach them? Is your projected share of the market identified, reasonable, and supported?

5. *Why do (or will) your customers buy? How much better is your product/ service?* Define the need for your product and provide references and testimonial support to enhance it. Try to be detailed in explaining the customer's benefit in buying your product.

6. *Do you have an unfair advantage over your competitors?* Focus on differences and any unique qualities. Proprietary processes/technology and patentable items/ideals are good things to highlight as competitive strengths.

7. *Do you have a favorable cost structure?* Proper gross margins are key. Does the breakeven analysis take into consideration the dynamics of price and variable costs? Identify, if possible, any economies of scale that would be advantageous to the business.

8. *Can the management team build a business?* Take a second look at the management team to see whether they have relevant experience in small business and in the industry. Acknowledge the fact that the team may need to evolve with the business.

9. *How much money do you need?* Financial statements, including the income statement, cash flow statement, and balance sheet, should be provided on a monthly basis for the first year and then quarterly basis for the following two or three years.

10. *How does your investor get a cash return?* Whether it's through a buyout or initial public offering, make sure your plan clearly outlines this important question regarding a harvest strategy.

A COMPLETE ASSESSMENT OF THE COMPONENTS

There are 10 components of an innovation plan. As you develop your plan, you should assess each component. Be honest in your assessment since the main purpose is to improve your innovation plan and increase your chances of success.[6]

TABLE 11-3 Innovation Plan Assessment

Directions: The innovation plan will help company executives to more adequately evaluate your business idea. This assessment tool can help you and your I-Team self-evaluate the innovation plan before it is submitted to senior executives. The brief description of each component will help you write that section of your plan. After completing your plan, use the scale provided to assess each component.

    5 = Outstanding—thorough and complete in all areas
    4 = Very Good—most areas covered but could use improvement in detail
    3 = Good—some areas covered in detail but other areas missing
    2 = Fair—a few areas covered but very little detail
    1 = Poor—no written parts

THE TEN COMPONENTS OF AN INNOVATION PLAN

1. **Executive Summary**—This is the most important section because it has to convince the reader that the innovation will succeed. In no more than three pages, you should summarize the highlights of the rest of the plan. This means that the key elements of the following components should be mentioned.

   The executive summary must be able to stand on its own. It is not simply an introduction to the rest of the innovation plan. This section should articulate the new venture concept clearly, describe its uniqueness, formulate the "fit" with the corporate innovation strategy, and demonstrate the future growth potential. Because this section summarizes the plan, it is often best to write this section last.

Rate this component:	Outstanding	Very Good	Good	Fair	Poor
	5	4	3	2	1

2. **Description of the Innovation**—This section should provide background information about your industry, a general description of your innovative concept, and the specific mission that you are trying to achieve. Your product or service should be described in terms of its unique qualities and value to the customer. Specific short-term and long-term objectives must be defined. You should clearly state what sales, market share, and profitability objectives you want your business to achieve.

Key Elements	Have you covered this in the plan?	Is the answer clear? (yes or no)	Is the answer complete? (yes or no)
a. What type of innovation will you have?			
b. What products or services will you sell?			
c. Why does it promise to be successful?			

Key Elements	Have you covered this in the plan?	Is the answer clear? (yes or no)	Is the answer complete? (yes or no)
d. What is the growth potential?			
e. How is it unique?			

Rate this component:	Outstanding	Very Good	Good	Fair	Poor
	5	4	3	2	1

3. **Marketing**—There are two major parts to the marketing section. The first is research and analysis. Here, you should explain who buys the product or service - or, in other words, identify your target market. Measure your market size and trends, and estimate the market share you expect. Be sure to include support for your sales projections. For example, if your figures are based on published marketing research data, be sure to cite the source. Do your best to make realistic and credible projections. Describe your competition in considerable detail, identifying their strengths and weaknesses. Finally, explain how you will be better than your competitors.

The second part is your marketing plan. This critical section should include your market strategy, sales and distribution, pricing, advertising, promotion, and public awareness. Demonstrate how your pricing strategy will result in a profit based on the type of corporate venture you are proposing. Make sure to validate your innovation's "fit" with the company's strategy for innovation.

Key Elements	Have you covered this in the plan?	Is the answer clear? (yes or no)	Is the answer complete? (yes or no)
a. Who will be your customers? (Target Market)			
b. How big is the market? (Number of Customers)			
c. Who will be your competitors?			
d. How are their businesses prospering?			
e. How will you promote sales?			
f. What market share will you want?			
g. Do you have a pricing strategy?			
h. What advertising and promotional strategy will you use?			

Rate this component:	Outstanding	Very Good	Good	Fair	Poor
	5	4	3	2	1

4. **Operations Segment**—In this segment it is important to describe the mode of this corporate innovation concept (internal, external, or cooperative) and outline its advantages. Operating needs, projected operating costs, and general plans for operations should all be considered in this section.

Key Elements	Have you covered this in the plan?	Is the answer clear? (yes or no)	Is the answer complete? (yes or no)
a. What is the mode of this corporate innovation?			
b. Have you outlined the advantages of thistype of innovation approach?			
c. Any operational needs in terms of facilities, or equipment?			
d. What estimates do you have for operatingcosts?			
e. Have you described the general operations of this new innovation?			

Rate this component:	Outstanding	Very Good	Good	Fair	Poor
	5	4	3	2	1

5. **Management**—Start by describing the management team, their unique qualifications, and how you compensate them (including salaries, employment agreements, stock purchase plans, levels of ownership, and other considerations). Discuss how your organization is structured and consider including a diagram illustrating who reports to whom. Also include a discussion of the potential contribution of the board of directors, advisers, or consultants.

Key Elements	Have you covered this in the plan?	Is the answer clear? (yes or no)	Is the answer complete? (yes or no)
a. Who will manage the business?			
b. What qualifications do you have?			

Key Elements	Have you covered this in the plan?	Is the answer clear? (yes or no)	Is the answer complete? (yes or no)
c. How many employees will you have?			
d. What will they do?			
e. How much will you pay your employees and what type of benefits will you offer them?			
f. What consultants or specialists will you use?			
h. What regulations will affect your business?			

Rate this component:	Outstanding	Very Good	Good	Fair	Poor
	5	4	3	2	1

6. **Financial**—Determine the stages where your innovation will require financing and iden-tify the expected financing sources (internal venture fund or outside equity sources). Also, clearly show what return on investment these sources will achieve by investing in your business. It is good to develop a budget for the venture. If the work is done well, pro forma financial statements could then be prepared to represent the projected finan-cial achievements expected from your venture plan. They also provide a standard by which to measure the actual results of operating your venture. They are a valuable tool to help you manage and control your business. Two key financial statements must be presented: an income statement (profit & loss) and a cash flow statement (cash inflows and outflows). These statements typically cover a one-year period. Be sure you state any assumptions and projections you made when calculating the figures.

Key Elements	Have you covered this in the plan?	Is the answer clear? (yes or no)	Is the answer complete? (yes or no)
a. Have you staged the funding needs so that executives can gauge the innovations' progression and expected needs?			
b. What is your expected monthly cash flow during the first year?			
c. What is your total expected business income for the first year? Quarterly for the next two years? (Forecast)			

Key Elements	Have you covered this in the plan?	Is the answer clear? (yes or no)	Is the answer complete? (yes or no)
d. What sales volume will you need in order to make a profit during the three years?			
e. What will be the breakeven point?			
f. What are your total financial needs?			
g. What are your funding sources?			

Rate this component:	Outstanding	Very Good	Good	Fair	Poor
	5	4	3	2	1

7. **Critical Risks**—Discuss potential risks before they happen. Here are some examples: potentially unfavorable industry-wide trends, unexpected innovation or development costs that could exceed estimates, sales projections that are not achieved. The idea is to recognize risks and identify alternative courses of action. Your main objective is to show that you can anticipate and control (to a reasonable degree) your risks.

Key Elements	Have you covered this in the plan?	Is the answer clear? (yes or no)	Is the answer complete? (yes or no)
a. What potential problems have you identified?			
b. Have you calculat-edthe risks?			
c. What alternative courses of action are there?			

Rate this component:	Outstanding	Very Good	Good	Fair	Poor
	5	4	3	2	1

8. **Harvest Strategy**—Ensuring the survival of an internal venture is hard work. An innovation team's protective feelings for an idea built from scratch make it tough to grapple with such issues as management succession and harvest strategies. With foresight, however, corporate entrepreneurs can keep their dream alive, ensure the vitality of their ventures, and usually strengthen their venture and the company in the process. Thus identifying issues involved with harvesting of the venture as well as management transitions are essential in the early stages (even if they are to change later on in the development of the venture).

Key Elements	Have you covered this in the plan?	Is the answer clear? (yes or no)	Is the answer complete? (yes or no)
a. Have you planned for the orderly transfer of the venture assets if ownership of the business is passed to this corporation?			
b. Is there a strategy for identifying potential harvest opportunities?			

Rate this component:	Outstanding	Very Good	Good	Fair	Poor
	5	4	3	2	1

9. **Milestone Schedule**—This is an important segment of the innovation plan because it requires you to determine what tasks you need to accomplish in order to achieve your objectives. Milestones and deadlines should be established and monitored on an ongoing basis. Each milestone is related to all the others and together they comprise a timely representation of how your objective is to be accomplished.

Key Elements	Have you covered this in the plan?	Is the answer clear? (yes or no)	Is the answer complete? (yes or no)
a. How have you set your objectives?			
b. Have you set deadlines for each stage of your growth?			

Rate this component:	Outstanding	Very Good	Good	Fair	Poor
	5	4	3	2	1

10. **Appendix**—This section includes important background information that was not included in the other sections. This is where you would put such items as resumes of the management team, names of references and advisers, drawings, documents, licenses, agreements, and any materials that support the plan. You may also wish to add a bibliography of the sources from which you drew information.

Key Elements	Have you covered this in the plan?	Is the answer clear? (yes or no)	Is the answer complete? (yes or no)
a. Have you included any documents, drawings, agreements, or other materials needed to support the plan?			

Key Elements	Have you covered this in the plan?	Is the answer clear? (yes or no)	Is the answer complete? (yes or no)
b. Are there any names of references, advisers, or technical sources you should include?			
c. Are there any other supporting documents?			

Rate this component:	Outstanding	Very Good	Good	Fair	Poor
	5	4	3	2	1

Summary: Your Innovation Plan

Directions: For each of the innovation plan sections that you assessed in the previous section on components, circle the assigned points on this review sheet and then total the circled points.

Components	Points				
1. Executive Summary	5	4	3	2	1
2. Description of the Innovation	5	4	3	2	1
3. Marketing	5	4	3	2	1
4. Operations	5	4	3	2	1
5. Management	5	4	3	2	1
6. Financial	5	4	3	2	1
7. Critical Risks	5	4	3	2	1
8. Succession Planning	5	4	3	2	1
9. Milestone Schedule	5	4	3	2	1
10. Appendix	5	4	3	2	1

Total Points: _____

Scoring:

50	—	Outstanding! The ideal innovation plan. Solid!
45–49	—	Very Good.
40–44	—	Good. The plan is sound with a few areas that need to be polished.
35–39	—	Above Average. The plan has some good areas but needs improvement before presentation.

30–34 — Average. Some areas are covered in detail yet certain areas show weakness.

20–29 — Below Average. Most areas need greater detail and improvement.

Below 20 — Poor. Plan needs to be researched and documented much better.

ORGANIZING AN ACTION PLAN

WHY ACTION PLAN?

There is no scarcity of good ideas. There is also no scarcity of good intentions. Why is it then that the shelves of organizational planning departments, university presidents, department heads, community services organizations, and countless other effective innovation people are stacked with plans that were never implemented? More importantly, why is it that so many entrepreneurs never seem to get their innovations off the ground.

The answer is often quite simple. Their innovation plans never actually included the last critical step—action planning. Action planning is the process of taking good ideas and breaking them into manageable steps that can be accomplished and measured. Action planning maximizes success and minimizes failure.

Action planning is often ignored because it is believed that there is "always a market for good ideas" or that the "cream will always rise to the top." Entrepreneurs and innovators are often so in love with their ideas that they can't understand why everyone is not begging to help them put the idea into action.

The reality is that the action planning and implementation phases are often the most difficult. Ironically, developing an action plan often seems to be an exercise in the obvious. That is, everybody surely knows what we have to do to get this idea in place. The action plan is the opportunity to test this assumption. It is the chance to put down in writing exactly how the idea is to be implemented and at the same time make sure that everyone involved knows all the steps.

At the end of this section you will find a set of forms that can be used for constructing your action plan. Please refer to them as you read this section.

INNOVATION ACTION PLANNING

Action planning is a clear process with no shortcuts. The steps below demonstrate this process:

- Choosing the team
- Naming and describing the specific goal to be accomplished
- Describing the current reality that forms the environment for the project
- Discerning the key actions that need to be performed
- Creating a calendar of actions and assignments for team members

Each of these outcomes is critical for the success of any project. Without accomplishing each of the above, innovation success is seriously jeopardized.

CHOOSE A TEAM

In most cases you will need the help of others to bring about meaningful change in your organization. The first step is to identify a group who also has an interest in improving your workgroup. These people can be technical experts, a banker, a lawyer, etc. The real key is that they want you to succeed and are willing to work.

LIST BELOW POTENTIAL TEAM MEMBERS:

1. _____

2. _____

3. _____

4. _____

5. _____

6. _____

7. _____

8. _____

9. _____

10. _____

DECIDING THE GOAL

Without specific targets, projects lose focus and flounder. When goals are not clear and specific, the steps to be taken are also not clear. In the space below, write a specific goal statement for your innovation. For example, a goal for a mail order business might be: "To have my first sales catalogue in the mail by June 1."

Name the goal: _____

_____

a. Strengths in your situation that lead toward the goal:

_____

_____

b. Weaknesses that threaten the accomplishment:

_____

_____

c. Potential benefits of pursuing this course of action:

_____

_____

THE CURRENT REALITY

The next step is to look at the environment of your business. You must be able to identify those aspects of the project that are its strengths and, at the same time, list the benefits that successful achievement of the goal will bring to the organization.

You also must be prepared to face up to its weaknesses and the potential threats that exist to the project. This process is called a force field analysis where you attempt to identify forces working in favor of success and those working against success. Based on this analysis, you must be able to determine if the balance of forces favors success.

A well-done force field analysis will allow you to align the critical resources necessary for the success of the project. Failure to perform this step may result in unanticipated resistance to a project or lack of an appropriate support base. It is often easier to deal with a problem if it is identified in advance.

Use the current reality worksheet to summarize the success and failure forces confronting your business. Don't be too concerned about the number of factors in each category. What is more important is the relative weight of the factors. A strong success factor may outweigh several irritating failure forces.

CURRENT REALITY WORKSHEET

Success Forces	Failure Forces
Strengths	**Weaknesses**
_____	_____
_____	_____
_____	_____
_____	_____
_____	_____
_____	_____
_____	_____
_____	_____

Success Forces	Failure Forces
Opportunities	*Threats*
_____	_____
_____	_____
_____	_____
_____	_____
_____	_____
_____	_____
_____	_____
_____	_____

DETERMINING KEY ACTIONS

The heart of the action plan is the identification of the specific actions to be performed. There is no one best way to accomplish this activity; however, the key is to assure that everyone on your team has an opportunity to provide input. Provided at the end of this section are multiple copies of action identification sheets. Ask each of your team members to take a few minutes and try to identify the action steps that must be taken in order for you to reach your business goal.

INDIVIDUALLY LIST THE TASKS THAT WILL MOVE THE PROJECT TOWARD THE GOAL (BIG AND SMALL ACTIONS)

_____
_____
_____
_____
_____
_____
_____
_____
_____
_____
_____
_____
_____
_____
_____
_____

ORGANIZING ACTION CLUSTERS

Once a large group of steps are identified, some editing must take place. Items that are the same can be eliminated as well as those which are not really necessary for project completion. Next, the action steps need to be organized into action clusters.

Action clusters are all actions that relate to one another in some way. For example, there may be several different pieces of financial information that need to be obtained. These can be grouped together in a "financial information" group. The same may be true for acquiring needed equipment. When putting steps into clusters, try to arrange them in the order in which they must be accomplished.

GROUP THE ACTIONS INTO SEVERAL CLUSTERS OF SIMILAR ACTIVITY

Cluster 1 _____
_____
*Actions:*_____
_____
_____
_____

Cluster 2 _____
*Actions:*_____
_____
_____
_____
_____

Cluster 3 _____
*Actions:*_____
_____
_____
_____

Cluster 4 _____
*Actions:*_____
_____
_____
_____

Cluster 5 _____
*Actions:*_____
_____

_____

_____
_____
_____

TIME FOR ACTION

This is a critical element in the process. Once you have organized the steps into clusters, you are ready to make decisions about when each step will be accomplished and by whom. In most cases, the steps will be performed by you, but there are several things that may have to be done by your banker, a supplier, or a contractor. By creating a graphic calendar of the action plan, you can make sure everyone knows his or her assignment and you can keep track of progress. A large chalk or grease board can be used to chart your success.

FIGURE 11-1   Action Planning

CALANDAR OF ACTION AND ASSIGNMENTS

(Atction Cluster)	(Completion Date)	(Person Resposible)

ACHIEVING SUCCESS

You now have an Action Plan that can be used as a tool for achieving the success you desire. You must now put this plan in motion. Everyone has assignments and deadlines. Your job is to build and maintain momentum for your plan.

You must:

- Keep everyone informed and motivated,
- Use milestones with specific dates,
- Update the plan when needed, and
- Acknowledge successes, even small ones.

Summary

This chapter has provided the "road map" for developing an effective innovation plan. Beginning with the important benefits of an innovation plan for the innovator and I-team as well as for the executive team that evaluates it, we then outlined each segment of an innovation plan. We also provided a complete assessment tool for self-evaluation of the plan. The chapter then described the importance of the action planning process and offered a tool for developing your own action plan. It is hoped that you will be able to utilize these tools in developing an innovation plan and an action plan for your organization.

INNOVATION-IN-ACTION

Innovation Strategy at Koch Industries

Executives have increasingly embraced corporate entrepreneurship as a strategy for revitalizing their organizations. Koch Industries is an excellent example of an organization that effectively employs a strategy for innovation, focusing on three core principles: creating a more supportive environment for innovation, enhancing the creative potential in each employee, and shaping and reinforcing the behaviors required to generate new products, processes, and businesses. Based in Wichita, Kansas, Koch Industries is one of the largest privately owned corporations in the United States, with $100 billion in revenue and more than 70,000 employees. The firm utilizes a self-developed concept called Market Based Management (MBM). According to CFO Steve Feilmeier, the MBM philosophy is "based on allowing the free market to create long-term value … executed by fostering internal entrepreneurialism. Koch Industries is much more interested in hiring people with the right values and beliefs than those with the right skills and knowledge, although [it is necessary that an employee develop] both dimensions" (Calabro, 2008). Specifically, Koch Industries employs the MBM strategy and lives a philosophy with five integral parts: vision, decision rights, knowledge processes, virtue and talents, and incentives (Koch, 2007).

(continued)

First, Koch focuses on vision and decision rights to create an environment that sets the stage for effective entrepreneurial strategy implementation. According to CEO Charles Koch, vision "begins and ends" with creating value and then implementing strategies that maximize the value for the long term. This value-added perspective is supposed to guide all activities. The firm operationalizes this vision by directing its priorities in two areas: those actions required for staying in business and being legally compliant, and "gap analyses" whereby the risk-adjusted present value of an opportunity is compared to the resources consumed. This quantitative gap analysis process ensures adherence to the vision of creating value. Koch Industries' employees live this vision by focusing on innovation, operations, trading, transaction excellence, and service to the public sector. An important aspect of the entrepreneurial environment at Koch, decision rights ensure that the proper individuals are in the proper roles, that they have the authority necessary to do their jobs, and that they are held accountable for creating long-term value. Decision rights are viewed as similar to the notion of property rights. Roles are clearly defined, and expectations and standards for behavior are provided. Koch believes that employees with the best "comparative advantage" should make the decision. According to Charles Koch, an individual gains a comparative advantage when he or she is able to perform an activity more effectively with lower opportunity costs. Company belief holds that everyone is unique, and should look for opportunities where they have the comparative advantage.

Second, Koch Industries emphasizes knowledge processes and virtue and talents. According to Koch, knowledge processes focus on creating, acquiring, sharing, and applying relevant knowledge, and developing systems for measuring and tracking profitability. As stated by CEO Charles Koch, "Knowledge fuels prosperity by signaling and guiding resources to higher-valued uses" (Koch, 2007, p. 101). Activities such as benchmarking, dialogue with specialists, and developing technology and business networks are hallmarks of identifying and creating knowledge resources in the company. Furthermore, employees are sought who have the specific knowledge to successfully perform their roles, and who are willing to share that knowledge with others. Finally, it is believed that knowledge also comes from assessing results. Developing quantitative profit and loss measures and better understanding the drivers of each is the keystone to this assessment. Focusing on virtue and talents ensures that people with the right values, skills, and capabilities are hired, retained, and developed to carry out the vision.

Lastly, Koch understands the importance of incentives to reinforce and shape desired organizational behavior. Company philosophy centers on rewarding people according to the value they create for the organization, not based on job title or tenure. According to Koch Industries, profit is a powerful incentive for entrepreneurs to take risks and satisfy consumer needs. Incentives are utilized to align employee interests with the interests of the company and society. Employees are paid a portion of the value they create. Furthermore, Koch Industries tailors each employee's compensation package to achieve maximum motivation. Employee needs, ability to create value, and time preference for compensation are considered when determining the compensation package.

Koch Industries' adherence to these five core principles has led it to be a global leader in the following sectors: refining and chemicals; process and pollution-control equipment and technologies; minerals and fertilizers; fibers and polymers (including Stainmaster and Lycra Spandex); commodity and financial trading and services; and forest and consumer products. The company's business interests originated in refinery machines and evolved into Koch Pipeline, Koch Alaskan Pipeline, INVISTA, and Georgia-Pacific. Koch Industries provides an illustration of how organizations can create a competitive advantage by implementing innovation and corporate entrepreneurship strategies. These strategies necessitate a top-down bottom-up approach, whereby senior management must set the entrepreneurial strategy and provide a supportive organizational environment structure to motivate the deliberate practices of innovation and entrepreneurship by employees at all levels of the organization.

References

Calabro, L. 2008. Koch Industries' Steve Feilmeier, "The CFO of the United States' largest private company explains what it's like to not worry about earnings," *CFO Magazine.* Retrieved from http://www.cfo.com/article.cfm/10317304?f=search.

Koch, C. G. 2007. *The science of success: How market based management built the world's largest private company.* Hoboken, NJ: Wiley.

Adapted from: Hornsby, J.S.and Goldsby, M.G.. 2009. Corporate entrepreneurial performance at Koch Industries: A social cognitive framework, *Business Horizons* 52: 413–419.)

Key Terms

Action Planning	Management
Appendix	Market Niche
Critical Risks	Marketing
Descriptions of the innovation	Marketing Segment
Executive Summary	Milestone
Financial	Milestone Schedule
Financial Forecast	Milestones
Harvest	Operations
Harvest Strategy	Planning
Innovation Plan	Risks

Discussion Questions

1. Describe each of the five planning pitfalls entrepreneurs often encounter.
2. Identify the benefits of an innovation plan (a) for an innovator and (b) for executive-level sources.
3. What are the three major viewpoints to be considered when developing an innovation plan?
4. What are some components to consider in the proper packaging of a plan?
5. Identify five of the 10 guidelines to be used for preparing an innovation plan.

6. Briefly describe each of the major segments to be covered in an innovation plan.
7. Why is the summary segment of an innovation plan written last?
8. Why are milestones important to an innovation plan?
9. Describe the "Action Planning" Process.
10. What is Innovation Action Planning?

Endnotes

1. For additional information on writing effective plans see: Timmons, J. A., Zacharakis, A., & Spinelli, S., *Business Plans that Work.* New York: McGraw-Hill, 2004.
2. Barringer, B. R. *Effective Business Plans.* Upper Saddle River, NJ: Prentice Hall, 2008.
3. Mason, C. & Stark, M. 2004. What do investors look for in a business plan? *International Small Business Journal* 22 (3): 227–248.
4. Based on: Kuratko, D. F.. 2009. *Entrepreneurship: Theory, Process & Practice,* 8th ed. Mason, OH: Cengage/Southwestern.
5. Based on: Kuratko, D. F. & McDonald, R. C.. 2007. *The Entrepreneurial)Planning Guide.* Bloomington, IN: Kelley School of Business, Indiana University.
6. Ibid.

ACCELERATING MOMENTUM: THE "I-SOLUTION"

SUSTAINING THE INNOVATION STRATEGY

A final challenge confronting senior-level managers is how to sustain any innovative momentum that is developed. More importantly, they need to accelerate that momentum so the innovative pace continues. There are two major aspects of this challenge: the role of managers and the role of the organization.

THE ROLE OF MANAGERS

As we discussed in Chapter 8, there are critical strategic roles that managers have in the innovation process.[1] Senior, middle, and first-level managers have distinct responsibilities with respect to each subprocess. Thus, organizations pursuing corporate entrepreneurship strategies likely exhibit a cascading yet integrated set of entrepreneurial actions at the senior, middle, and first levels of management.[2] At the senior level, managers act in concert with others throughout the firm to identify effective means through which new businesses can be created or existing ones reconfigured. Corporate entrepreneurship is pursued in light of environmental opportunities and threats, with the purpose of creating a more effective alignment between the company and conditions in its external environment. The entrepreneurial actions expected of middle-level managers are framed around the need for this group to propose and interpret entrepreneurial opportunities that might create new business for the firm or increase the firm's competitiveness in current business domains. First-line managers exhibit the "experimenting" role as they surface the operational ideas for innovative improvements. An important interpretation of previous research has been the belief that managers would surface ideas for entrepreneurial actions from every level of management, especially the first-line and middle levels. Therefore, managers across levels are jointly responsible for their organization's entrepreneurial actions.

In order to maintain this "entrepreneurial mind-set," managers must assume certain ongoing responsibilities.[3] The first responsibility involves *framing the challenge.* In other words, there needs to be a clear definition of the specified challenges that everyone involved with innovative projects should address. It is important to think in terms of, and regularly reiterate, the challenge. Second, leaders have the responsibility to *absorb the uncertainty* that is perceived by team members. Entrepreneurial leaders make uncertainty less daunting. The idea is to create the self-confidence that lets others act on opportunities without seeking managerial permission. Employees must not be overwhelmed by the complexity inherent in many innovative situations. A third responsibility is to *define gravity*—that is, what must be accepted and what cannot be accepted. The term *gravity* is used to capture limiting conditions. For example, there is gravity on Earth, but that does not mean it must limit our lives. If freed from the psychological cage of believing that gravity makes flying impossible, creativity can permit us to invent an airplane or spaceship. This is what the entrepreneurial mind-set is all about—seeing opportunities where others see barriers and limits. A fourth responsibility of entrepreneurial leadership involves *clearing obstacles* that arise as a result of internal competition for resources. This can be a problem especially when the entrepreneurial innovation is beginning to undergo significant growth. A growing venture will often find itself pitted squarely against other (often established) aspects of the firm in a fierce internal competition for funds and staff. Creative tactics, political skills, and an ability to regroup, reorganize, and attack from another angle become invaluable. A final responsibility for entrepreneurial leaders is to keep their *finger on the pulse* of the project. This involves constructive monitoring and control of the developing opportunity.

An organization's sustained effort in corporate entrepreneurship is contingent upon individual members continuing to undertake innovative activities and upon positive perceptions of the activity by the organization's executive management, which will in turn support the further allocation of necessary organizational antecedents.[4]

THE ROLE OF THE FIRM: REENGINEERING ORGANIZATIONAL THINKING

The dynamic entrepreneurial organizations of the twenty-first century will be ones that are capable of merging strategic action with entrepreneurial action on an ongoing basis.[5] This type of entrepreneurial organization could be conceptualized in the "new thinking" that is needed by today's leaders.. As has been shown in much of the recent literature, the strategic mind-set must lean toward the more innovative concepts in leading organizations today. It is important to recognize a critical factor that Covin and Slevin[6] point out. The *"hardware" side of organizations* (strategy, structure, systems, and procedures) is the contextual framework within which individuals take their behavioral cues. The *"software" side of organizations* (culture and climate), while more subtle and informal, is the locus for the acceptance or rejection of true entrepreneurial activity. Leaders cannot simply send an edict to the organizational members that entrepreneurial activity and innovations are to take place. Rather, they must focus on the development of an entrepreneurial climate to facilitate the entrepreneurial actions of organizational members.

To establish an entrepreneurial mind-set, organizations need to provide the freedom and encouragement required for employees to develop their ideas. This is often a problem in enterprises because many top managers do not believe entrepreneurial ideas can be nurtured and developed in their environment. They also find it difficult to implement policies that encourage freedom and unstructured activity. But managers need to develop policies that will help innovative people reach their full potential. Establishing this new thinking includes identifying *explicit innovation goals* which are mutually agreed on by the employee and management; establishing effective *feedback* and *positive reinforcement* so that innovators or creators of ideas realize what rewards exist; emphasizing *individual responsibility* because accountability is critical to the success of any innovative program; creating *reward systems* for innovations to enhance and encourage others to risk and to achieve; and accepting and dissecting *failures* so that individuals feel free to experiment without fear of punishment, and learning then takes place as failed projects are examined closely in real time.[7]

ASKING THE KEY QUESTIONS

What can a corporation do to reengineer its thinking to foster the innovative process? The organization needs to examine and revise its management philosophy. Many enterprises have obsolete ideas about cooperative cultures, management techniques, and the values of managers and employees. Unfortunately, doing old tasks more efficiently is not the answer to new challenges; a new culture with new values has to be developed. Although each enterprise must develop a philosophy most appropriate for its own entrepreneurial process, a number of key questions can assist in establishing the type of process an organization has. Organizations can use the following questions to assess their enterprise. Applying these questions helps them feed back to the planning process for a proper approach.

- *Does your company encourage innovative thinking?* Will individuals receive the corporation's blessing for their self-appointed idea creations? Some corporations foolishly try to appoint people to carry out an innovation when in fact the ideas must surface.

- *Does your company provide ways for innovators to stay with their ideas?* When the innovation process involves switching the people working on an idea—that is, handing off a developing business or product from a committed innovator to whoever is next in line—that person is often not as committed as the originator of a project.

- *Are people in your company permitted to do the job in their own way, or are they constantly stopping to explain their actions and ask for permission?* Some organizations push decisions up through a multilevel approval process so that the doers and the deciders never even meet.

- *Has your company evolved quick and informal ways to access the resources to try new ideas?* Innovators usually need discretionary resources to explore and develop new ideas. Some companies give employees the freedom to use a percentage of their time on projects of their own choosing and set aside funds to explore new ideas when they occur. Others control resources so tightly that nothing is available for the new and unexpected. The result is nothing new.

- *Has your company developed ways to manage many small and experimental innovations?* Today's corporate cultures favor a few well-studied, well-planned attempt to hit a home run. In fact, nobody bats 1,000, and it is better to try more times with less careful and expensive preparation for each.

- *Is your system set up to encourage risk taking and to tolerate mistakes?* Innovation cannot be achieved without risk and mistakes. Even successful innovation generally begins with blunders and false starts.

- *Are people in your company more concerned with new ideas or with defending their turf?* Because new ideas almost always cross the boundaries of existing patterns of organization, a jealous tendency to "turf protection" blocks innovation.

- *How easy is it to form functionally complete, autonomous teams in your corporate environment?* Small teams with full responsibility for developing an innovation solve many of the basic problems, yet, some companies resist their formation.

Developing a corporate innovative philosophy provides a number of advantages. One is that this type of atmosphere often leads to the development of new products and services and helps the organization expand and grow. A second is it creates a workforce that can help the enterprise maintain its competitive posture. A third is it promotes a climate conducive to high achievers and helps the enterprise motivate and keep its best people.

This new millennium has been characterized as an age of instant information, ever-increasing development and application of technology, experimental change, revolutionary processes, and global competition. It is now an age filled with turbulence and paradox. The words used to describe the new innovation regime of the twenty-first century are: *Dream, Create, Explore, Invent, Pioneer,* and *Imagine*! As scholars and researchers dedicated to the field of entrepreneurship and corporate innovation, we believe this is a point in time when the gap between what can be imagined and what can be accomplished has never been smaller. It is a time requiring innovative vision, courage, calculated risk taking, and strong leadership. It is simply *"the innovative imperative of the 21*st *Century"*.[8]

Haier's Process of Consumer-Based Innovation

Corporate innovation is a continuously evolving process for any organization. Today there are many successful companies using consumer feedback to spawn "design innovation." One such company is Haier, a Chinese major home-appliance manufacturing company. Haier was founded in 1984 and for over seven years produced one single refrigerator model. In the early 1990s, they adopted a diversification strategy rather than rely on this single-product strategy. Since then Haier has grown rapidly to become the fourth-ranked white appliance manufacturer in the world. Haier is the world market share leader in two of the largest major home-appliance industries, and they manufacture appliances in over 96 unique product categories worldwide. Haier's culture of innovation has also led to more than 7,000 patents.

One of the major reasons for Haier's success has been an ability to design innovations based on consumer feedback. Starting in 1999, Haier has developed into a horizontally structured organization. One of the goals of this structural change was to reduce the distance from the company's engineers and managers to the customers and end users. Reducing this distance was crucial to obtaining the information flow of customers' individualized demands.

This information flow from the consumer to Haier's managers and engineers has led to many customer-oriented design innovations. When the Chinese government distributed over 2 billion US dollars in subsidies to rural consumers for buying home appliances, Haier took advantage. Based on extremely unique consumer feedback from these rural consumers, Haier invented several new appliances. Many rural consumers were complaining that excess dirt was clogging up their washing machines. Many of these consumers were farmers and these farmers were washing potatoes and vegetables in their new washing machines, which was indeed the cause of the clogging. The customers thought that these washing machines should be able to wash other items beyond normal laundry. Instead of telling the customers to stop this behavior, Haier instead asked their engineers to modify their existing products. New washing machines were designed with wider pipes that would not clog with dirt or vegetable peels. New products were designed and manufactured that could wash laundry, potatoes, and vegetables. Haier even took these iterations a step further. They began designing washing machines that could wash and peel potatoes, and they developed a washing machine that could make cheese from goats' milk.

On the refrigerator side of new products, Haier launched a "design the icebox yourself" campaign. This campaign invited both existing users and potential users to participate as co-innovators and has since resulted in more than 1 million customized orders per year.

Hundreds of similar design innovations helped Haier win the market leadership in China's rural provinces, and this led to billions of dollars of new revenue. Although several other factors have contributed to their success, the ability to increase the acceptability of its products among rural Chinese was a significant cornerstone to Haier's success.

Source: Adapted from: http://www.plm.automation.siemens.com/CaseStudyWeb/dispatch/ viewResource.html?resourceId=11003; http://www.jamieandersononline.com/uploads/Serving_ the_World_s_Poor.pdf; http://www.springerlink.com/content/x0h5710767117r4/fulltext.pdf; http://www.haier.com/images/pdf/backgrounder.pdf; http://blogs.forbes.com/china/2010/06/17/ haier-a-chinese-company-that-innovates/ websites accessed January 8, 2011.

Key Terms

Absorb the uncertainty
Clearing obstacles
Explicit innovation goals
Framing the challenge

Gravity
"Hardware" side of organizations
Innovative imperative
"Software" side of organizations

Discussion Questions

1. Briefly describe the roles of managers in the innovation strategy.
2. Describe how senor, middle, and first-line managers impact entrepreneurial actions.
3. Identify the four responsibilities of managers in maintaining the "entrepreneurial mind-set."
4. Explain "gravity" in terms of an entrepreneurial mind-set.
5. Describe the "hardware side" of organizations.
6. Describe the "software side" of organizations.
7. What five important steps help an organization establish innovative thinking?
8. Identify some of the key questions that need to be asked in order to assist in the planning of any innovative activity.

Endnotes

1. Floyd, S. & Lane, P. 2000. Strategizing throughout the organization: Managing role conflict in strategic renewal, *Academy of Management Review* 25: 154–177.
2. Kuratko, D. F., Ireland, R. D., Covin, J. G. & Hornsby, J. S. 2005. A model of middle level managers' entrepreneurial behavior, *Entrepreneurship Theory and Practice* 29 (6): 699–716.
3. McGrath, R. G. & MacMillan, I. 2000. *The Entrepreneurial Mindset.* Boston, MA: Harvard Business Press.
4. Morris, M. H., Kuratko, D. F. & Covin, J. G. 2011. *Corporate Entrepreneurship & Innovation.* Mason, OH: Cengage/SouthWestern Publishers.
5. Ireland, R. D., Hitt, M., Camp, S. M. & Sexton, D. L. 2001. Integrating Entrepreneurship and Strategic Management Actions to Create Firm Wealth, *Academy of Management Executive* 15 (1): 49–63.
6. Covin, J. G. & Slevin, D. P. 2002. The Entrepreneurial Imperatives of Strategic Leadership. In M. Hitt, R. D. Ireland, M. Camp & D. Sexton (eds.), *Strategic Entrepreneurship:Creating a New Mindset* (pp. 309–327). Oxford, UK: Blackwell Publishers.
7. Based on: Kuratko, D. F. 2009.*Entrepreneurship: Theory, Process, & Practice,* 8th ed. Cengage/South-Western Publishing.
8. Kuratko, D. F. 2009. The Entrepreneurial Imperative of the 21st Century. *Business Horizons* 52 (5): 421–428.

APPENDIX A

A COMPLETE INNOVATION PLAN—"*SUROs SURGICAL COMPANY*"

TABLE OF CONTENTS

EXECUTIVE SUMMARY
COMPANY

Suros Surgical Systems ("Suros" or the "Company") manufactures minimally invasive medical devices for biopsy and tissue removal focused currently on the breast surgical market. Suros launched the product in April of 2002 and is now approaching sales of a million dollars per month and breakeven operations. Suros is seeking $7 million in investment capital primarily to grow its sales and marketing organization to take advantage of the market opportunity and achieve significant market share.

PRINCIPAL PLATFORM TECHNOLOGY

Suros has developed a surgical platform technology with specific applications for minimally invasive biopsy and tissue removal that provides significant clinical and economical solutions in interventional health care. The current market focus is breast biopsy; however, Suros believes there are opportunities in other biopsy and tissue removal applications. The technology has proven to be clinically safe, easier to use for physicians and technologists, and superior to current technologies, with its speed and efficiency. It is expanding the current vacuum-assisted minimally invasive surgical biopsy and tissue removal market through improved treatment range, improved economic return, and its ability to provide histologically and pathologically viable tissue core samples for accurate diagnosis.

BREAST BIOPSY MARKET DEVELOPMENT

Suros has revolutionized the breast biopsy market in two phases over a 15-month period. First, Suros introduced new and improved technology in April 2002. Second, Suros announced the first commercially available MRI-compatible breast biopsy procedure in May 2003. With these two events, Suros has the potential to significantly change the market mix of the 1.4 million breast biopsy procedures performed annually in the United States. The vacuum-assisted breast biopsy market is currently about 350,000 procedures per year. The balance of the current market is 350,000 core or needle biopsies and 700,000 open surgical biopsies. Management believes the total addressable U.S. market for Suros devices is moving toward $500 million annually.

Design and development of the ATEC™ (Automated Tissue Excision and Collection) breast biopsy and excision system was intended to address ongoing clinical weaknesses in existing biopsy technology, with all methods of imaging the breast. The ATEC™ addressed the stereotactic and ultrasound imaging arena—where 50 percent of the patient biopsy volume exists—and *also* the magnetic resonance imaging (MRI) sector where vacuum-assisted breast biopsy was not previously possible.

Suros capitalized on the unique attributes of ATEC™ in the traditional ultrasound and stereotactic market by expanding the market options and increasing patient comfort and throughput. By adapting its improved technology for applications never before available in the breast biopsy market, Suros became the first and only company in the world to commercially market a vacuum-assisted breast biopsy system compatible under all three imaging modalities—ultrasound, stereotactic, and MRI.

MRI-guided breast biopsy with ATEC™ is viewed by leading breast imagers as one of the most important advancements to women's health in the last decade. This ultrasensitive imaging modality is typically used for the most high-risk patients to visualize abnormal breast lesions at the earliest possible stage that cancer can be detected. The MRI breast scanning market has doubled each year for the past three years and this growth rate is expected to continue. The Suros ATEC™ system has already been installed in more than 30 of the leading institutions across the United States that traditionally advances and endorses the adoption of new technology in the health care market.

ATEC™ SYSTEM

Suros launched the ATEC™ system in April 2002 and it has been successfully used in more than 20,000 ultrasound, stereotactic, and MRI-guided biopsy procedures at more than 150 hospitals and breast centers across the United States. Notable institutions using the ATEC™ include Memorial Sloan-Kettering Cancer Center, Mayo Clinic in Jacksonville, Florida, Stanford University, Thomas Jefferson University, UCSD, UCI, University of Pennsylvania, Indiana University, Elizabeth Wende Breast Center, Stamford Health System, Lynn Sage Breast Clinic, and Breast Imaging of Oklahoma.

The ATEC™ system is a single-needle insertion process that allows access to targeted breast lesions through a small skin nick. It offers numerous features not found in competing products, allowing for outpatient diagnostic biopsy options for a more diverse patient population, improved patient throughput, and increased compatibility with vendor partners.

INTELLECTUAL PROPERTY

The Suros intellectual property portfolio represents a significant competitive advantage over current biopsy device manufacturers, with its technology and patents providing a solid foundation for growth opportunities in a variety of surgical areas, including liver, lung, ENT, urology, and neurosurgery. Suros now holds 15 patents (five issued since fall of 2000) and has a number of other patents pending or in the final application stage. Suros has FDA 510k clearance for additional surgical markets, which include general neurosurgical and ENT surgical markets as well as breast surgical market.

COMPETITION

Ethicon Endo-Surgery, a subsidiary of Johnson & Johnson Company, markets the Biopsys system (Mammotome) with estimated annual sales of approximately $100 million. The Mammotome was the first minimally invasive vacuum-assisted breast biopsy device introduced into the breast surgical market arena seven years ago. While the device provides vacuum-assisted, minimally invasive biopsy capabilities like the ATEC™, Suros believes the ATEC™ system has significant and notable clinical and user advantages. One of the most important and clinically relevant distinctions between the ATEC™ and all other market competitors is the ATEC™ system's unique compatibility with all three imaging modalities of MRI, ultrasound, and stereotactic. Suros also competes with companies using a radio frequency (RF) approach to breast biopsy that has more limited applications, as well as open surgical biopsy, a much more invasive biopsy approach that has greater risk to patients.

OFFICERS AND DIRECTORS

James Baumgardt	Chairman of the Board	Former President, Guidant NA Sales Chairman, Guidant Foundation
Jim Pearson	President & CEO	Former SVP, Equipment Services (NA) Medibuy ,CEO of Summit Medical
Rich Rella, CPA	Chief Financial Officer	Former CFO, Pictorial and Shepard Poorman Communications
Eugene Henderson	Corporate Counsel and Director	Senior Counsel, Founder, Henderson, Daily, Withrow & DeVoe

Michael Miller	Vice President of Engineering and Director	Cofounder, Promex (disposable medical device manufacturer), Manager, RCA/GE
Joseph Mark	Vice President Product Development and Director	Cofounder, Promex
Timothy Goedde, MD	Medical Director and Board Director	Instructor, American College of Surgery Surgical oncologist, Midwest Breast Center
Michael Hall	Director	Managing Director of Periculum Capital and previously Vice President of Marketing for Biomet, Inc.
William Ringo	Director	Chairman of Intermune, Inc., Retired President of Oncology and Critical Care Products at Eli Lilly
Phyllis Greenberger	Director	President and CEO of Society for Women's Health Research

FINANCIALS

($M)	2002A	2003E	2004F	2005F	2006F
Income Statement					
Revenue					
Breast	2.4	8.5	26.3	66.6	101.7
Other	—	—	—	2.4	7.0
Total Revenue	2.4	8.5	26.3	69.0	108.7
Gross Margin (%)	44	59	68	69	66
EBIT	(1.8)	—	3.0	18.5	34.9
Headcount	20	44	159	259	357

PRINCIPAL INVESTORS & STRATEGIC PARTNERS

Suros has raised a total of $7.6M in Series B & C and Convertible Debt financing. The outside investors include Rose-Hulman Ventures, Twilight Venture Partners and accredited individual investors.

TRANSACTION AND USE OF PROCEEDS

Suros is seeking $7.0 in equity financing. The purpose of the financing is to accelerate the growth in sales personnel and support, and expand the manufacturing capacity of the company. Suros has the resources currently to maintain profitable, rapid growth, but believes it has a significant market opportunity and desires to grow to the dominant market share by 2006.

INVESTMENT CONSIDERATIONS

- Platform technology with (5) FDA 510k clearances in interventional medicine, addressing multiple markets including the fastest-growing segment of breast biopsy (vacuum-assisted breast biopsy).

- Addressable breast biopsy and excision market approaching $500 million annually in the United States. International sales of the breast device as well≈as other platform markets represent significant additional market opportunities.

- First-to-market advantage in a progressive and quickly evolving MRI market with patent pending and proprietary technology. Suros has the only commercially available MRI-compatible biopsy device available for interventional breast cancer diagnosis. This biopsy capability provides the earliest stage breast cancer detection in the most high-risk patients.

- Strong IP portfolio, 15 issued patents, multiple patents pending with significant barrier to entry.

- Demonstrated demand—$10 million annualized revenue run rate after 19 months of sales.

- Attractive business model—capital, add-on, and disposable sales.

- The products maintain high gross margins with no product price erosion since launch.

- Outstanding customer adoption and approval, with leading surgeons, radiologists and institutions serving as advocates for Suros' technology, including Mayo Clinic, Memorial Sloan Kettering, Stanford, UCI, UCSD, Northwestern, University of Pennsylvania, Thomas Jefferson, I.U. Medical Center, University of Wisconsin, and The Methodist Hospital of Houston.

- Industry-experienced management team with proven track record.

- Internal development and design team.

- Efficient use of capital (only $7.6 million invested to date)

- Multiple exit options including IPO; numerous logical potential acquirers achievable within three years.

MARKET OPPORTUNITY

SUROS PLATFORM

Suros has developed a surgical platform technology, ATEC™, with far-reaching applications in interventional medicine. Its specific uses for minimally invasive biopsy and tissue removal provide significant clinical and economical solutions for use in multiple surgical specialties. The advancement of the Suros platform technology in the improvement of patient care is comparable in significance to the arrival of x-ray technology. Patient benefits of the ATEC™ include: reduced procedure time, less pain, less expensive, no breast disfigurement, fast and accurate diagnosis, reduced emotional trauma, and faster recovery time. Physician and health care provider benefits include: greater throughput, lower total cost, superior patient care, increased market size, and attractive established reimbursement. The ATEC™ system includes a console and related single-use disposable handpieces. The ATEC™ breast biopsy system is compatible with all three imaging modalities: ultrasound, stereotactic, and MRI, making it the most versatile system available accommodating a diverse patient population that was previously underserved.

DOMESTIC BREAST SURGICAL MARKET

The total number of breast biopsies performed in the United States annually is approximately 1.4 million[1], growing at 4–6 percent per annum. The Suros technology platform currently addresses the fastest-growing segment of the breast biopsy market: minimally invasive procedures. Given the impressive clinical results, favorable reimbursement, upward economic trends, and reduced pain associated with minimally invasive biopsies, this segment is significantly faster growing at 20–25 percent per year. Currently, over half of all U.S. breast biopsies are minimally invasive, using either vacuum-assisted or core/spring-loaded needle techniques.

The breast biopsy procedures market on an annual basis breaks down as follows:

Open surgical biopsy (OSB)	700,000
Core needle biopsy (CNB)	350,000
Vacuum-assisted breast biopsy (VABB)	350,000
Total biopsy procedures	1,400,000

[1]From *Start Up: Windhover's Review of Emerging Medical Ventures*, July 2003, page 28.

The clinical case for vacuum-assisted breast biopsy (VABB) procedures over core needle biopsy (CNB) and open surgical biopsy (OSB) is compelling. First, VABB is the recommend biopsy approach by the American College of Surgeons (ACS). Second, VABB is faster, less invasive, and economically superior. Core needle biopsy is typically a longer and more painful biopsy procedure that involves multiple needle insertions to retrieve tissue samples, which at times can yield an inconclusive diagnosis. An open surgical biopsy procedure requires hospitalization, is more expensive, has a longer recovery period, and since 80 percent of all biopsies are negative, OSB is less attractive to the patient, physician, and health care institution.

There are approximately 3,500 U.S. hospital or breast centers now offering vacuum-assisted biopsy capabilities in the United States, while there are a total of 6,500 potential hospital and breast center sites for minimally invasive biopsies. Additionally, there are 1,100 other private radiology center sites and 5,300 MRI center sites that could utilize the ATEC™ technology. As vacuum-assisted technology, such as the Suros ATEC™, becomes better known, its market penetration is expected to overtake open surgical biopsy, due to the numerous patient and institutional benefits.

MRI MARKET OPPORTUNITY

Historically, vacuum-assisted biopsies have been performed only in the ultrasound and stereotactic modalities—where 50 percent of all patient biopsy exists—and not with MRI. Primarily this is because previously available vacuum-assisted technology interfered with MRI images and their interpretation and were incompatible for use in the MRI environment, making it impossible to use VABB for MRI biopsy. In 2003, Suros introduced and commercialized the first-ever MRI compatible vacuum-assisted minimally invasive biopsy solution. The Suros technology is so unique that method and apparatus patents have been filed and are pending issuance. The combination of the ATEC™ equipment and the introducer apparatus allow Suros to offer the significant advantage of MRI breast biopsy averaging 30 minutes or less. This is a critical and unique advantage in an environment where MRI magnet time is expensive and heavily sought after within each institution.

MRI-guided breast biopsy with ATEC™ is viewed by leading radiologists as one of the most important advancements in women's health in the last decade. This imaging modality is typically used on the most high-risk patient to visualize breast lesions at the earliest possible stage cancer can be detected. It particularly benefits younger women, who typically have more dense breast tissue and require a more sensitive screening test. For this patient population, and for those women with a family history of breast cancer, MRI is the most effective cancer-screening test available. It also represents a significant growth opportunity for Suros, as well as a competitive differentiator and barrier to entry for competitors.

The MRI market includes 5,300 MRI centers, with 1,150 (23 percent) offering MRI breast scanning. The Company estimates that 60,000–80,000 breast scans were performed in these centers last year. This market has doubled each year for the past three years and its growth rate is expected to continue. This type of scanning growth rate without a legitimate biopsy option prior to the Suros ATEC™ system is amazing—the only other options before the ATEC™ were OSB or an extremely slow CNB. Suros stands to benefit substantially from this positive trend as the only vacuum-assisted biopsy solution in the MRI breast arena. ATEC™ for MRI has already been installed in more than 30 leading institutions across the United States that traditionally drive new technology adoption in the health care market.

BENIGN TUMOR EXCISIONAL OPPORTUNITY

In addition to vacuum-assisted minimally invasive biopsy used to detect cancer, the ATEC™ is also used for excisional biopsy, or the removal of all visible evidence of benign tumors. As ATEC™ becomes more pervasive in minimally invasive biopsy and physician experience with the device grows, ATEC™ use for the removal of benign tumors will likely increase dramatically. The potential market size for excisional biopsy includes the majority of the 700,00 open surgical biopsies performed annually. It's important to note that while 80 percent of all biopsies are negative, the majority of patients desire to have the suspicious area completely removed and therefore tolerate OSB. The ATEC™ has the capability to act as a biopsy as well as an excisional tool due to the unmatched speed in which it can remove tissue. For the patient, the speed of the ATEC™ translates to a 1–2 minute excisional procedure that would be 10+ minutes with any competitive technology. The option of OSB for benign tumor removal is clearly less favorable.

NEUROSURGERY MARKET

Suros is developing a minimally invasive intracranial surgical system, utilizing its proprietary patented ATEC™ technology platform. The prototype is being developed by the founding Suros development team in conjunction with the Rose-Hulman Institute of Technology. Although there are fewer intracranial procedures performed in the United States than breast biopsies, the market potential for Suros is significant. There are more than 220,000 cranial procedures performed annually and over 190,000 newly diagnosed patients with brain tumors each year.

The existing device for removal of tissue in the brain was developed more than 20 years ago and has key drawbacks, including heat generation, restricted line of sight and poor ergonomics which limit its use in the market. Despite these issues, management estimates that ultrasonic aspirators have annual sales volume of approximately $100 million. As with breast procedures, the neurosurgical market encounters certain product-capability/surgeon-need gaps that Suros can capitalize upon, leading to a market leadership position. For example, the precise high-speed blades of the Suros device allow the surgeon to perform tissue removal much faster and with increased precision than with existing ultrasonic devices. Second, the current market device fragments the tissue such that laboratory studies cannot be performed. The Suros Intracranial System will maintain the removed tissue in a condition where histology and pathology can be performed. Third, the Suros device hand piece will have the ability to function using straight or curved blades without degradation of power at the tip where delicate surgical control is required. This important engineering breakthrough improves surgery speed, surgeon comfort, and field of vision for surgical precision.

Suros has received early feedback that its product design will be embraced by neurosurgeons and interventional radiologists and is seen as an improvement over the current product. Neurosurgeons have already tested the Suros intracranial prototype in similar media and will begin testing it on patients in Q4 of 2003 and Q1 of 2004. Suros is preparing for a formal product launch in 2005.

OTHER MARKETS

The Suros technology provides a solid foundation for growth opportunities in a variety of other surgical areas for which it has FDA clearance, including gastrointestinal, pulmonology, ENT (ear, nose and throat), liver, and urology. Suros is researching product designs to address these markets and expects to have commercially viable products to address unmet market needs.

PRODUCT
THE ATEC™ SYSTEM

The ATEC™ Breast Biopsy and Excision System is a minimally invasive biopsy device allowing access to targeted breast lesions through a small percutaneous opening only a quarter of an inch wide. Unlike conventional biopsy devices, the ATEC™ system includes a lightweight, pneumatically controlled disposable handpiece that features a nonclogging and nonoccluding cutting blade design. Among its advantages over other competing products, the ATEC™ system is fully automated and compatible with all surgical visualization techniques now available to breast surgeons and radiologists, while providing pathologically viable tissue samples. The Suros breakthrough technology creates tangible economic and diagnostic benefits for its customers. For example, ATEC™ expands outpatient diagnostic biopsy options for a more diverse patient population, improves patient throughput, offers greater compatibility with installed equipment, and enjoys attractive, established reimbursement.

ATEC™ product advantages include:

- first commercially available vacuum-assisted system compatible with MRI
- first and only completely disposable system
- first and only fully automated system
- first and only closed system to limit exposure to bodily fluids for improved staff safety
- first and only system with continuous aspiration and lavage technique to minimize hematoma
- smallest vacuum-assisted needle
- fastest biopsy system (by a factor of 10) at 14 cores per minute—average number of biopsies per patient 8 to 12
- one-minute setup and cleanup time—easy for technologists

- 7-ounce handpiece that is much easier for physicians to use in the handheld arena
- true 12 and 9 gauge needles in standard, petite, long, and extra long lengths, allowing replacement of 14 gauge needle (most invasive) and service to diverse patient needs.

The Suros ATEC™ system consists of both reusable and disposable components. Standard package units include an ATEC™ console that controls and pneumatically powers a single patient use handpiece, the ATEC™ handpiece, and various adapters and disposable parts. The console is priced at $38,500 for stereotactic and ultrasound units and $55,000 for MRI. Suros believes that one strong indication of the market's acceptance of our technology is the fact that we are selling capital units at or near list price despite significant pricing pressure from competitors, including the fact that in some cases, competitors are giving equipment away in exchange for disposable usage commitments.

Various console components, each sold separately, allow the ATEC™ system to be seamlessly used with popular stereotactic and MRI equipment already installed at client sites, while at the same time improving patient care and staff safety. For example, the MRI Introducer Set facilitates the introduction and removal of fluids and tissue from the target site—including anesthesia and blood—but minimizes the exposure of the fluids to the adjacent medical equipment and medical staff.

In the most common breast biopsy modality, stereotactic, Suros offers the ATEC™ Adapter that provides the ability to lock the handpiece into the stereotactic table to inhibit movement and maintain registration with the biopsy site throughout the biopsy procedure. The Adapter facilitates the removal of the handpiece and inner cannula, while leaving the outer cannula in position within the patient's tissue to serve as an introducer for biopsy site markers and therapeutics. This greatly assists the visualization of the biopsy site during and following the biopsy procedure.

ATEC™ System Product Line for Stereotactic

Product	Price
ATEC™ Breast Biopsy System Handpiece—9g and 12g in a variety of lengths and configurations (standard, petite, long, and extra long)	$250
ATEC™ ATECMARK Biopsy Site Identifier—9g and 12g	$75
ATEC™ Needle Guides for most stereotactic units	$10
ATEC™ Tissue Filters	$5
ATEC™ Stereotactic Adapter for use on a variety of stereotactic systems	$5,500
ATEC™ Breast Biopsy System Console and components (including footswitch, suction canister, holder, and power cord)	$33,000

ATEC™ System Product Line for Ultrasound

Product	Price
ATEC™ Breast Biopsy System Handpiece—9g and 12g in a variety of lengths and configurations (standard, petite, long, and extra long)	$250
ATEC™ ATECMARK Biopsy Site Identifier—9g and 12g	$75
ATEC™ Tissue Filters	$5
ATEC™ Breast Biopsy System Console and components (including footswitch, suction canister, holder, and power cord)	$33,000

ATEC™ System Product Line for MRI

Product	Price
ATEC™ Breast Biopsy System Handpiece—9g and 12g in a variety of lengths and configurations (standard, petite, long, and extra long)	$350
ATEC™ ATECMARK Biopsy Site Identifier—9g and 12g	$75
ATEC™ MRI Introducer Set (sheath, stylet, localizing marker)	$195
ATEC™ Tissue Filters	$5
ATEC™ Breast Biopsy System Console and components (including footswitch, suction canister, holder, and power cord)	$55,000

Suros has developed the only commercially viable, fully automated vacuum-assisted biopsy device currently available for use in the MRI environment. The Company launched this system officially on May 13, 2003, and has already installed more than 30 systems in such opinion-leading institutions as Memorial Sloan-Kettering Cancer Center, Stanford University, Thomas Jefferson University, Mayo Clinic, University California San Diego, University California Irvine, Lynn Sage at Northwestern, Indiana University, Elizabeth Wende Breast Center, University of Washington, Stamford Health System, and University of Pennsylvania. These institutions employ many of the most published doctors in the field of vacuum-assisted and MRI-guided biopsy in the world. The Suros ATEC™ device takes a 60–90 minute procedure currently performed with a core or spring loaded device and reduces it to 30 minutes or less. The clinical indications for use of MRI point toward the highest risk patients, such as women with a family history of breast cancer or those previously diagnosed with cancer. Using MRI as the screening method allows visualization of breast lesions at the earliest possible stage cancer can be detected. MRI-guided breast biopsy with ATEC™ is viewed by leading radiologists as one of the most important advancements in women's health in the last decade.

Please see Appendix 2 for an illustration of the ATEC™ product line for breast biopsy.

COMPETITION

Ethicon Endo-Surgery, Inc. (Ethicon), a subsidiary of Johnson & Johnson company, markets the Biopsys system, the first minimally invasive surgery device introduced into the breast surgical market arena about seven years ago. The company's estimated annual sales of the Biopsys system are $100 million, making it the current industry sales leader. While the device provides vacuum-assisted, minimally invasive biopsy capabilities, Suros believes the ATEC™ system has significant and notable clinical and user advantages. One of the most important and clinically relevant distinctions between ATEC™ and all other market competitors is the ATEC™ system's unique compatibility with all three imaging modalities of MRI, ultrasound, and stereotactic. In addition, Suros is the only company offering a fully automated tissue excision and biopsy device. Full automation translates to increased throughput for the facility and improved patient satisfaction due to decreased procedure time. The ATEC™ product line is substantially superior in treatment range, speed, market utility, and flexibility.

Suros faces competition from other start-up companies such as SenoRx and Neothermia that support a radio frequency (RF) approach to biopsy. The reaction to these products has been less than favorable with questions as to its ability to treat the majority of patients and its ability to provide a pathologically viable tissue sample.

Suros also competes indirectly with open surgical biopsy, currently the most common type of breast biopsy performed in the United States. The procedure is highly invasive, time consuming, and painful for the patient. It carries greater patient risk and requires significantly longer recovery time compared to minimally invasive procedures, such as vacuum-assisted biopsy methods like the ATEC™ which can be performed in the physician's office on an outpatient basis. Consequently, there is an expected migration away from open surgical biopsy and a gravitation toward minimally invasive alternatives which are supported by women's advocacy groups and forward-looking health professionals. Suros continues to play an active role in the education and training efforts underway throughout the country to accelerate this natural evolution.

Please see Appendix 1 for a detailed competitive comparison.

FUTURE PRODUCT DEVELOPMENT

Building on the rapid and successful adoption of the ATEC™ system in the breast biopsy field, Suros is researching and developing new products to better serve its initial market and to expand into new markets. With respect to breast biopsy, Suros is preparing to introduce a second-generation console.

The new console offers improved design, simplified controls, and a substantially lower manufacturing cost. It is also considerably smaller and lighter, reducing facility space requirements and shipping costs. The console will be portable enough for sales representatives to carry to sales calls and tradeshow events.

With respect to future markets, Suros has developed a functioning prototype for intracranial surgery and is canvassing feedback from leading neurosurgeons. Initial feedback has been highly encouraging, with live patient surgical procedures planned for Q4 of 2003. Suros is anticipating a commercial launch into this market during 2005. The company will create a sales channel to sell its new product line in the neurosurgical market and has recently retained a product manager.

TECHNOLOGY AND INTELLECTUAL PROPERTY

Suros has five FDA 510k clearances for three distinct surgical platforms: general surgery (including, but not limited to, breast biopsy), neurosurgery, and ENT.

Suros is pursuing a "technology platform" approach to its protection of intellectual property, taking advantage of both method and apparatus utility patents. The Company now holds 15 U.S. patents (3 issued since fall of 2000), and has multiple patents pending on its technology.

Suros is also pursuing both an offensive and defensive IP strategy, utilizing pending status for filing updates as well as continuation-in-part applications. The Suros counsel on intellectual property matters is Terry Rader, a partner at Rader Fisman & Grauer of Bloomfield Hills, Michigan. Rader has extensive experience in the medical device industry and has developed a plan for protecting the company's technology in existing and future markets, including international and other surgical platform areas.

A list of all patents, issued and pending, is available.

SALES AND MARKETING

Since its launch, the ATEC™ system has been successfully used in more than 20,000 ultrasound, stereotactic and MRI-guided biopsy procedures at more than 150 hospitals and breast centers across the United States. Suros will work with these industry thought leaders to develop and implement regional and national training courses that will follow the model that "doctors teach doctors and doctors sell doctors" approach. This domino theory of adoption has proven successful for many medical technologies in the past and thus provides Suros with a high degree of confidence in its approach.

The user market in the United States as well as Suros' market penetration currently breaks down as follows:

	Total Institutions (2003)	Operating Breast Sites (2003)	Suros Installed Sites (2003)	% Penetration (2003)
Hospitals/ Breast Clinics	6,500	3,500	130	4
Private Radiology Centers	1,100	1,100	0	0
Private MRI Centers	5,300	1,100	30	3
TOTAL	12,900	5,700	150	3

Suros will use a direct sales force and a combination of co-marketing agreements to obtain projected market penetration sites and revenue targets. Co-marketing arrangements in the medical field are common and can be lucrative for both organizations, if implemented correctly. Suros has recently signed an agreement with a national developer and supplier of medical imaging systems that will significantly increase the market presence of the Suros ATEC™ system. The agreement with Bedford, Massachusetts-based Hologic, Inc. gives nonexclusive distribution rights in the United States for the ATEC™ system. The ATEC™ system is fully compatible with Hologic's stereotactic breast biopsy systems. This combination approach with Hologic will provide for more than 70 sales representatives and 40 clinical technologists representing Suros in one form or the other in 2004.

Suros has worked aggressively at defining and marketing to opinion-leading surgeons and radiologists who focus on breast disease management in their practice. The company has utilized the experience and expertise of its medical advisor, Dr. Timothy A. Goedde, a leading private practice surgical oncologist, to help it gain product acceptance and credibility in the market. Other industry leaders who make up the Suros Medical Advisory Board, and many prominent physicians throughout the country who use the ATEC™ system, have provided testimonial support for the clinical advantages and technological superiority of the system. The Suros marketing approach focuses on the distinct clinical and economic advantages of its product. Sales are supported by a direct clinical team that concentrates on customer education and retention.

Suros also capitalizes on its unique market position as the only vacuum-assisted biopsy device compatible with all three breast imaging modalities. Specifically, Suros is able to sell its stereotactic and MRI systems on a bundled basis at leading institutions. This marketing approach has generated success in nearly all of its MRI placement facilities.

After successfully installing the ATEC™ system at a client facility and training its medical team, Suros strives to promote the system's use on a repeat basis. As a result, component and handpiece sales per site are steadily increasing. The Suros goal is to maintain an average rate of $45,000 to $60,000 per site per annum in handpiece sales and a corresponding $7,200 in ancillary sales.

Suros customer care is oriented toward maximizing satisfaction, repeat use, and positive word of mouth. Customers consistently applaud the quality of Suros products and its customer and clinical support team.

While Suros has established an impressive market position in the United States after only 19 months of selling its breast biopsy product line, it has a tremendous opportunity to accelerate its growth. Suros has been able to generate a total of $10 million in revenue from selling to only a small percentage of available client sites. It has achieved 6 percent market share by calling on only 15 percent of the available market to date. The Suros team is committed to rapidly pursuing this immediate market opportunity and is actively hiring additional seasoned sales and clinical representatives as well as implementing nonexclusive co-marketing agreements to improve its coverage and market penetration.

The Suros superior technology, compatibility with installed equipment in all three imaging modalities, and the inherent product benefits of the ATEC™ are becoming widely recognized in the market as setting a new industry standard in vacuum-assisted breast biopsy. The Company's strategy of converting the most prestigious institutions across the country is succeeding. The ATEC™ is fast becoming the choice of leading surgeons and radiologists, making it the *de facto* standard in the breast biopsy market.

INTERNATIONAL SALES

Suros will also begin tapping international breast biopsy markets in 2004 through a strategy of aligning its direct sales in the organization and indirect sales through strategic marketing partnerships. The company is currently in negotiations with potential strategic partners with global sales capabilities.

OPERATIONS AND MANUFACTURING

FACILITIES

Suros occupies a total of 7,400 square feet in Indianapolis, Indiana, with a three-year lease that expires in May 2005. The cost is $11 per square foot. Suros anticipates a move to larger facilities in the second quarter of 2004. The Company rents no space outside of Indianapolis.

MANUFACTURING PROCESS

Suros pursues a hybrid outsourcing and in-house production strategy based on achieving the lowest cost of goods and the highest quality control. Suros outsources the production of its console units, receiving 10 to 15 units per month, with the capacity to grow according to anticipated demand. Suros is currently working with a production partner on the imminent roll-out of its next-generation console, which will greatly lower product and distribution costs.

Suros completes the manufacturing and assembly of the disposable handpieces at its Indianapolis headquarters. The Company's production capacity is 5,000 units per month at its current facility. This has been accomplished by outsourcing many of the product's components, which allows the Company to concentrate on the more sensitive product aspects and ensuring that all production is completely tested to specifications.

To date, the Company has produced and delivered over 20,000 handheld units with more than 99.5 percent satisfactory performance in the field. The Company believes it can increase the success rate and reduce production costs of handhelds by more than 15 percent in the next 12 months by converting production to a flow process and embedding quality procedures into the daily production process.

ORGANIZATION AND MANAGEMENT

ORGANIZATION

Suros currently has 45 employees nationwide. Suros has identified key management slots to fill some of which are related to the proposed financing. An organizational chart listing the current management as well as key additions is included in Appendix 3.

EXECUTIVES

James R. Baumgardt
Chairman of the Board

Baumgardt is the President of Guidant Foundation, Chairman of the Board for Rose-Hulman Ventures, LLC, a partner of Twilight Venture Partners, LLC, and was previously President of North American Sales at Guidant Corporation.

Jim Pearson
President & CEO

As President & CEO of Suros Surgical Systems, Inc., Jim Pearson has positioned the company to a leading market presence in vacuum-assisted breast biopsy systems in less than 18 months. Key accomplishments include fielding an experienced management team, raising over $7,000,000 dollars in capital, generating over $8,000,000 dollars in revenue in first full operating year, launching the world's first vacuum-assisted MRI product, and securing a profit in Suros' first operating year. Prior to joining Suros, Pearson served as Senior Vice President of Equipment Services for North America for Medibuy in San Diego, a supply chain health care exchange backed by Kleiner, Perkins, Caufield & Byers, and Sequoia Capital. Medibuy raised over $177,000,000 million in capital and was later sold to Global Health Exchange. While at Medibuy, Pearson was responsible for its complete "Equipment Life Cycle" offering and managed the equipment division at a satellite office in Cincinnati, Ohio. He grew the equipment division from 1 employee to over 40 in a three-year period, developed and launched Medibuy's "eAuction" website for the buying and selling of used capital equipment from and to health care providers, completed multiple hospital liquidations while establishing the equipment division as the leading revenue generator in its first two years. Pearson was also the founder and CEO of Summit Medical, Inc., a privately held specialty capital equipment distributor. Summit's capital was contributed directly by Pearson and reached a profitable operating position within 18 months. In doing so, he secured long-term distribution contracts with B&K Medical Systems, ESC Sharplan Lasers, Amertek Stabilization, Candela Lasers, Care Wise, and Ultraguide; developed a direct sales team; and was either #1 or #2 in sales for each company represented. Summit was later sold for equity and capital to Medibuy.

Richard M. Rella, CPA
Vice President & CFO

Rich Rella brings more than 25 years of diversified financial and operational experience working with entrepreneurial companies, providing leadership in building the infrastructure of the company. Prior to joining Suros, Rella was the CFO of Pictorial, Inc., a textbook publishing and software development company. During Rella's tenure at Pictorial the company grew from $14 to $30 million in revenue over six years and went through two ownership changes. Prior to Pictorial, he was the CFO of Shepard Poorman Communications Corporation, a printing and publishing company. During his tenure at Shepard Poorman, the company grew from $17 million to over $80 million over five years on a consolidated basis. The growth was the result of aggressive organic growth and three strategic acquisitions. Rella began his career with the regional CPA firm of Drees, Perugini and Company (now part of BKD). After six years in the Ft. Wayne office, he was named the managing partner of the Indianapolis office and over six years grew the office from 4 professionals to 20 and earned the distinction of being named one of the 25 largest CPA firms in Indianapolis.

Kent Smith
Vice President of Sales and Marketing

As Vice President of Sales and Marketing of Suros, Kent Smith brings a well-rounded background of success in rapid-growth organizations, experience, and results to the Suros management team. Prior to joining Suros, Smith was President and CEO of Cytomedix, Inc., a start-up health care biotechnology company specializing in growth-factor technologies for chronic wound care in San Diego, California. While at Cytomedix, Smith was responsible for bringing the company out of bankruptcy, developing a national independent sales channel while commercializing a new product for sale in the chronic wound market, and initiating the strategy to defend the company's intellectual property rights. Prior to Cytomedix, Smith was Senior Vice President of Suppliers at Medibuy.com, an Internet portal which raised over $177 million in capital. Prior to this, Smith spent over 20 years with Baxter Healthcare in various executive and sales management roles, including President of Baxter Japan's Cardiovascular Business, VP/GM of Baxter Japan's Hospital Business, VP/GM of Baxter's Specialty IV Business, and VP of Operations for the Hospital Supply Division of American Hospital Supply which was acquired by Baxter in 1986. He started his career as a sales representative for Burroughs Wellcome and Company.

Eugene L. Henderson
General Counsel and Director

Gene Henderson is the founding partner of Henderson, Daily, Withrow and DeVoe, an Indianapolis-based legal firm dealing with corporate and business matters. The firm has extensive experience in the health care, technology, and insurance industries. Henderson has been active in the formation and founding of Indiana entrepreneurial companies and has served as an officer, as counsel, and as a member of the Boards of Directors of several such companies.

Joseph L. Mark
Cofounder
Vice President, Product Development and Director

Joe Mark has been named a "Health Care Hero" in his hometown of Indianapolis for his role in developing groundbreaking clinical advancements in tissue excision devices. Mark has built his career on developing innovative products that improve patient care and provide the medical community with the most efficient and clinically advanced methods of gross, precise biopsy tissue removal. His prior experience has primarily been with medical device manufacturers.

Michael E. Miller
Cofounder and Director Engineering Services

Miller is a partner in Promex, Inc. Before joining Promex, he was Manager of Resident Engineering at RCA/GE/Thompson in Torreon, Mexico. He has various patents issued and has established himself as a leader in the engineering field.

Timothy A. Goedde, MD, FACS
Medical Advisor and Director

Dr. Goedde is a world-class surgical oncologist and instructor for the American College of Surgery, teaching postgraduate courses in breast ultrasound and stereotactic biopsies. He is the Medical Director for the Midwest Breast Center in Indianapolis.

Tony Wibbeler
National Sales Director

Tony Wibbeler brings a successful track record to Suros in both sales and management. He has developed and implemented the Suros sales strategy with impressive results—growing the ATEC™ breast biopsy and excision system customer base to more than 150 in the first year of sales. Prior to joining Suros, Wibbeler was a top performer of B&K Medical Systems and the leading sales representative for Summit Medical, Inc.s

Robert M. Gaffney
Director of Operations

Bob Gaffney brings 25 years of experience in medical-device design, development, and manufacturing. Previously he served as Senior Director and Site Manager for Nellcor Puritan Bennett Corporation, a manufacturer of cryogenics systems, where he was responsible for plant operations, product development, and support operations. Earlier in his career he was an engineer at American Hospital Supply Corporation and Becton Dickinson Corporation.

Jeffrey Garrison
Director of Clinical Strategy & Education

Jeff Garrison leads the Suros education and clinical strategy initiatives. His efforts guide Suros's corporate focus in providing relevant clinical data, educational tools, applications training, clinical paper publications, and training courses with its industry partners to position Suros as the clear choice in vacuum-assisted tissue excision and collection. Prior to joining Suros, Garrison served as Vice President of Sales and Marketing at NoInk Communications, a software development firm with products supporting the health care industry. Garrison was also President of Summit Medical, Inc.

Sue Hetzler
Director, Public Relations & Marketing

Sue Hetzler manages the Suros product and corporate marketing functions and serves as the primary media liaison and spokesperson for the company. She develops all Web-based communications and is the corporate contact for consumer and industry inquiries. Hetzler is a 20-year public relations and marketing professional with experience in secular and Catholic news media, association and military public affairs, and corporate marketing.

OUTSIDE DIRECTORS

William R. Ringo, Jr.
Ringo is currently chairman of Intermune, Inc. He recently retired as President of Oncology and Critical Care Products for Eli Lilly and Company in Indianapolis. He has served in various capacities with Eli Lilly since 1973.

Michael G. Hall
Hall is Managing Director of Periculum Capital Company, LLC, an investment banking and merchant banking company in Indianapolis. He was previously Vice President of Marketing and a Director of Biomet, Inc., manufacturer and distributor of orthopedic implants and related instrumentation.

Phyllis Greenberger, MSW
Greenberger is President and CEO of the Society for Women's Health Research, a Washington D.C.–based advocacy organization. Prior to becoming its Executive Director in 1993, she was a founding member of the society.

INSTITUTIONAL VENTURE INVESTORS AND SHAREHOLDERS

Periculum Capital Company, LLC
Periculum is a leading investment banking and merchant banking company based in Indianapolis. Periculum's primary investment banking services include merger and acquisition services and raising capital for growth and corporate acquisitions. The principals of Periculum have considerable experience in developing and financing medical product companies. Periculum was involved in the initial

development of Suros, provided the initial capitalization to incorporate Suros, and has sourced all its current financing.

Rose-Hulman Ventures, LLC

Rose-Hulman Ventures (RHV) is a technology-based business incubator and product-development center with unique rapid-prototyping and design engineering capabilities. Affiliated with the leading undergraduate engineering school in the country, Rose-Hulman Institute of Technology is located on a 180-acre, campus-like setting in a 35,000 square-foot building at Aleph Park in Terre Haute, Indiana. RHV manages over $50 million for venture investment and also leverages in-kind services for equity in portfolio companies.

Twilight Venture Partners, LLC

Twilight Venture Partners (TVP) is an Indiana-based, early-stage global venture fund focused on medical devices and biotechnology. Formed in September 2002, TVP has already invested in four companies: locally based Suros Surgical Systems, ComChem, BioStorage Technologies, and Given Imaging based in Israel. TVP's principals are experienced venture investors, entrepreneurs, and former senior corporate executives with proven track records, unique business relationships, and a combined century of life science industry experience.

PROFESSIONAL ADVISORS

KPMG

Suros has used KPMG as its audit partner since its inception. KPMG provides Suros with ongoing consultation, financial audit services, tax advice, and access to valuable entrepreneurial resources through its national network.

Henderson, Daily, Withrow & DeVoe

One of the leading law firms in Indianapolis, Henderson Daily provides a full range of legal services to a diverse national and international clientele, including publicly held companies, small businesses, and high-net-worth individuals. The firm provides Suros with corporate legal counsel.

Rader, Fishman & Grauer PLLC

Rader, Fishman & Grauer is a national law firm that advances the marketability of intellectual assets for global corporations and emerging enterprises. The firm's IP management services include strategies for intellectual asset protection, acquisition, exploitation, valuation, and dispute resolution. Its worldwide practice areas include patents, trademarks, litigation, copyrights, U.S. and foreign portfolio management, technology and e-commerce, trade secrets, and unfair competition. Rader Fishman is advising Suros on its global IP strategy.

CAPITALIZATION

The following table details the capitalization of Suros as of September 30, 2003, and the pro forma capitalization of Suros, assuming the sale of $7 million of Series D Preferred Shares:

	September 2003 (unaudited)	
	Actual	*Pro Forma as Adjusted*
Short-term debt, including current maturities:	$50,000[1]	$50,000
Convertible debt, excluding current maturities and accrued dividends[2]:	2,350,000	2,350,000
Shareholders' equity		
Common Stock, no par value, authorized 5,000,000 shares, issued and outstanding 1,300,000 shares	26,422	26,422
Series A Redeemable Preferred Stock, no par value, authorized 288,000 shares, issued and outstanding 287,448 shares, redeemable at the option of the Companycompany commencing in 2020	287,448	287,448
Series B Convertible Redeemable Preferred Stock, no par value, authorized 4,077 shares, issued and outstanding 4,052 shares	4,052,000	4,052,000
Series C Convertible Redeemable Preferred Stock, no par value, authorized 1,000 shares, issued and outstanding 568 shares	778,348	778,348
Series D Convertible Redeemable Preferred Stock,		7,000,000
Total shareholders' equity	5,144,218	12,144,218
Total capitalization	$7,544,218	$14,544,218

[1] Represents principal amount currently outstanding on the company's line of credit with Fifth Third Bank, which has a total commitment of $500,000.

[2] Accrued dividends on the Series B and C Preferred Stock were $774,051 at September 30, 2003.

FINANCIAL PLAN

PROJECTED INCOME STATEMENT AND KEY ASSUMPTIONS

The plan's revenue assumptions are as follows:

Breast Surgical Market:

- 18 capital unit sales per sales representative per year.
- 190 disposable units per installed unit per year.

	2002A		2003E		2004F		2005F		2006F	
Revenue	$ 2,366	100%	$ 8,458	100%	$ 26,296	100%	$ 69.098	100%	$ 108,680	100%
Cost of Goods Sold	1,387	59%	3,460	41%	8,350	32%	21,462	31%	37,059	34%
Gross Profit	979	41%	4,998	59%	17,946	68%	47,636	69%	71,621	66%
Operating Expenses										
Research & Development	–	0%	326	4%	1,147	4%	2,538	4%	3,908	4%
Sales & Marketing	–	0%	2,867	34%	10,676	41%	21,711	31%	26,506	24%
General & Administrative	2,789	118%	1,736	21%	3,084	21%	4,870	7%	6,341	6%
Total Operating Expenses	2,789	118%	4,930	58%	14,907	57%	29,119	42%	36,754	34%
Operating Income (Loss)	(1,810)	–77%	69	1%	3,039	12%	18,517	27%	34,866	32%
Other Income (Expense)										
Other Income (Expense)	(9)	0%	15	0%	83	0%	82	0%	254	0%
Interest Expense	–	0%	(97)	–1%	(164)	–1%	(164)	0%	(164)	0%
Total Other Income (Expense)	(9)	0%	(82)	–1%	(81)	0%	(83)	0%	89	0%
Income (Loss) before Income Taxes	(1,819)	–77%	(14)	0%	2,958	11%	18,435	27%	34,956	32%
Provision for Income Taxes	–	0%	–		(330)	0%	(7,097)	–10%	(13,456)	–12%
Net Income (Loss)	$ (1,819)	–77%	$ (14)	–77%	$ 2,628	10%	$ 11,338	16%	$ 21,500	20%

- $28,700 effective capital per-unit sell price (direct sales) in 2003 decreasing at an average of 13 percent per year to an average effective per-unit sell of $19,000 in 2006.

  - Average sell price reduction assumed to be 20 percent per year
  - Effective sell price reduction mitigated by gradual mix shift to higher priced MRI units

- $276 effective handpiece price in 2003, decreasing at 3.6 percent per year to an average effective per-unit price of $247 in 2006.

  - Average sell price reduction assumed to be 5–7 percent per year
  - Effective sell price reduction mitigated by gradual mix shift to higher priced MRI units

- 3 percent annual attrition rate in active sites

- Suros' domestic market share (disposable units):

	Percent of Market (%)	Procedures
2003	6	21,000
2004	12	52,000
2005	31	168,100
2006	45	309,300

- Disposable unit sales breakout (including international):

	Stereo/Ultrasound	MRI	Total
2003	20,200	800	21,000
2004	49,200	3,400	52,600
2005	157,100	15,200	172,300
2006	283,200	35,500	318,600

- Number of installed capital units (domestic):

	Stereo/Ultrasound	MRI	Total
2003	126	35	161
2004	480	140	620
2005	1,140	360	1,500
2006	1,750	620	2,370

- International Sales for the forecast period:

(Includes Stereotactic/Ultrasound and MRI)

	Installed Sites	*Disposable Units*	*Total Revenue*
2004	23	600	$.5 million
2005	157	4,200	$4.3 million
2006	363	9,300	$9.6 million

The plan's assumptions regarding staffing are as follows:

Headcount by Area

	2003	2004	2005	2006

Operations

	2003	2004	2005	2006
Supervision and indirect expenses	8	21	22	24
Production expenses	10	40	96	160
Research & Development	2	5	9	12

Sales and Marketing

	2003	2004	2005	2006
Executive Management	1	1	1	1
Sales Management	0	4	7	9
Sales Representatives	8	40	45	51
Clinical Applications	4	20	23	24
Customer Service	2	5	15	23
Other	4	11	21	31

General and Administrative

	2003	2004	2005	2006
Executive Management	2	2	2	2
Accounting	2	5	7	9
Human Resources	0	1	3	5
IT	0	2	5	5
Other	1	2	3	3
Total Headcount	44	159	259	357

Headcount by Product Line/Division

	2003	2004	2005	2006
Breast	44	158	244	324
Neurosurgical & Other	0	1	15	33

- Three-year average compensation per sales representative is $130,600.
- Average compensation (including fringe benefits costs) per FTE (full time equivalent) excluding production staff and commissions:

2003	$78,200
2004	$74,000
2005	$72,100
2006	$73,200

PROJECTED CASH FLOW STATEMENT AND KEY ASSUMPTIONS

Cash Flow from Operating Activities:	2002A	2003E	2004F	2005F	2006F
Net Income (Loss)	$ (1,819)	$ (14)	$ 2,628	$ 11,338	$ 21,500
Depreciation and amortization	192	309	548	767	925
Compensation element of non–qualified options	171	51	60	–	–
Changes in Working Capital					
Accounts Receivable	(526)	(1,045)	(6,424)	(5,345)	(4,837)
Inventory	(540)	(356)	(3,053)	(2,890)	(378)
Other Current Assets	(23)	8	–	–	–
Accured Payroll and Commissions	496	(39)	1,954	1,040	356
Accured Payroll and Commissions	418	383	655	661	(60)
Deferred Revenue	64	87	679	1,115	669
Accured Income Taxes	–	–	–	–	–
Changes in Working Capital	(111)	(963)	(6,190)	(5,420)	(4,250)
Net cash provided by (used in) operating activities	(1,567)	(616)	(2,954)	6,684	18,175
Net cash provided by (used in) investing activities	(364)	(557)	(1,739)	(800)	(769)
Net cash provided by (used in) financing activities	752	2,549	6,520	–	–
Net increase (decrease) in cash	(1,179)	1,376	1,828	5,884	17,406
Cash, beginning of period	1,658	479	1,855	3,686	9,567
Cash, end of period	$ 479	$ 1,855	$ 3,683	$ 9,567	$ 26,973

The plan's assumptions regarding cash flow are as follows:

- Raising $7 million Series D in Q1 2004.
- Includes servicing interest on Convertible Debt.
- Cash "low water mark" is over $1 million.

PROJECTED BALANCE SHEET AND KEY ASSUMPTIONS

Current Assets:	2002A	2003E	2004F	2005F	2006F
Cash & Marketable Securities	$ 479	$ 1,855	$ 3,683	$ 9,567	$ 26,973
Accounts Receivable, net	526	1,571	7,995	13,341	18,178
Inventory	603	958	4,102	6,902	7,280
Other Current Assets	45	38	38	38	38
Total Current Assets	1,653	4,422	15,727	29,847	52,468
Property & Equipment	793	1,156	2,894	3,694	4,463
Less: Accumulated Depreciation	(101)	(294)	(746)	(1,416)	(2,245)
Net Property & Equipment	692	861	2,148	2,278	2,218
Net Intangible Assets	481	559	463	366	270
Total Assets	$2,826	$5,843	$18,338	$32,491	$54,956
Current Liabilities					
Note Payable	$ –	$ –	$ 20	$ 20	$ 20
Accounts Payable, trade	609	528	2,482	3,523	3,879
Accrued Payroll & Commissions	466	330	1,463	2,123	2,063
Deferred Revenue	64	151	830	1,944	2,613
Accrued Income Taxes	–	–	–	–	–
Other Current Liabilities	–	519	41	41	41
Total Current Liabilities	1,139	1,528	4,836	7,651	8,617
7% Convertible Notes	–	2,350	2,350	2,350	2,350
Divident Payale	503	864	1,249	1,633	2,018
Stockholders' Equity:					
Common Stock	1	26	86	86	86
Preferred Stock	5,117	5,332	11,832	11,832	11,832
Retained Earnings (Deficit)	(3,934)	(4,258)	(2,015)	(8,938)	(30,053)
Total Stockholders' Equity	1,184	1,101	9,904	20,856	41,971
Total Liablilities and Stockholders's Equity	$2,826	$5,843	$18,338	$32,491	$54,956

The plan's assumptions regarding balance sheet items are as follows:

- Accounts Receivable is forecasted at 75 days for capital equipment sales and 45 days for disposable sales.
- Inventory is forecasted at 60 days on hand for capital-finished goods and 40 days for disposable-finished goods and raw materials.
- Accounts Payable is forecasted at 30 days for inventory purchase.
- 2004 Capital Expenditures include $750,000 for furnishings and equipment plus $250,000 in tooling costs for new console development.

APPENDIX 1

Competitive Landscape Technology Overview

	Vacuum Assisted		Redio Frequency			Cryogenic		other	
	Suros	Ethicon	SenoRx	Nothermia	Rubicor	Sanarus	BIP Gun	Open Surgical	Spring Loaded Core
MRI	Yes	No	No	No	No	No	Yes	No	No
Stereotactic	Yes	Yes	No	Yes	Yes	No	Yes	N/A	Yes
Ultrasound	Yes	Yes1	Yes	Yes	Yes	Yes	Yes	N/A	Yes
U/S Ease of Use	Easy	Difficult	Medium	Medium	Medium	Difficult	Medium	N/A	Medium
Office Procedure	Yes	Yes	Yes	Yes	Yes	Yes	Yes	No	Yes
Petite/Thin Breast	Yes	No	No	Kind of	No	No	No	No	No
Chest Wall Lesions	Yes	Yes	Yes	No	No	No	Yes	Yes	Some
Small Needle	Yes	No	No	No	No	No	Yes	N/A	Yes
Compatible w/ Marker	Yes	Yes	Yes	No	?	No	No	N/A	Yes
Tissue Acquisition Time	3.5 seconds	30 seconds 3 minutes	1 minute	7 seconds	45 seconds	1–4 minutes/specimen	30 seconds	1 hour or more procedure	1–4 minutes/specimen
Automated Tissue Collection	Yes	No	No	No	No	No	No	No	No
Excision	Yes	Difficult	No	Difficult	Difficult	No	Yes	Yes	No

(continued)

	Vacuum Assisted		Redio Frequency			Cryogenic		other	
	Suros	Ethicon	SenoRx	Nothermia	Rubicor	Sanarus	BIP Gun	Open Surgical	Spring Loaded Core
Closed System	Yes	No	No	No	No	No	No	No	No
Single Pass Biopsy	Yes	Yes	No	Yes	Yes	Yes	No	Yes	No
Risk of Infection	Low	Medium	Low	Medium	Low	Low	Low	Medium	Low
Core Integrity	No	No	Yes	Yes	Yes	Yes	No	No	No
Penetrate Dense Tissue	12 G	Bat Wing	Yes	Yes	Yes	No	Yes	Yes	Yes
Problem With Dry Tap	No	Yes	No	No	No	No	No	No	No
Possible Burn Artifact	No	No	Yes	Yes	Yes	No	No	No	No
Implants	Yes	Yes	No	No	No	No	Yes	Yes	Yes
Grounding Required	No	No	Yes	Yes	Yes	No	No	No	No
Transmissability Issues?	No	Yes	No	No	No	Yes	Yes	No	Device Dependent

APPENDIX 2

Product Illustrations

Handpiece and Console for Ultrasound and Stereotactic Modalities
Demonstration of Handpiece in use in MRI Setting

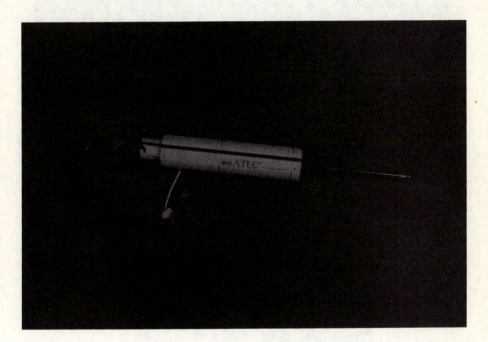

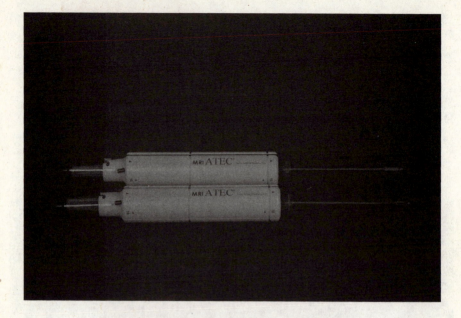

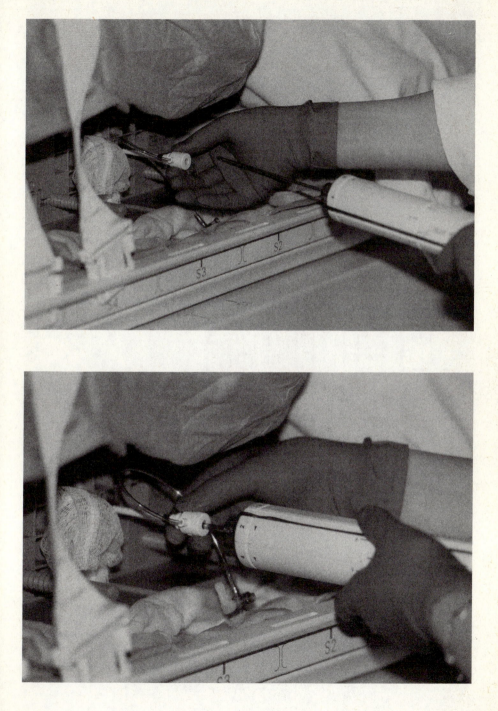

APPENDIX 3

Organizational Chart

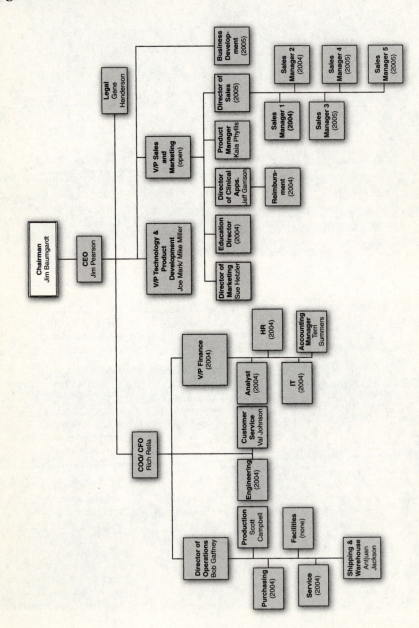

CASE MAP

The following case map provides suggested case studies that focus on many different aspects of innovation acceleration. These cases are drawn from three main sources that provide a catalog of many teaching cases related to innovation and entrepreneurship.

Case	Details	Issues	Summary
INNOVATION AT CIRQUE SOLEIL	Website:icmrindia.org/ casestudies/catalogue/ Business%20Strategy/ BSTR269.htm Publication Date: 2007 Case Length: 16 Pages	Innovation Strategy, Marketing, and Growth	The case discusses various innovations at Cirque du Soleil (Cirque), the Canada-based circus entertainment company.
XEROX PARC: INNOVATION WITHOUT PROFIT?	Website:icmrindia.org/ casestudies/catalogue/ Business%20Strategy2/ BSTR150.htm Publication Date: 2005 Case Length: 16 Pages	History, Structure, and Culture's impact on Innovation Implementation	PARC, the research arm of Xerox Corp., was set up to invent future technology. However, Xerox failed to capitalize on its innovations and blamed the casual/flexible culture of PARC.
DANIMAL IN SOUTH AFRICA: MANAGEMENT INNOVATION AT THE BOTTOM OF THE PYRAMID	*Source:* Ivey/GIBS Website: adobe.com/ products/acrobat/ readstep2.html Publication Date: January 21, 2011 Case Length: 15 pages	Innovation in Developing Countries, Social Marketing and Positioning	The case focuses on innovation in the South African dairy industry, focusing on an innovative new yoghurt product, Danimal, a product created specifically for the market at the base of the pyramid. It explains how management of the product line embodied the various innovation opportunities and challenges presented.

Case	Details	Issues	Summary
TAINO CON-STRUCTION SUPPLIES: MANAGING INNOVA-TION RISKS AT AN SME IN A SMALL, DEVELOP-ING NATION	*Source:*Ivey Website: adobe.com/products/acrobat/readstep2.html Publication Date: October 13, 2010 Case Length: 16 pages	Innovation, Managing Industry Change, Family Business, Green Products	Taino Construction has to make several strategic decisions that can guide the firm during very difficult times for the construction industry. They are trying to find ways to capitalize on the company's innovations and international advantages.
DESIGN CAREERS OF ALAN YIP AND WINNIF PANG	*Source:*Ivey Website: http://www.adobe.com/products/acrobat/readstep2.html Publication Date: October 13, 2010 Case Length: 15 pages	International Marketing, Product Design/Development, Entrepreneurial Marketing, Opportunity Recognition	This case describes how two Hong Kong product designers chose their respective paths and achieved design excellence and celebrity status.
EARCHECK	Arthur M. Blank Center for Entrepreneurship ©Babson College, 2009 www3.babson.edu/ESHIP/research-publications/facultycases.cfm	Innovation, Obstacles to Success, Key Hires, Teams	The focus of the case is on EarCheckk's evolution from start-up to several subsequent ownership situations. The obstacles to commercialization are highlighted.

If you are interested in exploring additional cases you can go to the following websites:

Babson: http://www3.babson.edu/ESHIP/research-publications/facultycases.cfm

IVEY: http://www.adobe.com/products/acrobat/readstep2.html

ICMR: http://www.icmrindia.org/

NAME INDEX

SUBJECT INDEX

E

EarCheck, 332
Economic deliverables, 148
Economists, engineers as, 126–127
Economy, creative, 147
Educational component of experience realm, 89
Electrical engineering, 128
Eli Lilly and Company, 314
Elizabeth Wende Breast Center, 297, 306
Employee development program, 180–181
Employee incentives, 72
Employee security, 221
Encouraging innovation, 30
Endorphin Café, 83–84
Energy level of innovator, 11
Engineering/engineers, 104, 123, 124–127
chemical, 127–128
civil, 128
computer, 128
disciplines of, 127–130
as economists, 126–127
electrical, 128
goal-oriented, 126
industrial, 128–129
main business of, 126
mechanical, 129
problem solving skills of, 127
Engineering Your Future (Oakes, Leone, and Gunn), 127
Enterprises, inside, 23
Entertainment aspect of experience realm, 89
En theos, 54
Enthusiasm, 54
Entrepreneur, experiential view of, 13
Entrepreneurial action, 3–4, 13
Entrepreneurial behavior, 13, 172
Entrepreneurial concept, 15
Entrepreneurial innovative actions, 167
Entrepreneurial mind-set, 290
Entrepreneurial motivation, 12, 12f
Entrepreneurial orientation (EO), 188, 197–198
Entrepreneurial planning, 264–265t
Entrepreneurial process, 44
Entrepreneurial readiness, 162–164
Entrepreneurial stress, 16–17
Entrepreneurship, 103f
collective, 33

concept of, 6
defined, 9–10
innovation, 168
organizational, 188f
research in, 15
strategic, 27–28
Environmental antecedents for innovation, 30–31, 189–190
Environmental Protection Agency (EPA), 254
EPCOT, 143, 152
Erector, 143
Escapism, 81
Escapist aspect of experience realm, 89
ESC Sharplan Lasers, 312
Esthetics, 89
Ethicon Endo-Surgery, Inc. (Ethicon), 298, 307
Eureka, 116
Eureka moment, 60–61
European Renaissance, 73
Evaluation, 47, 61–62
Event creativity, 63
Everyday Creativity, 249
Everyday Edisons, 146
Executive summary, 267, 281
Expectations, 250–251
Experience prototyping, 151–153
Experiences, 72, 89–90
Experiential view of entrepreneur, 13
Expertise, 49–51
Explicit innovation goals, 291
Exploitation, 6
Extension, 7
External corporate venturing, 28
External research and development (R&D), 77
ExxonMobil, 135

F

Facebook, 88
Fact-finding, 81–83
Failures, 11, 291
Fatalities, industrial, 101
Feasibility, 108–109, 135
Features, 241
Fed Ex, 150
Feedback, 106, 114, 291
Fellow employees, 26–27
Financial forecast, 268
Financial information group, 276
Financial statements, 268, 284–285
Firms role in innovation strategy, 290–291
First-level managers, 198
Flexibility, 110

Flexible mind, 110
Focus, 110–111
Focus groups, 230
Folklore, 16
Food Network, 146
Forcing style of conflict management, 217
Ford Edsels, 107
Forming stage of team formation, 211–212
Fortune 500 companies, 45, 106
Framing the challenge, 290
Functionality teams, 209
Fused Deposition Modeling (FDM), 139

G

Gamblers, 16
G-code, 140
Geico, 247
General Electric (GE), 71
General Motors, 125
"Give and take" approach, 77
Given Imaging, 315
Global Health Exchange, 311
Global innovative challenge, 3
Goal orientation, 10, 126
Goals
of action plan, 273–274
explicit innovation, 291
innovation, 291
life, 79, 80–81
realistic, 263
social, 79–80
Google, 28, 36–37, 73, 106
SketchUp, 132, 147
Gravity, 18, 290
Great Pyramids of Egypt, 101
Green Fuel Alternatives, 254–257
Group development, 211f
GUI (graphical user interface), 77
Guidant Corporation, 311
Gyrus ENT, 133

H

Handspring Inc., 139
Hard Rock Café, 90
"Hardware" side of organizations, 290–291
Harley-Davidson, 148, 236
Harris Directory, 231
Harvard Business Review, 150
Harvard Business School, 43, 49
Harvard University, 88
Harvest strategies, 268, 286
Hasso Plattner Institute, 111
Henderson, Daily, Withrow and DeVoe, 313, 315